SHERIDAN'S NIGHTINGALE

THE STORY OF ELIZABETH LINLEY

SHERIDAN'S NIGHTINGALE

THE STORY OF ELIZABETH LINLEY

ALAN CHEDZOY

a&b

Published in Great Britain in 1997 by
Allison & Busby Ltd
114 New Cavendish Street, London W1M 7FD

A catalogue record for this book is available from the British Library

ISBN 0 74900 264 6

Designed and typeset by N-J Design Associates
Romsey, Hampshire

Printed and bound in Great Britain by
WBC Book Manufacturers Ltd
Bridgend, Mid Glamorgan

For Gillian
who is music to me

Contents

PART 3
One True Lover

Acknowledgements

The name of Elizabeth Linley has hitherto been kept alive chiefly by the biographers of her husband, Richard Brinsley Sheridan. Of these, the books by W. Fraser Rae (1896) and Walter Sichel (1909) are outstandingly rich in information and have proved invaluable, as has the pioneering work on the Linley family published by Clementina Black in 1911. The only previous biography of Elizabeth Linley by Margot Bor and Lamond Clelland (1962) is helpful but brief.

Particularly useful have been: Cecil Price's superbly edited volumes of Richard Brinsley Sheridan's letters and his edition of Sheridan's plays; William LeFanu's collection of letters by 'Betsy' Sheridan; and the unpublished letters of Elizabeth Linley to her friend, Mehetabel Stratford Canning, edited by John A. Gillaspie, in the possession of Bath Central Library. Roger Fiske's work on English theatre music of the eighteenth century has also proved of great help, as has Carola Oman's biography of Garrick and W. Macqueen Pope's researches on the history of the Drury Lane Theatre. I have consulted many other works all of which can be found in the Select Bibliography.

I am especially indebted to the following institutions and individuals: the Bath Central Library, and Bath & North East Somerset Library & Archives Services; the Bath City Council Leisure Department; the Bristol Central Library; the British Library; the Trustees of the Dulwich Picture Gallery; the London Library; the National Portrait Gallery; the National Trust Waddesdon Manor; the Oxford University Press; Reed Book Services Ltd, Rushden, Northants; and the Victoria & Albert Museum Picture Library; Jack Bennet of Raheny for introducing me to Sheridan's Dublin; Paul Hubbard for musical advice and research on the Bristol Hotwells; Hugh Jacques, the Dorset County Archivist; Mrs Anne Sheridan for advice and the loan of vital materials; Mr Mike Timmins of Albemarle Row, Hotwells, Bristol; Giles Waterfield previously of the Dulwich Picture Gallery; my assiduous editor Vanessa Unwin of Allison & Busby; and my wife Brenda for her enduring encouragement and patience.

A.C.

Introduction

Among the paintings housed in the Dulwich Picture Gallery is a series of portraits of the Linleys of Bath painted by Thomas Gainsborough, a close friend of the family. The Linleys were prominent people in the musical life of the city in the late eighteenth century. They were celebrated for their good looks and their musical talent, and described by the distinguished musicologist Dr Charles Burney as 'a Nest of Nightingales' after he first visited them and heard the children play and sing. Time, however, proved that the Linleys carried a fatal inheritance. Gainsborough's pictures hint that they already suspected it. The father, Thomas Linley, is depicted at the age of about forty, just looking up from a score; he is handsome but his manner appears severe with a touch of melancholy about it. His son Tom looks knowing and confident, but his physique seems fragile, as if all his promise will serve merely as a temptation to fate. And though Samuel and William are good-looking boys there is something wistful about them.

Finest of all the portraits is a rather mysterious, full-length study entitled *The Linley Sisters*. It depicts two girls in front of an earth bank which bears primroses and trails leaves. It looks as if they have just finished singing a duet. The younger one, seated on the right, wears a golden brown dress and holds a musical score on her lap. She has a bright, cheerful look and gazes boldly towards us. Her elegant sister on the left is standing up and leaning on a guitar; her dress is ice-blue and her long delicate arms emerge from a profusion of lace. She looks away into the distance but her thoughts are obviously inward. Her gaze is serene, soulful, other-worldly. Even among her handsome siblings she is the supreme beauty.

What is she thinking about? At the time when the picture was being painted she was subject to a sexual harassment so remorseless that it terrified and exhausted her. In order to escape it, a few days after Gainsborough finished his work she took a decisive step and set out on the greatest adventure of her life.

Her name was Elizabeth (or Eliza) Linley. She was one of the most famous singers of her time and by the age of eighteen was already something of a cult among those who went to hear her. But her career ended abruptly when she married a playwright of genius. Her career is succinctly summarised in Roger Fiske's *English Theatre Music in the Eighteenth Century*:

> Elizabeth, Sheridan's wife, was among the finest sopranos of the century, but there will be little about her in this book partly because she specialised in oratorio, partly because, after her marriage, her husband forbade her to sing professionally.

What happened to Eliza after she walked out of Gainsborough's picture that day? Her story is full of incident. It tells of great beauty, a superb voice and theatrical triumph; of sexual abuse, elopement, duelling and true love. Her father was her master and her husband her rival, and because they exploited her she rebelled against both of them. She was ogled by a king and propositioned by two of his sons. Undergraduates mobbed her and stern Protestants worshipped her as a saint or even a goddess. Before she was twenty her life-story became the subject of a West End farce, and after she married Richard Brinsley Sheridan he made their courtship subject of his comic masterpiece, *The Rivals*. She is somewhere present in all her husband's great comedies. In later years he took her with him into the world of politics and high society where she got to know many of the illustrious figures of the age. She witnessed great scenes from the nation's history and played an important part in a struggle for the Throne. Eliza walked precariously through the decadent world of eighteenth century aristocratic society and when late in her life she found romance, she was soon obliged to give it up. Yet all the time her one true lover was waiting for her in Bristol at the Hotwells. After her death the moralists made her a saint once more but simultaneously utilised her story as an awful warning to young women.

Eliza's life is usually presented as a mere adjunct to that of her husband. In these pages I have therefore tried as far as possible to witness truly what she was. Marriage to a genius is always difficult but was especially so for Eliza because she too was an artist and needed to be heard.

Alan Chedzoy
Weymouth 1997

PART ONE

The Beauty of Bath

CHAPTER 1

Incident at the Théâtre Feydeau

It was when he was seated in the Théâtre Feydeau that Edward Fitzgerald saw the dead woman. At first he was not too surprised: for months past she had filled his dreams and all day he had been drinking hard. That evening his blood was singing with wine and patriotic speeches, and memories of her face and voice repeatedly came into his thoughts. Nevertheless another glance at the nearby box gave him a jolt. She was still there. He closed his eyes to steady himself. The house was hot and he had felt a little faint for some time but now he seemed to be having hallucinations. He concluded that the excitements of this, the most momentous day of his life, had heated his fancy to a fever pitch, and that perhaps in a little while the auditorium would have steadied itself and the woman would have gone. Twice he breathed deeply and opened his eyes again.

To his relief everything now seemed normal. At that very moment the musicians were entering. Bowing to the audience, they were greeted with a burst of applause. The piece to be performed that night was an operetta by Cherubini which seemed exactly suited to the city's buoyant mood. As soon as the musicians struck up the over-ture the audience began to hum and sway to the cheerful tunes. It was 1792, the first year of the Republic, and the citizens of Paris were breathless with enthusiasm and hope. It was as if the city had been reborn. Fitzgerald became aware of his young friend Sir Robert Smith – plain Bob Smith now – smiling sidelong at him. He grinned back sheepishly. And only when all other eyes were concentrated on the stage did he permit himself to snatch a glance sideways through the *loge grilleé* to the box beyond.

Nothing extraordinary met his gaze. In the glare of the stage candles he could make out a stylish middle-aged woman. Beyond her

1

were the haloed profiles of two other figures to whom she whispered occasionally while pointing at the musicians. From the diverse movements of this pair Fitzgerald perceived them to be young women, both apparently in the charge of the older lady, but he could see very little of them within the darkness of their box. Suddenly his heart turned over. For the girl furthest from him bent forward into the light and inclined her head in his direction. He glimpsed that mass of dark chestnut hair in which he had so many times buried his face, the elegant neck he had gently stroked, and that heart-breakingly delicate complexion of the most beautiful face he had ever kissed. Startled, he turned away. His mind reeled. How could it be that here in the Théâtre Feydeau sat the woman he had left pregnant and dying in England only ten months previously? He had come to France to forget her. Now here she was again, his lost love Eliza Linley, wife of the philandering playwright Richard Brinsley Sheridan.

Lord Edward had been in France for about three weeks. He had come determined to shake off his grief by burying himself in the historic events shaking the country. He wanted to discuss them first hand with the greatest living English revolutionary thinker, Tom Paine, so as soon as he arrived in Parish he had sought him out. To his delight, Paine proposed that Fitzgerald should lodge with him. Edward found himself sharing breakfast, dinner and supper with the sage, when they would debate how the doctrines of Liberty, Equality and Fraternity might be applied throughout the entire civilised world, even in such a backward place as Edward's native Ireland. Between meals Edward read Rousseau, visited the theatre, attended the meetings of the Assembly, and walked about the streets. Everywhere he observed how the energies of the people had been released by revolution so that, as he wrote to his mother, there had been nothing like it save 'Rome in the days of its conquest'.[1]

For the first time since Fitzgerald had heard of Eliza's death in the summer the pall of gloom over him began to lift a little and his senses to quicken. He was still only twenty-nine and not yet ready to surrender to a life of grief. For all his interest in revolutionary principles, Fitzgerald was a practical man and a soldier, and needed to be doing something again. Yet he was not clear how he might participate in the great events around him since in France he was a foreigner and could never be more than an observer of another people's revolution.

Besides, he felt himself to be something of a hypocrite. Here he was, enjoying the title of Lord Edward Fitzgerald and the privileges it brought him, while all the time pretending to support a great egalitarian revolution. He could not deny that he was the fifth son of James Duke of Leinster, the premier duke of all Ireland, yet Fitzgerald wanted to have done with titles. He was excited by a glimpse he had enjoyed of a simpler more egalitarian society than that at home. In the remote backwoods of North America he had encountered people who seemed not to need social superiors to shape their ideas. One old couple he had met lived about sixty miles from the next settlement, deep in the forest. They were self-sufficient, their lives dignified and serene. When he had chanced upon them in the woods they greeted him as a fellow human being and therefore an equal. They simply had no concept of social superiority. It was from meetings with such people that Fitzgerald had taken to reading Rousseau, the philosopher who believed even savages might be 'noble' and whose works had enabled him to understand the struggle for equality now being waged in France.[2]

When he had first arrived in Paris Fitzgerald made the acquaintance of an English aristocrat who, like himself, was an enthusiastic supporter of the revolution. With this new friend, Sir Robert Smith, he sometimes discussed the self-contradiction implicit in remaining an aristocrat and simultaneously supporting the revolution. Then one day the two young men learned about a rather unusual dinner that was to be given in the city and agreed that they might go and make a sensation there.

So it was that on the afternoon of 18 November Fitzgerald and Smith attended a banquet at the Hôtel de White. As at many other dinners at that time the assembled revolutionaries seemed chiefly intent upon proving their patriotism by consuming as much of the French grape harvest as they were able. Soon the diners were hammering on the table and roaring approval of the toast; 'The armies of France; may the example of its citizen soldiers be followed by all enslaved countries, till tyrants and tyrannies be extinct'. At this point Fitzgerald and Smith looked hard at each other. Was it a disloyalty to their own King and country to pledge their support to such a toast? They decided to ignore the question. By that time bottles were being passed so quickly that the wine ran red from the mouths of patriots taking up strains of popular French revolutionary anthems. The *Carmagnole* followed hard upon *Ça Ira* and afterwards most triumphantly the *Marseillaise*. From a distance, a monarchist spy sent to observe these events might have taken this for

3

yet another dinner held to celebrate the proclamation of the Republic and the victories of its citizen armies in Savoy, Nice and the Austrian Netherlands. On drawing nearer however he would have been puzzled by the muttered conversations along the tables, for these were not in French but English; Fitzgerald and Smith were sitting among their fellow countrymen.

Other revellers soon arrived. There were deputies from the Convention, generals of the various armies of the Republic, and representatives from many nations where word of the revolution in France had stirred the minds of radical spirits. Each of these was welcomed in turn by the English chairman, Mr J. H. Stone, and talk soon turned to the way in which the French experiment might be exported to other countries. Edward met a fellow Irishman among the guests named General Dillon who rose to propose another toast; 'The people of Ireland; and may Government profit by the example of France, and Reform prevent Revolution'. The General it seemed still considered himself a loyal subject of King George III and only wanted the authorities at home to take heed of what would happen if they did not introduce reforms.

As one toast quickly followed on from another Fitzgerald and Smith waited for an appropriate moment in which to make their dramatic gesture. It came shortly after the diners had raised their glasses once again, this time to pledge themselves to 'the speedy abolition of all hereditary titles and feudal distinctions'.[3] At this point first Edward and then his friend rose to his feet, each formally renouncing his title. Their words were greeted with enormous outbursts of cheering and renewed bawlings of the *Marseillaise*. At last, with much backslapping and embracing, the dinner came to an end. He who had been Lord Edward Fitzgerald, scion of the most ancient Irish house of Geraldine, walked out onto the evening boulevards as plain Citoyen Edouard Fitzgerald. In an alcoholic haze he and Smith now strolled among the crowds of citizens and soldiers, tradesmen, prostitutes and beggars in order to try out their shiny new liberties. But soon they grew sleepy and needed a sit-down. So they turned into the Théâtre Feydeau.

Now Fitzgerald sat in a box with his heart pounding, hardly daring to look again at the young woman alongside him. Of course when he thought about it he knew that she was not, could not be his lost love. Eliza was thirty-seven when they had parted whereas the girl he had glimpsed looked less than twenty. But the resemblance between them was amazing. Another glance confirmed his thoughts. This was a much younger woman, though her slender, vulnerable figure seemed achingly familiar to him. He had to know who she was.[4]

After the performance he made some discreet enquiries. To his surprise he discovered that he already knew of the older gentle-woman. She was Madame de Sillery, Comtesse de Genlis, a celebrated novelist who had until recently been living in England. More than once he had been invited to meet her and her charges at the Sheridans' house at Isleworth. On those occasions he had declined, confiding to his friends that he had a horror of learned ladies, but now everything was changed.

Madame de Genlis was in Paris with very different motives from those of Fitzgerald. While he had travelled south to greet the revolution, she was heading north to get away from it; while he had renounced his title, she was trying to save a branch of the royal family; and while he might saunter carefree along the boulevardes, she was engaged in the perilous business of safely conducting two young noblewomen through the roaring streets of the revolutionary city.

Her party was to spend just one night in Paris. Madame had calculated that it was all the resting-time they needed there during their long coach journey from the south of France to Belgium. For safety's sake she thought that even that night would be better spent at the theatre than in the hotel. By the following day she expected to be well on her way towards the Belgian border with her charges and shortly after that she hoped they might board the packet to England where they would be safe. The two young women she was protecting were both of the highest social rank; in fact they were Bourbons, though this was a great secret. One was her pupil, Mademoiselle d'Orleans, the daughter of the Duke of Orleans. He was the sole member of the Royal Family who had pronounced himself sympathetic to the revolution and he had recently styled himself plain Philippe Egalité. As an aristocrat he was still aware that his family was in danger and had decided to send his daughter out of the country.

But it was the identity of the other young woman which most aroused Fitzgerald's interest. He learned that Eliza's double was named Nancy – though everybody called her Pamela. Madame treated the girl as her ward, claiming that she had been born in Newfoundland of parents named Seymour or Sims. Nevertheless it was said that Pamela was really Madame's illegitimate daughter and that the father was Philippe Egalité himself. It was this discovery which most disturbed Fitzgerald. He had never met the girl but understood that this was the same Pamela of whom Eliza had spoken during the previous spring when Madame de Genlis and her charges had been guests at the Sheridan home. Even as Eliza lay dying, she told him that he should forget her and marry Pamela. Fitzgerald, mad with love and grief, at first would not even look at the portrait of the girl that she showed him. Nevertheless she persisted. Although at the time he had flatly declined to meet the girl, Eliza's words now came back to him from the grave. The remarkable resemblance between the two women added to his fascination: Pamela was Eliza reborn.

Once his mind was made up Edward Fitzgerald was always bold and decisive. Next morning he sent his black servant Tony round to Madame with his card. She was flattered enough to put off her departure a little to receive 'Lord Edward' the title he temporarily resumed while courting Pamela. So impressed with him was Madame that despite the danger she arranged to spend another night in Paris to entertain him and afterwards permitted him to accompany her little party on the road to Rancy and Tournai. On the second evening he formally requested her permission to propose. At once Madame explained there was a difficulty: the girl was already engaged. She told him that Pamela had no money of her own and was going into a foreign land where she needed a provider and a protector. During their recent visit to England Madame had found such a man and accepted a proposal of marriage on Pamela's behalf. She admitted that the man was a widower, twenty-four years older than Pamela, but that he moved in the highest English society and was a Member of Parliament. Moreover she calculated that he must have been wealthy because he owned the famous Drury Lane Theatre. He was Irish like Lord Edward. She enquired whether perhaps the Milord knew of him. His name was Monsieur Sheridan.

CHAPTER 2

All Geniuses

Thirty years before the incident in the Théâtre Feydeau, concerts of a rather different sort were regularly advertised by two children in the city centre at Bath. Visitors to the Pump Rooms were frequently approached outside by a girl and boy asking them to buy tickets. They were exceptionally beautiful children, the girl about eight years old and her brother about two years younger. The tickets they offered were for subscriptions to a series of performances in the Pump Rooms by the Bath music master Thomas Linley. His lodger, the artist Ozias Humphry wrote in a description of the scene that the features of the girl 'prevailed upon the motley visitors of Bath when she gracefully held up her little basket with her father's benefit tickets at the door when they passed in and out of the Pump Room.'[1] It was a doubtful wisdom which sent two such attractive children into the streets on business. The great pleasure-city of Bath attracted many dissolute visitors, and careful parents would have recognised the moral danger to children. But Linley rarely considered the matter. He was interested in only two things: his musical career and money. He never failed to sacrifice his children in the pursuit of either.

When she had sold as many tickets as she could, the girl would carefully put away her takings and make her way home through Bath streets, hand-in-hand with her brother, jostling with visitors, horses, shopkeepers, chairmen, dressmakers, milliners, confectioners, actors and musicians. At last the children would cross the quiet close of the ancient Abbey before turning into busy Pierrepont Street with its shops and rushing carriages. Just off here was Pierrepont Place – otherwise called 'The Portico' – with its four columns supporting an archway. Beyond was little Orchard Street where they lived.

It was a quiet place except when the New Theatre opened its

doors at six-thirty and then later emptied its crowds out onto the street. And sometimes on a still summer night a last playgoer shuffling home up Orchard Street would stop in amazement at the cacophony of sound emanating from a tall old house near the Portico.[2] Through the open windows would come the crying of a baby, the noise of children quarrelling, the raised voices of a mistress scolding her maid, the scrapings of a violin from one room and harpsichord notes from another. But most remarkable of all was the sound of a young girl's singing coming high and clear from an upper sash. Even though simply running through her scales her notes were so liquid and fresh and charged with such an emotional intensity that for a moment her listener would stand transfixed. Then with a shake of the head he would go on. He had just passed the house of the Linleys.

They were an established Bath family. The music teacher Thomas Linley needed such a spacious house because his wife had given birth to twelve children over a period of eighteen years. The first, who died in infancy, had been christened George Frederick after the composer Handel, whom Linley admired above all others. The oldest of the surviving children was the girl who had sold tickets and sung from an upper room. Her name was Elizabeth Ann. In the family they called her Eliza.

Eliza Linley was born in Bath, probably in a house on Abbey Green, on 5 September 1754. She was baptised twenty days later at St Michael's Church. Her first home was on the Green but when she was about twelve the family moved to the eleven-roomed house in Orchard Street rented from a Mr Duperre for ten shillings a year. They remained there for the rest of her childhood.

Eliza was brought up in a home full of babies. The ages of her younger siblings is indicated by their baptismal years: Thomas 1756, Mary 1758, Thurston 1759, Samuel 1760, William Cary 1761, Maria 1763, Ozias Thurston 1765, the twins Jane Nash and Charlotte 1768, and William 1771. Only eight of the children survived into adulthood.[3] When in the early years the Linleys could not afford a maid, Eliza was required as the eldest to help with the housework. She went shopping, made beds, washed dishes, bathed and dressed her small brothers and sisters, gauffered her father's dress shirts, lit fires, and helped with the endless, endless mending of clothes. It was probably a good thing that Mrs Linley was an unintellectual woman for she needed all her practical resources to cope with her daily round of household duties. People said she had a quick temper, hardly surprising given her domestic situation. Linley may have had a small amount of financial help from his father, the prosperous Bath builder William Linley, but even so Mrs Mary Linley was obliged to make every possible economy. From 1762-4 she took as a lodger a young artist named Ozias Humphry. He became very fond of his landlady and often invited her up to his room to sing to him while he sketched one or other of her children. Humphry's drawing of her depicts a pleasant-looking if rather plump woman of about thirty; in her youth Mary Johnson had been considered rather pretty.[4]

To secure more living space in the crowded house some of the children were sent away to be educated. Both Eliza and Mary went to school in Wells for three or four years, and lodged with relatives. Jane Nash was also at school in Wells because later on she confided to her fiancé that she had lived in the country till she was about thirteen. Despite these efforts the Linley household remained crowded, shabby and noisy. Thomas Linley had no peace there. To a man with such a fine ear, life at Orchard Street must have been torture.

Linley was born two years before his wife in 1733 at Badminton in Gloucestershire. As a boy he was brought to Bath by his father and from the first he devoted his life to music. Some said that he had studied with a certain Signor Paradisi in Italy when he was young, though it is difficult to see how he could ever have found the money to do so. He loved music so much that when still a lad he became assistant to the organist at Bath Abbey, Mr Chilcot. His chief duty was to pump the organ but his musical talent was quickly detected and Chilcot, an excellent teacher, made him a full apprentice. As an organist, and harpsichordist of outstanding ability, as well as a fine tenor, Linley was able to set himself up as a music master in the city where, although still quite young, he was in great demand as a tutor for lady visitors. One who came to him in 1763 was Mrs Frances Sheridan, the charming wife of the famous Drury Lane actor Thomas Sheridan.

Eliza adored her father. He was still only twenty-one when she was born and in many ways the father and daughter grew up together. Linley was tall and dark with finely cut features which were inherited by Eliza, Tom, Mary and Samuel. Rather reserved with strangers, the music master would become animated when discussing music, while a poignant tune could reduce him to tears. But in defence of his business interests he could be quarrelsome and petty.

By the mid-1760s Linley was beginning to prosper. His growing reputation attracted more and more pupils and the public concerts he inaugurated at the Pump Rooms for fashionable audiences were not only profitable but served as excellent advertisements for his tutoring. At no time however did he neglect the musical education of his own children who were much more talented than any of his paying pupils. Eliza became a singer, Tom a violinist, Mary a singer and actress, and Samuel, after a Bristol debut aged six in which he danced the hornpipe at a performance of *King John*, took lessons from another Bath music master named William Herschel and was declared to have 'displayed great musical genius by his successful culti-vation of the oboe'. Soon Linley's older children ceased to be a drain upon his purse. On the contrary, their talents became significant assets in his household economy. This was especially true of Eliza.

Ozias Humphry was perhaps the first to feel her charm when she was still only a little girl. At the age of eight she could sing all the songs from such popular entertainments as *Thomas & Sally*, *The Beggar's Opera*, *The Chaplet* and *Love in a Village*. He wrote, 'These she would sing so sweetly that many a day at [his] solicita-tion, she chanted them, seated at the foot of his easel looking up at him, unconscious of her heavenly features.'[5] About this time her father became aware of the commercial possibilities of her looks and decided to send her out on the streets to sell concert tickets. As far as we know Eliza walked through these moral dangers unscathed.

As a child she had a delicate physique but she seems to have been healthy enough. If in her youth she sometimes complained of fatigue it was because her father worked her so hard. In fact when he discovered that it was the fragility of her appearance that made her especially attractive to concert-goers, he exploited the situation by arranging for her to sing the more pathetic arias.

As Eliza grew older she was aware of her good looks but she never consciously used them to charm and manipulate others. There was a gravity about her which informed her beauty with a moral qual-ity, apparent especially in her adolescence. The radical politician John Wilks, who was a noted womaniser, sensed there was something fine in her. After a dinner party where he had met Eliza and Mary he wrote to his own daughter; 'I still think' [that she is] 'superior to all the handsome things I have heard about her. She does not seem in the least spoiled by the idle talk of our [male] sex, and is the most modest, pleasing and delicate flower I have seen for a long time.'[6] In private with her brothers and sisters however Eliza was often lively and high-spirited with a will of her own. If her father pushed her too hard she could surprise him by suddenly rebelling.

Eliza was artistic in many ways; she sketched, wrote poetry, was an excellent mimic and a skilled instrumentalist. But it was her singing which brought her general admiration. Linley's teaching had strongly emphasised simplicity and directness. The professional musician Charles Dibdin, who shared Linley's views concerning the characteristics of fine singing, recorded in his *Professional Life* that his pupils were 'taught nothing more than correct expression, and unaffected pronunciation of words; the infallible and only way to a perfect singer'. He argued that the force and meaning of the words of a song should be stressed, as in speech. Dibdin considered Madame Mara and Elizabeth Linley to be the finest singers of his day 'because they were taught on this principle'.[7] But there was more to Eliza's singing than correct emphasis; her tone had a heart-breaking poignancy. In later years her sister-in-law remembered 'something angelic' in her voice, a beauty of expression which lent 'such additional charms to our sister's singing'. She possessed 'that same peculiar tone that I believe is hardly to be equalled in the world'.[8]

Recognising his daughter's ability to attract audiences, Linley put her to work by arranging concerts for her throughout the West Country. Her programme consisted mainly of pieces from Handel oratorios though she sometimes condescended to Arne's settings of Shakespeare's songs. She rarely sang anything lighter and never anything remotely amorous or skittish. When singing Handel her gravity of manner and purity of tone gave her a saintly expression. Linley knew there was money in that. His musical friend William Jackson, who was organist of Exeter cathedral, tried to sum up the young singer's appeal:

> Her voice was remarkably sweet and her scale just and perfect; from the lowest to the highest note the tone was the same quality. She had a great flexibility of throat, and whether the passage was slow or rapid the intervals were always precisely in tune. Her genius and sense gave a consequence to her performance which no fool with the voice of an angel could attain; and to those extraordinary qualifications was added a most beautiful person, expressive of the soul within.[9]

Meanwhile Linley had even higher hopes for Tom, and planned

to give him the best musical education that money could buy. He engaged a fellow Bath musician named David Richards to give Tom violin lessons. The boy's professional debut took place at the Bath Assembly Rooms in 1763. On 25 July in the same year *Boddely's Bath Journal* advertised a concert at Loggan's Rooms at the Hotwells where at the end of the first act a concerto on the violin was to be performed by a Master Linley who was a child of only seven years old. The boy was also to join a trio with his father and a Mr Higgins at the end of the second act.[10] Later Tom was sent to study with a friend of his father, Dr William Boyce, who was organist and composer to King George III and kept a house at Kensington Gore. At the end of each Bath season Tom went to stay with him for intensive coaching. Boyce was 'so captivated by the Child's Genius and disposition' that he agreed to teach him for five years. Very soon he reported that Tom had made 'astonishing progress'.

It was probably Boyce who procured parts for Tom and Eliza in their London debut at Covent Garden. The masque, entitled *The Fairy Favour* with music by J.C. Bach, had been devised for the first theatre visit of the future Prince Regent, four-year-old George, for it had been thought that he would enjoy the performance better if the cast consisted entirely of children. The libretto by Hull told how Titania had lost her boy but eventually found him again in a castle by the Thames. Tom Linley was the star. He played Puck, danced a hornpipe and performed a violin solo.[11] Of the two it was Tom who attracted the greater notice. On 3 February *The London Evening Post* reported:

> Nor can enough be said of the little boy, who plays the part of Puck; his singing, playing on the violin, and dancing the hornpipe, are all beyond expectation, and discover extraordinary abilities in one, who must be considered a child. [12]

On the nineteenth of the same month Tom was also reported to have played a violin solo at a concert by command of their Majesties King George and Queen Charlotte.

But Linley's ambitions for Tom went further than that. He understood that a young violinist could receive the finest training only in Italy and so he resolved to send his son there. Tom was only twelve but his future was already decided. His last concert in England was probably the benefit he played for Eliza on 21 May 1768. That month a Linley family friend, Thomas Gainsborough, painted a portrait of Tom with Eliza, later known as *Miss Linley with her brother Tom*. On 11 May Gainsborough wrote to his friend William Jackson about his subjects, asking: 'I suppose you know the boy is bound for Italy at the first opportunity.'[13]

Tom's subsequent departure was the first small break-up of the Linley family and it grieved Eliza deeply. She was fond of her brother. They had grown up together, they looked like each other, they performed in concerts together and shared the same sense of humour. Tom's cheerfulness had provided much of the fun in her life, and she was to miss him terribly.

Tom remained in Italy studying the violin until 1771 when he was fifteen. The fact that his father could afford to keep him there is evidence of the increased prosperity of the Linley family. Tom went first to Leghorn to be taught by the famous violinist Nardini. When Nardini moved to Florence to become Director of Music at the Ducal court Tom went with him. Nardini was not one of the exhibitionist school of virtuosi later popularised by Paganini. On the contrary his playing emphasised the qualities prized by the Linleys: clarity, sweetness and expression. Tom felt very much at home with his tutor and his regard was reciprocated. Apparently he was his master's favourite pupil and they gave concerts together in Florence, where Tom lived the life of a young gentleman. He enjoyed entertaining visitors from England, among them Dr Burney who had first glimpsed him among the 'nest of nightingales' in Bath.

Tom's intelligence, good looks, high spirits and bounding confidence, when added to his extraordinary musical ability, brought him not only admirers but true friends in Italy where he was often referred to as 'Il Tommasino'. Among the many who fell victim to his lazy Linley charm were an Austrian gentleman and his son who called on him one spring day in Florence in 1770. The boy was then just sixteen, older than Tom whom he called 'Little Linley'. Musical Italians considered these two lads to be 'the most promising geniuses of this age'. On 12 April 1770 the Austrian wrote to his wife from Rome to tell her of the meeting between Tom Linley and their own boy. It was Wolfgang Amadeus Mozart:

In Florence we came across a young Englishman, who is a pupil of the famous violinist Nardini. This boy, who plays most beautifully and who is the same age and the same size as

13

Wolfgang, came to the house of the learned poetess, Signora Corilla. The two boys performed one after the other through-out the whole evening, constantly embracing each other. On the following day, the little Englishman, a most charming boy, had his violin brought to our rooms, and played the whole afternoon, Wolfgang accompanying him on his own. On the next day we lunched with M. Gavard, the administrator of the grand ducal finances, and these two boys played in turn the whole afternoon, not like two boys, but like men! Little Tommaso accompanied us home and wept bitter tears, because we were leaving on the following day. But when he heard that our departure would not take place until noon, he called on us at nine o'clock in the morning and gave Wolfgang with many embraces the following poem, which Signora Corilla had to compose for him the previous evening. Then he accompa-nied our carriage so far as the city gate.[14]

While Tom was away, Eliza drew even closer to her younger sister Mary who was about three-and-a-half years her junior and who shared Tom's sense of fun. Mary's professional career began as a comic actress in winter of 1769 when she was just eleven. She appeared in a piece called *Man and Wife* at Covent Garden. The *Freeholder's Magazine* specially praised her 'great humour and vivac-ity'. The playwright and theatre manager George Colman was so impressed with her that he wanted to sign her up for a season at his summer theatre in the Haymarket, the home of Italian opera. Linley refused. He wanted musical, not theatrical careers for his children. As far as he was concerned the theatre was a source of moral danger for his daughters and like most respectable professional people at that time he regarded actresses as little better than prostitutes. Besides he believed he could make much more money from Mary as a singer. So Mary soon became a professional specialising in orato-rio. The craze for Handel's music had by no means died down by 1770 and a talented young soprano had ample opportunity to make money. Her voice was thought to be very fine, second only to that of her famous sister. In the spring of 1771, Gainsborough commenced his portrait of Eliza and Mary which was later named *The Linley Sisters*.

There were even more Linley prodigies in the pipeline. In 1770 Samuel was ten years old and already a veteran of the stage and a talented oboeist. He too was soon recruited to perform in his father's concerts. Even little Maria, only seven years old in 1770, was receiving singing lessons from Linley and showing considerable promise. These Linley children were not only good-looking musical prodigies, they also possessed a pronounced sense of humour and an infectious confidence. Before Tom had gone to Italy a visitor once called at Orchard Street and heard the girls sing. Afterwards he innocently inquired of little Tom whether he was also musical. 'Oh yes!' the boy replied. 'We are all geniuses here, sir'.[15]

By the age of seventeen Eliza had acquired a considerable reputation as a soloist throughout the south western counties. In 1770 both she and Mary performed at the Three Choirs Festival, and even though she was so young her father demanded a performance fee of £100 and got it. Well aware that his elder daughter had become a little goldmine, he had already taken the precaution of making her his apprentice and was therefore entitled to pocket every penny she earned. As a result, Eliza's life soon became a never-ending treadmill of practice and performance.

She had also become something of a cult figure after a curious happening one evening in Salisbury Cathedral in 1770. It was a miracle and no one expected it. Worshippers at an English cathedral seldom expect miracles. The congregation that evening had not gathered for an act of worship but for a recital of sacred music. All they knew was that a celebrated young singer was to perform arias from Handel's *Messiah*. When Eliza appeared her audience was not disappointed. She was still very young but her obvious confident composure suggested that she was already a complete professional. Her hair was dark chestnut in colour, her figure delicate, and her complexion very pale. It must have seemed to her audience that such a slight girl could never hope to fill the great nave of Salisbury with its sound. They were wrong. The musicians took up the strains of the aria: 'Rejoice greatly, O daughter of Zion, shout, O daughter of Jerusalem'. High above them a soprano voice sounded. It was not especially powerful but such was its clarity that it was audible throughout the cathedral. Most remarkable of all was its tone of such an extraordinary sweetness that the voice became the perfect instrument to match the soulful expression of the singer's radiant face. The girl was soon lost in her song. Had it not seemed a little too Romish and blasphemous on a cold Salisbury evening, local people might have thought they had a saint among them.

Then came the miracle. What happened next was reported by the local newspaper:

At a Salisbury music meeting . . . while Miss . . . was singing the air in the oratorio . . . 'I know that my Redeemer liveth', a little bullfinch that had found means . . . to secrete itself in the cathedral, was struck by the inimitable sweetness, and harmonious simplicity of her manner of singing, and mistaking it for the voice of a feathered chorister of the woods, and far from being intimidated by the numerous assemblage of spectators, it perched immediately on the gallery over her head, and accompanied her with the musical warblings of its little throat through a great part of the song.[16]

It was an epiphany. Word of the duet went fast round the cathedral town and this in turn increased the public's fascination with the youthful singer and her brilliant brothers and sisters.

With such extraordinary young talents at his command, Thomas Linley's regular concerts at the Bath Assembly Rooms became very popular events and were frequently sold out. Up until about 1767 he had had to struggle to feed his family and pay his bills but shortly after Eliza came home from her school at Wells and Tom joined her on the concert platform Linley could count on ever increasing profits. In time Eliza's annual fees alone were probably enough to pay the expenses of the entire family. Although in later years Tom and Mary began to earn considerable sums, because they were minors, their father kept everything his children earned. The fortunes of the Linleys rapidly improved. In 1767 he twice placed advertisements in the *Bath Chronicle* for the lease at Orchard Street, describing the house as 'neat' and 'convenient' 'next to the Portico' and possessing 'hard and soft water'. The notices did not attract any offers to the landlord Mr Duperre in Orange Court or at his snuff shop in Wade's Passage. But four years later by June 1771, the Linleys had left Orchard Street. Their lease up, they had moved to a brand new house in the Royal Crescent. Thomas Linley and his daughter were going up in the world.

CHAPTER 3

Entertaining Strangers

When the Linleys arrived at the Royal Crescent work was going on all around them.[1] The architect, John Wood the younger, had taken seven years to complete his masterpiece. The daytime noise was tremendous while gangs of navvies, masons and carpenters dug, sawed and hammered, and the road rumbled with huge carts bringing sacks of mortar, blocks of limestone and great lengths of uncut architrave. But above it all the serene roof-line of one of the most stunning terraces in Europe was slowly rising above the Somerset hills into the clear sky. No doubt Linley complained that he could not hear his pupils play and regularly regretted that he had ever left Orchard Street. Secretly, however, he was proud of his new address and delighted to be able to show that he had at last arrived in genteel society.

But the Linleys were in a curiously isolated social position. Linley's professional work brought him into daily contact with the gentry and even the nobility but as a music master he was little more than a superior servant. Nor was he the social equal of the professional men, the doctors and lawyers who tended to the wealthy people flocking to Bath. At the same time the Linleys were far too cultivated to mix easily with the local tradespeople. But even if the good looks and obvious gentility of Linley and his elder son and daughter tempted a hostess to invite them, the thought of Mrs Mary Linley would soon have stifled the impulse. There was something undeniably 'common' about her, something that would not do. So despite their growing affluence the Linleys were rarely invited out save as professional musicians and they entertained few guests themselves.

An exception came on an October evening in 1770. It was a meeting which although she did not realise it was to transform Eliza's life.

17

A few weeks beforehand, an ageing actor and widower, Thomas Sheridan, had come to live in Bath with his family. There had been an uneasy acquaintance between the Sheridans and the Linleys for years. As a return for the music lessons Linley had given to Mrs Sheridan, Eliza had recently been hired by Thomas Sheridan to supply the musical interludes to his London poetry readings which he referred to as his 'Attic Entertainments'. So when Linley asked the Sheridans up for supper he could be sure that at least these fellow artists would accept. More than that, he relished the opportunity to show off his splendid new house to an old colleague and rival, especially as he rather pleasurably suspected that while his own career was flourishing, Sheridan's was fast going downhill.

So that evening the Sheridans walked up from their rented house in Kingsmead Street[2] and were duly greeted by the Linleys in their splendid surroundings. If the shabby old actor were taken aback by the grandeur of the terrace house, he did not show it. Linley presented his wife, then Eliza aged sixteen, Mary aged eleven and Samuel who was only nine. In response Sheridan introduced his sons and daughters one by one and Eliza dutifully shook hands with them all.

In 1770 Thomas Sheridan was still only fifty-one but looked older, and yet his rather faded appearance was contradicted by his grand manner. He was in every sense an actor. He did not so much speak to people as address them in a strangulated sing-song. In order to tune up he would regularly clear his throat and then deliver his words in a curious monotone with odd and rather unexpected emphases. To the young Linleys he was affable and condescending but when he talked to their father he was dogmatic and obviously prepared to tolerate no argument. He relaxed only when introducing his elder son Charles, a self-confident young man of twenty who was clearly his father's pet. But Richard Brinsley aged nineteen, the seventeen-year-old Alicia and her twelve-year-old sister Ann Elizabeth were all passed over as if they were of little consequence.

After the Sheridans had admired the drawing room the two families sat down to start a conversation. It was initially a little strained while the two fathers contended for supremacy. Sheridan rather stiffly informed them all that he had come to Bath to seek new pupils to learn his 'system' of elocution (he called it 'orthoepy'). To hear him one would have believed that he was still a successful lecturer attracting many rich pupils. He even made it appear that he was doing the population of Bath an immense favour by offering them his services. Proudly he informed them all that Charles was now helping him in his great educational project of reforming society through elocution. Even Richard Brinsley was allowed to take a few pupils. He expressed total confidence that as the Bath season went on he would be overwhelmed by young gentlemen eager for lessons but in this he was not totally honest. However, he needed to keep up appearances in front of Linley. He was also fishing for Linley's help. The music master had extensive contacts in the city and Sheridan hoped to recruit new pupils from among them.

The assembled company listened respectfully to all this while Mrs Linley, pregnant and practical, bustled about the room filling cups and snuffing candles. And as the tea things went round Linley had his turn. He positively glowed with the account of his success. His practice, he claimed, was continually expanding especially with the higher class of people. His concerts were usually sell-outs, he was taking as many pupils as he had time for and his own children were exceeding all expectations with their talent. He was most proud of his absent son Tom who, studying under Signor Nardini in Italy, was regarded by his master as a musical genius. Linley had little doubt that when the boy came home he would shake the musical world. Then there was his Eliza (she coloured up at the mention of her name) who was enchanting the public with her oratorio singing. Mary was also a singer and young Sam who was only nine was making progress as an oboeist. He also informed his guests that at that very moment whole cradlefuls of Linley genius were asleep upstairs: young Maria, Ozias Thurston and Jane Nash aged six, four and one respectively, all of whom would undertake musical careers. Perhaps, he enquired politely, the Sheridans might like to hear his children perform?

So the music started. Mary sang and Samuel obligingly puffed out a tune upon the oboe. But pride of place was given to sixteen-year-old Eliza who, as her father accompanied her upon the harpsichord, sang favourite pieces from Handel while the Sheridans sat round and watched the candle-flames mooning in the spoons. Her general demeanour was rather timid but when she came to perform she was totally assured. And as her rich and vibrant young voice filled the Bath drawing-room that autumn night even Thomas Sheridan softened a bit. Then she changed the mood and introduced some old English songs and they all joined in the choruses. After that came more tea and refreshments.

A meeting between two such lively and artistic young families as the Linleys and Sheridans could only be a success. And despite the rivalry and stiffness between the fathers, the atmosphere soon relaxed and the chatter began among the young people. Eliza and Alicia were almost of the same age and by the end of the evening the Sheridan girls both called Eliza by her familiar name. She had learned to call Alicia 'Lissy' and Elizabeth 'Betsy'. The two fathers watched uneasily at this sign of a developing friendship among their girls for neither wished to encourage it.

For all his apparent affability, Sheridan despised Linley and would not have dreamed of calling upon him had not he desperately needed the musician's contacts. At best he considered Linley to be a provincial music master who made his fortune by getting his children to sell tickets in the street and allowed his own daughters to give public performances after which they might be propositioned by any man. The Sheridans, on the other hand, were descended from an ancient Irish house which had numbered its bishops and scholars of distinction. He believed that it was a condescension on his part even to visit Linley and he certainly did not desire any friendship to grow up between their children. Paradoxically, Linley was also against any such friendship though Sheridan would have been outraged to learn the music master's reasons. Linley believed that Sheridan was headed for professional and financial failure. This would not have been serious had Sheridan enjoyed a private fortune but he had nothing save a small Civil List pension. More than once he had been forced to return to the stage though he affected to despise the acting profession. Even as an actor Sheridan's glory days were over. He no longer rivalled David Garrick at Drury Lane, nor could he fill a London hall with his poetry readings. Linley understood well enough Sheridan's reasons for coming to Bath. He was in desperate search of a new audience.

Linley was especially contemptuous that Sheridan had brought up his children unable to support themselves. He was determined that each of his own children would be able to make a living out of the music business. When Tom returned to England he was obviously going to be a great success on the theatre and concert stages, and even at that time Eliza alone could earn £1,000 a year with her singing. By contrast, not one of Sheridan's two sons and two daughters was equipped to earn a penny. Teaching elocution was clearly no foundation for a regular income. The Sheridan children had few prospects and Linley did not want his children mixing with them.

Such thoughts were remote from the more generous responses of the younger people. As the Sheridan girls clattered and chattered down the hill that night, round the Circus, along Gay Street and through Queen Square, Alicia's voice was raised high with enthusiasm at the recollection of Eliza's singing. Her father stopped her short. There would, he said, be no further visits to the Royal Crescent. Charles, however, was absorbed with feelings which disturbed him. He was generally impervious to female charm but now the image of a young girl and the thrilling vibrancy of her voice had begun to possess his mind. What young Richard Brinsley thought is not recorded. He probably found the Linleys rather dull for they were not especially receptive to the sort of witty remarks on which he secretly prided himself. As for their music, people seemed to like it but he had no opinion. Nevertheless when he next wrote to his London friend Mrs Angelo, after reporting that his family were settled in 'a very neat house, pleasantly situated, and very cheap', he informed her of the private party with the Linleys and added that one of the young women present had sung 'like an angel'.[3] Not that he was any judge of singing. He was practically tone deaf.

Eliza Linley too, as she carried her candlestick up the grand staircase of their new house, was pleased at the prospect of a friendship with Alicia Sheridan. She was not sure how frank she could be with Alicia but at least she now had someone of her own age with whom she could talk things over. For though none of her family suspected it, Eliza was in the most desperate trouble. She was daily threatened by danger and disgrace. Nor could she see any way out of her situation.

CHAPTER 4

An Enemy

Who were the Sheridans? Soon after the party at the Royal Crescent, Eliza Linley's life became so closely interwoven with the story of this family that they must be introduced.

Thomas Sheridan was a famous man but by 1770 was bitter and cantankerous, long believing that his life was a failure. His body language proclaimed it: his voice was often harsh, his manner peremptory and his gestures heavy and clumsy. Everywhere he went, he was dogged by the conviction that his vast talents had gone unrecognised by the public and neglected by his friends. Often he suspected that people were laughing at him and this he could not bear. He had come to Bath painfully aware that in London there sat in a coffee house a great and influential man who spent much of his time ridiculing him.

Privately Sheridan was conscious that there might be something ridiculous in himself. Yet why this should be was not clear to him. He was not a man of narrow concerns. On the contrary he had lived his life in pursuit of an ideal. Ever since boyhood his mind had been preoccupied with poetry, especially the sound of the words of the greatest poets in the English language. As a result he had been passionately determined to share that experience with others. For years he had kept this faith and now he believed he was entitled to respect.

Sheridan was proud of his family. Among his ancestors he numbered clergymen, bishops, a minister of the crown and even the private secretary of a king, yet somehow in his own life this had counted for nothing. He was the son of a great scholar and the godson of one who had been the most famous man in Ireland, but these connections had done him little good. For years he had written books and given lectures to prove how the entire system of education for gentlemen might be transformed into something better, yet people did not want to listen to him. Now he was lonely, getting old and almost penniless, and he had come to Bath in one last desperate attempt to repair his finances. His mood was grim. Resentment at others and disgust with himself contended with each other to spoil any peace he might have had.

The Sheridans were of protestant Irish stock and they possessed a marked talent for self-publicity. In the early seventeenth century a certain Father Denis Sheridan, parish priest of Kildrumferton, defected to the Anglican Church and helped Bishop Bedell translate the Bible into Erse. [1] Of his four sons, two became bishops though one was deprived of his sees in 1711 for refusing to take the oath of allegiance to William and Mary. Another son had been secretary to the exiled King James II and was believed to have married one of the King's natural daughters. When he was later accused of complicity in the 'Popish Plots' and required to answer the charges before the Irish House of Commons, he turned the hearing into a show-trial, proudly claimed to have descended from one of the 'ancient families' in Ireland, applied for Habeus corpus and was freed.

Dr Thomas Sheridan (1687-1738), father of the Thomas Sheridan we have met, was a classical scholar and a fool. He was a nephew of the bishops, a schoolmaster, a translator of classical texts, a writer of comic verses and a layabout. He graduated as Doctor of Divinity in 1726, married, and later opened a school at King's Mint House, in Capel Street, Dublin. As a scholar he was a wonder; as a businessman a disaster. His wife, Elizabeth MacFadden, brought him £500 as a dowry but also a crowd of poor relations whom the Doctor had to support. Another part of her marriage portion was Quilca House in County Caven but this was in such a derelict state that it reduced Sheridan's fortunes even more. An account of the housekeeping there suggests that Mrs Sheridan was no better at managing practical affairs than her husband. Dean Swift said that there was only one lock and a half in the whole house; the key to the door was lost; the best bed threatened to collapse beneath the sleeper; the furniture was rickety; the empty bottles uncleanable; the full ones stuffed with rags; the street door hung upon one hinge and a great hole in the floor threatened to break the leg of anyone foolish enough to walk across. Such was the estate of the Sheridans.

Neither the Doctor nor his wife were capable of ordering their affairs and as time went on they got more and more into debt. An additional burden were the nine children whom Mrs Sheridan produced at a rate of one a year, four of whom survived. Then the Doctor had a stroke of luck; Dean Swift got him appointed chaplain to the Lord Lieutenant, Carteret. Unfortunately the Doctor's notorious vagueness contrived to turn the opportunity first into farce and then scandal. At his induction sermon Dr Sheridan took as his text 'Sufficient unto the day is the evil thereof', forgetting that that particular day was the anniversary of the Hanoverian succession. A Whig spy reported the matter and the Doctor was dismissed as Carteret's chaplain. He got on no better as a schoolmaster and the number of his pupils began to fall off. His friend Swift wrote in his epitaph: 'This good-natured improvident man . . . remained a punster, a Quibbler, a fiddler and a wit'. The Doctor said of himself: 'I am famous for giving the best advice and following the worst'.[2]

He first met Jonathan Swift in 1713 when the latter arrived in Dublin to become Dean of St Patrick's. They became instant friends and constant companions. Swift wrote part of *The Drapier's Letters* and *Gulliver's Travels* at Quilca House. Yet somehow the Doctor contrived to spoil even this friendship. Apparently Swift had asked him one day to keep notes on his (Swift's) displays of avarice for the purpose of reprimanding him about it. Without the slightest sense of tact, the Doctor did precisely this and was surprised when Swift eventually got tired of it and turned him out of the Deanery. When Dr Sheridan died Swift composed a sharply worded epitaph. He had, said the Dean, only two great ends in life: 'To spend his cash and lose his friends'.

Thomas Sheridan (b.1719) was the Doctor's third son and it was he who took the family to England and into the theatre. He was given a splendid start in life. Even after his godfather Swift had quarrelled with his father, the Dean continued to take an interest in Thomas and arranged for the boy to be awarded a scholarship to Trinity College Dublin. The young Thomas displayed scholarly leanings like his father and for a time it was assumed that he too would be a schoolmaster and perhaps a clergyman. He was the chief hope of the family. But he had been sent to school in England for a time, and while there the lonely boy sought company by attending the London playhouses. At Drury Lane, Covent Garden, the Haymarket or Goodman's Fields the curious playgoer might often have spied him sitting among the audience in his Westminster King's Scholar's uniform. He was stage-struck. And this passion persisted even after he came back to Dublin. At Trinity College, instead of gravely applying himself to his books and cultivating the useful acquaintance of visiting clergymen, the young student Sheridan spent his time writing a farce entitled *Captain O'Blunder or the Brave Irishman*, acting in college plays and reading Shakespeare aloud to admiring fellow undergraduates. He loved to perform, to strike attitudes and to declaim the lines of Shakespeare in lofty tones. He was high on dramatic poetry. And when the time came for him to leave college he would not hear of going into teaching. He was set on becoming an actor. In January 1743 Thomas Sheridan made his debut at the Theatre Royal, Dublin, as Richard III.

It was this step which Sheridan subsequently regretted. He gradually came to realise the loss of social status he had suffered by going on the stage. Initially he disguised this consequence from himself, pretending that his becoming an actor was really an educational project superior to mere school teaching. He was going to instruct the whole world. As one early biographer put it: 'The young man began to entertain the romantic idea that oratory constituted the first of human achievements; and that by perseverance he should be able to strike out new lights for the improvement of nations, instead of confining himself to the humble employment of instructing boys'.[3] But his experience of the actor's life soon destroyed any such illusions. His own father may have been unsuccessful, even a bit of a joke, but no one denied that he was a gentleman. As an actor, however, he could not command such respect. In the mid-eighteenth century both in Dublin and London actors were still regarded by middle-class people as little better than the rogues and vagabonds of the Elizabethan travelling companies. Such people were not fit company for gentlemen and especially ladies. Thomas Sheridan, graduate of Trinity College, soon began to feel this demotion very keenly.

But he loved his new life and the opportunity it gave him to exercise his talent for speaking verse and at night when he walked out onto the candlelit Smock Alley stage and gazed into the black cave of the auditorium, for a while he was able to put all his regrets about this choice of profession to the back of his mind. Here he was king, sometimes quite literally, playing Richard III, Richard II or Lear. Slowly he learned his craft; how to wring the heartstrings of an audience with passionate yet artful renderings of Shakespeare's speeches. His art took on new subtleties. While he worked out interpretations of the great classical roles, he became a very fine actor indeed.

Within two years Sheridan was manager of the Smock Alley theatre, responsible for hiring youthful talent from England for the summer seasons in Dublin. He brought over the brightest new stars from Drury Lane and Covent Garden, the ravishing Peg Woffington and an incandescent new talent named David Garrick. However, try all he might, there was little Sheridan could do to stop the frequent fights between the young bloods and the footmen in the upper gallery, and the impertinent behaviour of those who had paid to sit on stage who insisted on their right to interrupt the action of the play, and to wander at will behind the stage and into the dressing rooms.[4] Sheridan did all he could to reform these customs and finally, and for the first time in any theatre, forbade anyone to go behind the scenes except for the cast. Many a young 'gentleman' objected to the fact that a mere actor should tell him how he should behave anywhere. On one occasion a drunken young man named Kelly clambered over the orchestra rail and forced his way into the dressing rooms where he assaulted an actress. When Sheridan tried to restrain him, Kelly started a riot.[5] For this he was tried, imprisoned and fined £500. But Sheridan was a true actor. Knowing the incident would give him a splendid opportunity to display his true gentility, he announced that Kelly had been treated over-harshly and successfully petitioned for the young man's release. As a result, Sheridan became the hero of Dublin overnight. One young woman was so touched by his nobility that she sent some sentimental verses about him to the local paper. Sheridan traced the author, a Frances Chamberlain, and soon after persuaded her to marry him. They had something important in common. Mrs Sheridan admired him passionately and he shared her opinion.

In Dublin however the theatre was rough and this tended to put off respectable middle-class family audiences. Box office takings were frequently very low. But Sheridan struggled on as manager of Smock Alley, investing nearly eight years of his small profits into the place. During that time Frances bore him six children, four of whom survived. Then disaster struck. On 2 March 1745, during a performance of Voltaire's play *Mahomet the Imposter*, some of the actors' lines inflamed the nationalist sympathies of the audience and there was a riot. The theatre was sacked, boxes torn out, the expensive curtains slashed and part of the theatre set on fire. At once Sheridan understood that years of profit, however small, had come to nothing. The landlords were now his creditors and he would have to work for years to repay them for the damage to their property.

There was one offer of help. The English government approved of his stand against the nationalists and sensing that he might become a useful spy, offered him a pension of £300 a year. But Sheridan refused: he knew that to accept this bribe would finish any hope he might have of appearing on the Dublin stage ever again.

With the hope of rebuilding their lives soon Sheridan was playing at Drury Lane where David Garrick now reigned. The great actor was very generous to his Irish friend and even allowed him to take over his favourite roles of Hamlet and Richard III. But there was something too haughty in Sheridan to appreciate the honour. Though he was well received by the Drury Lane audience he could never reconcile himself to being regarded as 'second only to Garrick'. Not surprisingly he and Garrick quarrelled.

For some years Sheridan continued as an actor in London and was largely successful but as he failed to match Garrick's audiences he became progressively disenchanted with his profession. He believed himself to be too much the gentleman to appear on the stage and his mind wistfully churned over the matter of what profession he could follow other than acting.

Then an idea struck him. He was after all a graduate of Trinity College and an authority on the speaking of Shakespearian verse. In his opinion this made him an expert on every aspect of spoken English. So he decided to set himself up as a teacher of elocution, or as he termed it 'orthoepy'. To promote the subject he would found an academy. On the evening of 6 December 1757 he presided over a public meeting at Fishamble Street, Dublin, where over two hundred 'Lords, both Spiritual and Temporal, Privy Councillors, Members of Parliament, Doctors of Divinity, Fellows of the College, and Gentlemen of Fortune' endorsed his idea enthusiastically. Some of them even agreed to subscribe to it.

In the event nothing much came of the project but Sheridan pressed on with public lectures. He began to take in pupils with a growing private practice, usually young gentlemen eager to make a career in parliament but embarrassed by their regional accents. At first he was successful and welcomed a number of eminent novitiates to his home in Henrietta Street, Covent Garden. He also gave solo readings of Shakespeare and Milton in lecture halls. These 'Attic Entertainments' were initially very popular, especially after he hired little Miss Eliza Linley to provide the musical interludes, and meant he could simultaneously demonstrate his regained gentility, make money, and advertise his lecturing business.

This self-proclaimed expert on spoken English also published a number of textbooks on language and speech, including works on the art of reading, a projected scheme for the publication of an English grammar and dictionary, and *A Plan of Education for the Young Nobility and Gentry* (1769) in which he advocated that the entire education system should be based upon his own principles of orthoepy.[6] For a time he thought he had succeeded in breaking away from his first degraded profession as an actor, believing that he was now the teacher and professor he should really have been in the first place. At last, he was a gentleman again.

As such he was obliged to keep house on a rather grand scale because his clients expected to be entertained lavishly. One of his friends was Dr Johnson whose *Dictionary of the English Language* had appeared in 1755. For some years Johnson was a frequent guest at Henrietta Street, attracted there not only by the good food but also no doubt by the considerable feminine warmth and charm of Frances Sheridan. The great man was rather more sceptical about Sheridan's new profession, and was especially sardonic about the claims of any Irishman to be an authority on the pronunciation of the English language. In order to ingratiate himself with the sage Sheridan offered to use his aristocratic contacts to get Johnson a pension of £300 a year. Johnson was suspicious. In his dictionary he had defined a pension as 'pay given to a state hireling for treason to his country'. But when Sheridan assured him that such a pension was not for anything Johnson was expected to do for a political party but for what he had done already for his country, Johnson accepted.

Then came their quarrel. It took place when Johnson discovered that Sheridan had already accepted a pension of £200 a year for himself. He was mortified to have accepted an honour that had already been awarded to one he regarded as so much his inferior. 'What!' said Johnson, 'have they given *him* a pension? Then it is time for me to give up mine'. It was true that he afterwards added that nevertheless he considered Mr Sheridan to be a very good man.[7] However, this qualification did not appease Sheridan when he heard it. Boswell reported that nothing could soothe his injured vanity. Refusing to meet Johnson again he started to cut him in the street. They both began to make spiteful jokes about each other in the coffee houses. According to Sheridan, Johnson had 'gigantic fame in these days of little men'. According to Johnson, 'Sherry was dull, naturally dull; but it must have taken him a great deal of pains to become what we now see him. Such an excess of stupidity is not in nature.' They never forgave each other.

Sheridan continued to cultivate influential friends in his own interest. Eventually his contribution to language teaching was recognised by Oxford University which in 1758 'incorporated' him as a Master of Arts. Edinburgh made him a freeman in 1761, and Cambridge University gave him a master's degree in 1769. It was all good advertising but orthoepy never paid as well as his acting, and after a time it went out of fashion. Meanwhile the gentle but resolute Frances Sheridan had done her best to contribute to the family income by turning writer. In 1761, with the help of her friend Samuel Richardson, she published a novel, *Memoirs of Miss Sydney Biddulph* which was a success, and shortly afterwards Garrick produced her comedy *The Discovery* at Drury Lane. But even the combined earnings of the two Sheridans now failed to match their expenditure and when their debts rose above £7000, and a Scottish lecture tour failed, they agreed to fly the country. In a plan to avoid their creditors, husband and wife took separate coaches down from Scotland to Dover, and there in September 1764 they embarked for Calais with three of their children. Richard Brinsley, a schoolboy at Harrow, was left behind.

None of them had ever been to France, they spoke no French and knew no one. Frances was terrified of foreigners and the unfamiliar place in which she found herself.[8] Thomas Sheridan had only his Civil List pension to rely upon but at least in France he believed they would be safe from creditors and he could not be sent to the debtor's goal. He wanted to find somewhere where they might live quietly on his tiny income, and where he would have the peace and tranquillity to write his textbooks which he would send to be published in England to repair both his reputation and his fortunes.

So began a series of adventures the family never forgot. Their lack of French caused a great many confusions at first but on the way to Paris they picked up on the road a destitute Italian named Baptiste and he became their guide and mentor. Even then there were misunderstandings. At one point Thomas Sheridan felt safe enough to go on ahead to Paris to secure lodgings for his family, leaving them in the charge of Baptiste. But when they all got into the coach to leave for Paris he shouted 'Hotel de Picardie' to the driver, and Frances only heard the word 'Picardie'. Assuming that they were going the wrong way and that she would never see her husband again, she had hysterics and the whole family were in terror until they pulled into the inn yard in Paris.

From there they headed towards Blois as a staging post to the south. They never left that town. By chance they fell in with an old Englishwoman named Miss Hemin and she persuaded Sheridan that Blois was cheap and just the place for an English family to settle. So began a peaceful life on the banks of the Loire. They all learned French. When the weather allowed, Thomas Sheridan worked out of doors in their sunlit garden, composing his *Grammar*, *Dictionary* and a handbook for French students wishing to learn English. Frances also worked every day. She added two more volumes to her novel *Sydney Biddulph*, wrote an oriental tale, *Nourjahad* and started a new comedy, *A Journey to Bath*. Meanwhile the little girls kept a pet lamb but eventually it had to be butchered after it was caught eating a page from their father's precious *Dictionary*.

From 1764 to 1768 they lived at Blois cheerfully. It was a frugal existence of a few hundred pounds a year. Frances would sit out of doors singing to her daughters and accompanying herself on the guitar, and in his best actor's manner, Sheridan would announce grandly that the air of the region was 'inconceivably fine' and that he could live better in Blois on £100 a year than on £500 in London. Unfortunately, however, the payments on his pension became erratic and Sheridan was obliged to write to his good friend in Dublin, Sam Whyte, to beg for a loan of £100. Sam not only sent the money but revealed that he had successfully placed a petition before the Dublin parliament which would protect Sheridan from arrest by his creditors. This meant that he might go back to Dublin and London to start work again as an actor and might eventually pay off his creditors and restore his own fortunes. The whole family could go home.

Then tragedy struck. Sheridan decided to go ahead to Dublin to secure lodgings for his family. But his leaving preparations agitated Frances so much that she was seized with a fainting fit and had to be put to bed. At first the prognoses were good but her condition sharply deteriorated. Within a fortnight she was dead. She probably had cancer.

The funeral was as picturesque as any incident in a gothic romance. Although Frances herself had been friendly with the local priest, Thomas Sheridan would not allow his wife to be buried in the catholic churchyard in Blois. A local protestant family offered a plot in their private burial ground, but this was some way out of the town and getting the coffin there was a problem, because it was thought that the cortège might antagonise the local catholic population. A family friend who was a colonel in the French army advised that the ceremony should take place in the dark with an escort of dragoons which he would provide.

One night a little procession set off across the moonlit valley of the Loire. First came the troopers holding aloft their flickering flambeaux, then Thomas Sheridan with his sixteen-year-old son Charles, and finally the plain cart bearing the coffin. In the graveyard the dragoons took up defensive positions among the tombstones, but there was no surprise attack and the cortège peacefully returned to Blois as the dawn broke.

Some days afterwards the family packed up their belongings and left Blois for Dublin. On the journey, Thomas Sheridan called in at a protestant convent at St Quentin where he left Alicia and Betsy until he might send for them. Then in the autumn of 1768 he and Charles took the boat to Dublin. They had been in France for four years.

Back in London they took lodgings in Frith Street, Soho, where the girls and subsequently Dick, joined the family. Once more Sheridan took up his lecturing career interspersed with bits of acting. For two more years he pursued the chimera of reforming education on the principles of the correct reading of English verse. He was still obsessed with the idea but people had ceased to listen to him. He had become a joke.

Desperate, he brought his family to Bath, understanding very well that if he should fail to recruit new pupils, his own children would be threatened with destitution. He could barely contain his chagrin. Sometimes he took out his temper on the girls and sometimes on Dick. But what he really needed was an enemy, a reliable and permanent object for his blame. And it was in Bath that he found the person who would slowly grow into that office. She was an inoffensive seventeen-year-old girl, utterly confused and bewildered by life, who would have been amazed to think that she could have aroused anyone's hostility. She was Eliza Linley.

CHAPTER 5

Lovers

Eliza's trouble was men. They were always telling her that they had fallen in love with her and she came to dread such confessions. For one thing she never quite knew what they meant. Some of them seemed to be talking about powerful feelings she had unwittingly aroused in them but others implied something entirely different.

Her good looks were her undoing. As a young girl she was often frightened and puzzled by the effect she had on men. She was never quite sure whether they were expressing admiration for her singing or a lecherous desire. Perhaps they were not always entirely clear about their own intentions. But as Eliza grew older she learned to distinguish the motives of a blushing young man who had come up to the stage to blurt out his admiration for her from those of the practised womaniser who stared at her coolly and slipped a little note into her hand proposing that they should meet later.

By the age of seventeen she was the unchallenged beauty of Bath. In fact she was such an object of gossip there that the city was sometimes swept by rumours concerning the love-life of its own 'fascinating warbler', as one observer called her. Her fame had quickly spread to other towns. Fanny Burney at a London concert noticed how Eliza 'engrossed all eyes, ears and hearts', while in Oxford her appearances created a sort of 'contagious delirium' among the students. When the rumour went round that Eliza had 'gone to Scotland with a young man of £3000 per annum' there were long faces seen all over the city.

As Eliza got older this situation became increasingly painful and though she was not tempted, she was sorely tried. But her parents remained oblivious to her plight. Her father never understood that as her employer he was subjecting his daughter to many dangers. As for Mrs Linley, she was too preoccupied with her pregnancies and housework without Eliza adding to her worries. Besides, the Linleys were staid people. How could Eliza tell them that from morning to night she had no peace from men? She even felt guilty that she was constantly exposed to unwanted flattery, doubtful invitations, passionate confessions, lewd remarks and immoral propositions.

In 1770 her current admirers included Mr Morris, a tenor with whom she was sometimes obliged to appear, and an indolent and wealthy young man called Watts. Then there was Charles Sheridan. She had first met him on the night his family called on the Linleys at the Royal Crescent. Eliza recognised at once that she had aroused his interest. It was all too depressingly familiar. From then on Charles tried to meet her as often as possible. A handsome if rather stiff twenty-year-old with an immense opinion of himself, he wanted to appear wise, though in fact he was merely calculating. He was very unlike his younger brother. Where Dick was quick he was plodding; while Dick was full of charitable feeling, he thought chiefly of himself and where Dick's ambitions soared, Charles simply wanted a good job. But though their natures differed, the two young men were quite close, and Charles felt free to discuss his passion for Eliza with his brother. Night after night they came back to the same subject: how could Charles with no wealth, profession or prospects hope to win the hand of such a splendid creature as Eliza Linley? Dick was a good listener but could give no encouragement. By contrast, when Thomas Sheridan heard of his son's infatuation he said a lot. He was ruthless. Did Charles not understand that a true gentleman could never consider marrying the daughter of a mere provincial music master, a girl who was little better than a common actress paid to display her charms to the public?

Despite this parental opposition, Charles persisted in making some sort of proposal to Eliza which provoked Linley into a burst of anger.[1] He reminded Eliza of just how much she could earn, and that her prospects were rising. He said that with her looks and unrivalled opportunities to display them she might marry anybody. He was certainly not going to let her go off with a penniless young man who was nothing but the elder son of a failed actor. Unknowingly the fathers agreed with each other. As for Eliza, she was only too relieved to be forbidden to marry a man to whom she was not attracted in the first place.

That autumn Charles Sheridan became very depressed and

remained so throughout the next year. Yet despite the fact that Eliza had never given him the slightest encouragement he carried on believing that she really did want to marry him. He was conceited enough to think that a rational young woman must prefer his obvious good looks and ability to those of any other man. When Eliza failed to respond, his injured pride could only account for it by supposing that she was as avaricious as her father and assessed any prospective husband purely on the basis of money.

But when he came to review his own prospects soberly Charles was obliged to admit that his passion for Eliza was inevitably a hopeless one. Both fathers were implacably opposed to the match, he had no income of his own, and no prospects to offer the girl. After pondering on his passion for weeks, Charles abruptly decided to give up all hopes of Eliza. Some time during the summer of 1771 he wrote her a letter of farewell and asked Alicia to give it to her. Then he retired to a farmhouse in the country about seven miles from Bath where there was no likelihood of regularly bumping into Miss Linley. He was determined to expunge her from his mind, and set about it with a routine of activities. Some time later, when the business had blown over, he even tried to solace his feelings by making a pass at Mary Linley.[2]

Charles Sheridan was shallow, pompous, self-centred and lacking any kind of emotional spontaneity. This shows how easy it was for Eliza to generate powerful feelings in even the unlikeliest people. Charles did not get over her immediately. Years later, even when a husband and father, he could still be upset when her name was mentioned.

How different from Charles' frigid passion was the awakening sexuality which Eliza provoked in Nathaniel Brassey Halhed! 'Nat' Halhed was an undergraduate at Christchurch, Oxford and came from a wealthy Oxfordshire family. Despite the fact that his father was a director of the Bank of England Nat always seemed to be in need of money, perhaps because he spent so much of his allowance on theatre tickets. He was a fine classical scholar but could never stick to anything, admitting cheerfully that one day's hard work might be undermined by several nights of 'dissipation', (by which he meant hard drinking). He was charming, sentimental, with wild hopes of achieving literary fame and becoming rich as a dramatist. He was always falling in love.

Nat was passionate about music; he rarely missed an Oxford concert. One morning he went to a recital of oratorio pieces given by a Miss Linley from Bath. He had heard that she was beautiful and was at first prepared to be amused by the effect she had on his fellow undergraduates. But after some minutes her powerful presence and deep feeling began to work on him too. He was startled to find that the young lady he thought he was in love with suddenly seemed to take second place to Eliza. With the frankness of youth he wrote to tell a friend; 'I dare not examine too closely whether I am in love with her (Eliza) or no. Were Dessy young enough for me to have serious hopes, I am sure I should not. But I am afraid that with her the fire of love must change for the gentle glow of friendship.' In all Halhed probably met Eliza on not more than three occasions but it was enough to change his entire life. After her visits he would sit quite still in his college room, while her poignant tones re-echoed in his memory. He was learning the meaning of suffering.

By a strange coincidence the friend that Nat Halhed had written to was Richard Brinsley Sheridan. They had been at Harrow together and were now engaged in a literary partnership conducted by correspondence.[3] When sending copies of his latest translation of Greek poetry Nat would usually enclose a covering letter containing all sorts of gossip. Naturally when he learned that Dick Sheridan knew the Linleys he could hardly wait to tell his friend about Eliza's success in Oxford. He cheerfully reported the sensation caused by her first concert in the city and also the general dismay evoked by the news that she had eloped. But his feelings became serious after one recital when he was personally introduced to her. In order to save postage, she had agreed to bring him a parcel from Dick Sheridan. In ecstasy Nat wrote to Dick: 'I received your packet by the fairest hands that ever inspired a harpsichord with sentiment and feelings.' Even Thomas Linley took a liking to the young man and invited him to Bath. Nat wrote to Dick: 'You need not doubt my resolution of visiting King Bladud [the mythical founder of Bath]; however wavering I might have been, you may guess I am determined by another view of Miss Linley'. He confided that he had 'promised the Linleys' to visit them in Bath as he was now on terms of 'personal intimacy' with them. He added; 'I have just been to hear [Eliza] rehearse. I am petrified; my very faculties are annihilated with wonder. My conception could not form such a power of voice – such a melody – such a soft yet audible tone! O Dick – '[4]

As for Eliza, she barely distinguished Halhed's adoring glances from those of the other students who crowded into her concerts, familiar as she was with the atmosphere of puppyish adoration which pervaded such occasions. She would see scores of undergraduates, most of them deprived of female company all their lives, now briefly permitted to gaze on her from a distance. These concerts were climactic events in which her final liquid notes would hang in an air heavy with adolescent yearnings, only to fall into a roar of cheering released from hundreds of young male throats. Some among her audiences were emotional romantics like Halhed, who asked for little except to admire her from afar; others were impertinent young men who would openly stare after her outside college gates, making it plain that their interest had little to do with oratorio. At such times her father would hurry her along. In Oxford she was not permitted to go out alone or to speak to any young man. She was kept prisoner.

By the spring of 1771 Halhed had become Eliza's devoted admirer but at this stage his feelings were fickle. Even as he wrote to Dick to admit that he could not 'get Miss Linley out of his head', he was finishing a fifty-line poem in 'heroic pastoral' measure about a 'very pretty girl' he had glimpsed in the Oxford music-room. Nevertheless his regard for Eliza was heightened by the encouragement he received from her parents and their invitation to visit them in Bath. After the unfortunate business with Charles Sheridan the Linleys discussed what was to be done with their daughter. Realising that she would not remain his apprentice for ever, Linley now seems to have hit on the idea of marrying her off to some rich man so that the whole family might share in her good fortune. Halhed looked like a good prospect; his father was something in the Bank of England. Eliza probably never realised that her parents wished to inspect Halhed as a prospective husband and may not have known that he was in love with her. As far as she was concerned, Nat Halhed was good company, and everything she liked in a young man. He was musical, charming, sentimental and a friend of Dick Sheridan.

The calculating Linleys were too busy for Halhed to visit them in Bath, but on 29 April Eliza was back in Oxford again when, as a complete change from the solemnities of her Oratorio season at Drury Lane, her father actually permitted her to perform for one night at the Music Hall. She sang a saucy song about suitors:

Well! Sirs, then I'll tell you without any jest,
The thing of all things I hate and detest;
A Coxcomb, a Fop,

A Dainty Milk-sop,
Who's essenced and dizzened from bottom to top,
Looks just like a doll in a Milliner's Shop.[5]

Halhed does not mention that he saw Eliza on this visit but it is hardly likely that he missed her. Shortly afterwards he received a letter from Dick enclosing a mote which Eliza had personally signed. It was probably little more than a conventional expression of her best wishes but it may be imagined just how much this lovesick boy would have treasured the scrap of paper.

Then on the 29 July 1771 came the blow to all Halhed's dreams of marrying Eliza. That day he wrote to Dick to tell him of the terrible news: his father had obtained for him a post as a writer, in the service of the East India Company. This would give him affluence and a job for life but he would have to go to India and live there for many years. He was still totally dependent on his father and he knew it was no good arguing. There was now absolutely no possibility of sharing his future with Eliza. His fate, he said, was 'positively determined'. He apologised for burdening his friend with his grief: 'the effusions of passion' he wrote, 'are never very entertaining to a third person'. When Dick passed the news to Eliza, Halhed's letter thus revealing to her for the first time the depth of his passions, she could only feel sorry for this poor young man. He was now suffering a breakdown. The brute fact that he must soon part with her for ever jerked Nat into the recognition that he was now madly in love. It was the first adult passion he had ever known and its immediate disappointment had a tragic effect. Dick wrote from Bath to console him, enclosing a note from Eliza. Halhed replied:

> I did not know the situation of my own heart, till I received your letter; but the sight of a signature from a hand on which .
> I could have wished to breathe out my soul, and some thought of the little care I took to express the peculiarity of my sensations when I had it in my power at Oxford, have put me in a situation very difficult to express – the Bath post-mark would at any time have made my heart flutter like a frightened bullfinch in a cage, yet if your letter had in the inside discoursed wholly on other topics, there might have been some chance that I should waive the melancholy reflections that now assault me. But your present epistle has unmanned

me. By heaven! it has almost put a period to my very functions, and I cannot see, speak, write, or think as I used to do, or as I ought to do.

O Dick, there are certain things (I perceive it too late) that attack me most forcibly on the thought of quitting my native country. I once hoped that my sensations would be few, and my pangs trivial. But they already overcome me by mere anticipation. What will be the consequences of them when the time, that fateful time comes, it is impossible for me to imagine.[6]

He added that he did not think that he would be able to see Dick before his departure for India, and as for Eliza 'of whom [he] dare not think but as a divinity', he was grateful for her good wishes. His final comments are (perhaps) deliberately ambiguous:

. . . as far as delicacy will permit, I would wish you – Dick, [to use] your own eloquence on this occasion for I well know the insufficiency of my own; and perhaps she may be inclined to yield attention to the readiness of your thoughts when the stale and trite methods of my sentiments might have unspired [sic] her with no other ideas but those of contempt and disgust.[7]

It is not clear here whether Halhed is advising Dick to use the 'readiness' of his thoughts to continue to press Halhed's suit or to make love to her on his own account. It seems most likely that Halhed was 'as far as delicacy permitted' turning the girl over to his friend. The last of *The Epistles of Aristenaetus* they had translated together and which was published only a few weeks after Halhed had written his letter to Dick is entitled: 'From a Lover resigning his Mistress to his Friend'. It contained two lines which seem to express Halhed's own mood:

I yield to you – what I cannot cease to love,
Be thine the blissful lot, the nymph be thine . . .[8]

By the time it came for him to depart from England, Nat Halhed was deeply depressed and embittered. He had a sense of having been used, though he could not say how. Nor could he understand why Eliza had only ever written those notes tucked into Dick

Sheridan's packets, instead of private letters. Halhed's passion was still so real to him that he hardly recognised that he had barely spoken to the girl and had never enjoyed an intimate moment with her. It existed solely in his own head, and in the words of some rather indiscreet letters he had written to Dick Sheridan. Even so, he felt rejected. He also suspected that he was just one of life's plodders, while Dick was one of those people blessed by talent and destined to succeed. He wrote a goodbye letter to his friend:

> But perhaps, Dick, the only reason and the only person in the world that could have the least influence in causing my stay, may have an equal share of power over and more participation with your destiny. If so, Dick I envy you more than I can express, and shall envy you, if I come to have mountains of gold at my disposal. . . I have been a very miserable creature, and in all probability am doomed to more misery than any I have yet felt. The only thing I can possibly induce myself to believe I possess is sensibility; and in such a situation as mine, when it has Eliza for its object, ought I to look upon it as a blessing? . . . But I believe, Dick, however fortunately you may be situated in the meridian sunshine of all that is worth thinking of in this world, that you still have humanity enough to sympathise with the torments of absence, and good nature enough to pity them. . . Adieu, Dick.

When time came for him to embark, Halhed was only just well enough to board the ship which was to conduct him from an icy England to the lush island of Madeira. But after a few years in the vast and mysterious subcontinent he was a success, enjoying a reputation as a translator, not of amorous Greek epistles, but of a series of oriental law books, the Persian version of the Gentoo code. However, the loss of Eliza seems to have had a debilitating effect throughout the whole of his early life: it was not until thirteen years later that he married Helena Ribaut, the daughter of the Dutch Governor of Chinsura.

As for his 'bequest' of Eliza, it could have no possible consequence. Eliza was not Halhed's to give, and Dick made no move at all to start courting her. In fact he seemed indifferent to her, which may have been a great relief to the girl who needed a friend rather than another admirer. As far as she was concerned, Nat Halhed's infatuation was yet another example of how her good looks provoked profound but unwanted feelings in other people. She did not wish to have this effect; she did not understand it: it alarmed and depressed her. But she could not waste too much emotion worrying about Halhed when she had another lover close at hand, not sweetly romantic like Nat, but persistent, lecherous and dangerous.

This was Thomas Mathews, or 'Captain' Mathews as he liked to be called. He first came to Bath in 1770 when he was twenty-six. Descended from an old-established Llandaff family, with estates in both Wales and Ireland, he was sometimes called 'the Irishman'. Mathews had served in the 86th and 56th regiments as an ensign but had resigned to get married. His wife Diana Jones was 'an heiress of Glamorgan' with an ancestral home at Fonmon Castle. It was Mrs Mathews' dowry rather than her husband's family annuity that enabled the Mathews to live a stylish life in Bath. And though his wife was a shy woman, Mathews himself went about the town a good deal and had the knack of making himself popular. He entertained fairly lavishly both local personalities and national celebrities. Very soon after his arrival in Bath, he made the acquaintance of Thomas Linley.

Eliza was only sixteen when Mathews first became a regular visitor to the Royal Crescent, and it was not long before he was such an intimate friend of the family that Linley asked him never to stand on ceremony but to walk right into the house when he wanted to. Presumably the music-master thought that he might profit from such a wealthy acquaintance. Mathews often did walk in and the Linley parents professed themselves delighted with their new friend. He was so attentive to them all, particularly Eliza, insisting that she only went about the streets on his arm and nobody else's'. For this the elder Linleys were especially grateful: even they were aware that their daughter might need some protection when walking in public. Occasionally Eliza would return these visits by calling upon the Mathews at Portland Place, perfectly proper because Mrs Mathews was always at home. There is no doubt that Eliza was at first flattered by the attentions of this fashionable officer some ten years older than herself but at just seventeen she was still too young to judge the propriety of the relationship. Nevertheless there was talk about it. People remarked that it was very unwise of Mr and Mrs Linley to allow their handsome daughter to go about so openly with a married man.

As Eliza grew older however, her feelings for Mathews changed. She dreaded to be left alone with him. On such occasions his jokes and flirtatiousness quickly gave way to sexually explicit behaviour. He was always trying to touch her, and he soon began to make suggestions that they should become lovers. She would have complained to her father had she not been terrified. For she knew very well that if Linley found out what was going on, he would have challenged Mathews to a duel and would stand no chance against the professional soldier. So she kept quiet about things and in private avoided Mathews as best she could. In public she dared not alter her behaviour to him too abruptly in case this should provoke suspicion.

A visitor to Bath in the summer of '71 might still meet young Miss Linley on the arm of Captain Mathews as they took a turn in the river gardens to see how the building of Pulteney Bridge was getting on. But as Eliza understood Mathews better, this forced intimacy grew more and more irksome. She had learned to detest the man who had subjected her to constant sexual harassment even as a child and was mortified that their friendship was the subject of Bath gossip. To be seen on his arm in the public streets had become a matter of deep embarrassment to her. When a group of disapproving ladies looked their way, Mathews would only laugh loudly and ostentatiously put his arm round her. He thought that she was his property and liked to advertise the fact.

So in that summer, at the age of only seventeen, Eliza found herself surrounded by a group of men intent on making demands on her. There was her father, who forced her to a never-ending grind of practice and performance; there was the cold fish Charles Sheridan, who was at that time sulking in the country because he could not have her; there was a hopelessly sentimental boy dying of love on board a ship in the middle of the Indian Ocean; and a heartless womaniser determined to ruin her. Things could hardly be worse.

But they could. One day her mother and father called her in to hear some wonderful news. They said that they had accepted on her behalf a splendid offer of marriage from a Mr Walter Long. He was very rich and just over sixty years old. When Eliza, bewildered, protested that she had never met the man in her life, they said they would soon put that right. She was going to meet him very soon.

CHAPTER 6

Farce

The scene was set in the drawing room of 11 the Royal Crescent, Bath on a sunlit morning in 1771. A splendidly dressed but pale and nervous young woman was sitting opposite the windows as if deliberately posed for a portrait by Mr Gainsborough. Another older woman fussed behind her chair performing little duties for the younger one, such as smoothing her blue silk dress, arranging the lace at her wrists and patting down her magnificent chestnut hair. But these services were unrequested and seemed only to annoy her daughter. Their conversation was repetitive and carried on in urgent whispers. The girl repeated that she would not see the visitor who was due in a moment and made as if to get up from her seat to leave the room. Over and over again her mother regularly responded that she must stay there and pushed her down again. Wearily the girl watched the motes rise and fall in the shaft of sunlight at her feet. Eliza Linley was waiting to meet Walter Long.

Her spirits were very low and she cared nothing for the fact that she was about to be introduced to the highest bidder on the local marriage market. At first she had flatly refused to hear of Long as a suitor. Her father, who had for many years taken it for granted that she would always do as she was told, was taken aback by the violence of her response. Rows and shouting matches followed and a few times, in her desperation, this gentle and amenable girl had almost come to raining blows on her father's face. Frequently these quarrels ended with her storming out of the room, slamming the door and rushing upstairs where she would collapse in a tear-stained heap on her bed. She simply could not understand how her father could do such a thing to her as to force her into marriage with this sixty-year-old bachelor. Surely he should have had some respect for

42

her feelings? And perhaps at times, after sitting and sobbing alone in her bedroom, she remembered that other girl in ancient Rome who had dedicated her virginity to God, and when her father insisted that she should marry, preferred death to breaking her vow. They boiled her in oil but through the entire ordeal she still sang hymns and they could only stop her singing by cutting her head off. This way Cecilia had become patron saint of musicians. Now Eliza secretly vowed that she too would rather die than marry this old man.

But as one spring day followed another her parents slowly undermined her will. Each morning she was greeted by her father's closed mouth and stony face over the breakfast table. And when Linley had gone off to his business Mrs Linley was left guarding Eliza. Throughout the long mornings she would follow the girl from room to room, scolding and arguing, and her theme was always the same. Eliza was a wicked ungrateful girl to disobey her kind father to whom she owed everything. She would break his heart with such disobedience. And it was all so silly because if only Eliza would think clearly about what was being proposed she would understand that Mr Long was a brilliant match and a grand connection for them all. He was one of the richest men in Wiltshire, reputed to be worth £200,000. If only Eliza would see sense about the marriage she would soon have a splendid home and an assured place in genteel society. Mrs Linley protested that she could not understand what the girl could have against Mr Long. And for a moment her voice flickered with suspicion. Had Eliza encouraged some other man, some penniless young adventurer? To tell the truth Eliza was a little flustered by this question and perhaps not entirely truthful in her answer. But when her mother was satisfied there was no other lover, she returned to the main attack. Surely Eliza must realise that in securing this match her fond father had only her best interests in mind?

As Eliza remained obstinate her mother hardened. Of course, she said, Miss hoity-toity Eliza Linley had never known poverty as her parents had done. She was used only to living in a grand house with plenty of money to feed her and put clothes on her back. But when she sipped her breakfast chocolate or stepped into a sedan-chair in the street, where did she think the money came from to pay for all this? When Eliza sobbingly responded that Long was too old for her, her mother was contemptuous. What did a difference in age matter? If a girl were to marry a rich man it was surely better that he should be old, so that she would not have to put up with him very long and might soon look forward to having complete control of his money for herself.

Still Eliza held out and the atmosphere at the Royal Crescent grew worse. Mrs Linley did not give up however; she now pretended to agree that perhaps Eliza was right in refusing a man she had never met, and perhaps not unreasonable in declining to accept him without having been introduced to him. But she argued that at least Eliza might agree to meet Mr Long, whom she surmised must have fallen in love with her daughter when seeing her on the stage. Surely, Mrs Linley persisted, this was a great compliment and Eliza should be grateful for it. By such arguments the parents ground her down and in the end Eliza gave in and agreed to meet him. But all the while, at the back of her mind, there grew the fierce resolve never to marry this old man.

In the drawing room at the Royal Crescent the clock ticked loudly, the sunlight from the window imperceptibly slanted a little more to the west and still Eliza waited. Then at last there came the sound of foot-falls and male voices in the entrance hall outside and Thomas Linley entered the room with an elderly man. He was introduced first to Mrs Linley and then to Eliza. Obediently she took the gnarled hand prof-fered to her but would neither look him in the eye nor respond to his remarks. Then, to her alarm, her parents left the room. But although Walter Long remained very respectful and complimentary in the remarks he made to her, she steadfastly declined to enter into conver-sation with him. Disappointed, he bowed his way out of the room and within a minute her parents returned, furious.

Now they re-doubled their campaign. Both of them regularly harangued her at home so that she got no peace from morning to night. Nor was her father averse to economic blackmail. He pointed out that she was still entirely dependent upon him, and that if she continued to disobey him he would have every justification for turn-ing her out into the gutter. What would she do then? Beg? At such moments her mother would chime in with observations that Eliza's dear father was only trying to provide for her when her looks and voice were gone. As a mere seventeen-year-old she did not know how to answer them. In the end she gave way.

When the news of her engagement to Long went round Bath there was despair among Eliza's many admirers. Charles Sheridan was bitter and felt justified for having said that Eliza was merely a fortune-hunter. As for Thomas Mathews, he was mortified at the thought that old Long would have the girl before he could. Neither of them guessed that their anguish at this marriage was nothing compared to Eliza's. She felt like a trapped animal.

In the spring of 1771 and for the first time she could remember, Eliza's father allowed her singing career to take second place to other concerns. To her surprise he even agreed to Long's request that she should give up her programme of engagements. At first he had resisted this suggestion, because whenever Eliza cancelled a concert he lost money. But Long's cheque book soon dispelled Linley's objections. The lovesick old bachelor announced that he would pay Linley £1,000 for the loss of his apprentice daughter's earnings in the period leading up to her marriage. That was the kind of argument Linley understood. He now professed to agree with the bridegroom that it was not proper for a lady of Long's elevated class to sing in public. Eliza was relieved. She had come to detest public concerts where people only came to stare at her instead of listening to her music, so for a time she was content that these old men should stop her singing. Soon afterwards it was publicly announced that Miss Linley was to withdraw 'from public exhibition'[1] and she had more time for the doubtful pleasures of fitting dresses, discussing changes to Long's house in Gay Street, and completing arrangements for the summer wedding. Her suitor was most generous. He paid for everything, and in addition presented his bride-to-be with jewels said to be worth a thousand pounds.

As the wedding day approached Elizabeth began to panic. At first there seemed little she could do to prevent it. She had already tried so hard to get her parents to change their minds that she knew it would be no good appealing to them. But her growing perception that she had had little share in determining her own destiny, that from the beginning her father had appointed himself as her master, and that now without her agreement he was proposing to hand her over to his successor, made her increasingly resentful. There followed yet more blazing rows with Linley in one of which she screamed at him that 'if she got married at all, she would do so to be free, and not to be a slave'.[2] It did no good. Her father was genuinely baffled by her attitude. Was he not doing his best to ensure that she would always have a good home? He did not really understand what she was complaining about.

It then occurred to Eliza that there remained one avenue of escape which still might be tried. It was not likely to be successful but she resolved to test it. Her idea was to throw herself upon the mercy of the man appointed as her husband-to-be. So she wrote a private letter to Long and told him that 'she could never be happy as his wife,[3] and that 'her reluctance to the proposed match (was on) the ground of her attachment to another and requesting that he would withdraw his suit in order to shield her from her father's displeasure'.[4]

Incredibly it worked. Many years later a lengthy account of the courting of Eliza Linley was published by her friend Alicia Sheridan. Other than her brother Dick, Alicia was better placed than anyone to know about these matters. Throughout the period from October 1770 to March 1772, she was Eliza's closest friend and enjoyed many intimate conversations with her. And it is Alicia's account which provides the remarkable information concerning Long. For according to her, when once he received Eliza's pleading letter he acted like a perfect gentleman. He did just what she asked. Out of pure consideration for her feelings, and without giving Linley any reason for his behaviour, he withdrew from the engagement.

Of course, when he once heard that the marriage had been broken off, Mathews was overjoyed and soon began to pester Eliza again. By contrast, Linley was outraged at the thought that not only had his beautiful daughter been rejected and made a subject of ridicule in Bath, and his whole family had just failed to marry into a fortune, but that he had lost a considerable amount of money in concert fees. So he sued Long. Surprisingly the whole business was settled with very little unpleasantness. Long could easily have exonerated himself from charges of breach of promise by producing the letter in which Eliza had begged him to break off the marriage. He never did so. On the contrary, as reparation he agreed to settle £3000 on Eliza so that when she came of age she would be able to indemnify her father against any loss of earnings he had suffered. He also decided that, as a leave-taking present, she might keep the jewels and clothes which he had given her.

Naturally the gossips round Bath found Linley's settlement with Long a rich source of speculation and jokes. Some even said that Linley had sold off his daughter for a while and now been paid for it. But in the upshot, though Eliza was made to look foolish, her reputation did not suffer. It was gentleman Long who took all the blame and shame upon himself. Some people said that he was a silly old bachelor who, when confronted with a real live breathing beauty, had lost his nerve. But in the face of this talk, still Long never so much as hinted that it had really been Eliza who had wanted to break off the match. Nor did he ever tell her parents that she had admitted to another 'attachment'. Whenever his name was mentioned in later times Eliza always spoke well of him.

In the summer of 1771 the story of Elizabeth's love life, coupled with the public's interest in her as one of the most famous singers of the day, began to provoke gossip far beyond Bath. It attracted attention even in London, and did not escape the notice of a one-legged man who, though he was not attracted to her beauty, soon became as great a torment to Eliza as any of her lovers. He was fifty-one years old and not specially interested in young girls because he was homosexual. In appearance and manner he was not prepossessing: he was short, fat, flabby, selfish and greedy. But he had an intelligent face, a bright wicked eye, a pronounced sense of humour and an infectious wit.[5] He had been visiting Bath when the Long business had been the talk of the town. He had never met Eliza, though he was a crony of the great actor David Garrick who knew the Linley family well. Yet while he personally did not wish Eliza any harm, he had no compunction in deliberately humiliating her in the eyes of society. He was the manager of the Little Theatre in the London Haymarket. His name was Samuel Foote.

During the late 1760s Foote had made a reputation for himself at the Haymarket by writing and producing comic plays in which he caricatured living celebrities. It now occurred to him that the goings on down in Bath of the famous singer Miss Linley would make a fine plot for a farce. With Foote the thought was parent to the deed. In a matter of days he knocked off a play and on 26 June 1771 the Haymarket presented the first performance of his new farce entitled *The Maid of Bath*. The plot was remarkably like the recent story of Eliza Linley. People liked the satire and the play was a huge success. It ran for twenty-four nights in London. Word of the production then quickly spread to Bath. It quickly made Eliza a laughing-stock.

The play tells of the adventures of a provincial opera singer Miss Linnet who is reluctantly engaged to be married to an old miser Flint while at the same time she is pursued by a notorious womaniser named Major Rackett. In the Haymarket production the part of Flint was played by Foote himself. Meanwhile in Bath no one was in any doubt about the real identity of the play's characters and indeed the prologue was written by David Garrick who had met all the Bath originals personally. It was even said that Garrick had encouraged

Foote to write the comedy in the mistaken belief that it would champion Eliza's injured reputation!

Foote had researched the Linleys thoroughly. Kitty Linnet had many resemblances to Eliza: they both had fine handwriting, lived in a house with a lodger, and kept maids. But it was Foote's portrait of the older Linleys that so distressed the family. For example Mrs Linley was presented as the mercenary and vulgar Mrs Linnet, always nagging her daughter to marry money:

> MRS LINNET: Yes Kitty, it is in vain to deny it! I am convinced there is some little, low, paltry passion, that lurks in your heart.
> MISS LINNET: Indeed my dear mother, you wrong me.
> MRS LINNET: Indeed, my dear Miss, but I don't. What else could induce you to reject the addresses of a lover like this? Ten thousand pounds a year! Gad's my life, there is no lady in Town would refuse him, let her rank be ever so –
> MISS LINNET: Not his fortune I firmly believe.
> MRS LINNET: Well, and who nowadays marries anything else? Would you refuse an estate, because it happened to be a little encumbered? You must consider the man in this case as a kind of mortgage.
> MISS LINNET: But the disproportion of years –
> MRS LINNET: In your favour child, the encumbrance will be sooner removed.[6]

In the play, Flint's miserly instincts are deliberately egged on by his cronies, jealous of his hold on Kitty Linnet, so that he withdraws his proposal of marriage to her and suggests that she should become his mistress instead. Unfortunately for him, he is overheard making this offer and is publicly disgraced. He therefore retires to the country to take comfort in the one real love of his life, money. At this point in the play Major Rackett sues for Kitty's hand but she rejects him and insists that he should marry Miss Prim, the little milliner he has seduced. As for Kitty, she does not get married at all.

The Maid of Bath provoked hilarity throughout the West Country but curiously no law suits. Linley could hardly have suggested that his daughter had been traduced by the play because the pert Kitty Linnet behaves impeccably throughout, and coolly sails through a sea of temptations undefiled. Furthermore he must have been aware that to make a fuss about Foote's comedy would only subject Eliza to even more derision. So he left it alone. Neither did Mathews go to law, perhaps because he felt that his actions would not survive a searching examination. The person who came off worst in Foote's hands however was poor old Walter Long, who was depicted as that 'old fusty, shabby, shuffling, money-loving, water-drinking, milk-marring old hunks, Mr Soloman Flint'. But though Long never shook off this label and for the rest of his life was known in Bath as 'Mr Flint', he seems to have put up with it cheerfully. As for Eliza, people still occasionally referred to her as 'Miss Linnet' or 'The Maid of Bath' for years after, prompted no doubt by Foote's frequent revivals of his comedy at the Haymarket Theatre during the years 1772-7.

Although Foote's satire made Eliza's life even more wretched for a season, Mathews did not spare her. During the autumn of 1771 it must have seemed to her that she could hardly avoid the man. He was always at her, begging, cajoling and bullying. Sometimes he would try to blackmail her by warning that if she continued to refuse to sleep with him he would make a defamatory public announcement about her and ruin her reputation. Sometimes he would try pathos instead and threaten to commit suicide. And still Linley remained too wrapped up in his music business to be aware of what was going on. It is difficult to believe however that Mrs Mary Linley did not suspect something, but if so she did nothing about it.

And as if all this were not enough of a farce, Eliza soon found herself involved in another dispute in which yet again she was made to appear ridiculous. Perhaps to make up for the recent period when he had lost her professional services, her father was now keener than ever to maximise her commercial potential, and this soon led him into a highly publicised quarrel with a rival music master.

William Herschel was a German organist who had come to Bath in 1766 from his native town of Hanover in order to avoid the miseries of the Seven Years' War. He made his living by taking pupils and giving concerts just as Linley did. In latter years however the two men had realised that there was sufficient trade in the city for both of them, and became civil if not friendly. Herschel accepted Sam Linley as an oboe pupil and even began to co-operate with Linley by putting on concerts. Their partnership did not last long. When the New Assembly Rooms (later the 'Upper Rooms') were opened in Bennet Street, just off the Circus, these premises soon became the most fashionable venue in the town and a prime site for concerts and there was considerable competition to book them for events. This was what they quarrelled about.

Herschel was so annoyed by Linley's subsequent behaviour that he published a piece about it in the *Bath Chronicle* on 6 January 1772:

MR HERSCHEL begs Leave to inform the Public that he has no other Reason for leaving the Concerts at the New Assembly Rooms than to avoid the very ungenteel Treatment he has received there from Mr Linley, not only in not allowing him at two of the Concerts a proper Desk for his Music, but obliging him at once, on account of that Deficiency, to place his Books upon the Ground.

Besides, when Mr Herchel [*sic*] consulted with Mr Linley for a proper Night to have his Concert so as not to interfere with Mr Linley's interest, it was agreed Mr Herschel should have it on the 8th of the Month; and after that Agreement he was so ungenteel as to take away that night from him, and to fix it for his Daughter's Concert without giving any other reason than that it would be more advantageous than some night before Christmas which he had fixed for that purpose.

As from the Illiberal Treatment and the whole Management of the Concerts it is but too evident to every real Connoisseur in Music, or Impartial Person that Mr Linley's views are entirely selfish and envious, Mr Herschel hopes the Public will not throw any Odium on him if for the future he renounces all Connection with a Character so totally opposite to his own.[7]

On 16 January, Linley's reply revealed that the real bone of contention between these two men was not the desk on which they placed their scores, nor even the bookings for the New Assembly Rooms, but the professional services of Eliza. For Herschel understood very well that she was the greatest draw in Bath. Tom and Mary were not adequate substitutes: a benefit without Elizabeth Linley was hardly worth staging:

In answer to Mr Herschel's Advertisement in this Paper of last THURSDAY MR LINLEY begs leave to inform the Public that the only Reason MR HERSCHEL assigned to him for his leaving the CONCERTS at the NEW ASSEMBLY ROOMS was on account of Mr Linley's refusing to let his eldest Daughter sing at a Concert which Mr Herschel intended to have for his Benefit; at the same time declaring, that it was not worth his while to play at the SUBSCRIPTION CONCERTS for a few Guineas unless his Benefit Concerts were made as good as Mr Linley's adding that he had as great a Right to expect Miss Linley should perform for him as a stranger (alluding to Mr FISCHER) and if Mr Linley would consent to her singing for him he would resign his Place in the Concerts. On his receiving a Refusal to the Demand, he accordingly did resign.[8]

Linley finished with some sarcastic remarks about the disputed music desk, a denial that he had ever agreed to concert dates with Herschel, and a reassurance that his rival need have no fear about their future business connections because there were not going to be any. Herschel replied again and the controversy ended.

There was one extraordinary consequence to this quarrel, nine years later. Embittered by his failure to secure the services of the musical star of Bath, Herschel's chief interest turned from music to astronomy. Whenever he had a free night from his concerts he now preferred to go into his Bath garden with his sister Caroline and proceed to map the stars. One evening in 1782 he gave his tube a twist and discovered his own 'star'. He had focussed upon a heavenly body which he could not immediately recognise but which he subsequently proclaimed to be a new planet. He called it 'Uranus'. In discovering it he doubled the size of the known universe.[9]

But back in 1772 when once more Eliza's name was paraded before the Bath public as the object of a petty dispute such heavenly matters were undreamt of. At home her father never stopped complaining about Herschel, and Mathews lay in wait for her behind every closed door. The situation was intolerable. She hated this kind of publicity. She had to get away.

Then an idea came to her. It was a plan which would free her from her father, Mathews, Herschel, Charles Sheridan and the whole pack of them. She quickly walked down to the Sheridans' house to discuss it with her new friend Alicia. At first Lissy was thrilled with the plan which she pronounced 'romantic' – a word which was just becoming fashionable. But on second thoughts she was more cautious. She thought Eliza's scheme was risky. Perhaps there were other ways of warning off Mathews. She suggested they should consult her younger brother, Dick.

CHAPTER 7

Local Hero

About ten years before Eliza was subjected to Mathews' harassment, another young victim faced regular scenes of torment at a school set on a hill near London. Harrow was fast becoming a fashionable academy for the sons of the gentry and the professional classes, and the scholars, quick to snuff out any interlopers, showed little tolerance for boys from poorer backgrounds. When it was rumoured that ten-year-old Richard Brinsley Sheridan was the son of an actor, he was soon made to pay for it. From that time on, whenever the two hundred or so boys milled about the exercise yard, Dick Sheridan would find himself in the middle of a jostling, jeering crowd. They taunted him for his Irish accent, his supposed acquaintance with actresses and the fact that his father was nothing better than a common actor. The confused little boy was told that with such connections he had no business at Harrow mixing with the sons of English gentlemen. Day after day the scene was repeated so that Dick's life was made a perpetual misery.

He was utterly bewildered. Only a year before that he had been at school in Dublin with his sister Alicia, while their parents had gone off to London with Charles. There he had made so little progress that the headmaster, Mr Sam Whyte, had pronounced him to be 'a most impenetrable dunce'.[1] Soon afterwards the two children had been sent to join their parents in London where Mr Sheridan had resumed his acting career. Yet Dick was packed off to school in Harrow, once again parted from the rest of his family. It was a grim place for a sensitive boy. He was fagged and bullied, he had no money with which to supplement his rations, he had to sleep three to a bed, and was threatened with regular beatings by some of the senior boys. Not surprisingly he became a 'low-spirited boy, much given to crying alone'.

Worse was to come. It seemed as if his family was about to desert him entirely. One day in September 1764, his father turned up at the school to stay the night with his friend the headmaster Dr Sumner. Thomas Sheridan had come to explain that he must fly the country and go to France. His creditors were after him, he said, and if he were captured he would be sent to a debtor's prison. The family could manage well enough on his pension in France while he wrote the *Grammar* and *Dictionary* which would make their fortunes. At first Dick listened to his father with delight until with awful conviction he realised that he was not to go with the others. His father confirmed it, telling him that he would stay at Harrow under the care of Dr Sumner.[2] He was on his way to meet his wife at a channel port where they would embark for France accompanied by Charles, Alicia and the baby Betsy.

Sheridan would not listen to his son's desperate pleas to go with them: Dick would be better off at Harrow surrounded by his school-friends and in the care of the headmaster. He told Dick that during the holidays he could count on any number of his father's friends to welcome him to their homes. In particular he mentioned Mr and Mrs Parker of Waltham Abbey and a 'splendid West-Indian' named Mr Aikenhead who was a very old friend and 'well-known as an amateur of fashion in the literary and theatrical history of the day . . . who had a villa at Richmond' and a smart town house. As it turned out, during the whole of the four years while his family was in France, Dick never once had an invitation to visit from any of these people.

Had he remained the tearful little boy who had first gone up to Harrow he probably would not have survived, but luckily he found an inner resource which preserved him. He did so quite suddenly, on an occasion when as usual he was surrounded by a jeering mob in the playground. Until that time his instinct of self-preservation had not been tested but he was passionately defensive of his father and would not hear a word against him. So it was a risky thing for the son of a fashionable London physician to tease him with the easy insult that he was nothing but 'a poor player's son'. Quick as a flash Dick shot back: 'Tis true my father lives by pleasing people, but yours lives by killing them.'[3] There was a burst of laughter all round and the bully was embarrassed.

It was a defining moment for young Sheridan. He realised that he could easily disarm any tormentor by use of repartee. So he began to rehearse a part for himself; he learned to disguise his unhappiness in a show of coolness and good humour. Any bully who threatened him knew that he ran the risk of a lethal retort which would earn him the ridicule of his schoolmates. Even the notorious disciplinarian Dr Parr was so nonplussed by his retorts that he forgot to beat him. Soon Dick's effrontery and amusing replies were famous throughout the school. The whimpering little boy had become a wit.

But underneath the surface Dick's emotional development had been deeply damaged. Throughout his childhood he was almost entirely deprived of affection. The sweet-natured, intelligent mother whom he was said to resemble died while in France, so that he had seen little of her; he hardly knew her at all. His elder brother had always been treated as the favourite and his sisters kept with their parents. Only he had been singled out to be sent away to school, and only he had been left in England. He had become a stranger to his family. Most painful of all however was his gradual realisation that his father had neglected and deserted him. Somehow Dick Sheridan learned not to feel things too deeply – though this calm was sometimes broken when he was swept away by a sudden passionate attachment often accompanied by jealousy and resentments. But as he grew older, he learned to hide his emotions beneath an air of suavity and worldly wisdom and to seek praises and attention by displaying his acumen on every possible occasion. It worked. Both men and women succumbed to his charm. Only his father remained immune.

Despite the neglect he suffered, Dick Sheridan remained a loyal, loving son. But his affection was unrequited, his father remaining impenetrably cold and distant. To tell the truth, he could barely hide his disdain.

By contrast Alicia adored her brother. She had not seen him for many years when at last he left Harrow and rejoined his family in Soho. He was seventeen then and Alicia two years younger. Suddenly the miserable schoolboy of her faint memories was transformed into an Apollo. Years later she wrote an account of that reunion:

We returned to England, when I may say I first became acquainted with my brother – for faint and imperfect were my recollections of him, as might be expected from my age. I saw him; and my childish attachment revived with double force. He was handsome, not merely in the eyes of a partial sister, but generally allowed to be so. His cheeks had the glow of health, his eyes – the finest in the world, – the brilliancy of genius, and were soft as a tender and affectionate heart could render them. The same playful fancy, the same sterling and innocuous wit, that was shown afterwards in his writings, cheered and delighted the family circle. I admired – I almost adored him. I would most willingly have sacrificed my life for him . . .[4]

There was little employment for Dick when he rejoined the family. His father quickly made it plain to him that there was no money either to send him to a university or article him to a profession. Sheridan hoped eventually to get a diplomatic appointment for Charles but at that time he had nothing to offer either of his boys other than to help him with his pupils. They became orthoepy teachers, though it was Lissy's opinion that Charles, the favourite, simply pretended to respect his father's grand scheme for reforming the human race. As for Dick, he found the elocution business ridiculous. His efforts at tutoring were hardly sincere. His first pupil was Harry Angelo, the son of Domenico Angelo, a family friend and a fencing master in Soho. Young Harry later recorded the very different teaching methods of the Sheridan father and son:

The elder Sheridan, who was constantly at my father's, drilled me for the [dramatic] parts which I occasionally performed. The manner of this celebrated teacher of elocution, however, was not quite so bland as that of his illustrious son, Richard Brinsley, who, I have said before, was the friend of my youth. He undertook to teach me to read with propriety . . . I was allowed to go and receive my lessons from him three mornings a week, at his father's house, the family then residing in Frith Street, Soho, within a hundred yards of my father's. Nothing could be more dissimilar . . . than the temper and manner of my two instructors; with the elder Sheridan all was pomposity and impatience. He had a trick of hemming, to clear his throat, and, as I was not apt, he urged me on with – 'Hem-hem heiugh-em, boy, you mumble like a bee in a tar-bottle; why do you not catch your tone from me? – Heiugh-heium – exalt your voice – up with it. "Caesar sends health to Cato". Cannot you deliver your words, hem-hem-heiugh-m-m-m, with a perspicuous pronunciation, Sir?

With his son Richard it was, 'Bravo, Harry; now again; courage, my-boy, – Well said, my young Trojan.[5]

When the family moved to Bath in the winter of 1769 Thomas Sheridan very soon found that his dreams of recruiting large numbers of new pupils there were entirely unfounded. Bath was the city of fashions and everybody knew that orthoepy had gone out of style. So Sheridan was forced to keep up appearances on his pitiful pension of £200 while attempting to work up a trade. He decided to give a year to the Bath experiment; if he failed in that time then he would have to try something else.

From the first things went badly. He had no extra pupils to provide his sons with work. They soon turned to other interests. Charles was quickly involved in his infatuation with Eliza and then went to live in the country. But Dick stayed in Bath. His lack of occupation infuriated his father who complained that the boy seemed happy enough to scribble poetry in his room and hang about the Bath coffee houses all day. To add to his annoyance, Dick, unlike his father, had the knack of being popular. His sisters idolised him and his breezy nature quickly made him new friends. Sheridan gloomily predicted that his son would come to a debtor's grave.

Lissy explained all this to Eliza. She said her father was not being fair. What was Dick supposed to do when no opening was offered to him? Besides, she said that Dick was already working hard at his chosen profession. Despite his father's contempt for the idea, he was determined to become a famous writer, and had already contributed a number of political letters to the *Public Advertiser* which people said were amazingly clever for such a young man. He had also started a literary partnership with his friend, Mr Halhed, of Oxford University. Together they had written a farce and even published a translation of an ancient Greek poet. Blushing, Eliza had to admit that she already knew of Mr Halhed.

In the autumn of 1771 Thomas Sheridan gave up all hope of establishing a successful practice in Bath and returned to the profession he despised. Rarely without offers to perform as an actor, he accepted one from a theatre in Dublin. Charles was still in the country, so Sheridan left his other three children in the house at Kings Mead Street to look after themselves. And it was precisely at this time, when his father was despairing of Bath, that Dick started the career which was to make him the talk of the city. Dick Sheridan was a fine mimic with a wicked sense of humour and a remarkably good ear. He had been tickled by the provincial speech and ideas he had come across in Bath. On 30 September the New Assembly Rooms was due to open. Dick sent some verses to the *Bath Chronicle* in which he gently satirised local manners at the 'ridotto'.

He had noticed with delight that the word 'ridotto' was so unfamiliar to the west-country burgesses that many of them thought it had something to do with a 'red otter'. Furthermore, some of the more bucolic guests cheerfully assumed that the 'octagon' where refreshments were served was some sort of pig-house or 'hogstye-gon'. So he put all this into a set of verses for the paper in the form of a spoof letter from a waiter, Timothy Screw, to his brother Harry who was a waiter at Almack's in London:

Nor less among you was the medley, ye fair!
I believe there was some beside quality there:
Miss Spiggot, Miss Brussels, Miss Tape and Miss Socket,
Miss Trinket, and aunt with her leathern pocket;
With good Mrs Soaker, who made her old chin go
For hours hob-nobbing with Mrs Syringo;

For sure, my dear Hal, you'll be charmed to hear,
That within half an hour all the tables were clear.
The rest, Hal, you know is forever the same,
With chatt'ring and dancing and all the old game
Cotillions in one room, country-dance in another,
In ev'ry room – folly confusion and pother;
With unmeaning questions, of, 'Which room's the hotter?'
And, 'Madam, how do you like the 'Rudotter'?'

To see Captain Plume dance - sure none can dislike him -
Wade's picture, I think, is purdigiously like him -
'Do you dance, sir, tonight?' 'No madam, I do not'
'I don't wonder at all, 'tis suffoking hot'.[6]

If his friends were worried that his verses might have given offence, they need not have been. Bath people were amused and delighted and reprints of his verses were subsequently advertised at a penny each. Dick became something of a local celebrity.

Next he turned his attention to a provincial buffoon named Miles

Andrews who had recently published lines on certain fashionable
ladies of Bath. Andrews' verse was so banal that it merited nothing
but ridicule. Attempting to praise Lady Margaret Fordyce and her
sister Andrews wrote:

> *Remark, too, the dimpling sweet smile*
> *Lady Margaret's fair countenance wears;*
> *And Lady Ann whom so beauteous we style*
> *As quite free of affected airs.*[7]

Dick Sheridan replied scornfully:

> *And could you really discover,*
> *In gazing these sweet beauties over,*
> *No other charm, no winning grace,*
> *Adorning either mind or face,*
> *But one poor dimple to express*
> *The quintessence of loveliness?*

And he concluded with some really lovely lines:

> *Marked you her cheek of rosy hue?*
> *That eye, in liquid circles moving;*
> *That cheek abash'd at man's approving;*
> *The one-love arrows darting round;*
> *The other blushing for the wound:*
> *Did she not speak – did she not move –*
> *Now Pallas – now the Queen of Love?*[8]

Alicia and Eliza read this over. Of course they knew who the
author was and they excitedly discussed his love-life. Was Dick
perhaps in love with Lady Margaret that he could write such verses
about her? If Eliza had thought this was proof then she must have
been taken aback on turning the page to find a mention of herself.
Admittedly it was rather backhanded compliment to her singing but
it was pleasing nevertheless. In scornfully dismissing Andrews as a
poet Dick conjured up the muses:

> *– Nay, should the rapture breathing nine,*
> *In one celestial concert join,*

Their sov'reign's power to rehearse,
Were you to furnish them with verse,
By Jove, I'd fly the heavenly throng,
Tho' Phoebus played, and Linley sung.[9]

The girls decided that Dick was too cautious to reveal his heart in his poetry. No doubt what passions he harboured he kept to himself. This was true, but though Eliza was unaware of it, Dick's quick eye had already taken in the drama of her relationship with Mathews, and he feared for her reputation. He even published some verses designed to defend her from the Bath gossip-columnists:

Oh, if Eliza's steps employ thy hand,
   Blot the sad legend with a mortal tear,
      Nor, when she errs, through passion's wild extreme,
Mark then her course, nor heed each trifling wrong.[10]

So Dick was not surprised when his sister came to him to tell him how miserable Eliza was being made by Mathews' conduct, and he agreed at once to try to help. Something had to be done: the situation was getting worse. Mathews was now often beside himself with passion and jealousy. He had threatened Eliza with rape, scandal and his own suicide, blackmailing her into continuing her calls upon his wife in order to keep up appearances. She knew that he only did this so that he might escort her home and proposition her yet again. Curiously, however, this happened less and less. For often as not, when she got to the Mathews', young Dick Sheridan would be there, leaning languidly on the mantlepiece, and talking about nothing. And naturally he insisted on escorting Miss Linley home. Mathews dared not object.

Even these measures were not enough. Mathews's behaviour became more blatant and outrageous. Eliza took Dick entirely into her confidence and begged him to tell the man to leave her alone. For many a twenty-one-year-old this might have been a formidable task, but Dick Sheridan readily agreed. He knew he was taking a risk because Mathews was hot-tempered and a noted swordsman. But they were drinking companions and had long played at being men of the world together. One night the two met in a quiet tavern and in front of a roaring fire discussed Eliza. And as the light from the candles danced round the wainscot, Dick coolly put to his friend that he really must not go on persecuting Miss Linley like this. He said that Mathews's pursuit of Eliza was nothing but 'cruelty, libertinism and fruitlessness'. Mathews would not have taken that talk from many people but somehow Dick Sheridan was so convivial that he did not take offence. He agreed to leave the girl alone.

For a short while he kept his promise, but soon he was pestering Eliza again and in her desperation she came once more to consult Dick Sheridan. By this time both of them were playing a game of bluff. Eliza had a plan in mind but could not say what she really wanted. Neither did Dick give any hint of what he was up to, but simply let the girl speak. He couldn't look Eliza in the eye when Alicia argued that it was his moral duty to support her friend in her scheme, however desperate it seemed. To Alicia's surprise he agreed to go along with the plan. His impassive face gave the impression that he had no feelings on the matter at all.

CHAPTER 8

Gone!

Throughout early March Eliza could barely contain her agitation at the thought of the grave step she was about to take. We can imagine how difficult it was for her because at this very time she was posing for Gainsborough in his studio, obliged to stand still for hours on end. Her father thought the family business needed advertising and could think of no better way of attracting London theatre managers than to have a joint portrait of his two nightingales, Eliza and Mary, exhibited at the Royal Academy. Linley knew Gainsborough was just the man to do it. He had been a family friend almost since he first came to live in Bath in 1759, and knew all the Linley children. Six years previously he painted Eliza and Tom together in beggar costume.[1] Accordingly the girls would brave the March showers every day and walk round to Gainsborough's studio, where Eliza changed into her ice-blue dress and Mary into her golden-brown one to pose for the picture. Gainsborough decided that Eliza should stand with the guitar and Mary should sit with a score on her lap. While her mind reeled with thoughts of Mathews, Dick Sheridan and the escape she was contemplating, Eliza stood patiently and the artist painted until the light faded.

He was very happy to be asked to paint the Linley girls. He was fond of Eliza and as a painter and lover of music deeply responsive to her pale, delicate looks and her plangent voice. During the course of his career he painted all the good-looking ones in the family: single portraits of Thomas Linley himself, Tom, Sam, Mary, Mary's husband, Eliza's husband and Eliza's son. He painted Eliza alone twice, possibly three times, and Eliza with her sister Mary, as well as her child portrait as a beggar with Tom. Years after Gainsborough painted *The Linley Sisters*, when both he and the Linleys were successful in London, he adopted a little boy of three, giving as his reason the fact that he resembled the Linley children.[2]

Few people who looked long and hard at Eliza could remain unmoved by her beauty. Gainsborough seems to have been haunted by it. His friend Thicknesse later remembered:

> After returning from the concert at Bath near twenty years ago, where we had been charmed by Miss Linley's voice, I went home to supper with my friend, who sent his servant for a bit of clay from the small beer barrel, with which he first modelled, and coloured her head, and that too in a quarter of an hour, in such a manner that I protest it appeared to me even superior to his painting.[3]

And as he painted, the observant Gainsborough sensed this young girl's inner thoughts. Besides he had talked to her, heard the gossip, and managed to put two and two together.

As March went on, Eliza became more and more difficult for her father to deal with. She sometimes seemed hysterical; she complained of headaches and breathlessness, and was obstinately reluctant to appear at concerts. A short-tempered man, Linley had little patience with all this fuss and did not see where it was leading. Things came to a head on the morning of 18 March when Eliza refused to get up. Linley sent up to tell her to get out of bed to come and prepare for her concert, but she replied that she had a headache. Finally she announced that she was too unwell to sing and that she positively would not go. Even her mother took her side. Linley knew he would have to give in, even though for him to turn up at the Assembly Rooms without Eliza would undoubtedly disappoint his audience. So grumbling away, Linley set off for the concert with his two younger children even though Tom and Mary were not adequate substitutes.

Then came the event which changed all their lives. Linley returned home three hours later to find his wife in a distraught state, sobbing and screaming and burying her head in her apron. At first he could not understand what the matter was but through her tears Mrs Linley blurted out that when she had gone up to Eliza's room with a drink the girl's bed was empty. Though the servants had searched throughout the house they could not find her. Eliza was missing.

At once Linley sent out search parties and made frantic enquiries but as the night wore on, and the replies came back, he came to an astounding conclusion. His daughter was not at a friend's house, nor was she walking the streets in a delirium, nor had she gone to drown herself in the River Avon. Shortly after he had left for the concert, Eliza had been seen in the Royal Crescent getting into a sedan-chair. It had taken her to the London Road where she got into a coach with two companions, a woman and a young man. The young man was Dick Sheridan.

Linley was swept up by conflicting emotions. Part of him wanted to shout round the streets that his beautiful daughter had been taken from him and seduced by that good-for-nothing young loafer. But another part urged him to keep quiet. If all this should be discovered then Eliza's reputation would be irretrievably ruined. He began to nurse a glimmer of hope. If he could find out where Eliza was going, even now he might chase after her and bring her home so that the whole business might be kept secret.

It was a forlorn hope. Bath was a small city and word quickly went round that Sheridan had gone off with Miss Linley. Some said that they had absconded to Scotland to get married. A shrewder view was offered by Thomas Gainsborough; on 31 March he wrote to his patron Lord Mulgrave:

> Miss Linley is walk'd off sure enough with young Sheridan; but He is not at the bottom of the mischief, he is supposed to be only half-way. M—ws is the scoundrel supposed (and with much reason) to have undone the poor Girl – it vexes me much; I could fight about it, because I was just finishing her Picture for the Exhibition. I feel for poor Linley much. Though in my opinion he did not quite take care enough.[4]

Because of the disgrace Eliza seems to have brought upon herself, the painting *The Linley Sisters* was not exhibited at the Royal Academy that year. The little clay head of Eliza which Gainsborough had modelled fared even worse. The day after he made it, a house-maid knocked it off the shelf and it smashed to pieces.

It was the Sheridans' landlord at Kings Mead Street who first discovered the family's predicament. When he called on the morning of 19 March 1772, he found Alicia and young Elizabeth (Betsy) Sheridan quite alone in the house. He knew that their father was still in Dublin, and that Charles, for some reason, had gone off to the country, but what perturbed him especially was to discover that young Mr Richard was not in the house. Alicia Sheridan soon let slip that her younger brother had left Bath the previous night, though she did not say where he was gone. The landlord may have suspected from this that the Sheridans were decamping one by one to avoid paying the rent; he was certainly concerned to find two young ladies living entirely unprotected in one of his own houses. Accordingly, he took it upon himself to send a message to the nearby village to ask Charles Sheridan to come home. He did so at once.

When he arrived Charles was astounded by Alicia's news: Dick and Eliza Linley had left the city together the previous night. Under his severe interrogation Alicia all but admitted that she had been party to their plan, and had even helped them with a little money she had saved from the Sheridan family housekeeping expenses. However she kept quiet about where they were heading because she feared that the fugitives might be caught and brought home again. Charles was sickened and enraged by the news because he was still in love with Eliza himself. Both his brother and his sister had betrayed him. It was too much for him to believe Alicia's repeated assertions that Dick and Eliza had not eloped but gone off because Eliza had to get away from a man who was pestering her, and Dick was merely her protector. He would return, said Alicia, after he had settled Eliza in a safe place.

In the meantime, one question of great concern to the runaways was whether Mathews would find out where they had gone and come after them. The weak points in their defence were Alicia, and Dick's friend William Brereton, the only people let into the secret of their destination. If either of these could be browbeaten by Mathews, then he might follow. Linley was not such a threat. Before quitting Bath Dick had left a letter for him telling him that Mathews had been pestering his daughter and that this was the reason she had gone off. Surprisingly Linley at once accepted the truth of these statements. In a letter dated 22 March, Brereton told Dick:

> The morning after you left Bath, Mathews came to me and has repeated his visits several times. It is impossible to give an account of his conversation, it consisted of many dreadful oaths and curses upon himself. . .
>
> The town has so little charity for him that they make (him) worse perhaps than he deserves. I carried two messages from

him to Mr Linley, but he would not hearken to a word about him. He said he had been deceived once and would never trust him more, since that he had heard so many reports to his prejudice that their meeting may be of bad consequence, and I shall endeavour by all means to prevent it. In my last conversation with Mr Mathews I ventured to affirm that he had nothing now to do but to settle his affairs and leave Bath with a resolution never to return again. This scheme (if anything he says can be depended upon) he solemnly promised shall be immediately put into execution. After which, I know Mr Linley's plan is to get his daughter to return to Bath, in order to put an end to the many wicked suggestions, which the malice of his enemies have propagated . . .[5]

Brereton was being too optimistic about Mathews. The man had no intentions of quitting Bath. What he wanted to do was discover the whereabouts of the runaways and to go after them himself. He repeatedly nagged Alicia and Brereton to tell him, but they held out. Up and down the streets of Bath he went knocking on the doors of all their acquaintances to find out. He hardly bothered now to disguise his true intentions towards Eliza, and openly complained when drinking with his cronies that young Sheridan had prevented him from having the girl. But soon public opinion in Bath began to set hard against Mathews.

Mathews did not take Brereton's repeated advice to leave the city. He continued to badger everyone he knew for information about the runaways, and made daily visits to any of the Sheridan girls he believed most likely to know where they were. Alicia was furious to be forced to listen to his uninvited diatribes against her darling brother, but he received a warmer welcome from Charles. Both men considered themselves to have been robbed of Eliza's favours by Dick and they strove to outdo each other in abusing him. Alicia hated such talk. She was outraged that Charles should join such an appalling man as Mathews in disloyally criticising their own brother in their own home.

Eventually, but too late, Mathews somehow got hold of the fugitives' address and wrote them several insulting letters. Then on Wednesday 8 April, three weeks after their flight, he publicly announced his contempt for Dick Sheridan in an advertisement in the *Bath Chronicle*:

Mr Richard S * * * * * having attempted, in a letter left behind him for the purpose, to account for his scandalous method of running away from this place, by insinuations derogating from my character, and that of the young lady, innocent as far as relates to me, or my knowledge; since which he has neither taken any notice of letters, or even informed his own family of the place where he has hid himself; I can no longer think he deserves the treatment of a gentleman, and therefore shall trouble myself no further about him than, in this public method, to post him as a L[iar], and a treacherous S[coundrel] . . .[6]

This public vilification of his own brother finally shocked Charles into realising what sort of person Mathews really was. It also re-awakened his sense of family loyalty. Three weeks had elapsed since Dick's disappearance with Eliza, and Charles's temper had cooled. Besides he had begun to reconsider the matter and come round to Alicia's view that Dick had only gone off with Eliza to protect her from the attentions of Mathews. Extremely guilty that he had ever allowed Mathews to cajole him into abusing a member of his own family, Charles accused him on one visit of improper conduct to Eliza and publishing a defamatory advertisement against Dick. Listening to their quarrel in the next room, Alicia and Betsy Sheridan were terrified that Charles would be drawn into a duel. But fortunately Mathews could see when he was beaten and walked out of the house. Shortly afterwards, having no remaining supporters in Bath, he left for London.

News of his departure came as a relief to the Linleys. Nevertheless it did not answer the question that by now they and all Bath were asking. Where were the runaways?

CHAPTER 9

Mrs Harley's Adventures

While Bath was still ringing with gossip, Eliza was enjoying the most romantic adventure of her life. On the night of 18 March, after her father had left for his concert, she had risen from her 'sick-bed' to answer a discreet knocking on the door. Just as Dick Sheridan had promised, it was a chairman come to convey her to a coach on the London Road. Dick had reserved coach-seats for them both and one for a servant woman paid to act as Eliza's chaperone on their journey to London. It was agreed that none of them would speak more than was necessary in the public coach but if they did speak, as a precaution Eliza would be referred to as 'Mrs Harley'. Along the London Road, they stopped to refresh themselves at the various inns which acted as staging posts. They approached London the following day, crossing Hounslow Heath, which was notorious for highwaymen. Sitting in a tightly-packed, unheated, squeaking, jolting compartment which smelled of sweat, stale breath and old leather, Eliza's mind teemed with images: of a sudden hold-up by a masked rider on the heath; of her father at home in Bath ashen with worry; and of Mathews's furious face after discovering that she had gone. But a sideways glance at the calm profile of Dick Sheridan comforted her. In the folds of her mantua she clutched her reticule even more tightly. It contained their precious savings; the pittance that Lissy had been able to spare from her housekeeping, and about £40 she herself had saved from the interest on Mr Long's money. They met no highwayman and the coach rattled safely into London in the late afternoon of 19 March.

Though Dick Sheridan had planned the journey, it was Eliza who had already chosen their destination. Alicia's stories of how the Sheridans had previously crossed the channel and settled in Blois had fired Eliza's imagination. After weeks of daydreaming it dawned on her that she too might escape to France where neither Mathews nor her father might follow her. She planned to take refuge in the very convent at St Quentin where the Sheridan girls were once left by their father. Running away would be quite an adventure, the sort of thing that happened in the novels she had read. She imagined that the convent would have a cloister, a crypt, and a dungeon, like Walpole's Castle of Otranto. Her romantic dreams, however, were offset by an uneasy awareness that she was unprepared for such a journey. She needed a protector, especially as she had no knowledge of the country, little money, and only a few words of French. That was why she had gladly accepted Dick Sheridan's offer to accompany her, despite the fact that he had never been to France, had less money and no French at all. Besides, she had a secret which seemed to override all such considerations.

The runaways first task when they arrived in London was to get some more money. They had enough to last a very short time in France. So they called upon Dick's London friends, the Ewarts, who were successful wine-merchants, for a loan. At the Ewarts' house Eliza was rather startled to find herself introduced by Dick to old Mr Ewart as 'an heiress who had consented to be united to him in France'[1]. Old Ewart pronounced himself charmed with her, though Eliza was not sure whether he admired her face or her supposed fortune. Ewart congratulated Dick on his new choice for he said that he had heard lately that his young friend had become entangled with a singer, a Miss Linley of Bath, who would have brought him nothing but trouble. The runaways went on empty-handed to another house where again Dick hoped to borrow money. Mr Field was an hospitable oil merchant, and when they called he was engaged in entertaining another young couple named Lamb. Years later the son of that marriage, Charles Lamb, in an essay entitled 'My First Play', wrote a brief account of the arrival of Sheridan and his charming companion:

We went [to the theatre] with orders, which my godfather F[ield] had sent us. He kept the oil shop [now Davies's] at the corner of Featherstone Building in Holborn. He was also known to and visited by Sheridan. It was to his house in Holborn that young Brinsley brought his first wife on her elopement from a boarding school at Bath – the beautiful

Maria Linley. My parents were present (over a quadrille table)
when he arrived in the evening with his harmonious charge. [2]

Lamb was of course wrong in two respects. The young Miss Linley
was Eliza, not her sister Maria, and she had not run away from a
boarding school but her father's house. But the gist of his story is
true.

Old Field was most helpful. He suggested that to prevent being
apprehended by the young lady's father, they should embark at once
on a ship for Dunkirk. He said that he could find them a passage in
a vessel because he knew a captain who would help. We do not know
for sure which port they left from but it was probably Dover. Field
accompanied them to the quay, handing them over to the captain
with instructions that the man was to take as much care of them as
if they had been his own children.

The voyage that followed plunged Eliza into the depths of misery.
The ship was small and the sea very rough. So wretched was she
from sea-sickness that she even forgot her terror of drowning. Her
illness was such that Dick, who had himself never been to sea before,
thought that she was about to die. Even between the waves of dreadful nausea and despair, however, Eliza sensed that her companion
was treating her with extraordinary tenderness. He never once left
her side, wiping her face clean and keeping her warm. She had
never experienced such compassion in a man.

As dawn came on the sea slackened and Eliza was able to go on
deck to watch the grey harbour riding in to meet them. She felt utterly
alone. The breakwater, the shapes of the buildings, the incomprehen-
sible speech around her, were all completely alien. She did not even
know where Dunkirk was on the map. It was a moment of terror and
despair. But Dick Sheridan bustled around her whistling away, and
conveyed her to a waterfront tavern where he urged her to take some
coffee and a brioche. Her courage revived. She noticed that though he
spoke no French he had the knack of getting people to understand him.
In fact they adored him. Waiters, ostlers, tavern-keepers and especially
servant-maids were only too ready to humour this cheerful, charming
young Englishman. He soon found out how they should continue their
journey. There were stage-coaches, he said, which would take them to
St Quentin via Calais and Lille. That afternoon Eliza found herself in
another coach jolting across the misty flat lands of northern France
until it pulled up for the night at Calais.

For the first time the fugitives were faced with the practicalities of their difficult adventure. The chaperone had been left behind in London: they were now only two. At Calais, awkwardly Dick Sheridan was obliged to book two rooms, which they sensed must have seemed odd to the inn-keeper. However much they maintained that Dick was merely Eliza's protector, they were unmarried and travelling together. They probably guessed the scandal created by their disappearance from Bath. Both knew that if their escapade were to get out it would almost certainly ruin Eliza's reputation and brand Dick as a heartless seducer. Yet as if deliberately courting disaster they seem to have agreed tacitly never to discuss the subject. But between themselves they scrupulously continued to preserve the fiction that they were not eloping together but that Dick was Eliza's knight-errant escorting her to a convent before he returned to England.

It was at Calais where at last they dropped all pretences. With a grave face, Dick sat Eliza down upon her little bed to listen to his serious confession. It changed everything between them. Up until that moment he had never given her a hint that his feelings for her were any more than those of a friend, but now to her astonishment and joy he admitted that he had been passionately in love with her for months.

What he said was entirely sincere. He had for a long time attempted to protect her from Mathews, and later wrote that as they had crossed the channel, and he had thought that Eliza might 'expire', he would 'assuredly have plunged with her body to the grave'.[3] But there was always something of an actor in Dick Sheridan which induced him to manipulate people. Long before they had set off for France he was aware of the consequences to Eliza's reputation should their escapade become public knowledge. Now he wanted to use the situation to blackmail her into marrying him. What he did not guess was that this naïve young girl was manipulating him. Eliza was undoubtedly running away from persecution but she had also engineered the whole escapade which threw them together. Alicia Sheridan described the scene:

After quitting Dunkirk, Mr Sheridan was more explicit with Miss Linley as to his views in accompanying her to France. He told her he could not be content to leave her in a Convent unless she consented to a previous marriage, which had all along been the object of his hopes, and she must be aware that after the step she had taken, she could not appear in England but as his wife.[4]

Perhaps Eliza was not as unaware of Dick's feelings as he thought. She had noticed how edgy he had become in the theatre at Calais when two French officers had stared at her, and he had complained afterwards that as he and she were not related he had no real right to protect her from such attentions. In fact, she had been in love with him all along, so much so that she had been prepared to risk her reputation and go to France with him. She knew that he was an honourable man and his treatment of her on the boat proved it. Besides, if she were to retain her reputation they must get married; inclination and prudence dictated it. Alicia continued:

Miss Linley, who really preferred . . . Dick Sheridan . . . greatly to any other person, was not difficult to persuade, and at a village not far from Calais the marriage ceremony was performed by a priest who was known to be often employed on such occasions.[5]

Neither Dick nor Eliza however regarded this ceremony as giving them the right to sleep together. In fact they were amazingly chaste throughout the whole adventure. For one thing, Dick was rather proud that he had honourably carried out his role as Eliza's protector. Picking up his brother's pomposity, on 15 April he wrote to assure Charles that; ''tho' you may have been ignorant for some time of our proceedings . . . (I hope you) . . . never could have been uneasy that anything could tempt me to depart even in thought from the honour and consistency which engaged me first'.[6] What he said was true but he chose not to add that he and Eliza were husband and wife. Few would have believed the extraordinary fact that though the young couple were married, deeply in love, and had the opportunity, they abstained from love-making. Most of those secretly married did so precisely because they wanted to become lovers lawfully.

Why did they abstain from love-making? For one thing, Eliza did not wish to upset her father. The ceremony was celebrated by a Roman Catholic priest, while they were both Protestant, and the marriage would never have been recognised by their families. Secondly, neither of them had reached the age of twenty-one and they were therefore minors who under English law needed their fathers' permissions to marry. Nevertheless, because Eliza was so intensely in love, she decided to go through with it. They promised to be faithful to each other but to keep their relationship secret until they were both of age. Such promises, repeated in the little village church in Picardy, would strengthen their love and resolve when perhaps their parents and all the world might in future oppose the match. In this she was right.

From Calais the two lovers journeyed on to Lille where they stopped; Eliza was ill. Ever an optimist, Dick wrote cheerfully to Charles: 'Everything on our side has at last succeeded. Miss L— is now fixing in a Convent where she has been entered some time. This has been a much more difficult point than you could have imagined, and we have I find been extremely fortunate. She has been ill, but is now recovered. This too has delayed me.'[7]

They remained at Lille for some ten days, at first staying in separate rooms at the Hôtel de Bourbon in the Grande Place. Here Eliza became much worse. She was never lacking in determination and courage but she was physically fragile and subject to fainting fits. No doubt the agitation of the elopement, the exhausting boat trip and coach travel, and the uncertainties of their journey were all too much for her. Luckily Dick soon struck up an acquaintance with an English physician, Dr Dolman, who lived in Lille. When he heard of Eliza's illness he volunteered to examine her.

After his first consultation he was grave. He produced a packet of white powder and instructed Eliza to take some in a glass of white wine twice a day. He also suggested that Dick should remain at the Hotel, while Eliza should come and live in his own household so that she might be nursed by his wife. They accepted. Within a few days the rest, warmth, and the expert care of the Dolmans, made Eliza feel better. But the Doctor's original concern was not misplaced. Dolman was the first doctor to recognise in Eliza's pale face the signs of that disease which was to become the curse of the Linleys. She was tubercular.

In Lille, Dick came to sit by Eliza's bedside every day to talk to her. One way in which he tried to get her mind off her present worries was by persuading her to tell him stories about her childhood. And so it was in the Dolman house, conversing in low tones in a little bedroom, that they first got to know each other. Eliza told Dick about her family, her musical life in Bath, and the drudgery of working for her father. When she spoke of Linley, she could not keep back the tears.

Dick calmed her, wiped her face, and to amuse her told her about his own early life: of his mother and their years in Dublin; of his misery when he was first sent to Harrow; and of how he had been abandoned when the rest of his family went to France. He told her of those who had befriended him at school, the headmaster Dr Sumner and his friend Dr Parr, both of whom would puff foul-smelling pipes while proclaiming to the boys the cause of liberty and the Whig party. Dick said that he was a Whig himself. Was she? Eliza did not know. She had never paid much attention to politics but was vividly aware of this sudden blaze of enthusiasm in her young husband. It seemed as if he could be anything he chose in life, and she determined to support him in whatever he wanted to do. She understood very well that because he was a man he could shape his life as he wanted: he had that freedom. And she was aware that though he had no money, no breeding, and no connections, he could write and speak better than anybody she knew and was also the most charming man she had ever met.

But each night Eliza tossed and turned. In her dreams she was in the boat again, and she woke in a sweat of apprehension about their present plight. All thoughts of the convent at St Quentin seemed to have faded with her illness, and despite the generosity of the Dolmans, the little money they had was running out. What were they to do? She did not have enough strength to decide. She could only lie on her bed in what seemed a dreadful inertia of will. Something had to happen.

Something did. On 24 April the door of her room opened and her father walked in. Linley had traced them through the letters Dick had written home. Eliza was terrified to see him, but also relieved. He was not angry with her but shame-faced because at last he under-stood the harassment she had received from Mathews. He also understood that he had not protected her as a father should. His life in Bath, he admitted, was too much taken up with his music and his business. Even more surprisingly, he showed little anxiety that his daughter's honour might be compromised. He took it for granted that though Dick was a scamp he was not a scoundrel. He acknowl-edged that Dick had behaved honourably in escorting her to France. Those last days in Lille were a time of forgiveness and reconciliation for father and daughter.

Nevertheless there was still a trial of strength between them. Linley was anxious to get Eliza home at once so that she might fulfil the concert engagements already made in her name. Eliza thought this over carefully. For the first time in her life she had a little power to try to get what she wanted from her father, and the experience was exhilarating. So she sat up in her sick bed and started to bargain with him. Before she agreed to go home, she made him promise several things. She pointed out that he overworked her and that this was undermining her health, so she wanted her concert programme reduced. He accepted the point. Next she demanded the right to refuse a booking when she did not want to do it. He agreed. Finally, she made her father swear that, once she had undertaken the engagements he had already made in her name, she should be free at any time to return to France and the convent. Truly alarmed by the sight of her sick face, he assented. He would have said anything to get her home.

The whole party then set off for England. Mrs Harley and her friends arrived on the Kent coast on about 29 April. Dick and Eliza had been away for nearly six weeks. But Eliza knew how to be discreet and never once did she utter to her father a word about her marriage. That was her secret.

CHAPTER 10

Hysterics

As soon as Linley travelled back with the runaways they were obliged to resume their old relationship. Once more they had to make out that Dick was merely Eliza's protector. Even then the suspicious Linley saw to it that they were kept as far apart as possible; throughout the entire journey home they were not allowed to be alone together. Perhaps their hardest trial came after they had disembarked and taken the evening coach to Canterbury. To pretend that they were not emotionally involved was not so difficult on a channel packet. There they could walk about and go on deck. But sitting opposite each other in a swaying coach and trying to avoid each other's eyes made things much more difficult. On arrival at the inn, Eliza went straight to bed, worn out by yet another channel crossing. Only afterwards did she discover that Dick had deliberately sat up all night, obeying a vow he had made to himself in France.

The following day they took the coach to London, and on the journey Thomas Linley tried to make Dick promise that, should they meet Mathews, he would not cause any trouble. Eliza glanced at Dick's face when he replied. He agreed, but did so with that sly look which she recognised as evasiveness. She knew he had no intention of keeping his word. They arrived in London at about nine o'clock. Once again Dick did not go to bed. When he had helped settle the Linleys into their rooms, he went out to look for Mathews.

Eliza could only guess what Dick was up to. She was aware that while they were in France Mathews had published an abusive letter about Dick in the *Bath Chronicle*, though they had not yet seen the actual words. And in Lille Dick had received two insulting letters from Mathews who had at last discovered their address. In one, Mathews had assured Dick that he (Mathews) could be found at any time, and that Dick need not 'deprive himself of so much sleep and stand on ceremony'.[1] Eliza's contempt for Mathews knew no bounds. He would only have sent out such a challenge if he had been pretty sure that there was little risk of Dick taking it up, since he was very young, and away in another country. But she also sensed the extent of pride in her young husband. Dick could not endure any slight to his honour, and loved to play the hero to an admiring public. Mathews had mistaken his man.

Unknown to Eliza, after receiving Mathews's letter, Dick had vowed that he would not 'deprive himself of so much sleep' on English soil until he had caught up with the man. As a result he was now about to rampage through the most intensive and sleepless week of his life. While he was full of action and heroics, Eliza spent her time sitting frantic with anxiety, whispering about him with his sisters, and scanning the *Bath Chronicle* for news of him. And all this time she had to feign indifference to the young man who was her husband. She was learning the only role assigned in her day to a woman in love – that of a passive spectator. While the man she adored acted out the rituals of heroism, all she was permitted was hysterics.

Dick's adventures started at the inn in London as soon as the exhausted Linleys fell asleep. He took down his pistols, crept out of the house, and went to call on his friends the Ewarts. By ten o'clock young Ewart had given him the very information he wanted. Mathews was in London, lodging with a Mr Cochlin at Whitefriars. Dick arrived there just past midnight, edgy from lack of sleep but driven on by furious indignation. His knocking on Cochlin's door produced no effect: he began to hammer. Eventually Mathews called out to ask who was there but after being told it was Sheridan fell silent. Dick hammered again. Then a rather different voice called out that the door could not be opened because the key was lost. Revenge was turning to farce. By two o'clock Dick had somehow got into the house at last, only to be confronted by Mathews in his night-shirt. Dick's rage against this half-naked man huddling by the embers faltered. Mathews was too cold to be aggressive, though his shivering may have been provoked more by the pistol he glimpsed poking out of Dick's pocket.

Mathews was totally apologetic. 'He dressed – complained of the cold, endeavour'd to get heat in him, call'd Mr S. his dear Friend, and forced him to sit down.'[2] He claimed he had been misrepresented. His advertisement in the *Bath Chronicle*, he said, had been published simply as information for the public, not as an insult to his young friend; Dick's real traducers were his brother Charles and 'another gentleman'. Finally at seven o'clock in the morning he suggested that Dick go home to bed. Dick returned to Mathews lodgings, where they agreed to publish joint explanations in the *Bath Chronicle* to end the public quarrel between them. Was there an end in sight? The only detail that Dick wanted to check was the actual wording of the advertisement.

A load lifted from his shoulders, Dick got up into the stagecoach next morning with the Linleys to return home. Eliza could not be cheerful. Every sign-post declaring the decreasing number of miles to Bath only confirmed her dread of the enforced separation from Dick, once they arrived. For the first time in over six weeks she would have to part from her sweet travelling companion and husband. Glimpses of the Somerset countryside through the stagecoach windows mingled with memories of other views from ferries, coaches and hotel rooms. But when the coach pulled up at the Bear Hotel on Saturday evening, she was obliged to step down, shake hands, and wish Dick goodbye with no more emotion than if they had only just met. She took her father's arm and walked up towards the Royal Crescent, while Dick, whistling in a display of insouciance, strolled down towards Kings Mead Street.

Once out of Eliza's sight, however, he doubled back and turned into the offices of the *Bath Chronicle* where the editor showed him the advertisement that Mathews had placed three weeks earlier. That stopped his whistle. For far from being the simple, informative piece that Mathews claimed to have written, here was a notice presenting him as a liar and a scoundrel. He saw at once that any correction that Mathews put in the paper could not make up for such an obvious insult.

Meanwhile Lissy was still living at Kings Mead Street with only her younger sister Elizabeth for company. For weeks they had been waiting for news of Dick, so that when he knocked at the door the two girls were overjoyed to see him. Lissy told him that their father was still in Dublin and that while Dick had been in France, Mathews had called almost daily to try to bully them into revealing his whereabouts. However she concluded triumphantly that they had not given away anything and Mathews had left town. Dick probably did not tell his sisters about meeting Mathews in London but as he listened to their tale of harassment he became even more furious with the man. He knew something else that would have to be done.

Next came a frosty meeting with Charles, who was still smarting at the fact that Dick had run away with the woman he loved. However, he was also feeling rather guilty that he had in turn been less than loyal in joining Mathews to abuse his brother. The two young men began to talk through their differences while their sisters rather apprehensively retired to the next room. Soon the girls became alarmed when they heard raised voices. They were terrified that their brothers were quarrelling about Eliza and might even fight a duel over her.

But when the door opened, and the men reappeared, they were perfectly affable both to their sisters and each other. To the girls' relief the entire family then sat down to an amicable evening. Alicia was never told explicitly, but guessed that they had started with recriminations and ended with apologies. Charles entirely accepted Dick's story that he had simply acted as Eliza's protector and apologised for the fact that he had initially taken Mathews' part. In the end he had realised the man was a scoundrel and would even have challenged him to a duel had he not left for London. He also apologised for allowing Mathews into the house to harangue poor Lissy. The two brothers then discussed Mathews' advertisement, and Charles was quite of Dick's opinion that it could not be allowed to pass. They decided upon a desperate remedy.

When Lissy and Betsy woke on Sunday morning they discovered that their brothers had left the house. Their bedclothes had not been slept in. Alarmed, the girls assumed the worst; they concluded that the previous evening their brothers had feigned reconciliation and left the house soon afterwards to fight each other. Alicia was terrified that at any time they might receive news of a duel, with one of their brothers dead and the other his murderer. Desperate to prevent tragedy, the girls hurried up to the Royal Crescent to consult the Linleys; if Eliza were the cause of this impending fratricide she might at least know where the duellers were fighting.

Eliza knew nothing and became faint when she heard of the danger Dick might be in. Questions were met with counter-questions, the talk in Linley's elegant drawing room changed from desperate, to panic-laden, to hysterical. Overcome with emotion, Betsy began to shriek. Soon the others were joining in. Eliza fainted, and when she came round, Lissy and Betsy fainted. Thomas Linley came back to the apartment to find a room full of hysteria; he hardly knew what to do. But fortunately his clear-minded lodger, a Presbyterian minister named Mr Joseph Priestly, set about reviving the girls with smelling salts. Reported to know something of science and medicine, no doubt he would have found a whiff of oxygen more effective, but his experiments did not discover that element until two years later. The only rational one in the room, he pointed out that they had no real evidence to suppose the brothers were duelling. The inconsolable girls could not explain these matters to a stranger and could only gaze out of the window. At last it was time to go. The sedan chair arrived, Alicia got into it, and Linley, hand in hand with Betsy, escorted the two girls home. Eliza was left to face her terrors alone.

The Sheridans, however, were not fighting each other. Charles had accompanied Dick to London so that his younger brother could challenge Mathews. Dick interrupted his journey long enough to drop an advertisement in the *Bath Chronicle* offices on the way and Eliza must have seen it the following day:

> Mr T Mathews thought himself essentially injured by Mr R Sheridan's having co-operated in the virtuous efforts of a young Lady to escape the snares of vice and dissimulation. He wrote several most abusive threats to Mr S.— then in France. He laboured with cruel industry, to vilify his character in England. He publickly posted him as a scoundrel and a Liar. – Mr S. answered him from France (hurried and surprised) that he would never sleep in England 'till he had thank'd him as he deserves.[3]

Charles and Dick arrived in London and made their way straight to the house of Dick's friend, William Brereton. From there Charles went to see Mathews but after two hours talk could not gain a decent apology from him. It now seemed that the stage was set for a duel.

It was the evening of 4 May. Dick first sent a challenge to Mathews to meet him in combat at Hyde Park. Mathews' acceptance came back and the two parties set out for the park. For some reason Charles stayed at Brereton's house to wait for the result of the duel. Dick's second was Brereton and his friend Mr Smith acted as a surgeon; Mathews was seconded by his cousin Captain Knight. A carriage and four was kept waiting at the park gate near the turnpike so that the winner might make a quick getaway.

That Mathews had agreed to this duel is not to be wondered at: all the circumstances were in his favour. He was seven years older than Dick and much stronger; he had been given a choice of weapons and had fixed upon swords rather than pistols because he had learned to fence in France and was considered 'very skilful in the science'.[4] As an army officer he had been allowed plenty of opportunity for practice with a foil. Dick was sustained by jealousy, indignation, plenty of courage, and the ever-present image of an innocent Eliza assailed by this man. But his advantage lay in the one or two useful tricks he had picked up from his father's old friend, the London fencing master Domenick Angelo.

Despite the fact that Mathews had good reason to be supremely confident, when it came to it he was curiously nervous. While Dick was content to fight almost anywhere, he kept objecting to the various locations suggested. The place originally chosen, the 'Ring' (later 'Rotten Row') did not suit him, nor did several other sites put forward by Dick's seconds. Complaining that these were either not flat enough or too public or unsuitable in some other way, Mathews became agitated by some army officers standing near the duelling party. He feared they might call the authorities, so the two parties retired briefly to the Hercules' Pillars inn and later adjourned to the Bedford Coffee House to wait for dark. Mathews continued to pay Dick elaborate compliments throughout, presumably trying but failing to get the duel called off. Finally they all trooped round to a private room at the Castle Tavern. There the combat took place.

It was hardly possible for any onlooker to make out the events with certainty. It was a small room, lit only by Ewart's flickering candle, making what happened next a matter of dispute. Duels are fast and furious affairs in which parries are almost too quick to follow. There are few neutral observers. All witnesses agreed, however, that as soon as the door was closed the assailants were at each other. Mathews' desperately ferocious assault was met with a series of expert passes: Sheridan was a young swordsman that old Angelo would have been proud of. Before long, to Mathews' amazement, Dick Sheridan succeeded in knocking his sword out of line. Sheridan then closed with Mathews, seized his foil, and held his sword-point at his opponent's breast.

At this moment Captain Knight rushed in to pull Dick back by the arm, crying out, 'Don't kill him!' Dick triumphantly claimed that Mathews's sword was in his power as Mathews himself called out

'I beg my life'. The combatants were parted. Desperate for any chance to end the business, Knight yelled, 'There He has begg'd his Life, and now there is an end to it.'[5] But when Ewart declared Dick to be the winner – since at the moment of interruption he had possession of both swords – Mathews complained that Knight's intervention had given him an unfair advantage. Irate and insulted, Dick told Mathews either to give up his weapon, or stand his guard again. At first his sulky opponent hung on to his sword but eventually handed it over. With a true sense of drama, Dick broke it and flung the pieces across the room.

Mathews was genuinely shocked by this breach of duelling etiquette. Breaking an opponent's sword was reckoned a mark of supreme contempt. Dick coolly replied to Mathews' protests that if he still wanted to continue he would lend him a dress sword. Mathews soon changed his tune; he could not draw on a man who had just spared his life. Dick persisted; Mathews must either take his guard again or agree to publish a full apology. In return Dick would keep secret the fact that he had broken Mathews' sword, thus saving him from dishonour. With bad grace, Mathews agreed and signed the apology. It was all over.

Meanwhile, back in Bath, a distraught Eliza, consumed with worry about Dick, was obliged to conceal her agitation from her parents. For their benefit, she had dismissed her recent hysteria in the drawing-room as something caught from Lissy and Betsy. But her father was still suspicious and even more determined to discourage her friendship with the Sheridan girls. He could not entirely forbid them entrance to his house; they were the children of an old colleague and were alone and in trouble. So for the moment he had to put up with their regular visits to his house for news. One morning in the midst of their worries, Alicia pushed past Linley's servant to announce that her brothers had come home.

If Eliza showed any sign of fainting again Alicia quickly reassured her that Dick was not only unhurt, he was victorious. She explained that once she realised that Dick's secrecy was a way of protecting her, all her anger subsided. It was no good, she said, no one could be angry with Dick for long. He had a way of talking you out of it. Eliza privately assented.

The following Thursday, at the breakfast table, Eliza's father grunted and passed her a copy of the *Bath Chronicle*. He was pointing at the following announcement, signed 'Thomas Mathews':

Being convinced that the expressions I made use of to Mr
Sheridan's disadvantage were the effects of passion and misrep-
resentation, I retract what I have said to his disadvantage, and
particularly beg his pardon for my advertisement in the *Bath
Chronicle*.[6]

Eliza's relief was profound. Dick was safe. When she heard that
Mathews had gone back to his estate in Glamorgan, it seemed they
were free of him for ever.

Dick Sheridan was the hero of Bath. His advertisements in the
Chronicle, the way he had protected Eliza from Mathews, their
romantic elopement, and whispers of a victorious London duel had
made him so. On 13 May his brother Charles wrote proudly to their
London uncle, Richard Chamberlaine, that Mathews' main insult
was the allegation that his brother 'had married Miss L(linley)'.
Charles understood exactly why Dick had been obliged to take
action against him; he was now 'applauded' by 'everybody' in the
city. In another letter he confessed untruthfully that he himself had
outgrown his 'ridiculous attachment' to Eliza.[7]

Amazingly, Eliza's own reputation had come to no harm as a
result of her recent French escapade and when she returned to Bath
she was received as the respectable Miss Linley. It was tacitly
assumed in local society that she was still a virgin. Little did they
realise she was a married virgin. This was partly thanks to her
father who treated his daughter as an innocent on the run from a
cruel seducer. But the rest of the credit should surely go to Dick
Sheridan and his ability to promote myths about himself. He still
maintained that he had accompanied Miss Linley to France simply
as her protector. Mathews was a villain, he was a romantic hero, and
Eliza the innocent heroine.

The one person most likely to take a harsh view of Dick's behaviour was his own father, but luckily something happened at that time
to change his mood. When Dick got home from France, news came
from Thomas Sheridan in Dublin to say that through the agency of
his friend Mr Wheatley, Charles was to be appointed Secretary to the
British Legation in Sweden. The old actor was coming home to
supervise his eldest son's departure. Dick was apprehensive; so far
the news of his French trip had been kept secret from his father but
when he learned about it, he was likely to be furious. However,
Sheridan could think about little else than Charles's new appoint-

ment. When he arrived home, Alicia's account of her brother's role as protector and his heroics in the duel was so glowing that the old man had to admit – albeit grudgingly – that his son had behaved honourably, if not with discretion. He even received Dick's French hotel expenses with uncharacteristic equanimity. It seemed as if nothing could upset him.

Nevertheless, these events put old Sheridan on his guard. Through the details of the story he realised for the first time how great was the risk of a marriage between the Sheridan and Linley families. If it did happen, it would be due to his own carelessness and he was not going to have that! He stood by his view that Eliza was little better than an actress, and he suspected that the likes of the Linleys would be only too happy to compromise his boy Dick in the sort of vulgar escapade they seemed to enjoy.

The Linley parents shared his apprehension. To them, Eliza was a treasure trove. A girl with her earning capacity might marry anyone she chose, even a peer. They were not going to let her waste herself on the penniless son of a superannuated actor.

Both fathers held the same view and took the same precautions and the couple were kept apart. Eliza was a wife and at the same time no wife. She could not even confide her secret to Alicia. Before they went to France, she and Dick might at least meet in company and chat in a friendly way but now they were obliged to pretend indifference to each other. In the drawing room of mutual friends such as the Lynns or the Roscoes, people watched them intently when they sat together. Eliza had to prepare a public face to meet their curious glances. She and Dick had not yet worked out how to write to each other in secret and as for meeting alone, that was impossible. For a young wife and husband it was all very frustrating.

CHAPTER 11

Love Letters

Eventually the young lovers found a spot where they might occasionally meet. Just across the river Avon on the eastern side of the city were the Spring Gardens. On these May mornings Eliza would get up stealthily from her bed, taking care not to wake Mary, dress, creep to the back door, and let herself out of the house. She could be sure that Messrs Sheridan and Linley were still asleep, and would steal down the almost-deserted streets to the river. There the bright spring sun would just be rising over Robert Adam's Pulteney Bridge, where masons and carpenters were busy mixing mortar and hammering away. It took considerable courage for this young girl to cross over the bridge at such an early hour and risk being noticed. But there at the Spring Gardens was a grotto constructed in the latest Romantic style, and in the grotto there was a stone seat, and sometimes on that seat she would find a piece of paper marked: 'For Laura'. This was what she had always come for.

Dick Sheridan was a great romantic. Whenever he could, he wrote Eliza verses in the fashionable pastoral style. In these he would picture himself as the deserted shepherd 'Horatio' and Eliza as the fickle nymph 'Laura'. But Eliza understood very well that each was a calculated apology for his jealous outburst. Since their return from France, Eliza had again become the centre of attention in all the Bath concert halls. Yet she was Dick's wife, and, he felt, his property. Propositions from other men aroused intense anger in him but because their marriage was still secret, he was powerless to do anything.

Dick's jealousy vexed Eliza. One May morning she opened a packet to find yet another set of verses. The lines, although insipid to modern ears, eloquently express the misunderstandings and quarrels suffered by the two lovers in these difficult days:

Uncouth is this moss-covered grotto of stone,
  And damp is the shade of this dew-dripping tree;
Yet I this rude grotto with rapture will own
  And willow, thy damps are refreshing to me.

For this is the grotto where Laura retired;
  As late I in secret her confidence sought;
And this is the tree kept her safe from the wind,
  As blushing she heard one grave lesson I taught.

Then tell me, thou grotto of moss-covered stone,
  And tell me, thou willow with leaves dripping dew,
Did Laura seem vexed when Horatio was gone?
  And did she confess her resentment to you?

Methinks now each bow as you're waving it, tries
  To whisper a cause for the sorrow I feel:
So hint how she frowned when I dared to advise;
  And sighed when she saw that I did it with zeal.

True, true, silly leaves, so she did, I allow;
  She frowned; but no rage in her looks did I see:
She frowned; but reflection had clouded her brow:
  She sighed; but perhaps, 'twas in pity for me.[1].

As well as self-pity, Dick suffered from intense mistrust. Initially he was insensitive to the great change that had come over Eliza since he had accompanied her to France. At one time she had been attracted to him; now she adored him. If he had truly understood how much, he would have had no reason for jealousy. But long years of rejection had scarred his emotional development, and although he sought constant attention and admiration, he never really trusted anyone. Eliza's spontaneous reaction to Dick's poem was to leave him one of her own in the grotto the next morning. She hoped it would reassure him of her love, as she had tried to many times.

The sweets of solitude to share
  With my dear youth I love,
Shall be my only joy and care,
  No more I wish to prove.

85

With him to wander o'er the mead,
  Which Spring hath newly drest,
And praise the power which thus decreed
  We should be truly blest.

I'll lead him from the noon-day heat
  Within some leafy bower.
Then soothe his soul with concord sweet,
  Or music's soothing power.

Or if a book still more amuse
  And ease his pensive mind,
Some favourite author will I choose
  Till he's to peace resigned.[2]

Eliza's verse is ingenious but stilted. But if Dick found his best expression in verse, it is in Eliza's letters that her true feelings come pulsing through. She was occasionally able to smuggle them to Dick with little keepsakes – a lock of hair or a portrait miniature. Unashamedly passionate, they vividly convey her life's desperation and tumult in those days. The following scribbled note to Dick breathlessly suggests all the drama and complexity of their covert relationship:

> For fear I should not be able to speak to you, I write to tell you I shall be at Mrs Lyn's this evening. Don't tell Lissy that you know of my being there, as I promised her I would not tell you. Only think of Captain Hodges! I am frightened out of my wits.[3]

Another was written shortly after they returned from France. They had spent an evening in the company of mutual friends and of course had not been able to speak openly. By the time Eliza got home she was bursting with passionate words. As soon as she reached her bedroom, she sat down to pour out her feelings to her lover. At this time of repression and denial neither of them was entirely sure of the other, and Eliza's note makes it clear that she too had her own jealous suspicions:

> Eleven o'clock. Though I parted from you so lately, and though I expect to see you again so soon, yet I cannot keep my

fingers from the pen but I must be plaguing you with my scrawl. Oh, my dearest love, I am never happy but when I am with you. I cannot speak or think of anything else. When shall we have another happy half-hour? I declare I have not felt real joy since I came back from France before this evening. Perhaps now, whilst I am writing and amusing myself by expressing the tender sentiments which I feel for you, you are flirting with Miss W., or some other handsome girl, or making fine speeches to [illegible] scold. I do not believe any such thing, but give me leave to doubt that I may with greater pleasure be convinced to the contrary. No, my life and Soul, I love you to such a degree, that I should never bear to see you (even in joak) [sic] show any particular attention to another.[4]

Now she was past all reticence in her letters, a matter which she was later to regret. Whenever she found time and opportunity she would take pen to paper and pour her heart out to this stranger she had married. And she was often obliged to write after exhausting days filled with rehearsals and performances, in a bedroom lit only by a flickering candle, letters informed with that same passionate simplicity and truth that people detected in her singing. This letter continues:

I really think Charles suspected something this evening. He looked amazingly knowing when I came down. Duce take his curious head. I wish he would mind his own business and not interrupt us in our stolen pleasures. Is it not amazing, my dear Love, that we should always have so great an inclination for what is not in our possession. . . .

Let me see, what have I more to say? – nothing but the same dull old story over and over again- that I love you to distraction, and that I would prefer you and beggary before any other man with a throne. I will call you Horatio – that was the name you gave yourself in that sweet poem – write to me then, my dear Horatio, and tell me you are equally sincere and constant. . . .

My hand shakes so at this moment I can scarce hold the pen. My father came into my room this moment, and I had just time to stuff the letter behind the glass. 'Twas well he did not take much notice of me, for I was. . . Goodbye, God bless – I will. . .

Another letter written a few days later complains about Dick's intention not to write to her for a week. This was probably during one of her concert tours when Dick thought the risk of discovery to be too great. She began the letter at midnight:

> Twelve o'clock. You unconscionable creature to make me sit up at this time to scribble nonsense to you, when you will not let me hear one word from you for this week to come. Oh, my dear, you are Tyrant indeed. Yet do not fancy I would do this if it was not equally agreeable to myself. Indeed, my dearest love, I am never happy except when I am with you, or writing to you . . .[5]

And even though Mary stirred impatiently in the bed and whispered that Eliza should put out the candle and come to sleep, still she sat there at the window in her nightdress, scribbling away as if for dear life. And though the quill would squeak and the ink sometimes smudge, her thoughts poured out swiftly onto paper as if she were actually talking to Dick. She told him everything that was on her mind and all her bits of gossip. She said she was trying to get out of singing at some of her father's private concerts, and reported that Miss Roscoe had recently told Mrs Linley openly that she agreed with the whole world that Eliza and Dick Sheridan would be married soon. She concluded:

> God bless you, my dear, dear love. I am so weary I must go to bed. There is but one thing that could keep me awake and that is your company. Once more adieu . . .

> Upon my knees, half nacked [sic], once more I am going to tire you with my nonsense. I could not bear to see this little blank without filling it up. Tho' I do not know with what, as I have almost exhausted the Budget of news which I had colected [sic] since our long absence. I do insist that you write to me, you lazy wretch, can't you take so small a trouble? I can receive your letter by the same method. My sister is very

impatient that I don't come into bed, but I feel more happiness in this situation, tho' I am half froze, than in the warmest bed in England.

In June 1772 the lovers were separated when Thomas Linley insisted Eliza should take a music tour to Chester, Cambridge and Oxford. Both Linley parents were to go and take Mary with them. When Eliza broke the news to Dick about the tour he was almost distraught with jealousy at the thought of her meeting innumerable adoring young men. So on the night before she left she wrote once again to reassure him.

Wednesday night, 12 o'clock. The anxiety I felt whilst in my dear Horatio's company tonight would not let me feel the pains of separation, but now that I am retired, and at full liberty to give way to my own unpleasing ideas, I cannot describe what I feel to be so long divided from you. Oh, my love, how vain are your doubts and suspicions; believe me, if I thought it possible for me to change my present sentiments of you, I should despise myself. Never shall you have the least reason to suspect my constancy or my love. I am in a very gloomy disposition tonight, but I will not give way to it. I will try to forget every disagreeable circumstance, and only look forward to those happy hours which I hope are still in store for us. With what rapture shall we meet, when we may do so without constraint, when I may live in your arms without the fear of parents, or (care for) the ill-natured world. I could write to you without ever leaving off, but my sister insists on my coming to bed. It is now near one o'clock, and I am to be up by five tomorrow, God bless you, my ever dear Horatio. Think of me while I am absent, and don't let any idea disturb your peace in regard to me, for while I live I can never cease to be your own Eliza.[6]

But once the tour started her days were so intense that it was almost impossible for her to find the time and energy to write. She was still only eighteen and her parents had total control over her: her mother was within her rights when she removed the candle in the bedroom after Eliza had undressed, saying it was to prevent her from reading and becoming overtired. But what is more likely is that she suspected that her daughter used some of her bedroom hours to write letters to an admirer. On 31 June, right at the end of her tour, somehow Eliza managed to find an opportunity to write from Oxford to explain why she had not written before.

> Oxford, Monday, 12 o'clock. How shall I account to my dear Horatio for my long silence? Will he permit me to excuse myself by pleading the continual hurry which I have been in since I parted from him? Indeed, nothing should have hindered my writing before but the shocking situation I was in, all day confined to business, and at night my mother took away the candle for fear I should read. It was an absolute impossibility to elude her vigilance. We came here this morning, and I have taken the first opportunity to assure you of my unabated love.[7]

She had to be so careful in her letter not to arouse Dick's suspicions and jealousy. Whilst mentioning that during her tour she had attended a public 'masquerade', she was at pains to emphasise that she had not wanted to go in the first place, that she had no option but to go, and that she did not enjoy a minute of it.

> While I was at Chester, I went to the Masquerade, but such a scene of confusion and fright I never saw, and sincerely hope I never shall again. Mrs Williams (whose husband was the principal leader in the affair) made it her business to insist on our going with her, and she was so pressing, my father could not refuse her. I own as I had never seen anything of the kind I had some curiosity, but it is perfectly satisfied. I would not go through the fatigue of another for the world. We had two dresses apiece. Mine was a pilgrim and a Spanish lady, Polly's a shepherdess and another pilgrim. The crowd was so great at the door, that, before I could get into the room, the fright overcame me and I fainted in the midst of them. On the return of my senses I found somebody going to pull me by my legs as you would a dead horse; this roused me, and I gave them a hearty kick.

> Luckily a gentleman that I knew came by who took care of me home, where I was going to pull off my finery and stay at home, but I was prevented by Mrs Williams who came to fetch

me to my mother and sister who had made their way through the crowd and was got safe. At last I got to this famous affair, but never was disappointment equal to mine, to see such a nonsensical puppet show. I walked about as tired of the Masquerade as I am at a long sermon. The impudent looks and speeches of the men were too much for me. I forgot that I had a mask on and really felt myself very much affronted at their ill-bred stares. So much for the masquerade.

Ironically it did not occur to either of them that far more threatening than any petty causes of jealousy was the effect the tour had on her health:

At Cambridge there was nothing but the music which was very fine. I was extremely ill for two days. I was taken ill in the church during the Oratorio of 'Samson'. I fainted and was carried out. This raised no small bustle among the Cantabs, as they call them. I need not describe them to you, they are a strange set; though, upon the whole, I really think they are more rational beings than the Oxonians. It seems there is to be a very great riot here on one of the nights. They don't like the music, and intend calling the Governors to account. How it will end God knows.

She ends with the usual declaration of love and devotion:

I have not been out since I came here. I shall be very happy when I am once more in Bath. I cannot tell how much I long to see you, to ask you a thousand questions. Oh, my dear Horatio, I have had many perplexing thoughts since I have been absent, but I will hope for the best. If I find you well and happy on my return I shall be content. It is much if I am not with you as soon as this letter. Till then receive my tenderest affections, and let me find you constant as I left you. If my prayers are granted, I shall once more embrace my Horatio, and convince him how sincerely I am his Eliza.[8]

Eliza would have fainted a second time had she known what was happening to her 'Horatio' back in Bath. For on the very night that she was writing to him from Oxford, another person was addressing a letter to him of a far less loving nature. William Barnett, acting for Mathews, was a natural trouble-maker who had recently gone to live in the Llandaff neighbourhood near Cardiff. There he had met Mathews, still smarting from the shame of his first duel with Dick Sheridan. It took little for Barnett to persuade Mathews that he would never regain his good name until he had re-fought his duel with Sheridan and beaten him. Once convinced, Mathews acted quickly. First he sent Dick an insulting letter and soon after turned up in Bath again accompanied by Barnett. And it was Barnett who carried the challenge to Dick by employing the specially unkind method of placing it in the hands of his sister Alicia.

For a while Dick Sheridan avoided confrontation with Mathews and Barnett. He was not obliged in honour to fight another duel. He remembered the words of his brother Charles, who wrote, 'You risked everything . . . where you had nothing to gain, to give your antagonist the thing he wished, a chance for recovering his reputation . . . he wanted to get rid of the contemptible opinion he was held in, and you were good-natured enough to let him do it at your expense.'[9] But eventually Dick's patience snapped when on the evening of 30 June Barnett handed him a letter demanding to know where he might meet Dick to arrange another combat with Mathews. Dick wanted to be done with Mathews once and for ever, so he agreed to meet on Kingsdown, Bristol. It was a fine morning, the first of July 1772.

From the White Hart, the two pairs made their way to Kingsdown, Mathews with Barnett as his second, and Dick Sheridan with Captain Paumier as his. Surprisingly, Mathews, famed for his swordsmanship, now chose pistols because he said he wanted to avoid a repetition of their undignified scuffle. But Dick recklessly insisted on rapiers. According to Barnett, Dick then attacked Mathews 'in a vaunting manner' and after two or three passes the combatants closed. In the ensuing struggle Mathews' sword snapped and they both fell to the ground. The point of Mathews' blade was stuck in the earth, but keeping him down with his heavy body-weight, he crouched over Dick and started hacking at him with the broken blade. Seizing hold of Dick's sword, he demanded that he beg for his life. When Dick refused, Mathews pulled the point of his own blade out of the earth and stabbed him in the face and neck some twenty or thirty times. Had not a bulky item in his breast pocket got in the way, Dick might have been mortally wounded. Even so he was growing weaker by the minute from extreme loss of blood. Paumier implored him: 'My Dear Sheridan, beg your life, and I will be yours for ever!'

'No, by God, I won't,' Dick replied, and passed out. It was only then that the seconds could part them. Mathews was helped into one of the chaises; he was fleeing to France till the whole affair had blown over. His last words were, 'I have done for him.'[10]

The semi-conscious Sheridan was carried to a stone-cutter's hovel on the down where he was given some water, quite convinced in his few moments of lucidity that he was dying. Meanwhile, the opportunistic cottager went outside and collected from the ground evidence of the duel; he had some vague notions of exhibiting it later to curious people. He picked up some bits of sword, one of Dick Sheridan's shirt-buttons, and a broken picture-frame empty of its miniature. It was this which had partially stopped Mathews' frenzied stabbing. Without this picture of Eliza to protect him, the blows would certainly have pierced Dick Sheridan's heart.[11]

CHAPTER 12

Doubts and Suspicions

Eliza was not told about the second duel. Her father did not want to upset her because he knew that when she learned of Dick Sheridan's blood ebbing away on Kingsdown, she would not be able to carry on with her engagements. So he ordered that the Oxford papers with their account of the fight should be kept hidden from her. Many in her audience had read them, however, and an undergraduate named Thomas Greville who attended one of these concerts later told Alicia that Eliza's appearance on the occasion 'inspired the greatest interest in the company present. As her ignorance of the duel and its consequences were known to every person, and her beauty, joined to the effect of her truly enchanting powers, could not fail of exciting a degree of sympathy in youthful and susceptible minds, when they thought of the heavy calamity that hung over her'.[1]

After the Oxford tour was over the family started out for home in a chaise. Still Eliza was not told. But as they drew near to Bath they were met, at Linley's pre-arrangement, by another chaise carrying the Reverend Panton, a family friend. A rather puzzled Eliza then changed from one vehicle to the other at her father's request. Both then trundled slowly onward to Bath. Alone with Eliza, Panton gently broke the news of the second duel and Dick Sheridan's injuries. Her response was immediate and intense: losing all sense of caution, she cried aloud: 'My husband! My husband!' She demanded to be taken to Dick's bedside, so that she might tend him day and night 'as his wife'.[2]

Meanwhile Dick was fighting for his life. After he recovered consciousness on Kingsdown, his friends had driven him straight to the White Hart in Bristol, where his wounds were dressed by Messrs

94

Ditcher and Sharp 'the two most eminent surgeons of the time'.[3] Because his father was still in London with Charles, it was his sisters, and particularly Lissy, who had to take full responsibility. So when they visited him and discovered that he was in great discomfort in the noisy hotel, they obtained permission from the surgeons to take him home to Bath where they intended to nurse him themselves. Less sympathetic was his brother Charles, who wrote on 3 July from London to express his displeasure that Dick had fought the duel, to tell him that all their friends in London condemned his decision to do so, and to regret that he was unable to lend his brother a few pounds. It was cold comfort for a desperately ill man but despite this fraternal lack of feeling, the devoted care of the Sheridan girls was rewarded. On 2 July *The Bath Chronicle* reported the duel adding that: 'Mr Sheridan received three or four wounds in his breast and sides, and now lies very ill'. On 4 July, the London paper *The St James's Chronicle* stated that: 'Sheridan is much wounded, but whether mortally or not is yet uncertain.'[4] But though the first paper had very much underestimated Dick's injuries, by the time the second came out he was already showing signs of pulling through. On 9th July *The Bath Chronicle* was able to inform its readers 'with great pleasure' that 'Mr Sheridan is declared by his surgeons to be out of danger'.[5]

So for the next few days Dick lay at home in Kings Mead Street recuperating under Alicia's care. The house was quiet and his room kept darkened. Lissy and Betsy came in regularly to wash his wounds and feed him gruel. They insisted that he must try to recover his strength, even bringing the occasional loving message from Eliza.

Eliza was suffering agonies of worry and remorse. Though Alicia was willing to pass on her messages to Dick, she dared not let Eliza see him, so apprehensive was she of what her father would say when he got back from London. Nor would Linley have allowed his daughter to visit Kings Mead Street. But after Eliza had suffered eight more days of desperate anxiety, Dick's friend Paumier passed her a note, from Dick, probably dictated to Betsy. Eliza at once wrote a reply for Paumier to take back to her injured husband:

> I cannot resist the opportunity of thanking my dear Horatio for his concern for me. Believe me I have not been in my senses these two days, but the happy account of your recovery has perfectly restored them. Oh! my dearest love when

shall we see you? I will not ask you to write as I am sure it must hurt you. I am going to Wells tomorrow. I am obliged to be there before my father returns, and I expect him very soon. I shall not be happy till I hear from you there. Oh! my Horatio, I did not know till now how much I loved you. Believe me had you died, I should certainly ( ) dressed myself as a man and chalenged [*sic*] M. He should have killed me or I would have revenged you and myself. I cannot stay to write more as Mr P is waiting. I suppose you can trust him. I will not write again till I hear from you at Wells as I do not know how to direct safely. God in heaven bless you my dearest Horatio and restore you once more to health and happiness and the arms of your Eliza.[6]

To her great distress she received no reply at Wells. She did not know that Thomas Sheridan had returned from London and put a stop to all letter-writing. He arrived home in a foul mood, very angry with Dick for fighting Mathews again for, he believed, unnecessary reasons. At first he positively refused to visit the sick bed himself, and announced that Dick could not receive anyone from outside the family, especially not Elizabeth Linley.

After a few days, old Sheridan cooled down. Even though he was partly willing to admit that Dick had at least acted honourably, he still wanted to vent his rage on somebody. He picked on Mathews, suggesting that Dick should bring a legal action against the man for assault, because Mathews' violent conduct on Kingsdown had exceeded the controlled homicide rules of duelling. He was also concerned that during the fight, Mathews had been wearing some kind of armour beneath his shirt, also contrary to the rules. However Dick declined to press charges, presumably because he did not want to give Eliza's name any more publicity.

The two fathers puzzled over Eliza's calls for her 'husband' when she first heard of Dick's injuries in the duel. But neither of them seems to have regarded the remark as anything more than an expression of what she wished to come about – and what they both intended to prevent. While still recovering, Dick had written to Linley with a formal proposal for his daughter's hand in marriage. His offer was rejected on the grounds that he was still a minor and could not legally enter into a marriage settlement, though had Dick been a man of good prospects, no doubt Linley would have found a way round these difficulties. The fathers agreed that Dick would be refused visits or letters from Eliza, and she should be sent away from Bath, banished to relations at Wells and Bristol. Dick was not even allowed to write to explain why he might not write to her! Perplexed and distressed by his silence, she wrote again from Wells:

> Saturday morning
>
> To what can I impute your silence? At a time, too, when you must be certain that I am in the most dreadful state of suspense . . . I was surprised not to find a letter ( ) when it was my particular request. I received a letter from my mother which has if possible increased my uneasiness. After telling me that my father and yours have had many serious conversations, she adds 'I could say more but I am not permitted.'
>
> I am ordered to stay here a week longer. My father wrote two or three lines at the bottom of my mother's letter, where he tells how your father has behaved and of your sending him a note, but he says that it is no use to him as you are under age, and he does not suppose it will be ( ) your power to keep your word . . . It is strongly reported that we ( ) and that I discovered it in my fright when I first heard of your duel. Then there is a long lecture with hopes that it is not true and that I will convince the world I have more spirit than prudence, etc.
>
> Now what am I to think of all this? Can you imagine, Horatio, that I can be easy under these circumstances? For God's sake write to me. Tell me what has happened and do not hide anything from me. I have been tortured with ten thousand apprehensions ever since your first letter. And now if possible I am more so . . . ( ) from you by the next post I ( ) to think my happiness is no longer ( ) to you. Therefore if you wish me still to believe you faithful do not fail to ( ) your sincere Eliza.[7]

She did not receive one line in reply. For the very first time she began to doubt Dick Sheridan's sincerity. Eliza's concern would have deepened had she known that Thomas Sheridan had recently compelled his younger son to take 'an oath equivocal' not to marry her.[8] Luckily for Eliza at this time Dick was naturally devious: his assurances were never to be relied on. He could always find arguments to defend broken promises. He could have claimed in this case that he need not respect the oath equivocal because it was extracted by compulsion, or he might say that he intended to keep it; already married to Eliza, he could not marry her in the future!

Throughout the months of July and August Dick was convalescent at home. Eventually he was allowed to get up and even pay visits with his family to the houses of friends. Once again Betsy was able to pass the occasional letter between her brother and Eliza. As for Linley, he could not keep his daughter in Wells for ever. Back in Bath Eliza would occasionally glimpse Dick across a drawing room floor. But their enforced separation bred suspicions. Dick was racked with jealousy once more because he knew that the Bath gossips frequently linked Eliza's name to new admirers, and that her parents were actively encouraging her to make a match with a rich suitor. And sometimes one or other of them would overdo the play-acting. On one evening Eliza's studied lack of interest in Dick and her close attention to a certain Mr R provoked such a spasm of jealousy in him that he dashed off a bitter note to her. She replied:

How can you my dear Horatio torment yourself and me with such unjust suspicions? My behaviour last night proceeded from the anxiety I felt in perceiving you look so remarkably grave. If I was prudent it was my father's conversation that made me so. He declared he would sooner follow me to the grave than see me married to you as you would ruin me and yourself in a short time by your extravagance. I knew he watched us last night; 'twas that which made me cautious. If I said anything in my note to offend you, impute it to my desire to have you esteemed by your father.

You cannot have any doubts in regard to R–. Believe me I have wrote to him to put an end to every future hope. I never can think of another. I do not know how to see you. My situation at present is very disagreeable. I am not suffered to go out without my father or mother, and I am so watched I can scarce find a moment to write. We must have patience. In the meantime assure yourself of the sincerity of my intention for I will ever be my dear Horatio's Eliza.[9]

A little mollified, the wounded lover resumed his secret letters to her. One day Paumier brought Eliza a packet by hand. In it was a poem from Dick, appropriating a line written by his old friend Halhed and developing it into a set of verses. For all its dated pastoral conventions, it was exactly calculated to express their own situation:

> Dry be that tear, my gentlest love,
>   Be hushed that struggling sigh,
> Nor season, days, nor fates shall prove
>   More fixed, more true than I.
> Hushed be that sigh, be dry that tear,
> Cease, boding doubt, cease anxious fear,
>   Dry be that tear.
>
> Ask'st thou how long my love will stay,
>   When all that's new is past?
> How long, Ah Delia, can I say
>   How long my life will last?
> Dry be that tear, be hushed that sigh,
> At least I'll love thee till I die!
>   Hushed be that sigh.[10]

These verses revived Eliza's faith in her husband. Here again was the tender lover she had married and who had twice risked his life for her. She sent an answer immediately:

> Think'st thou, my Damon, I'd forgo
> This tender luxury of woe,
> Which better than the tongue imparts
> The feelings of impassioned hearts;
> Blest if my sighs and tears but prove
> The winds and waves that waft to love.
>
> Can true affection cease to fear?
> Poor is the joy not worth a tear!
> Did passion ever know content?
> How weak the rapture words can paint!
> Then let my sighs and tears but prove
> The winds and waves that waft to love.[11]

By the end of August Charles had left for Sweden and Thomas Sheridan was making preparations to return to the Dublin stage. But he still had the problem of what to do with his daughters and his impecunious son. He decided not to take them to Dublin, but to send the girls to the convent at St Quentin where they had lodged many years before. Dick would go with them as their escort and then might stay on to learn something of the language. Just as the plan formed in his mind however, Sheridan learned something else that changed it. His anger knew no bounds when he discovered that despite Dick's oath he and Eliza were still corresponding with each other – aided by Betsy and Paumier. Betrayed by his own son, and concluding that such a liar was morally unfit to be the protector of young girls in a foreign country, he changed his plans. He decided to take his daughters to Dublin with him, and send Dick to Waltham Abbey to stay with the Parkers and study something useful.

For the last time before he left Bath, Dick broke his promise not to communicate with Eliza, and sent her a letter assuring her of his love. In replying Eliza seems to have believed that she would be waving him off on the Irish boat. Her farewell letter is a truly Romantic document, written at midnight by the light of the moon and in pencil because her cruel mother had removed her inkstand. Her principle concern was still to soothe her lover's suspicions:

> Tuesday night, 12 o'clock
>
> You see to what shifts I am reduced. I have lost my ink, but I hope you will understand me as I could not resist the inclination I had to thank my dear Horatio for his sweet letter – but is it possible you can ever believe I can change or bestow one serious thought on any object or any other person in life? My whole soul is devoted to you, nor would I change my present situation to be wife to any man. Yet though I despise the ties that govern vulgar souls, yet I must look sometimes towards a time when I hope it will be in my dear Horatio's power at least to make me his in every sense of the word . . . But as it is we must submit till fortune puts in our power to be happy in our own way.
>
> How could you tease me about Miss C—? Indeed, my love, if you believe her you would hurt me very much, as I give you my word and honour I never gave her the least reason to

think that you was of the least consequence with me more than a friend. Nor could the hints that Lissy dropt proceed from anything I ever said, as I assure you I never have nor ever will make a confidant of anyone; Be easy then my dearest love, on that head, as I am resolved for once to convince you that I can keep a secret. How beautiful at this moment does the bright moon appear! Yes, my Horatio, it was conscious that thy Eliza's thoughts were wholly fixed on thee, nor can any other idea remove thy loved resemblance from my heart. I feel I love you every day more tenderly, I cannot support the idea of a separation, and yet I have sometimes horrid thoughts about your going to Dublin. Oh, my loved Horatio, what will then become of your Eliza? But I will not make myself unhappy with imaginary evils. If you love me, and will always be constant in every situation, I will yet be at peace and in that hope even, it is impossible but I must be happy. 'One woe doth tread upon another's heels; so fast they follow.' I had before lost my ink, and now my candle is just burnt out. God bless you, my dear, Dear Love; believe me tenderly and sincerely your Eliza.[12]

Yet the waning moon might have given her pause for doubt. It was the emblem of change. After an absence between them of many months perhaps Dick Sheridan might not remain as faithful as he said he would.

CHAPTER 13

At Waltham Abbey

Shortly before Dick left Bath, Eliza persuaded him to meet her secretly one last time in the Spring Gardens. He arrived in a frantic state, talking wildly. What he had to say stunned her. He announced that they must break of their courtship and forget their so-called 'marriage'. He said that Sheridan had insisted that they should not correspond and that he had to agree. It was only common-sense; their fathers would never let them marry and they were both still entirely dependent. Letters would only prolong the agony. His talk was so desperate that eventually Eliza agreed that they should not write to each other. But even as she made her promise she knew that she would never give him up and suspected that he felt the same way. When the time came to part, Eliza could barely contain her tears. As she slipped away from their familiar grotto, Dick stood there in an agony of grief, watching her go, her slight shoulders hunched in misery. She glanced back at him once more, then turned towards the Bridge. In an instant her blue dress and chestnut hair were lost in the press of people. Soon afterwards both lovers left Bath, she for Wells and he for Waltham Abbey.

Dick arrived in Essex on 28 August 1772 and stayed at Hill Farm, the home of old friends of his father, the Parkers. They welcomed him warmly, but from the first day he was desperately miserable. Determined to honour his promise not to write to Eliza, he spent the whole of his first day in his room, scribbling letters home to almost anyone other than Miss Linley. He was barely able to contain the grief he felt at her loss. He wrote 'wholly *entre nous*' to his sister Betsy to tell her of further debts he had run up which his father would soon receive, but added that he was now 'planning Prudence and all the Cardinal Virtues'. He sent his regards to his

102

Bath friends, the 'Breretonites, Morganites (and) Walshites', in fact to anyone he could think of other than the Linleys.[1] He wrote to tell his father that he had arrived and was snugly lodged in the town though he would have preferred to be in the country. Excusing himself from writing previously to Eliza when he had promised not to, he claimed that there had been circumstances which had made it impossible for him to discuss 'that connexion' with 'proper candour'. But with a determination to punish himself he went further: 'I can now have no motive in solemnly declaring to you that I have extricated myself, and that on this subject you shall never again have the smallest uneasiness.'[2]

Waltham was a small country town famous chiefly for its Norman Abbey where King Harold was interred, and also as the home of John Foxe, author of the *Book of Martyrs*. Dick Sheridan too suffered deeply there, but for a cause in which he did not believe. He remained at Waltham Abbey from the autumn of 1772 till the following March, for most of that time keeping his promise to his father not to write to Eliza. Instead he poured out his heart in letters to a seventeen-year-old Oxford student named Thomas Grenville, the younger brother of George Grenville. Thomas Sheridan had recently cured Buckingham of a stutter. During these visits to Bath, Buckingham and Dick Sheridan had become firm friends. These letters were received in Bath, then Ireland, and finally in Christchurch College, Oxford to where Thomas returned in November.

The first, written on 30 August shows Dick in despondency, desperately trying to put away thoughts of Eliza yet hungry for any scrap of news of her. Maudlin sentimentalities about friendship and love, and confessions that he is suffering from 'excessive melancholy' suddenly giving way to an impassioned cry:

> I hope you have seen her, I hope you have talked to her; if you have, and should again I am sure that your own Feelings will suggest to you what I would say. Tell me she is happy; if she is otherwise tell her to be so. – O upon my soul, it were the Part of an Angel to come down from Heaven, to watch over her, and reconcile her mind to Peace. I wish Dying could assure me of the Power to come from Heav'n to her with that Happiness, which I fear she will never know Here. It is impious to say it, but I should exchange a Robe of Glory for her Livery.[3]

There is a recognition here that, whatever his own suffering, Eliza's would be greater. In this he was right.

Tom Grenville had heard Eliza sing at Oxford. Like many other young men who were smitten with her, he was only too ready to keep an eye on her as best he could. His reports to Dick Sheridan were sent, of course, all in the name of friendship. So when on 4 September he glimpsed Eliza in Bath, he wrote at once to tell Dick that despite the fact that Eliza was unwell, her father had insisted that she make her usual appearance at the Three Choirs' Festival. Grenville added: 'She is gone to Winchester and Gloucestershire, and she appeared but once since your departure from Bath and then only for a very short time.' He went on:

> Believe me it is not the common offer of complaisance when I say it is now my first and principal wish that it were in my power to reconcile your mind to the loss of what you so much regret, or what I fear is and must be impossible, and make you happy in each other. Why was her fate so cruel as so early in life to bring upon her the imputation and censure of the world?[4]

Such banal reflections were little calculated to lessen Dick's misery and in these early days at Waltham Abbey he was depressed most of the time, not surprisingly imparing his physical health. In late September he complained of toothache and other minor complaints. He told Grenville that he had; 'for this fortnight [been] very confined and in too much pain either to employ or entertain [him]self.' The boy Grenville sagely responded by recommending to him 'that tranquillity of the Mind, which is indeed the Health of the Soul', though this sort of talk did Dick little good other than to make him ponder even more on the nature of his own unhappiness. Naturally he denied that his illness had anything to do with losing Eliza, but sometimes he would grow tired of all their philosophising and cry out in despair:

> I am sick without society – my love is almost the only feeling I have alive, 'Amo ergo Sum' – is the confirmation of my existence . . .
> But what shall I say of this attachment! to hope for happiness from it, I must agree with you, 'is and must be impossible'.
> – I have received a letter from her, since I wrote to you

(Counterband) fill'd with the violence of Affection, and concluded with prayers, commands and entreaties that I should write to her. I did not expect such a Desire, as she had acquiesced to my determination of not corresponding . . . I cannot now do it: – for to tell her why I am right is to plunge into wrong: – to tell why I did resolve, is to break my resolution, yet to deny her and not excuse my denial is a hard mortification . . . – I am determined not to write . . . How strange is my situation: if I consult my Reason, or even one half of my Feelings I find conviction that I should wish to end this unfortunate connexion – what draws the knot, rejects the influence of reason, and has its moiety of the Feelings (dearest! tenderest!) with the Passions for its hold. Perhaps then it is best that there is an artificial, but powerful bond that keeps me to the other Party.[5]

He entreated young Grenville to become a good friend to Eliza for his sake, though curiously warns him – as he did not with Nat Halhed – of the risk that in so doing he too may become entangled in a 'Love Net' and fall in love with her himself.

The days went by at Hill Farm while Dick Sheridan lay on his bed thinking of Eliza, or reading letters from Alicia which mentioned every item of Bath gossip except the one thing he wanted to know. Sometimes Mrs Parker would persuade him to come down and sit with the family, and he would take his place by the fireside and smile, pretending to listen to the conversation. He smiled as the clock ticked and he would decline a game at cards and smile, and smiling he would take the hand of an inquisitive neighbour come in to meet the famous Mr Sheridan, and smiling he would decline supper while Parker talked to him about his father, and everybody would be so kind so that he would go to bed smiling. Then came another wretched night. Alone beneath the counterpane, a solid misery would sit on his chest while Eliza's pale face haunted him. He dreaded that he should never see her again, picturing her even now up late in Bath, ringed by a crowd of laughing men, each one intent upon possessing her. So he would toss and turn into the early hours when at last he would fall into a doze, and a tepid autumn sunlight whitened his window.

In October Grenville wrote to tell his friend that he was going to Ireland for a fortnight, and to set Dick's mind spinning with jealousy:

I cannot send you any news of her though she has returned from Gloucester a week, I have not been able to see or hear of her, though I have endeavoured to do so. I dread the Oratorio expectations; the theatre and the company are not calculated for her amusement but how many are there who will think it calculated to promote the most villainous intentions; for so I must call all which tend only to a selfish gratification at the expense of the fair one's happiness, or which must from the soft-eyed virgin, etc.[6]

But Dick Sheridan had too much life in him to allow him to simply sit down and die of love. He knew that he had to make an effort to motivate himself again, and to turn his thoughts to something life-giving and creative. On 30 October he apologised to Grenville for his previous gloomy letters and talked of the reappearance of his 'Sun of Health'. 'I assure you,' he wrote 'I have now better Health, and mere animal Spirits, than I remember to have had. I keep regular hours, use a great deal of Exercise, and study very hard. There is a very ingenious Man here, with whom, besides, I spend two hours every evening: In Mechanicks, Mensuration and Astronomy, etc.'[7]

Dick had made up his mind to spend his time at Waltham usefully. He was painfully aware that he had learned very little in his years at Harrow, and that he was nothing more than an averagely ignorant young man. So he started to study voraciously for the first and only time in his life as if to fill his mind with things to think about other than Eliza Linley. He filled a small quarto book of nearly a hundred pages with an abstract of the history of England, and worked his way through Sir Philip Sidney's *Arcadia* and Sir William Temple's works. Unfortunately, thoughts of Eliza would persist in breaking in on his concentration, printed words fading in the recollection of her face.

30 October 1772 was a very significant date for Dick Sheridan: his twenty-first birthday. From that time onwards he was his own master in law, and theoretically free to marry whomsoever he wished. But there was no estate for him to inherit, and no bequest from his ancestors. He was still just as dependent upon his father, his prospect of marrying Eliza as remote as ever. Curiously he did not refer to his birthday when he wrote to Grenville that day, nor did he mention Eliza save for one mysterious remark: 'You will observe that I have

omitted saying anything *de Amore, aut de Cecilea mea (utinam quidem mea esset!)* I have kept absolutely to my resolution. But (from a late accident) I will defer saying more 'till I see you.'[8]

By November Dick seems to have partially regained his habitual good spirits, and to have broken out of the geographical confines of Waltham Abbey. He wrote three times to Grenville that month to recommend an 'easy unpremeditated style' in letter-writing, telling his friend that he was in London staying at the Bedford Coffee House and going to plays, and to let him know of his plans for the future. He set his heart on becoming a lawyer like Grenville, though to do this he knew he would still have to overcome his father's opposition. He told Grenville that he was studying very hard; he intended to make himself master of French and Italian; he was going to spend the following summer in France; and he would soon enter his own name as a student at the Temple. He breezily announced that his old schoolmate Lord George Townshend had recently promised to do something for him, and that he might even consider an offer of a temporary post in the diplomatic corps, though he did not intend to be an under-secretary at some obscure embassy for life. Meanwhile, he invited him down to Essex to spend a few days with him. 'You shall hunt and Shoot and Study in the prettiest rotation imaginable – At night you shall go on stargazing Parties, and with Ladies two [*sic*]: and conclude the Day with very good wine, and Pipes if you choose them.'[9] He had started flirting, though rather cynically.

If Dick sat on a precarious perch of optimism, a letter he received shortly afterwards soon knocked him off it. On 8 December he wrote to Grenville about two pieces of news which had cast him into despair. Firstly he had learned that Paumier had signed an account of his last duel with Mathews. Written by Barnett, it largely upheld Mathews's version of the event. Dick felt betrayed; now no one would believe his own view of how things were. Nor was he sympathetic to Paumier's excuse that Mathews had threatened to challenge him if he did not sign:

> I wait but for the Post from Bath, when I shall seek the bottom of this Treachery and if I do not revenge it, may I live to deserve it.[10]

But there was worse news for which he unfairly blamed Grenville:

by way of Consolation I find added to this Account that Your Friend, Sir T. Clarges, is either going to be married to or run away with Miss L. Excuse this vile disjointed scrawl.. I know not what to write, for upon my soul I believe I am distracted as greatly [as] I think I am injured.[11]

This was the torment he could hardly endure. Never mind that he had told Eliza there was no future for them and that they must forget each other, nor that he had no claim on her, never saw her, and did not even answer her letters. The thought of her with another man was still a torment to him. He dreaded that soon he would hear that she had married Clarges. At the same time he burned with resentment at her ingratitude. Had he not twice risked his life for this woman who was now intriguing with another man? Disgust and self-pity welled up in him. It was all that the Parkers could do to dissuade him from setting off for Bath to challenge Mathews to a third duel.

So he moped out his dark winter days in a small town at the end of a long muddy road in Essex. He read, he wrote, he watched the raindrops trickle down his window-pane, and he tried hard not to think of Eliza. By the end of January he had still heard no more of her affair with Clarges. As for the Paumier/Barnett business, he was tired of the whole set of them and decided to take no further steps in the matter. His depression returned after yet another disappointment. Lord George Townshend had encouraged his ambitions of surpassing his brother Charles as a diplomat and gaining the love and approval of his father. But after some time and many promises, Townshend had to admit he had no such diplomatic post for Dick. Dick felt so enormously let down that he became unwell again.

The only hope he could cling to was that he might still become a successful lawyer. In the New Year of 1773 he wrote to tell Grenville that he hoped that his name would soon be entered at the Temple, the 'great Gate of Power'. In February he was still waiting; presumably his father was holding out against his plans. But Dick now 'pressed so earnestly' and gave his father 'such solemn assurances of determined application to the study of the law' that he gave way. He also agreed to Dick's new proposal that instead of visiting France, in the spring he should go on a reading vacation to 'retire a few hundred miles Northward on a party with Messrs Coke, Blackstone and Co.'[12] Dick hoped to call on Thomas Grenville in Oxford on his way to Yorkshire.

Dick's name was not entered as a member of the Middle Temple until 6 April 1773. However, in the weeks preceding he made several trips to London, ostensibly concerning his prospective career. But a new prospect was opened to him which Thomas Sheridan had never anticipated. Dick had realised that the annual oratorio season at Drury Lane was fast approaching where the principle singer was to be none other than Eliza Linley. She would be only an hour's ride from Waltham Abbey! The mere thought of it set his pulses racing.

CHAPTER 14

Lady in Distress

Utterly miserable and unable to keep her promise not to write to Dick, Eliza sent him two letters in the autumn of 1772. Each begged an answer. She received no reply. Worse still, she began to hear rumours which appalled her. A Miss C——y (Carey?) from Bath who had been staying at Waltham Abbey recently returned home to a city eager for news of its hero Dick Sheridan. Miss C. duly obliged people with a pack of gossip, so taken aback was she by the undue attention she was receiving. She hinted that Dick was involved in an affair with a married woman, a Mrs Mary Lyster, the wife of a Waltham surgeon, to whom he had shown his private letters from Miss Linley. Eliza felt sickened. Her last scrap of faith in Dick Sheridan disappeared.

Her parents had not allowed her the respite she so clearly needed. She was still virtually a prisoner, and an unremitting round of concerts and tours was blithely arranged for her by her father. Nor had her parents abandoned their ambition of finding her a wealthy suitor. They soon came up with another candidate. Sir Thomas Clarges was a musical enthusiast and had fallen in love with Eliza when he had first heard her sing. In fact he seemed ideal. The Linleys encouraged him so much that soon after he had been introduced to Eliza, he proposed. To his amazement she turned him down flat. So at the very time when Dick believed that Eliza was eloping with Clarges, the disappointed baronet was packing his bags to take a grand tour to France and Italy.[1]

Some of Eliza's admirers were less honourable in their intentions. One day there was a knock at the Linley's door. The music master was delighted to welcome a very grand titled lady. But she would speak only to Eliza, and in private. Mystified, Linley found

110

himself bundled out of his own sitting room. The door closed, the two women confronted each other. Lady A. handed Eliza a letter from Lord G——r (Grosvenor?) in which he invited her to become his mistress. He offered her his 'heart and fortune' but regretted that he could not make her his wife because he already had one. To her amazement Lady A. was shown the door in a manner which aristocratic ladies did not usually experience from mere tradesmen. The local paper subsequently published what were supposed to be Lord G's letter together with Eliza's dignified reply:

MY LORD – Lest my silence should bear the most distant interpretation of listening to your proposals, I condescend to answer your infamous letter. You lament the laws will not permit you to offer me your hand. I lament it too, my lord, but on a different principle – to convince your dissipated heart that I have a soul capable of refusing a coronet when the owner is not the object of my affection – despising it when the offer of an unworthy possessor. The reception your honourable messenger met with in the execution of her embassy saves me the trouble of replying to the other parts of your letter, and (if you have any feelings left) will explain to you the baseness as well as the inefficacy of your design. L—y.[2]

In late February 1773 Eliza left Bath for London with her family to sing in the lenten oratorios. The concert-bills announced a performance of *Judas Macchabaeus* at the Theatre Royal on 26 February, featuring 'Miss Linley, Mrs Weichsel, Miss Mary Linley, Mr Norris and Mr Parry' and 'End of the First Act A Concerto on the Violin, by Mr Thomas Linley.'[3]

The Linley girls were a great success. At home the proudly loyal *Bath Chronicle* reported that they carried 'all before them' and that London audiences were 'riveted to the Drury Lane Oratorios alone.' Covent Garden and the Haymarket theatres it said were 'little frequented on the Wednesday and Friday (Oratorio) evenings' while at Drury Lane it estimated that a single night's takings probably exceeded £500.[4] Fanny Burney attended Eliza's first performance on 26 February and seems to have revisited the theatre throughout March. She was extremely enthusiastic about Eliza's talents and reported that the town 'has rung with no other name this month'.[5]

Handel's music was still very popular with English audiences in the late eighteenth century but this hardly explains the enormous success of the oratorio season at Drury Lane in 1773. No doubt some spectators enjoyed these oratorios in the right religious spirit, but it was in fact Eliza's sexual appeal that brought in the crowds. Many came simply to look at the pretty Linley girls as objects of curiosity. Fanny Burney noted the current rumours about Eliza in her diary: (the young singer was) 'believed to be very romantic . . . [and] has met with a great variety of adventures and has had more lovers and admirers than any nymph of these times'. Fanny added: 'She has long been attached to Mr Sheridan . . . a young man of ( ) very well spoken of, whom it is expected she will speedily marry. The applause and admiration she has met with can only be compared to what is given to Mr Garrick. The whole town seems distracted about her. Miss Linley alone engrosses all eyes, ears, and hearts.'[6] She added slyly:

> Had I been for my sins born of the male race, I should have certainly added one more to Miss Linley's train. She is really beautiful; her complexion is a clear lovely animated brown, with a blooming colour on her cheeks; her nose that most elegant of shapes grecian; fine, luxurious, easy-sitting hair, a charming forehead, pretty mouth and most bewitching eyes. With all this her carriage is modest and unassuming and her countenance indicates diffidence and a strong desire of pleasing – a desire in which she can never be disappointed.[7]

Eliza was now the talk of London and the focus of society gossip. One young nobleman went as far as publishing amorous verses about her in the press.[8] And because she sang sacred songs, even clergymen felt safe enough to succumb to her charms. *The Bath Chronicle* duly reported one event attended by the Linley girls: dinner with the Lord Bishop of Bristol at the Deanery House, St Paul's. The newspaper added the hope that the two young ladies might soon be introduced to the choir at St Paul's 'and promoted to Minor Canonries'.

On 13 April the same newspaper announced that the Linley family had received the ultimate accolade: a private concert for the King and Queen:

Yesterday se'enight Mr Linley, his son and elder daughter,

were at the Queen's concert at Buckingham House; Miss Mary Linley, being ill could not attend. The King and Queen were particularly affable; his Majesty told Mr Linley that he never in his life heard so fine a voice as his daughter's nor one so well instructed; that she was a great credit to him, and presented him with a £100 bank note. No one attended the concert but their Majesties, the children and one lady. It continued five hours, yet no one sat except the two performers who played the harpsichord and the violin-cello.[9]

Eliza's health was never robust. She was required to stand through-out the three-hour concert in what must have been an exhausting ordeal for her. George III on the other hand found it a stimulating occasion. He was very attracted to this young girl and made a point of attending a number of her later performances. Horace Walpole wrote to tell Lady Ossory on 16 March that the King had ogled Miss Linley 'as much as he dares to do in so holy a place as an oratorio and at so devout a service as "Alexander's feast".'[10] These occasions now set the King pondering on how he might enjoy a more intimate relationship with Eliza. Meanwhile throughout the month of March he had to be content simply to view her from the Royal Box at Drury Lane.

To Eliza all this meant little. Despite the adulation she enjoyed, she was close to a breakdown over Dick Sheridan. She thought about him night and day even though she believed he had betrayed her, and though she despaired of their relationship. In yet another letter she let him know of the pain he had caused her, demanding he return her letters. This time he replied. His letter has not survived but from her response it is clear that Dick explained his silence by point-ing out obedience to his father, and claimed that he had not received her letters, and that he had never been involved with Mrs L. But he politely declined to return Eliza's letters. She bitterly replied:

I have been so deceived by you and by everyone that it has almost deprived me of my reason, but I have paid too, too dear for my experience ever to put in your power or anyone's to impose on me again. I did not expect that you would attempt to vindicate your conduct. You cannot to me. Think! oh! reflect one moment on what I have suffered, and then judge if I can again consent to risk my life and happiness. For

113

God's sake, S—n, do not endeavour to plunge me again into misery. Consider the situation I am in. Consider how much your persisting to refuse my letters will distress me. Reason, honour, everything forbids it. This is not a sudden resolution, but the consequence of cool, deliberate reflection. You are sensible it is not from caprice, but when I tell you I have lately had some conversation with Miss L. and Miss C—y, you will not suppose I will be again deceived. Farewell! If you value my peace of mind return my letters.[11]

Dick Sheridan was reluctant to return Eliza's love letters, probably because he intuitively understood that to do so would finally end their relationship. Instead, when he was next in London he went round to Drury Lane and left a packet for her at the stage door. Only when she was alone in her room could Eliza open it. With trembling fingers she found a note from Dick saying that he would not return her letters until she was able to swear to him that she loved another man. It was the ultimate test of her feeling.

Her agonised reply proved to be the most important letter she ever wrote:

Thursday night, 12 o'clock.
I did not think to have opened another letter of yours but was deceived by your telling the maid they were my papers. I am too well convinced you have art and eloquence sufficient to impose on one less credulous than me . . .

Why S—n, will you thus distress me? Why endeavour to disturb that repose which for some time I have tried to court? I conjure you by all you hold dear, cease to persecute me. I never can be yours. There are now insuperable bars between us. Do not let the mistaken notion of pity impose on you. You are Deceived. You know not your own heart – it is not in your nature to be constant, especially to one who is so much in your Power, but if you still persist in thinking your happiness connected with mine, I now assure you it is not in your power to make me happy. I have gone through such scenes from my infancy of distress Disappointment and Deceit, it has taken from me that keen sensibility which has been the fault of all my misfortunes. My Heart is no longer susceptible of Love; 'tis dead to every tender feeling. You think I hate you, Heaven

knows I do not, but I cannot love you nor any Man. Your cold-
ness, your neglect, your contempt at a time when I stood so
much in need of consolation to support me, prey'd on my
mind, and the convincing proofs I have since received of your
Behaviour completed my cure. I saw you in such a light, I
could not but despise you, but tho' I do not now look upon
you in that light, I own to you I do not love. What was it that
first induced me to regard you. You are sensible that when I
left Bath I had no idea of you but as a friend. It was not your
person that gained my affection. No, S—n, it was that delicacy,
that tender compassion, that interest which you seemed to take
on my welfare, that were the motives that induced me to love
you.

When these were lost, when I found you no longer the man
my fair imagination painted you, when, instead of respect, I
found myself spoken of with contempt, laughed at, made the
Sport of your Idle Hours, and the subject of your Wit with
every Mileners [sic] Prentice in Bath! When I was convinced of
this, how could I love, how could I continue blindly to esteem
the man who had used me so basely. In regard to your omis-
sion in writing to me, I assure you, that is the least crime my
heart accuses you of, but I assure you I wrote twice, and put
the letters in the Post Office myself, they could not miscarry.

I beg'd, I entreated you to write; but receiving no answer,
I again renew'd my request, and urg'd it by every sacred tie.
In answer to this, P[aumier] showed me what you had writ to
him, where you desire to know if I insisted on your breaking
your promise to your father and where you offer to come to
Bath. I own I was hurt. What could I have said more than I had
already done? Were not my entreaties and supplications sufficient to prevail (if your own affections were not strong enough
to prompt you) but you must ask if I insisted on your compli-
ance? You know, S—n, I could not insist, I had put it out of
my power. I told you, before we Parted, that I might Desire,
request but should never insist on anything from you. Your
proposal of coming to Bath I looked upon as mere Words, as
you was well assur'd your father would not permit it. Besides
how ridiculously contradictory did it appear that you, who

held a promise so sacred as to refuse writing, would yet break thro' every tie of honour to see me . . .

To Eliza's surprise, Dick's recent letter had been laced with jealousy. He seemed to suspect her of carrying on love affairs with almost everyone she had met, including his previous friend Paumier, whom he now disliked. Eliza dismissed Dick's suspicions; Captain Paumier, she assured him, behaved to her with the 'strictest friendship' and was 'a worthy man':

At present you see everything through a mist of passion, but let reason once more chase the cloud of suspicion from your mind, and you will think with me that P— has not deserved your resentment.

I do not judge from appearances. If I did, I should be weak enough to listen to your plausible excuses, but, S—n, I cannot be again deceived. I am altered in every respect. I look back on my past conduct with Horror; I cannot be happy, but yet I trust I shall not be miserable.[12]

By February 1773 old Sheridan had at last woken up to the fact that his younger son and the still dangerous Miss Linley were now living only a few miles apart. Dick told Grenville that his father was apprehensive because 'all the Counties in the Neighbourhood of London were within the magic Circle of a formidable Enchantress who was to keep Lent there'.[13] But he added like one startled into a new life:

Eliza is within an hour's ride of me, and must have been for some time. Yet upon my honour, I have and do industriously avoid even knowing that particular Place that is blest with her inhabiting – I was obliged to go to London the other day – and I protest to you, no country Girl passing alone through a church-yard at midnight, ever dreaded more the appearance of a Ghost than I did to encounter this (for once I'll say) terrest(r)ial being – But – I can't not [sic] say anything on this subject on paper.[14]

Eliza wrote again:

I am acquainted with your Behaviour to your father and Lissy. I know by what means my Letters were made Publick. In short there is not a circumstance, nor a disrespectful word of yours that I am not acquainted with, tho' I did not get but little intelligence by Miss C. It is useless therefore your endeavouring to extenuate your behaviour. I cannot look upon you in the light I formerly did. Besides, supposing you was even to convince me you had never been guilty, I never could be yours. The remorse, the Horror which I feel when I reflect on my past conduct, would not permit me to marry the man who would have it so much in his power to upbraid me. After this declaration I hope you will no longer refuse returning me my letters; be assured this is the last you will ever receive from me.

You say you will not give them up till I declare I love another man. Do not distress me so much as to continue in that resolution. Believe me, I am incapable of loving any man. They cannot be of any use to you. Do not think I shall alter my resolution, or that I am to be terrified by your threats. I will not think so basely of your principles as to suppose you meant anything by them. There are insurmountable obstacles to prevent our ever being united, even supposing I could be induced again to believe you.[15]

Her words gave him new grounds for hope. Now that he considered them more closely he saw innumerable tell-tale signs that Eliza still only wanted to be reassured of his love. But then his eyes fell upon words which appalled him. The Linleys had taken advantage of this poor girl's wretched state and bullied her into promising on her knees that she would never marry him. Worse still, her father had extricated from her a reluctant agreement that she would accept a proposal from the first respectable man who made her a good offer. She had hoped that there would be no takers, but she was wrong.[16] She admitted:

My father before we left Bath, received proposals for me from a gentleman in London, which he insisted on my accepting. I endeavoured to evade his earnest request, but he urged my promise in such a manner that I could not refuse to see him (at least). He has visited me two or three times since we have been there. He is not a young man, but I believe a worthy one. When I found my father so resolute, I resolved to acquaint the gentleman with every circumstance of my life. I did, and instead of inducing him to give me up, he is now more earnest than ever. I have declared it is not possible for me to love him, but he says he will depend on my generosity – in short there is nothing I have not done to persuade him to leave me but in vain. He has promised my father not to take my fortune, and you may be assured that this circumstance will have great weight with him. You see how I am situated. If this was not the case, I could never be your wife, therefore once more I conjure you to leave me and cease persecuting me.

My father has this minute left me. He knows I am writing to you, and it was with the greatest difficulty I pacified him. He was going immediately to your lodgings. He has given strict orders to Hannah to bring every letter to him. You will make me eternally miserable if you persist after what I have told you. Be assured I will not open any letter of yours, nor will I write again. If you wish me to think my happiness is dear to you, return my letters. If not, I cannot compel you, but I hope your generosity will not permit you to make any improper use of them. For God's sake write no more. I tremble at the conse-quence.[17]

Great anguish passed through Dick as he stood in the pale sun-light reading Eliza's words. He was close to losing the most precious thing in his life. Linley had triumphed and Eliza had given in. But as her words scorched into his mind, once again he was convinced that this was not really a letter of farewell, but a last desperate plea for help. She was begging him to deliver her from a dreadful fate.

All doubts and evasions disappeared from his mind. Begging the loan of Parker's horse, he galloped off down the windy April roads towards London. As he splashed through the Essex mud he hardly noticed the stream of life about him, the carts and the coaches and the workless farm labourers with their pitchforks over their shoul-ders. His mind was filled with another image which consumed him with despair: Eliza dressed in white in a small Covent Garden sitting room with an elderly man hanging over her. Disgusted, he shuddered at the decrepit courtesies he knew she had to endure. He shouted against the wind to urge his horse faster and belaboured her with his whip, dreading that he would be too late and would arrive to find Eliza married. On he rode, without stopping, until his exhausted and trembling mare pulled up sharp at the stage door of the Drury Lane Theatre.

What happened in the ten days following the Royal concert on 3 April is a matter for conjecture. Subsequent events and romantic rumour have partly filled in the gaps, since there were no further letters between Dick and Eliza, and the relevant pages are missing from Alicia (Lefanu) Sheridan's account of their courting.[18]

When Dick arrived in London Linley denied him entrance to the Drury Lane Theatre. And even when at last Linley agreed that he might be admitted, it was on the condition that he should not attempt to obtain private interviews with Eliza after the performances. For several nights running Dick's only way of seeing her was to sit in the stalls listening to her lovely voice ringing out round the auditorium. He hit on a ruse to disguise himself as a coachman so that he could speak to her as he drove her home.

Eventually Linley allowed them to meet in his presence, probably in a private room at the Bedford Coffee House which Dick used as his headquarters in London. It was a great mistake. They were supposed to talk about returning Eliza's letters but Dick used the occasion to propose to her once more. Now he was of age and might speak for himself.

From then onwards this passionate young man confronted Linley daily at the theatre with a mixture of arguments, threats, pleas and a persuasive charm. Linley found them difficult to resist. Meanwhile at home his daughter was threatening suicide should she be forced to marry an old man she did not love, rather than Dick Sheridan, whom she did. Eventually Linley could take no more of it. Having protected his own financial interests in his daughter, he stopped trying to make her see sense and simply gave in.She could do as she wanted. Perhaps this was partly due to the new Romantic age. Ten years before, Edward Gibbon's father had forbidden his son's sentimental attachment to a young woman and the boy had simply submitted. In Eliza's generation however, young people were beginning to give first consideration not to their parents' wishes but to their own feelings.

On 8 April 1773 Eliza sang at a charity concert for the

Foundling's Hospital, and on 12 April gave her last public performance in London, a benefit performance for her brother Tom at the Haymarket Theatre. Then on 13 April at the parish church of St Paul's Covent Garden, and in a double wedding with Ewart and his bride, Elizabeth Ann Linley, a minor, with her father's consent, married by licence, and in the presence of Thomas Linley and John Swale, Richard Brinsley Sheridan Esq. The service was conducted by the Reverend Daniel Boote, Doctor of Divinity.

Only one person of significance was absent from the ceremony. Thomas Sheridan, still in Ireland, did not even know that it was taking place. Besides, he trusted his son not to do anything foolish. Had not Dick given him his solemn oath that he would never marry Miss Linley?

PART TWO

A Theatrical Marriage

CHAPTER 15

Bliss and After

One night close to midsummer's eve, a young woman sat in her bedroom in a cottage deep in the Buckinghamshire countryside. She remained quite still on the edge of the bed, staring into a bowl, scarcely daring to breathe. By the light of a single candle which stood on a table nearby she could just make out the simple appointments of the room: a chair, a chamber-pot, two pictures and a window seat. Above the cottage, a thin starlight silvered its thatch and whitened the path but failed to penetrate the dark woods. Save for the occasional call of an owl, the house was enveloped in an intense silence. A passer-by would hardly have made out the candle-light at the bedroom window but countless little white moths beat their heads against the glass as if wanting to get in.

From time to time Eliza wiped her burning forehead with a hesitant, nervous movement, as if she were trying to escape some foul beast that stalked her. Breathing as quietly as possible, she tried to pick out the sounds of the house; she heard her sister clumping along the bare boards past her room, and a creaking bedroom door. Voices murmured from the parlour below where her masters sat deciding her fate. There was the scrape of a poker, a burst of masculine laughter and the abrupt pop of another cork.

Suddenly the beast sprang and Eliza was seized by a spasm of coughing and spluttering. There was an abrupt sound of footsteps and the door burst open to reveal Mary with a candle flaring in her hand, her face pale as a moth. In a moment her arms were round her sister while she breathed words of comfort. But Eliza's whole body was wracked with spasms, and she was oblivious to everything except heaving and hacking into the bowl at her mouth. After several intensive waves of coughing, her lungs began to ease, her gasping subsided, and she felt once more the sweet sweat on her face.

Mary wrapped her in a blanket and wiped her forehead with a damp flannel. She looked at Eliza as if looking for an answer. Obediently her sister held up the bowl for inspection. As Mary brought the candle closer they both saw something dark at the bottom of the vessel. At that moment there came another burst of laughter from below. The men downstairs had heard nothing.

It was a bitter moment in a honeymoon which had seemed to many onlookers like the end of a fairy tale. When once the news of the Sheridan wedding broke, the press showed considerable interest in the whereabouts of the celebrated singer Elizabeth Linley and her gallant young husband. They were a glamorous couple. On 16 April 1773 the *Morning Chronicle* had reported their wedding and also that 'after the ceremony [the bride and groom] set out with her family and friends, and dined at the Star and Garter on Richmond Hill; in the evening they had a ball after which the family and friends returned to town, and left the young couple at a gentleman's house in Mitcham, to consummate their nuptials'.[1] Three days later the editor of the *Bath Journal* reprinted the item adding that he knew it would be of special interest to his many readers who had closely followed every ramification of the Maid of Bath's story and who would now rejoice in its happy outcome.

From Mitcham the newly-weds disappeared from public view for more than a month. They went briefly to Barrow's Hedge in Surrey, and then came to the Buckinghamshire hamlet. There they hired a cook and a gardener, and settled down to live the simple life. About a month after their arrival, Dick Sheridan wrote to Thomas Grenville and gave him a brief glimpse of his honeymoon days.

> I should inform you first that I have for some time been fixed in a grand little Mansion situated at a place called East Burnham, about 2 mile and $1/2$ from Salt Hill . . . Had I hunted five years I don't believe I could have hit on a Place more to my mind, or more adapted to my present situation; were I in a descriptive vein, I would draw you some of the prettiest Scenes imaginable. I likewise waive the opportunity of displaying the rational and delightful scheme on which our Hours proceed. – On the whole I will assure you, as I believe it will give you more pleasure, that I feel myself absolutely and perfectly happy . . . If I thought it would be entertaining to you I would send you an account of the arrangement of my

Household which I assure [you] is conducted quite in the manner of plain Mortals, with all due attention to the Bread-and-Cheese – Feelings – I have laid aside my Design of turning Cupid into a Turnspit's Wheel, and my meat undergoes the indignity of a Cook's handling.[2]

The tone-deaf young husband concluded with an ironic comparison of Eliza's powers to those of the god Orpheus, who, according to legend, could literally move mountains and trees with his entrancing music:

I have even been so far Diffident of my Wife's musical Abilities as to have Carrots and Cab[b]ages put in to the Garden Ground; and finding that whatever effect her Voice might have upon the Sheep on the Common, the Mutton still obstinately continued stationary at the Butcher's, I have design'd to become indebted to the Brute's abilities.[3]

Throughout May and early June, while the pink hawthorns bloomed and the bold hedge parsley creamed its way around their garden plot, the honeymooners remained alone at the cottage, blissfully happy and wanting no visitors. Only occasionally was their idyll broken, when Dick would have to ride off to London on business. After one such trip he came back and presented her with some lines of poetry written in a listless hour at an inn:

> Teach me, kind Hymen, teach – for thou
> Must be my only tutor now
> Teach me some innocent employ,
> That shall the hateful hours destroy,
> That I this whole long night must pass
> In exile from my love's embrace.
>
> True she is mine, and, since she's mine
> At trifles I should not repine;
> But oh, the miser's real pleasure
> Is not in knowing he has treasure;
> He must behold his golden store
> And feel, and count his riches o'er.
> Thus I, of one dear gem possesst

125

And in that treasure only blest
There every day would seek delight
And clasp the casket every night.'[4]

Eliza was probably pleased and flattered by the compliment that Dick saw himself 'of one dear gem possesst'. At this time and for many years to come she remained besotted by her husband, and quite incapable of adopting a critical attitude toward him.

Dick's disappearances to London were always to the same purpose, to borrow money. For the moment, their only regular income derived from the interest on Eliza's portion of the £3,000 made over to her by Mr Long. The marriage settlement arranged by their solicitor John Swale, dated 10 April 1773, stated that £1,050 three per cent Consols should be 'transferred to Swale and Linley In Trust, to pay the Dividends to Mrs Sheridan for her Life'.[5] The interest on £1,050 would have amounted to just £31.10 shillings per annum, and apart from that all the young couple could depend on were the few hundred pounds Eliza kept back of the 'Long' money, and £50 which Dick had borrowed from Swale. They had few prospects and their financial situation seemed perilous. Though Dick had entered his name at the Middle Temple for the Hilary (Spring) term, Eliza was soon made to understand that her husband no longer looked towards the law as a future career. Despite that, he was bounding with energy and confidence. When Eliza voiced her fears for the future he quickly dismissed them. She may have seen a note he wrote to Grenville at this time and would have been as puzzled as Grenville by the words: 'As for the little Cloud which the peering eye of Prudence would descry to be gathering against the Progress of the Lune, I have a consoling Cherub that whispers me, that before They threaten an adverse Shower, a slight gale or two of Fortune will disperse them.'[6] But where was this gale of good fortune to come from? Dick would not say: he would never discuss money matters with his wife.

Not that Eliza was really concerned about finances during their summer idyll at East Burnham. She knew that when it came to it, she was quite capable of earning an income which would keep them both in relative luxury. As a singer she could command fees of at least £100 a night. It was true that recently she had despised the work, but that was due to her father's dictatorial ways, the exhausting tours, and the never-ending sexual harassment to which she had been subjected. Now that Dick would be her manager, everything would be better. There would be plenty of money.

She had two previously arranged commitments to sing; after Convocation at Oxford University in July and at the Three Choirs' Festival at Worcester in September. Then, while she was still at East Burnham, her father told her that she had received another stupendous offer. The proprietors of the Pantheon, James Wyatt's immense Byzantine pleasure palace recently completed in Oxford Street, were willing to pay her a fortune: 'one thousand two hundred guineas for twelve nights at the Pantheon, 1,000 guineas for the oratorios, and 1,000 guineas for Giardini's concerts', a total of 3,200 guineas each season, a contract which was to continue for seven years.[7] Eliza at once saw the chance to make up to her young husband for all the hardships he had suffered on her behalf, and she went to tell him, enormously excited. His response amazed her. He greeted the news coolly, and airily informed her that far from accepting it, as her husband he had decided that he would never permit her to sing in public again.

For a moment she was taken aback. But on reflection she thought she understood his motive and was moved by it; he was worried about her health and the strain her concerts put on her. It was gratifying to have someone at last who was concerned about her, but Dick was not being realistic. Quietly and lovingly she spelt it out to him: if she were not to sing professionally they would have no money to live on. But it made no difference. He would not even discuss it and insisted that he was the only person to decide whether or not she should continue singing in public. He had already made up his mind that she would not.

Some biographers of Richard Brinsley Sheridan have suggested that Eliza had already agreed not to sing in public, even before she married him. All the evidence however points to the contrary. Sheridan's earliest biographer, Watkins, reported that

> he never intimated his resolution of withdrawing her from that pursuit till after their marriage . . . The interdiction was totally unexpected by her friends, who considered it as an act of severity and insult on the part of a man who could neither boast pedigree nor property . . . Even Mrs Sheridan was anxious to secure an income by her vocal powers; and she earnestly entreated her husband to relax from his opposition,

so far as to allow of her occasional performance, until their circumstances should render it unnecessary. But he still continued inflexible.[8]

Eliza was perfectly familiar with her legal situation. As a minor and an apprentice she had no existence in law when bound to her father. Now she was a wife, her husband had succeeded to her father's powers: he was in effect her new 'master'. In this case, however, she entirely, and perhaps wrongly, trusted Dick to act in her best interests. Even so, she was taken aback by his decision and his disdain for the Pantheon offer. His explanation – in so far as he was prepared to account for his motives at all – was extraordinarily simplistic. He believed that now she had become Mrs Sheridan, she was no longer a singer for hire but a gentleman's wife. As such there was no question of her performing in public. To do so would mean compromising *his* social status.

And it was chiefly the thought of his own dignity that made Sheridan write to a Mr Isaac of Worcester, cancelling the agreement and refusing to allow Eliza to appear in the Three Choirs' Festival. Later he defended his decision to Linley who had set up the initial contract:

He [Isaacs] had enclosed a letter . . . for my wife, in which he dwells much on the nature of the agreement you had made for her eight months ago, and adds, that 'as this is no new application, but a request that you [Mrs S] will fulfil a positive engagement, the breach of which would prove of fatal consequence to our Meeting, I hope that Mr. Sheridan will think his honour in some degree concerned with fulfilling it'. – Mr- Storace, in order to enforce Mr. Isaac's argument, showed me his letter on the same subject to him, which begins with saying, 'We must have Mrs Sheridan, somehow or other, if possible! – the plain English of which is that, if her husband is not willing to let her perform, we will persuade him that he acts dishonourably in preventing her from fulfilling a positive engagement. This I conceive to be the very worse mode of application that could have been taken; as there really is no common sense in the idea that my honour can be concerned in my wife's fulfilling an engagement which it is impossible that she should ever have made.[9]

Dick's argument was based upon the legality that once Eliza had become a married woman, any contract which her previous 'master' had signed on her behalf was no longer valid. Previously she had been her father's property; now she was his:

> Nor (as I wrote to Mr. Isaac) can you, who gave the promise, whatever it was, be in the least charged with the breach of it, as your daughter's marriage was an event which must always have been looked to by them as quite as natural a period to your right over her as her death.[10]

This piece of bravado was written by a young man who had recently fought two duels and was still fired up with the sense of his own honour. In possessing Eliza, Dick Sheridan found for the first time in his twenty-two years of life that he was in a position of power. The sensation was intoxicating. Titled people were begging him to allow his wife to appear at concerts, and like some great man it was his whim which would decide their happiness. But he was still determined to signal to all the world that he held his honour in greater value than money. Though his own father was an actor, he had passionately maintained that he was also a gentleman. Now he too could insist on his rightful status. But he could not resist playing with Linley's hopes:

> As to the imprudence of declining this engagement, I do not think even were we to suppose that my wife should ever on any occasion appear again in public, there would be the least at present. For instance, I have had a gentleman with me from Oxford (where they do not claim the least right as from an engagement), who has endeavoured to place the idea of my complimenting the University with Betsey's performance in the strongest light of advantage to me. This he said, on my declining to let her perform on any agreement. He likewise informed me, that he had just left Lord North [the Prime Minister and Chancellor of the University] who, he assured me, would look upon it as the highest compliment, and had expressed himself so to him. Now, should it be a point of inclination or convenience to me to break my resolution with regard to Betsey's performing, there surely would be more sense in obliging Lord North (and probably from his own application) and the

University than Lord Coventry and Mr Isaac. For, were she to sing at Worcester, there would not be the least compliment in her performing at Oxford. Indeed, they would have a right to claim it.[11]

The ever-cautious Linley replied on 15 May, pointing out that if Eliza were to sing at Oxford, Dick had no reason to refuse to honour her Worcester commitment as well. He suggested that Dick should 'wait upon' both Lord Coventry and Lord North. But his son-in-law had throughout his life exhibited a genuine and perhaps foolhardy contempt for money. His ownership of Eliza enabled him to feed this vanity in all sorts of ways. For example, his father had not been able to afford to send him to the university, but here he was at the age of twenty-two with Oxford begging that he should 'compliment' them by allowing his wife to sing there. Even more satisfying was the fact that the Prime Minister, Lord North, had to take time off from the American War to consult the wishes of young Mr Sheridan. Eliza was worth far more than riches to him; she would prove his passport into the great world.

There was however another reason why Dick Sheridan refused to allow his wife to sing: jealousy. He feared that on stage she would attract the sexual attentions of other men. Old Sheridan's views about actresses had implanted in his son the conviction that no real lady might ever perform on the public stage and still retain her reputation. There were still hundreds of Mathews in the world. Dick was even wary of an approach from the King himself. To his surprise, George III had instructed his agents to offer Mr Richard Sheridan the post of manager of oratorios at the Theatre Royal, Drury Lane. Dick, however, was well aware that there was no reason why he should be offered such a post except as the husband of the celebrated Eliza. He remembered her account of how she had sung at court, where George had stared at her suggestively and over-tipped her father with £100 note. Sheridan 'declined the offer very civilly and peremptorily' and suggested to the King's agent that as Mr Linley had 'twenty Mrs Sheridans more' at home, he should be offered the job. He was not.[12]

As the summer went on, Eliza became more and more alarmed at Dick's resolution that she should not perform at Oxford or the Three Choirs Festival, not only because it reflected on her professional reputation but also on that of her father who had made the bookings. The matter worried her so much that she became unwell. She begged Dick to change his mind, or at least to discuss the matter with Linley. In mid June he agreed to meet the music master at the honeymoon cottage with his daughter Mary.

Relations between Linley and Dick Sheridan were now very good except for the one vexed issue of Eliza's musical commitments. The two men spent long hours in the parlour drinking wine and talking over her future. Linley was enormously excited by the immense sums offered by the Pantheon's proprietors and was set upon changing Dick Sheridan's mind on the matter. Meanwhile Eliza was delighted to take morning walks with her sister through the Buckinghamshire countryside. Soon however Eliza had to stay indoors because she was indisposed. She suffered days of high temperatures and listlessness, followed by nights of coughing. During these attacks Mary sat up with her while her husband and father stayed downstairs. At times Eliza dreaded that she might learn her fate from the bottom of her spitting bowl. Ironically, it was perhaps because of her delicate condition that Dick agreed to reconsider his decision about her bookings, but only if her health improved. The news cheered her up at once and her coughing stopped.

Despite the growing affability between them, Linley could not persuade Dick to let Eliza accept the enormously rewarding offers she had received from the Pantheon and other theatres. But eventually his nagging, aided by the subtle flattery of Lord North, persuaded Sheridan to honour Eliza's previous commitments. So, not without a sigh, one bright July morning the young couple left East Burnham for the last time and followed a handcart carrying their goods to Oxford. In the lane's turning Eliza looked back once at the thatched cottage and wondered if she would ever again be as happy as she had been there.

But their spirits were cheerful as they started out on their new married life. In Oxford they were treated as celebrities. Eliza appeared in an oratorio entitled *The Prodigal Son*. Then on 9 July, she and Mary sang Italian songs and pieces from Handel together to an audience of about 3500 people at Convocation. The philosopher, Dr James Beattie, described the concert as the 'finest and most magnificent musical entertainment I have ever seen'.[13] It was a triumph.

The question of the Three Choirs' Festival was still to be settled. For a little while longer Dick kept people waiting for his decision.

His mind was made up eventually by two invitations they received: one to stay with the sixth Earl of Coventry at his home at Croome during the festival period in September, and another invitation for July from the prominent merchant banker Stratford Canning and his wife. This last one tipped the balance. The advantages to these grand hosts were evident. Sheridan could hardly accept these invitations and yet refuse to let his wife sing at the Festival. What was more, as a temporary resident, the famous Mrs Sheridan would be obliged to perform briefly for her fellow guests. The social-climber in her husband could not resist such opportunities and at last allowed Eliza to sing at Worcester.

Eliza enjoyed these visits very much. She especially liked Mrs Mehetabel Canning, a kindly and upright Irish woman with whom she soon became close friends. In fact at both the Cannings' and at Croome the Sheridans were treated with the greatest courtesy. At first Eliza was considered to be the celebrity while Dick was merely her husband. But then she noticed a curious pattern emerging. His dubious reputation as a duelist was soon forgotten as one lively dinner-table conversation followed another. Groups of diners would bend to catch his latest remark and shouts of laughter would rise from the people sitting around him. His words were whispered along the tables for others to admire.

Eliza was delighted that her husband was considered a wit for she wanted everyone to hold him in the same great esteem as she did. This also suited Dick, who quickly realised that his wife's reputation might serve as his stepping-stone to fame. He had no intention of supplying a footnote to history as merely the husband of Eliza Linley.

Yet in their private conversation he was still adamant that once she had fulfilled her commitment at Worcester he would never let her sing in public again. If she pointed out once more that her singing career was their only source of income, he would mutter something about making a living by writing for the press. She knew that though he would not recognise the reality of their financial situation, he would soon be forced to face up to it.

In September came the Three Choirs' Festival at Worcester. Dick had let it be known that these would be Eliza's farewell appearances. Afterwards *The Gloucester Journal* reported that: 'At the close of this Meeting she [Eliza] took leave of an admiring public, in the full lustre of unrivalled talents, leaving the minds of her enraptured audience impressed with a remembrance not soon to be eradicated of her sweet and powerful tones, and charmed with her generosity and benevolence'.[14] Unsurprisingly Dick insisted that she should emphasise her newly-acquired gentility by refusing the payment her father had so arduously negotiated on her behalf, so she put the hundred guineas in the collection plate. They had no money to live on but he could not resist this very theatrical gesture.

Eliza was not especially upset about the money. She knew that she was at the height of her powers as a singer and her receptions at Oxford and Worcester had left her with a warm glow of achievement. Anticipating an even more successful career, she was confident that once her husband saw sense she could make an ample living for them both. Only on rare occasions now did she reflect upon those desperate summer nights at East Burnham, when she had sat staring at blood in a bowl as if trying to divine her fate.

CHAPTER 16

Miscarriages

One April evening in 1773 an aging actor sat morosely inspecting his features in the dressing room mirror of Cork's principle theatre. What he saw did not please him. As he wiped away the last vestiges of Richard Crookback he revealed a terribly old and tired face. Thomas Sheridan was still touring Ireland with his interpretations of Shakespeare, while his son was enjoying a month of love at East Burnham. It was desperately hard for a man of fifty-four. Every few days he was obliged to sit for long hours in a hired carriage, as it creaked wearisomely along muddy roads from one small town to another. He had to endure primitive inns, indigestible meals, grubby bedlinen, uncivil servants, long hours of work and low company. He would arrive in a town tired out, take too many glasses of wine while roasting himself at the tap-room fire, sleep fitfully, walk through his moves on an unfamiliar stage next morning, and in the evening would play Hamlet or Richard III for four hours. He hated the life: he hated the theatre. But he had to keep on in order to maintain the four unemployed children he had left behind in Bath. The compensation for such a vagabond life was demonstrating his considerable powers to provincial audiences and receiving the occasional invitation from local gentry eager to meet a famous actor.

On this particular evening he had just such a treat to look forward to; a reception at Lord Muskerry's. The sight of his own pale, drawn features depressed him. How could he look his best? He decided to apply a little more rouge than usual. At Muskerry's party he could forget his life of drudgery and enjoy the pleasure of fine wines, delicious food and polished manners. These people would understand and respect the fact that he was a Master of Arts of both English universities, a scholar, and a teacher of educated speech. Above all they would treat him not as a common actor but as a gentleman. He luxuriated in the thought. At that moment, however, there was a knock at the door. In the glass he glimpsed his dresser come into the room with a letter. It was from England, in Alicia's handwriting. He broke the seal and impatiently scanned the contents. All at once, he felt as if his world had collapsed. His son Dick had married the actress Linley.

At first stunned, and then very angry indeed, he knew now that he had been betrayed. While Dick was promising not to marry that woman he was planning all the time to do so. He had always trusted Dick's word as a gentleman, and the thought of such deceit brought the old actor to his feet. So consumed by rage was he that he could hardly think of anything else all evening, even when Muskerry paid him a particular compliment, or when his hostess handed him a glass of specially fine Madeira. He would not forgive his son and he would never recognise that Linley woman as his daughter-in-law.

When Dick sent him a letter explaining his conduct, Sheridan did not answer. Instead on 20 April 1773 he wrote to Charles: 'I consider myself now as having no son but you.'[1] He also wrote to his daughters, commanding them to give up their friendship with Miss L. Dick was very grieved at his father's response, begging Thomas Linley to intercede for him. Since Linley had forgiven them both, he could not understand why Dick's own father could not do so. But on 5 May, Linley replied to Dick that there was 'small Prospect of a Reconciliation'; Sheridan could not 'be easily induced to forgive' Eliza.[2] In fact the old man hated his new daughter-in-law.

As autumn came on the newly weds could no longer trespass upon the hospitality of Eliza's wealthy friends. Nor could they consider returning to their honeymoon cottage at East Burnham. They had to make a living, and all Dick's plans to do so depended upon being in London. Dick and Eliza had friends and acquaintances in the capital and so it was comparatively easy to find lodgings among them. They proposed to spend the winter in Marylebone High Street with the musician Stephen Storace and his wife while looking for a house of their own.

The Storaces were an attractive, easy-going Anglo-Italian family earning their living from the arts. Stephen Storace, a double-bass player from Torre Annunziata near Naples, had first come to London some thirty years earlier to seek his fortune. He was something of an impresario and had served as musical director at Smock Alley

Theatre in Dublin when Thomas Sheridan was manager. He had been a partner in Johnson's Music Hall, had played in the orchestra at the Marylebone Gardens, and the King's Theatre in the Haymarket. Later on he had performed annually at the Three Choirs' Festival and had participated in all Eliza's appearances there.[3]

Elizabeth Storace was the daughter of John Trusler, for many years proprietor of the Marylebone Gardens. Trusler was prevented by theatre patents to put on plays in the Gardens so he had provided his patrons with music, fireworks and cakes. Elizabeth Storace proudly informed Eliza that twenty years previously her pastries had been famous. She showed her an old newspaper advertisement which announced that: 'Mr Trusler's daughter continues to make the Rich Seed Cakes, so much admired by the Nobility and Gentry'. The paper later advertised that Miss Trusler would be offering 'almond cheesecakes in a small size at 2s per dozen. Six or eight make a Dich, and are hot every day at one o'clock'.[4] Eliza pondered the fact that by diversifying in her arts, her landlady had helped her husband's career, whereas she herself could do nothing but sing.

There were two children in the Storace household: eleven-year-old Stephen Junior who was showing great promise as a violinist and later studied the instrument in Italy, and eight-year-old Ann Selina Storace, (known as 'Nancy') who already exhibited a precocious talent for singing. Stephen Junior eventually became an opera composer. In Ann Selina, Eliza detected a great likeness to herself.

When only seventeen she appeared at La Scala. Nancy's history, however, serves as an intriguing counterpoint to that of Eliza. Whereas the older girl's career was entirely directed by men, Nancy became a liberated, cosmopolitan woman who no one dared to order whether or not to sing. As an adult she became a famous soprano, performing in Austria, Germany and Italy, and was later a star of Drury Lane. All this however was long after that autumn when Eliza and her new husband first came to lodge with the Storaces in Marylebone.[5]

Eliza was quite at home there. The Storaces were her sort of people; cheerful and artistic. The very air they breathed was music. But as the spring came on, the Sheridans decided to look for a home of their own. They soon discovered a suitable property and the *Morning Post* for 4 February 1774 announced that Sheridan had 'taken a house in Orchard Street'.[6] Thomas Linley provided the furniture.

They now found themselves living in a very fashionable district still under construction; the adjacent Portman Square was completed just as they moved in. At the north end of Oxford Street paving stones gave way to green fields, while to the south, roughly on the site of the present Marble Arch, stood the gallows at Tyburn. In Orchard Street Eliza became familiar with both the most fashionable and the most brutal features of eighteenth century life. A woman of her fastidious sensibility probably turned with disgust from some of the desperate sights in the thoroughfares, such as the felons who arrived after a three-mile march jeered on by spectators from Newgate to Tyburn, for public whipping, branding or even the gibbet.

The chief problem for the young couple in Orchard Street was paying the rent. They knew they could expect no help from Sheridan and only a little from Linley. So Dick had to abandon any last hopes of the law and became a freelance journalist. Years later he wrote: 'I had no time for such [legal] studies. Mrs Sheridan and myself were often obliged to keep writing for our daily leg or shoulder of mutton, otherwise we should have had no dinner'.[7] Knowing that Eliza could write, he persuaded her to co-operate in composing items for the press. He even tried to convince her that it was she who had willingly agreed to give up singing in favour of writing, and presented her with some verses of congratulation:

ON HIS WIFE CEASING TO SING
Does my Eliza cease to sing
Or tires my love to touch the string?
Behold, she knows with equal skill
To grace the Muse's nobler will.[8]

He had the effrontery to claim that she wrote better than she sang:

Hear but her voice! amaz'd you'd swear
The soul of Music centres there!
Read but her verse, and You'll confess
Her song did raise your wonder less:[9]

Patiently Eliza waited for him to come to his senses. She was sure that he could never earn from his writing anything like the annual sum they would need to maintain a genteel lifestyle, let alone the fortune she could earn with her voice.

Meanwhile word began to get round in fashionable society that the charming Mrs Sheridan had stopped performing in public because her husband would not permit her. It even reached old Sheridan's arch-enemy Samuel Johnson. Boswell recorded their conversation on the matter:

> We talked of a young gentleman's marriage with an eminent singer, and his determination that she should no longer sing in publick, though his father [he means his father-in-law] was very earnest she should, because her talents would be liberally rewarded, so as to make her fortune. It was questioned whether the young gentleman who had not a shilling in the world, but was blest with uncommon talents, was not foolishly delicate or foolishly proud, and his father truly rational without being mean. Johnson, with all the spirit of a Roman senator, exclaimed, 'He resolved wisely and nobly, to be sure. He is a brave man. Would not a gentleman be disgraced by having his wife singing publicly for hire? No, sir, there can be no doubt here. I know not if I should prepare myself for a public singer, as readily as let my wife be one.'[10]

At this time Dick was also writing something more weighty than journalism. In November 1774 he informed his father-in-law that he had 'been very seriously at work on a book, which [he was] just now sending to the press', and which he thought would do him 'some credit'.[11] The book he referred to was a commentary on Lord Chesterfield's *Letters* of which Johnson had already proclaimed that they 'teach the morals of a whore and the manners of a dancing-master'. Dick was probably equally critical but we cannot be sure because his book was never published.

Soon after they were married Eliza became pregnant. Naturally they were both very pleased, but her condition worried her family. On 15 November her father wrote to tell Dick that 'We [Linleys] are all in great anxiety to hear from you in regard to Betsey's health.'[12] This was because they feared that her physique was too fragile to withstand the shock of childbirth. They were right. Punishing days of moving house and frantic writing took their toll; shortly after their move to Orchard Street she had a miscarriage. She was so ill that for a time her doctors despaired of her life. The *Morning Post* reported that young Sheridan had many plans, but he cautioned that these would only come about 'if his wife recover[ed]'.[13] So seriously did Linley now consider the situation that he actually begged his son-in-law to abstain from further sexual relations with Eliza, believing that she suffered from a 'seminal weakness' probably inherited tuberculosis. He commanded Dick that he: 'must absolutely keep from her, for every time you touch her, you drive a Nail in her Coffin'.[14]

During February Eliza lay in her bedroom listening to carriages rumbling in the fashionable streets outside. She was determined to get well soon so that once again she might help Dick with his daily struggle to pay for their 'bread and cheese'. She nagged him without mercy whenever he came in to see her to let her sing again in public. In the end he gave way – only partially – and agreed. He had to; their debts were increasing alarmingly. But Sheridan could not give way without saving face. Accordingly, he put word around that he had previously meant she might sing to genteel audiences but not in public places, such as theatres and concert halls where she might be insulted. To prove the point he informed the *Morning Post* that his wife would 'give concerts twice a week to the nobility' at Orchard Street.[15] From March onwards, Eliza, and sometimes Mary, sang their arias to delighted audiences. Fanny Burney attended one and observed that 'the highest circles of society were attracted to them by the beauty, fashion and talents of Mrs Sheridan. Entrance to them was sought not only by all the votaries of taste and admirers of excellence, but by the leaders of ton and their followers and slaves.'[16]

Sheridan liked to make out that these were private parties to which he welcomed the aristocracy, but in reality the 'guests' paid to get in. A certain Mrs Delaney wrote to her friend Mrs Port in April 1774 to inform her that she had experienced the greatest difficulty in getting a ticket for her friend Lady Mort, such was the interest in the concerts among prospective subscribers. 'Who would have imagined' asked Mrs Delaney disengenuously, 'I could be an instrument for obtaining favour among the bon tons.'[17] As more and more people came Sheridan's finances revived a little, so that later in the year he could afford to build a special music room onto the house. But these genteel soirées were hardly the triumphant return to the professional musical world which haunted Eliza's dreams.

Nevertheless, with their glamorous lifestyle the Sheridans were still spending far more than they earned, and it came as a considerable relief when they received invitations from wealthy friends to spend the summer months at their houses. Once again the Cannings invited them to Putney and Lord Coventry to Croome. But most flattering of all was that from the acknowledged leader of the social world, Georgiana, the young Duchess of Devonshire. By late spring Eliza felt well enough to go visiting again but was still doubtful whether to accept the invitation to Mrs Sheridan and her husband from Chatsworth. She feared that Dick would be snubbed, but as he seemed eager to go she accepted. Such invitations meant months of free accommodation in splendid surroundings and relief from money worries. The visits also allowed Eliza to postpone the showdown she meant to have with Dick about his refusal to allow her a singing career.

Some years later Lady Cork revealed to Tom Moore that when Dick Sheridan first went to Chatsworth he was considered 'an ugly, awkward-looking man' and that though the Duchess wanted 'to have Mrs Sheridan at her house she did not like to have her husband come too, for she considered him a mere player.'[18] Sure enough, when the Sheridans arrived, Eliza was the immediate focus of attention while Dick was ignored. But once again, though Eliza's nightly performances continued to be greeted with warm applause, she noticed that Dick's table conversation began to provoke considerable laughter, and that people clustered round to hear him. Soon he was the star and his fellow guests delighted in his wit. As for Georgiana, she was captivated by him. His triumph with the Duchess was so pronounced that she kept Chatsworth empty days after the guests had left, simply to listen to Sheridan's conversation. Had Eliza had less confidence in her husband she might have been jealous of her hostess; and had she been less loyal to Dick she might have resented the way in which he had supplanted her at Chatsworth; and had she been more perceptive she might even have noticed that in a curious way her husband seemed to regard her as his rival. But she did not. Loving him as she did, she simply rejoiced in his success.

As the summer weeks went on the Sheridans progressed from Chatsworth to Putney to Croome. Splendid ladies were caught in the long mirrors of the great salons smiling in the candlelight as Mrs Sheridan sang delightful songs for her supper. Her performance seemed deeply poignant to them, not just because of her soulful voice and her face, so soft beneath the candles, but also because it was clear that she was expecting a child. But a guest with good hearing might also have detected faint bursts of laughter from the dining room where some of the heartier spirits had preferred to stay on listening to Mr Sheridan.

In November it was time for the Sheridans to leave for London. For hours on end Eliza was jolted down the London road in Lord Coventry's carriage, blasted by severe draughts. As soon as she got home she went to bed. But the damage was done: she lost her baby. On the fifteenth of the month Dick wrote to Bath to inform Linley: 'I must promise to you that Betsey is now very well, before I tell you that she has encountered another disappointment and consequent indisposition . . . However she is not getting entirely over it and she shall never take any journey of the kind again.'[19] Dick did his best to keep his word and the Sheridans soon acquired a horse and little carriage with a groom who could double-up in the house.

Dick tried to reassure Linley on another point: 'I inform you of this now, that you may not be alarmed by any accounts from some other quarter, which might lead you to feel she was going to have such an illness as last year.'[20] He was referring to consumption. Linley was only partly convinced.

CHAPTER 17

Rivalry

During the first week of November 1774, Eliza lay in bed recovering from her miscarriage. Her mind was filled with anxiety about her and her husband's financial position. Since her illness there had been no recitals at Orchard Street, yet Dick had gone on recklessly running up bills. She now dreaded that unless he changed his mind and let her take up a contract at the Garden or the Pantheon, they would soon become bankrupt.

But when she tried to discuss her fears, he airily claimed to be working on a project that would solve all their financial problems. The only thing she was to worry about, he said, was getting well.[1] Ever since they were at Croome he had been scribbling a comic play which he said would make their fortune. Upon this slender hope their prospects rested. But Eliza had far more knowledge of the theatre than her husband, and knew that he was deluding himself. Without hurting his feelings, she tried gently to explain to him that it was a very difficult matter to write a successful play, and even more so to get it accepted. Managers rejected hundreds of scripts every year, some from established dramatists. And even when a new comedy was put on, often as not it failed or was forgotten after a few nights' run.

His reply took the wind out of her sails. He said that Tom Harris, the manager of Covent Garden, had already commissioned him to write a comedy and wanted to put it on in the New Year. All he had to do was write it. That he had been doing, scribbling away in the afternoons in the library at Croome while she was resting. He had even tried out some of his lines on dinner-guests there, and they had found them amusing. Now all he had to do was to put his head down and finish the piece. Harris was impatient for it.

Dick Sheridan's notion of writing a comedy first came to him at Bath when his father had shown him a manuscript he had brought back from France.[2] It was in Frances Sheridan's faded handwriting, and proved to be the first three acts of a comedy entitled *A Journey to Bath*.[3] Of course Dick already knew about his mother's career as a dramatist. Garrick had admired her both as a woman and a writer, and in February 1763 had produced her first comedy *The Discovery* with considerable success.[4] Unfortunately her second play *The Dupe* lasted only one night, perhaps because an embittered actress brought a mob into the house to howl the play off the stage. Even while the Sheridans were preparing to cross the channel to escape from their creditors, Frances was working on a third comedy, the first three acts of which she sent to Garrick. To her dismay the great man rejected it on the grounds that it had no 'fable', was not unified and had 'no humour'.[5] This was *A Journey to Bath*.

For some time Dick forgot all about his mother's play but once he re-read it he realised that his mother had written it with extraordinary prescience. It anticipated the love story Dick had just played out with Eliza. Set among the same lodging houses, streets and squares of Bath which they had frequented, one scene even took place in the Spring Gardens grotto where he used to leave poems for Eliza. And just as they had had to struggle against the dictates of their parents, so in his mother's play the love of young Lucy Tryfort and Edward Bull was obstructed by an older generation. Mrs Tryfort anticipated the less than grammatical Mrs Mary Linley, always trying to bully her daughter into taking a rich husband:

> MRS TRYFORT: (You are) . . . a silly chit that might be a
> countess (if you) had the grace to deserve it.
> LUCY: I don't desire it.
> MRS TRYFORT: That's for you, Miss, a foolish metamor-
> phosis![6]

Dick would not accept Garrick's verdict on the play. In his opinion there was plenty of humour in it, witty lines, sharp plotting and good characterisation. With a bit of revision something might be done with it. So he decided to tinker about with the script – regarding the comedy as he did his mother's only legacy – and then offer it to a theatre manager.

But when in the summer of 1774 he looked through it, a better idea came to him. Why should he not devise a more up-to-date play set in the same city? And what better story could he find than the tale of his own recent escapades courting Eliza? It should be a story of elopements, duels and young love. Bath should furnish the scene and Eliza's courting the plot.

During the weeks at Croome he was spurred on by the definite prospect of production. The fact that Tom Harris had commissioned the play from so inexperienced an author was not merely a measure of Dick Sheridan's persuasive abilities but also a recognition of the drawing power of the subject matter. With a shrewd commercial sense Harris appreciated that the public was still very interested in the story of the Maid of Bath and her romantic lover, and that playgoers would be willing to pay good money to see a dramatic version of Eliza's adventures especially written by her husband. It would positively pull in the crowds.

On 17 November Dick wrote to his father-in-law:

There will be a Comedy of mine in rehearsal at Covent Garden within a few days. I did not set to work on it till within a few days of my setting out from Crome, [sic] so you may think I have not, for these last six weeks, been very idle. I have done it at Mr Harris's [the manager's] own request. It is now complete in his hands, and preparing for the stage.[7]

For good measure he assured Linley that Harris was in no doubt that the play would be successful and that 'the least shilling he could expect from it was six hundred pounds'. Nor did Dick propose to be modest. Though the fashion of the time was for playwrights not to advertise their names as the authors of plays, he wrote that he intended to make public the authorship of the play, so that his friends would be alerted to turn up and clap.

However, there was one matter he mentioned to nobody. That was the existence of *The Journey to Bath*. He did not want to acknowledge the debt he owed to his mother's comedy, and feared that once discovered, *The Journey to Bath* might prove a powerful rival to his own play. But he had nothing to worry about. His production completely eclipsed any residual memories of his mother's play so that, as far as can be traced, in the two hundred and twenty years since it was written, it has never been presented on stage.[8]

Rehearsals began early in December. Each evening Dick would return from Covent Garden to Orchard Street bubbling over with excitement, eager to tell Eliza all about it and eager to get on with his rewrites. Ecstatically he told her that Harris had picked a first-class cast including five of the players who had recently triumphed in Goldsmith's *She Stoops to Conquer*. Edward Shuter who had played Hardcastle was now to be Sir Anthony Absolute; John Quick the comedian who had created Tony Lumpkin was to play Bob Acres; Mrs Green the original Mrs Hardcastle was to appear as Mrs Malaprop; Lee-Lewes a 'graceful and spirited comedian' who had played Marlowe was to have the part of the mischievous servant Fag; and the elegantly beautiful Mrs Bulkeley who had created the part of Kate Hardcastle was to be Julia, the character modelled on Eliza herself. Dick announced that with such a cast no play could fail. After long deliberations he decided to call it *The Rivals*.

Sheridan was always an excellent self-publicist. Over the Christmas and New Year period he made sure that a great many people in London society were aware of his opening night of 17 January at Covent Garden. He went round talking up its prospects as much as he could, pointing out to anybody who would listen that very few young playwrights had ever received such encouragement from a theatre manager as he had received from Harris. He even enthused over the actors. Shortly after the first production, the *Morning Chronicle* reported that *The Rivals* had been 'deemed the *ne plus ultra* of comedy' in the Covent Garden Green Room.[9] Even Harris's rival manager, Drury Lane's David Garrick, wrote to a friend to tell him that 'Sheridan's Comedy has rais'd great Expectations in the Public'.[10] Everything was set for a theatrical triumph.

Shortly before the first performance Eliza opened a letter from her sister Mary in Bath:

> My dearest Eliza,
> We are all in the greatest anxiety about Sheridan's play, – though we do not think there is the least doubt of its succeed-ing. I was told last night that it was his own story, and therefore called 'The Rivals,' but I do not give any credence to this intelligence.
>   I am told he will get at least £700 for his play.[11]

But suddenly a reaction against the play began to set in and Harris's early confidence started to drain away. He had heard that they could expect trouble on the first night from two different factions: one a set of jealous dramatists who had tried for years – unsuccessfully – to get their plays accepted by the Covent Garden management and had now discovered that an inexperienced rival had simply walked into Harris's office and been taken up; and the second a contingent of thugs from Bath, probably led by Mathews' friend Barnett, who believed that the play would expose Mathews' recent lewd courtship of Miss Linley. Rumour had it that they would break up the first night's performance to prevent Mathews' libel or ridicule.

When Harris got wind of these trouble-makers he tried to head them off. On the morning of production he published a notice in *The Gazetteer*: 'It having been reported that the story of the new comedy of *The Rivals* was not a fictitious one, we have authority to assert, that such a report is entirely void of foundation, and there is not the slightest local or personal allusion whatever throughout the piece'.[12] No one believed him. The *Town and Country Magazine* was positive that the plot bore a similarity to a 'certain affair at Bath, in which the celebrated Miss Linley (now Mrs Sheridan) was the subject of rivalship'.[13]

When Eliza learned that *The Rivals* was partially based upon her love affairs in Bath she was very apprehensive indeed. Foote's play had already given her more than enough of the wrong kind of publicity, and now the London public was to be regaled with a further instalment of her love-life. She could not understand why her husband thought it immodest for her to sing in a Handel oratorio but had no compunction in putting her character into a comedy for people to snigger at. But Dick went out of his way to reassure her that she was represented by the dignified heroine, Julia, who appeared in only a few of the least comic scenes and was plainly not there to be laughed at.

Dick had started his story where Foote's farce had left off, so that *The Rivals* was a sort of sequel to *The Maid of Bath*.[14] His play presented the chief elements of their own history: young lovers, repressive parents, elopements and duels, all set among the parades, parks and genteel apartments of the pleasure-city. Eliza had no difficulty in recognising most of his characters. He had depicted his own father as the irascible, irrational, apoplectic old buffer, Sir Anthony Absolute, with a clever young son who can run rings round him. Sir Anthony was as dictatorial and peremptory as his son Jack was cheerful and devious. Like Dick, Jack Absolute was a bit of an actor, able to assume a variety of guises. Cowardly Bob Acres was perhaps

146

Mrs Sheridan as St Cecilia, Sir Joshua Reynolds, The National Trust, Waddesdon Manor and the Courtauld Institute. The portrait exhibited at the Royal Academy in 1775 helped to promote the Linley cult.

Thomas Linley the Elder, 1733-1795
Thomas Gainsborough, by permission of the Trustees of
Dulwich Picture Gallery. Eliza's beloved father and
music master.

Thomas Linley the Younger, 1756-1778
Thomas Gainsborough, by permission of the Trustees of
Dulwich Picture Gallery. Tom Linley was Eliza's child-
hood companion and the hope of English music.

Drury Lane Theatre 1776. The Victoria & Albert Museum

Richard Brinsley Sheridan
John Russell, National Portrait Gallery.

Memorial tablet to Elizabeth Linley and her
family, Wells Cathedral. (Author's collection)

a rather unfair portrait of Mathews, and the fire-eating Sir Lucius O' Trigger a skit on Barnett. The heroine Lydia Languish was a more general sketch of one of those young ladies in Bath whose conversation was largely sustained by the sensational novels she borrowed from a lending library, rather like Alicia Sheridan. Mrs Malaprop was recognisable to Eliza as one of those newly-rich, vulgar women who crowded the Pump Room, though she was rather uneasy that sometimes she sounded a little like her own mother.[15]

The scenes between Julia and her jealous lover Faulkland were modelled on the desperate occasions when Eliza had unsuccessfully begged Dick to believe that he had no cause for apprehension simply because her parents were trying to marry her off to a rich husband. Whereas Julia was gentle and long-suffering, Faulkland and was beset with morbid suspicions which caused her great anguish. In this characterisation, Dick had been especially honest, for though he preferred the world to think of him as the jovial, devil-may-care Jack Absolute, they both knew he had sketched the other, darker side of his nature. By presenting himself not only as dashing Jack but also the exasperatingly insecure Faulkland, it was as if he was trying to apologise for some of his previous behaviour.

In her heart of hearts Eliza was ambivalent about her husband's new venture. Although she could do little but wish him well, she was also aware that if he became a successful playwright, he would never again allow her to resume her singing career. These conflicting emotions agitated her so much that in the end it was agreed that she would not go to the first night. She was still recovering from her recent indisposition, and Dick feared her health might not withstand the heat of the theatre and the excitement of the occasion. So on 17 January 1775, while other society women looked out their silks, and laced, perfumed and powdered themselves to visit Covent Garden, she sat quietly in Mehetabel Canning's sitting room in Slough. The *London Chronicle* reported 'there never was so much crowding known as at the new comedy of *The Rivals*' (and) 'never so many ladies and people of fashion at a first night's representation for a long time'.[16] It was a brilliant occasion. It was also a disaster.

The hissing started during the first scene. Later the *Morning Post* revealed that Sheridan's enemies had taken 'particular care to station serpents in every corner of the house, in order to nip the young adventurer in the bud'.[17] 'Mr B—d [Barnard-Barnett]' had tried to 'create a prejudice against the performance by every mode that malevolence could suggest'. Things went badly for Mrs Green whose peculiar language as Mrs Malaprop merely irritated them, and also for Ned Shuter – as Sir Anthony Absolute – who had not mastered his lines. As a result the repartee between him and Jack simply did not work. Worst of all was the reception for Lee as Sir Lucius O'Trigger. He had hardly attempted to learn his part, and when stuck for a word he simply 'filled up the chasm with numberless oaths' which, though they never appeared in the script, he clearly thought appropriate for any Irishman. Even well-disposed members of the audience were at first restive, then irritated, and at last hostile. The usual playing time in those days was three hours, so it was only to be predicted that towards the end of the fourth hour the actors could hardly be heard above the commotion. Lee was hit by an apple; exasperated, he went forward to demand of the audience: 'By the pow'rs, is it personal – is it me or the matter?' It was both.

To everyone's relief the play finally came to an end, though with an accompaniment of groans and jeers. In a characteristic piece of bravado Harris at once went out in front of the curtain to announce that, as advertised, the play would be repeated the following night but this only provoked further uproar. In the event the second performance was cancelled.

Sheridan's night was spent among wine bottles and sympathisers, but long before he had got up the following day, news of the disaster at Covent Garden was widespread in the city. Soon the awful reviews trickled in. *The London Packet* considered the plot 'ill-conducted and intricate'; the play was 'by no means destitute of merit' though whatever value it had was outweighed by 'the author's want of knowledge of the stage' and inability to construct a play.[18] The *Morning Chronicle* declared that amid the welter of imperfections it was possible to discover the 'trace of a man of genius, the gentleman and the scholar', but added that 'the fable was neither happily chosen nor skillfully conducted, nor were the characters faithfully copied from nature'.[19] The Sheridans found the last comment particularly ironic because those who broke up the performance did so on the grounds that the characters were based on actual people. *The Public Ledger* was even more severe; 'The Rivals as a Comedy requires much castigation, and the pruning hand of judgement, before it can ever pass on the Town as even a tolerable piece. In language it is defective to an extreme, in Plot outré, and one of the Characters (Mrs Malaprop) is an absolute exotic in the wilds of nature.'[20] For good measure their critic added that in the middle gallery at Covent Garden several of the spectators were to be observed 'in a profound sleep'.

At Slough Eliza got up early to hear the news. When she was told of the fiasco at Covent Garden her emotions were in turmoil: she did not know whether to be sorry or relieved. But at any rate she felt that she could now be sure of one thing: because he had failed in the theatre Dick would have to let her resume her singing career. So even when she sat down to write him a note of condolence, she could barely prevent her relief coming through. It was the most remarkably indiscreet letter she ever wrote:

> My Dear Dick, I am delighted. I always knew that it was impossible you could make anything by writing plays; so now there is nothing for it but my beginning to sing publickly again, and we shall have as much money as we like.[21]

The time had come for Sheridan to make the most critical decision of his life. Before he received Eliza's letter he was tempted to give up playwrighting altogether and to find some easier trade, but her tone stung him. Was she proposing that she should keep him for life? In a sudden vision he saw a dreadful humiliating future. Obliged to follow Eliza about from one theatre to another, he was permitted merely to look on from the wings as she bowed to tumultuous applause. He foresaw a growing estrangement between them, whilst she attended grand receptions at splendid houses without him, and read little notes from simpering admirers. The thought was unendurable. His mind made up, he scribbled a reply to Eliza: 'No, that shall never be.'[22]

Pondering the dreadful reception his comedy had received, Dick came to the conclusion that he himself was partly to blame. He had dashed it off in a breezy way, so that it was poorly constructed; the highly-professional Harris had had no say in its composition; and he had allowed it to over-run. Characters like Mrs Malaprop, funny at first, had gone on far too long. The play's racy language and suggestive allusions smacked of Restoration drama which the public had long grown out of and were now used to seeing in their censored versions. All of these factors created a restlessness in the audience, which was easily exploited by the trouble-makers.

When Eliza returned home on 19 January she found her husband in the drawing-room at Orchard Street totally absorbed in revising his comedy. On the same day the *Morning Post* announced:

> The comedy of the *RIVALS* at Covent Garden, is withdrawn for the present, to undergo some severe prunings, trimmings and patchings, before its second performance: the Author, we are informed, seeing the general disapprobation with which it was received, was very desirous of withdrawing it entirely, but the managers would not consent to it, determined to stand the event of a second embarkation, let the consequences be what they may.[23]

For the next ten days most of Dick's waking moments were occupied in revising his play. Whenever she looked into the music room at Orchard Street, Eliza would find him surrounded by pages of script. After flashing her a brief smile he would once again return to his mutterings and scribblings. Every so often he would utter a sudden exclamation, shuffle his pages together, seize his hat and stick from the hall, and rush off to see Harris at the Garden. Clinch had replaced Lee in the part of O'Trigger, and the cast were relearning their parts page by page as he took the rewrites into the theatre. But there was not much time: the second performance of *The Rivals* had already been announced for 28 January.

Eliza was probably allowed to attend the second performance because Dick no longer feared that Barnett's gang would turn up to make trouble. But she knew, and she knew that Dick knew, that it was his last chance to succeed as a dramatist. If the play failed this time then he would have to find another way to make his living.

On the night of Saturday 28 January 1775 the Covent Garden audience stamped in from the snow-covered streets to find the candles already lit and the great chandeliers lifted to the ceiling. The orchestra could hardly be heard at first, so great was the chattering in the pit. The boisterous footmen in the gallery were cheering on bets for another failure. Suddenly the music stopped, the curtain went up on a street in Bath, and an impudent servant stepped forward to shout: 'What! – Thomas.' The audience hushed at once to hear the actors. The comedy had begun.

In many ways what Eliza then witnessed was her own story. One character she recognised immediately from his turn of phrase and fantastic teasing manner. Jack Absolute was pretending to accept any wife his father would suggest for him:

> Sir, I repeat it; if I please you in this affair, 'tis all I desire. Not
> that I think a woman the worse for being handsome; but, Sir,
> if you please to recollect, you hinted something about a hump
> or two, one eye, and a few more graces of that kind – now,
> without being very nice, I own I should rather chuse a wife of
> mine to have the usual number of limbs, and a limited quan-
> tity of back; and tho' one eye may be very agreeable, yet as the
> prejudice has always run in favour of two, I would not wish
> to affect a singularity in that article.[24]

Though it was Woodward who spoke the lines, there was no mistaking her own husband's talk. And as the play went on she identified
others that she knew. It was the oddest sensation. Here on a stage
in London walked the people she knew at home in Bath. Sir Andrew
had the peremptory manner of Dick's own father; Sir Lucius was
Barnett to the life; and Mrs Malaprop really was at times embar-
rasingly like her own mother. She even spotted references to herself:

> FAULK: Do you remember what songs Miss Melville sung?
> ACRES: Not I indeed.
> ABS: Stay now, they were some pretty purling streams
>   airs, I warrant; perhaps you may recollect: – did she
>   sing – 'When absent from my soul's delight?'
> ACRES: No, that wa'nt it.
> ABS: Or – 'Go, gentle Gales!' – 'Go, gentle Gales!' (sings)
> ACRES: O no! nothing like it. – Odds! now I recollect one of
>   them – 'My heart's own will is free'. (sings)
> FAULK: Fool! fool that I am! to fix all my happiness on such
>   a trifler! S'death! to make herself the pipe and ballad-
>   monger of a circle![25]

And here were Faulkland and Julia playing out in comedy the sting-
ing jealousy which had driven Dick to risk his life twice in duels.

Such a highly public display of her own affairs both alarmed and
fascinated Eliza. She feared that once again the audience might
despise this slight tale of love-making. As the play proceeded she
glanced nervously round the house, quickly realising that she had no
longer any cause for concern. From the pit to the galleries laughter

reverberated all round Covent Garden. In revising his play Dick had freed some joyous, delicate bird of its earthly encumbrances, so that it rose in the air a thing of magic and delight. *The Rivals* was a huge success, and the audience loved it.

Despite this wonderful reception, both husband and wife awaited the press notices with some trepidation. They need not have worried. The papers were enthusiastic. The *Morning Post* pronounced the piece to be a 'good comedy' and the *Morning Chronicle* congratulated the author on making good use of his time between the two performances. Though it still could not pronounce the play a 'comic *chef d'oeuvre*', the paper believed that *The Rivals* gave good reason to hope the author would soon produce a 'capital play'.[26] The *London Evening Post* remarked upon the volume of applause the second performance had received, and in a later edition described how though he had been assailed 'by the serpents of envy' on the first night, 'Mr Sheridan, Hercules-like, even in the cradle of genius . . . had torn . . . the serpents asunder by the vigour of his mind.'[27]

But of all the praises heaped upon the play perhaps that which gave the greatest pleasure to Dick was a blunt comment reported as having been made by a balding, elderly playgoer during the second performance. After the first act David Garrick had turned to a friend to remark: 'I see this play will creep'. By the end of the performance, after repeated rounds of applause, he amended this to: 'I see this play will run.'[28]

From that night onwards the success of *The Rivals* was phenomenal. In an extraordinarily good outing for a first play it ran for sixteen performances. Back in Bath the Linleys rejoiced. Mary wrote:

> Bath, January, 1775
>
> It is impossible to tell you what pleasure we felt at the receipt of Sheridan's last letter, which confirmed what we had seen in the newspapers of the success of his play. The knowing ones were very much disappointed, as they had so very bad an opinion of its success. After the first night we were indeed all very fearful that the audience would go very much prejudiced against it. But now there can be no doubt about its success, as it has certainly got through more difficulties than any comedy which has not met its doom the first night. I know you have been very busy writing for Sheridan, – I don't mean copying but composing: – it's true, indeed; – you must not contradict

me when I say you wrote the much-admired epilogue to 'The Rivals'. How I long to read it! What makes it more certain is, that my father guessed it was yours the first time he saw it praised in the paper.[29]

Mary was soon to have a chance to read the play because the first of many pirated versions came out in February. In March *The Rivals* was produced in Bath, and Mary reported that she had never heard 'anything go off with such uncommon applause' and the clapping began in each scene before the actors spoke. But Eliza expected it: *The Rivals* was a Bath play about Bath people and naturally Bath loved it. The play's success however extended far beyond that city. In August Mary wrote again to tell them that people were turned away at the box office in Southampton where 'there never was any thing so universally liked'; and that the play had enjoyed a similar triumph in Bristol.

After the splendid reception afforded to his play, Dick Sheridan seemed permanently elated. With a new gaiety he stepped out to receive the congratulations of well-wishers in the street, or of knots of admirers in the entrance to the theatre. But one night, through the spy-hole in the Covent Garden curtain he glimpsed his father and sisters in the audience. His heart turned over. In the interval he could not pluck up enough courage to approach, and only 'gazed upon them from a distance with a breaking heart'. He could only guess at his father's emotions. Was Sheridan proud of his younger son? Or did he feel that in the character of Sir Anthony Absolute he had been ridiculed? Would he come behind the scenes afterwards to give Dick his blessing and congratulations? Thomas Sheridan did not go back stage, nor did he give any sign of what he was feeling. But his reflections were probably grim. That very night his status in the theatre had changed. Before *The Rivals* he was still Sheridan the celebrated actor, the orthoepist, the one-man-show. Afterwards he was merely 'old' Sheridan, or – as Samuel Johnson jokingly referred to him – 'Old Sherry'. From then on he would be simply Richard Brinsley Sheridan's father.

Dick watched the old man shuffle out among the stream of play-goers and he wept. He did not dare go after him, even though he wanted to beg his forgiveness. When he got home that night he was so downcast that Eliza asked him what was wrong. Telling her what happened, he could barely stop himself from bursting into tears again. He confessed to her that it grieved him badly 'to think that there sat his father and sisters before him, and yet he alone was not permitted to go near them or speak to them.'[30] Somehow he made Eliza feel that she was to blame.

She was confused about a lot of things. Though she had never before regarded her husband as her rival, it seemed that nowadays he had won the contest between them. Although she was relieved that they had an income, and proud of her husband's achievement as a playwright, these feelings were accompanied by a profound sense of loss. She had finally recognised that Dick's success meant the end of her musical career: she would never sing again in public. The trouble was that music had for so long been the most important part of her life, and she had no idea of how to go on without it.

CHAPTER 18

At Play

The Sheridans were famous. 1775 was their *annus mirabilis*. To many it seemed that there was an almost palpable glamour attaching to this young couple upon whom the gods had showered such gifts. She was radiantly beautiful; he was clever and brave. He could fill theatres with laughing people; she could hold thousands captive with her lovely voice. Young and talented and cheerful, they were supremely blessed with good fortune, and made people feel that anything was possible. Above all it was their love story which caught the public imagination, and because readers wanted to know more about them, the press continued regularly to report their doings. People sensed that this brilliantly attractive pair represented a new style, a new tone in society. They were – what was the word? – romantic.

That spring, London society welcomed a new literary lion that had come to be petted. Frequent invitations from the most elegant addresses arrived at Orchard Street, requesting the pleasure of the company of Mr and Mrs Sheridan at all sorts of receptions and balls. As the summer came on there were invitations to spend weeks at a time at various great houses. Dick accepted such offers with alacrity. Secretly he was rather flattered by the change in tone he detected in their wording. Where previously invitation cards had implied that he was included as a mere adjunct to his famous wife, now he was a rising star whom everybody wanted to gaze upon. Nevertheless they were still equal stars, and nothing pleased him better than to enter a drawing room with Eliza on his arm, to see every head turn when their name was announced, and to amuse one set of admirers with his wit, while watching her beauty charm others at the opposite end of the salon. In one sense he regarded Eliza as the visual measure of his success calculating that people must be impressed by his talent in capturing such a ravishing creature. She was his prize possession, and he liked to demonstrate his power over her. When in company people pressed her to sing, she would just glance at him for a nod or an imperious shake of the head which would signify his decision. Henry Angelo recollected that even during the Sheridans' first Christmas at Orchard Street when they were entertaining the Linleys and Angelos as guests, 'Mamma Linley asked her daughter to sing a certain little favourite air but a single glance from her juvenile lord and master, kept her mute'.[1]

Among the Sheridans' new acquaintances was a fifty-two year old portrait painter from Devon who had become the first president of the recently established Royal Academy. In the course of his success-ful career Sir Joshua Reynolds had painted a number of society ladies including Mrs Crewe, Mrs Bouverie, the ladies Waldegrave, the Duchess of Rutland and the Duchess of Devonshire. Eliza agreed to sit for him in the spring of 1775, probably at his house in Leicester Square. Sir Joshua always idealised his society ladies as tortured saints or martyrs of centuries past, each thereby associated with their virtues and each portrait endowed with extra solemnity and signif-icance. This was flattering to even the most protestant-minded aristocratic women. Mrs Crewe had already been depicted 'as Saint Genevieve' while Mrs Quarrington had been presented to the world as a reincarnation of St Agnes.

Reynolds painted Eliza in profile, sitting on a stool and playing at a keyboard. Her dark solemn eyes are absorbed with her private thoughts and above the instrument there is a cloud puffing out gusts of what is presumably inspiration. Two cherubs above her right shoulder, their eyes fixed upon musical scores, appear to be singing to the tune she plays. Of course people knew that these cherubs were really the little children of Mr and Mrs Cootes, the Sheridans' neigh-bours in Orchard Street, but that did not diminish the ethereal appeal of the infants. As for the choice of saint, for once Reynolds did not have to invent an association.

Six years previously in London, Thomas Sheridan, at one of his 'Attic Entertainments' for the public, chose to read Dryden's *Ode to Saint Cecilia* and to harmonise with his theme, Eliza had sung Purcell's setting of the Cecilia poems. From that time onwards people some-times referred to her by the name of this patron saint of musicians. Inevitably, Reynolds called his picture 'Mrs Sheridan as St Cecilia'.[2]

When exhibited at the Royal Academy exhibition in 1775 the portrait was a great success. The image of Eliza as a saint was to impress itself on people's memories for many years to come. Reynolds himself thought so highly of it that long afterwards he declared it 'the picture he would choose, if his fame was to be fixed on any single work'.[3] It hung in his studio for sixteen years and had such an emotional value that he would eventually only sell it cheaply to Eliza's husband, telling him 'It is with great regret that I part with the best picture I ever painted.' Reynolds was more than a little in love with Eliza himself.

Critics agreed with his high regard for both the picture and the sitter. One wrote that: 'the portrait of Mrs Sheridan in the character of St Cecilia possesses the beauty and simplicity of the Antique'. Even more enthusiastic was young Samuel Johnson, Reynold's nephew, just up from the country, who wrote home to his relatives as witness to one of Eliza's sittings: 'Her picture is going forwards, and I assure you it is quite a sight worth coming from Devonshire to see. I cannot suppose there was ever a greater Beauty in all the world, nor even Helen or Cleopatra could have exceeded her.'[4] Going to see Mrs Sheridan at the Academy soon became the thing to do. By coincidence the painting was on show while *The Rivals* was playing in the theatres. Whether one went to the comedy first, or to be enraptured by Eliza's beauty as 'St Cecilia', each seemed to be a commentary on the other. There was still plenty of gossip surrounding the Sheridans and more than one intrigued lady declared that it was difficult to reconcile the stories they had heard of Eliza's many lovers in Bath with the saintly appearance of the virgin on the wall.

In February this virgin became pregnant again. As soon as he learned of it Dick insisted Eliza take every precaution. She must give up wine and cards and going about and receptions and balls and late hours and London. The last idea seemed to obsess him. He wanted to send her away at once, and suggested that she go down to Bath to stay with her family for a few weeks. Eliza resisted. She felt quite well and was beginning to enjoy their new social life.

Fanny Burney glimpsed them at a reception given by the society hostess Mrs Cholmondeley, and reported that Dick Sheridan had a fine figure 'and a good although I don't think a handsome face. He is tall and upright, and his appearance and dress are at once manly and fashionable, without the smallest tincture of foppery or modish graces. In short, I like him vastly, and think him in every way worthy of his companion'.[5] Many other women agreed. But Fanny's most sincere admiration and sympathy were reserved for Eliza: 'She is much more lively and agreeable than I had any idea of finding her; she was very gay and unaffected, and totally free from airs of any kind'. Fanny was: 'absolutely charmed at the sight of her. I think her quite as beautiful as ever, and even more captivating; for she has now a look of ease and happiness that animates her whole face . . . the elegance of Mrs Sheridan's beauty is unequalled by any I ever saw, except Mrs Crewe's.'[6]

This last woman was soon to become very important in the Sheridans' life. Along with the Duchess of Devonshire and Mrs Bouverie, Frances Anne Crewe was one of the most celebrated Whig hostesses of the day. At bottom she was ruthless, but possessed a serenity and softness of manner which made her very attractive to men. The portrait of her sitting under a tree by Gardner suggests a determined young woman, perhaps rather over-dressed. Her figure is graceful, her complexion clear and she has intelligent if rather calculating eyes. Her husband John, first Baron of Crewe, and a Whig member for Stafford, rarely spoke in the house or anywhere else for that matter, but Frances made up for it, talking nearly all the time. A staunch Whig supporter, she gave receptions for politicians in Grosvenor Square, and also at other houses in Hampstead, Bath, and at the family seat, Crewe Hall in Cheshire. She was always on the look-out for bright young men whom she thought might be useful to the party. But her interest in Dick Sheridan soon became more than political.

It was the Duchess of Devonshire who introduced the Sheridans to Mrs Crewe while launching them into the great world of Whig society. Georgiana had always admired Eliza's singing, but now that she had also learned to appreciate Dick's wit, became a strong supporter of his plays. Though not a conventional beauty, Georgiana had enormous charm. David Garrick, wrote of her to a friend: 'the Grace of Devonshire is a most charming, exquisite, beautiful young creature. Were I five and twenty I could go mad about her; as I am past five-and-fifty I would only suffer martyrdom for her'. Horace Walpole was rather more detached on the subject, but noticed that 'her youthful figure, flowing good nature, sense and lively modesty, and modest familiarity make her a phenomenon.'[7]

Though their social ranks were very different, Eliza soon made a good friend of the Duchess. Six years younger than Dick and three years younger than Eliza, she still retained some of the wild spirits of a tomboy. She had a mass of golden hair, bright blue eyes, a sharp nose and a mouth which, had she been a servant would have been called 'wide' but as she was an aristocrat was described as 'generous'. Her eighteenth birthday on 7 June 1775 was also her first wedding anniversary. Fanny Burney considered Georgiana's husband the Duke of Devonshire to be 'ugly'; nevertheless in the eyes of many people his wealth and position made him the first match in England. But he was unable to respond to Georgiana's deep affection. He was a marital iceberg so cold that when once Georgiana attempted to sit on his lap in front of her mother the Duke jumped up in disgust and left the room.[8]

Despite or perhaps because of this, Georgiana determined to pursue the greatest pleasures that her elevated rank afforded. Tremendous charm and instinctive generosity of spirit soon made her a leader of English society. She captivated people of all classes and both sexes including even Marie Antoinette, and as an arbiter of fashion she was spirited and independent enough to put her mark on it. She disliked the ostentation of elaborately hooped dresses, preferring simpler cuts which followed the lines of the body and were later to influence 'Regency' styles.[9] Her disposition was naturally responsive to that new mode of feeling called 'romantic'.

Inevitably this lively passionate girl was soon beset with temptations. She gave in to only one: gambling. As soon as the cards were dealt she was consumed by the excitement of the event and lost all concern for the money she was losing. On first becoming a Duchess she had assumed that she would have access to unlimited financial resources. But after only one year of marriage she was so afraid to tell the Duke how much money she owed that her mother Lady Spencer had to do it for her. The Duke had paid up without much complaint but Georgiana was unable to stop there, launching herself upon a sea of gambling debts which was to pound away at her for the rest of her life.

So when in summer the Sheridans strolled the great rooms of Devonshire House, or Chatsworth, Georgiana's guests were already seated at the card tables set out beneath the massive chandeliers, ready for serious gambling. Games of whist or faro would go on until the small hours while large sums of money would change hands. Although he was a weak-willed man, Dick Sheridan disliked gambling – cards interfered with talk – so he never took a hand. The

Sheridans were better off now, but still without any capital, and a fascinated Eliza, unable to match the huge sums passing across the table, had to eke out the few guineas from her purse to make sure they lasted the evening.

Eliza found Georgiana intriguing. Everybody knew that the young Duchess was not happy in her marriage and yet she continued to show great sympathy and concern for other people, including Eliza. And there was far more to her than her beauty and charm. She was cultured and aristocratic; she wrote and read verses in French and Italian; and she took a profound interest in literature and the affairs of the day. Eliza had never had an intellectual woman friend before, and Georgiana both alarmed and attracted her. This young woman actually had opinions of her own, and it was said that she dared to discuss literary matters with Dr Johnson as an equal. She was also a politician – at least as far as any woman could be. When in London she made Devonshire House the social centre and unofficial headquarters of the Whig party. There she introduced Dick and Eliza to some of the brightest Whig luminaries. One was a rather haughty, difficult man in his late forties named Edmund Burke. Another was intensely ugly and fat, but made up for his looks by extraordinary charm and affability. He was the *de facto* Whig leader, Charles James Fox. He took to Eliza immediately.

In March Dick was away from home much of the time, busy with new projects at Covent Garden, leaving Eliza bored and often lonely. Without her private concerts – they had stopped when *The Rivals* succeeded – she had little to do, and few acquaintances save for the visits of her husband's friends. She missed her family a great deal. Sensing her homesickness, Dick was quick to suggest yet again that she should go down to spend a few weeks' holiday with her parents in Bath. There she would not have to put up with visits from strangers but could have all the rest she wanted among the people she loved best. When she objected that he would have nobody to look after him, he answered that he had a good many new friends now and would not lack company or a cooked dinner. This made her uneasy. Of course she longed to see her father and Mary and Tom, but she was loath to leave Dick alone in London at the mercy of his numerous female admirers. Though she hardly liked to admit it to herself, she was jealous and suspicious.

At last she went to Bath. Almost every day she would lie with her feet up on the settee in the sitting room at the Royal Crescent with the delicious treat of opening yet another packet from Dick in London. He told her about preparations at the theatre for his new play *St Patrick's Day*, reported Harris's comments and how the comedian Clinch was rehearsing his part. He wrote about dinners and receptions he had gone to, who he had met and what they had said. One of the most glittering of these occasions was a grand Ball given by Mrs Crewe in Grosvenor Square. Dick's description of the event made Eliza very uneasy, because she could imagine him surrounded by a group of superbly-dressed aristocratic women who did not disguise the fact that they found him very attractive. As if anticipating her concern, Dick's next letter enclosed a set of verses telling her how much he missed her. It was just like those he had written when they were courting.

The shepherd Silvio could not believe it was spring:

He scorn'd the sky of azure blue,
   He scorn'd whate'er could mirth bespeak;
And chid the beams that drank the dew,
   And chid the gale that fann'd his glowing cheek.
Unpaid the season's wonted lay,
   For still he sigh'd and said it was not May.[10]

When finally convinced by a nymph that the woods really are green, the nightingale really is singing and the bee really is buzzing, Silvio gives the reason for his truculence:

Pardon (said Silvio with a gushing tear),
'Tis Spring, sweet nymph, but Laura is not here.

Of course Laura-Eliza found this all very flattering. Even so she could not quieten her jealous fears. Her only relief was to write a set of verses in reply in which she pictured Dick as a swain among nymphs, re-enacting the judgement of Paris. She imagined him choosing between the enchantresses around him and presenting the prize to the most beautiful of all.

To Silvio

To other scenes doth Silvio now repair,
   To nobler themes his daring Muse aspires;

Around him throng the gay, the young, the fair,
  His lively wit the list'ning crowd admires.

And see, where radiant Beauty smiling stands,
  With gentle voice and soft beseeching eyes,
To gain the laurel from his willing hands,
  Her every art the fond enchantress tries.

When she wrote these verses Eliza was just twenty-one, four months pregnant and parted from her husband for the first time. In many ways she was still a naïvely poetic girl, provincial, middle-class, and very vulnerable. Her recent history seemed like a fairy story to her, with Dick as the handsome prince. She felt that the whole world knew of their romance and his gallantry. It was hardly credible that he should be unfaithful to her now and break the circle of their charmed life. Yet her delicate moral perception was startled at the libertine attitudes of many of his new friends, who expressed sentiments in fashionable London salons which would have shocked and repelled her circle in Bath. And though Dick seemed to find such remarks amusing, she disliked them.

That her young husband still loved her she did not yet doubt but she knew that he was weak and something of a snob. Her worst fear was that his vanity might prove his undoing, since she had seen the animation with which he responded to the flattery of beautiful and titled women. He might even take a serious mistress from among them. The question was, which one? In her playful reply she only dared hint her fears:

What various charms the admiring youth surround,
  How shall he sing, or how attempt the praise?
So lively all – where shall the bard be found,
  Who can to one alone attune his lays?

Behold with graceful step and smile serene,
  Majestic Stella moves to claim the prize;
'Tis thine,' he cries, 'for thou art Beauty's queen'.
  Mistaken youth! and see'st thou Myra's eyes?

'Pardon, bright nymph', (the wond'ring Silvio cries,)
  'And oh, receive the wreath, thy beauty's due –

His voice awards what still his hand denies,
   For beauteous Amoret now his eyes pursue.

Somehow this vapid versifying seemed inadequate to express what she really wanted to say, but Eliza played the pastoral game for thirty-six verses. Various 'nymphs' appear as rivals for Silvio's affections and for each nymph she invented a name: 'Stella' was the Duchess of Rutland, 'Myra' the Duchess of Devonshire, 'Flavia' Lady Craven, and 'Jessie' the Countess of Jersey. The portrait of the welcoming beauty with her 'gentle voice' and 'soft beseeching eyes' was unmistakable; 'Amoret' was Frances Crewe. Eliza had correctly identified their new friend as her most serious rival.

So the packets and the verses, the nymphs and the shepherds, the hints and the anxieties, passed again and again between the Royal Crescent and Orchard Street. These delicate sentiments were handed from one grubby groom to another, crammed into mail-boxes, hauled by sweating teams of horses, and swayed in carriages and were rained on along the Great West Road. By late May Eliza had had enough of wondering what Dick was up to. Despite the risk of another miscarriage, she took a coach herself and followed her letters home.

CHAPTER 19

Family Matters

Two hundred miles across the Mediterranean from Cartagena lies the little Algerian port of Tenes. Local fishermen know that here sudden storms can be whipped up in a matter of minutes and that these can sometimes prove fatal to foreign mariners. Uncounted wrecks lie in the African ooze, encrusted by shells and patrolled by brightly coloured fish, among them the remains of a small yacht which once carried valuable freight. In its cabin is a wooden box, and in that box there may still be a treasure, though one not so durable as coin or precious stone. Were that box now to be raised from its watery prison and opened up, the chances are that it would contain nothing but pulp. But if by some good fortune the contents have survived salt water, conger and crab, several packages would be found containing a number of manuscripts written in a faded hand.

Two of these are playscripts, and the others the libretto and score of a comic opera. They are old songs which have lain silent for years beneath the warm waters; their words have an eighteenth century ring:

Gentle Maid, ah! why suspect me?
Let me serve thee, then reject me.
Canst thou trust, and I deceive thee?
Art thou sad and shall I grieve thee?[1]

This song was first devised by three young people sitting in a London drawing room in the summer of 1775. Richard Brinsley Sheridan wrote the words, his brother-in-law Tom Linley set them to music, and Eliza first sang them. It was she who had got these two men to work together and who copied out the manuscript.

164

In May, Dick's new farce *St Patrick's Day* was presented at Covent Garden. He had written it for the benefit of Lawrence Clinch, the actor who had saved *The Rivals*, now, according to Dick, a poor man in distress. Once again Dick had recycled the story of his elopement with Eliza. His hero, Lieutenant O'Connor, was a charming adventurer like Jack Absolute, with a bit of Irish. One of his lines even sounded like Dick himself; 'I must marry the Girl first, and ask his consent afterwards'.[2] The audience, previously so critical of *The Rivals*, was now much easier to please. *St Patrick's Day* had been a great success.[3]

This favourable reception had put Dick in a buoyant mood when he welcomed Eliza home from Bath. Though she found their new life in some ways delightful, she was still rather lonely. She was even more anxious about money. Dick's unreliable income was barely enough to support their present style of living and he would never discuss financial troubles. Now, in her fifth month of pregnancy, she had no one with whom she could talk over her worries. Her own family were still in Bath. She missed them all so much. At the Royal Crescent there was music from morning to night but here in Orchard Street she might go a whole day without hearing a single note. Since becoming pregnant, she had been forbidden to visit the opera; Dick said it was too risky in her condition. Her only hope was that sometime soon her father might agree to take a house in the capital, where he had always wanted a career. But he was too cautious to throw over his successful west-country practice without a lot of consideration.

There was one other shadow over Eliza's life: her husband's fidelity. He knew so many people – so many women – and was always rushing off to increasingly secretive appointments. She sometimes feared that he regretted marrying the daughter of a provincial music master when he might have done much better for himself.

In Bath she had thought hard about a solution to all these problems. Her chief aims were to save her marriage, to keep Dick profitably occupied, to find a new source of money for them, and to bring the Linleys to London. What she needed was some project which would unite Sheridan comic genius with Linley musical talent, making a profit for them both. Then in a flash she hatched the perfect plan: Dick should write a comic opera and her father should set it to music. It would induce Linley to spend some time in town, bring music back into her house, keep Dick busy and get the two men she loved best in the world to work together in the interests of the whole family.

While in Bath she had discussed the scheme with her father. Linley was doubtful, pointing out that there had been no successful comic opera in London since John Gay's *Beggar's Opera* in 1728. But Eliza turned his objection on its head reminding him that Gay's opera had run for a record sixty-five nights, and adding that she saw no reason why the combined musical and dramatic talents of Thomas Linley and Richard Brinsley Sheridan should not do as least as well as John Gay. Linley knew it might be months before Eliza could go back on the stage and he may have been further influenced by the degree of desperation in his daughter's face. He had come to like and even admire his son-in-law, therefore he had no personal objections to Eliza's plan and told her that he would think about it.

Once back in London Eliza had to sell the scheme to Dick. He was immediately enthusiastic about it and characteristically appropriated it as his own. He was soon to be heard breezily claiming that he was writing a comic opera which would make fortunes for them all. Linley was still hesitant; his bread and butter depended on his remaining in Bath and his teaching obligations there would leave him little time for coming up to London to supply an entire score for a project of doubtful success. Dick countered this by deciding that a number of songs would be set to traditional tunes. By midsummer, Linley had agreed to compose most of the score, and to rehearse and conduct the Covent Garden band. So Dick started to work on a libretto of an opera to be called *The Duenna*.

Having at last committed himself, Linley instantaneously got cold feet. The awful thought that he might offend David Garrick frightened him into fits. No one in theatrical London dared risk the disapproval of this famous actor-manager. He had dominated his profession for some twenty-five years. Linley knew him personally: it was Garrick who awarded him the annual oratorio contract at Drury Lane. Always an admirer of Eliza's singing, he was still looking for an opportunity to book her for opera, and during her recent holiday in Bath Linley hinted to him that her husband might soon be persuaded to let her sing again in public. Consequently, on 20 April Garrick wrote to George Colman in London to tell him in the fashionable mock-conspiratorial language of Farquhars's *The Beaux Stratagem* 'I will tell you a Secret Brother Martin shall make your hair stand on End! – I believe I may engage the blood of the Lindleys [*sic*] – don't let one syllable of this transpire till ye deed is don!' But of course the deed was never done because Eliza was pregnant and her husband had not changed his mind. Linley was embarrassed and to make matters worse he had committed himself to mounting an opera at Covent Garden, the rival to Garrick's Drury Lane. He was desperately worried that Garrick might consider such an action as disloyal, and as a result would withdraw both his friendship and the lucrative oratorio contract.

In late May Covent Garden closed its doors for the season and Eliza and Dick prepared to welcome Linley to Orchard Street. He did not come! All they got were letters explaining that he was too busy but assuring them that they could expect him very soon. This was not much help. Dick was tone deaf and could not work on the opera alone; he could do little more than describe the melody he required. So the onus of giving the musical advice fell on Eliza. In fact without her help the project would have failed entirely. She copied out Dick's script and scored the songs from the scraps of composition her father had sent through the post. But it was not enough, and in the end she persuaded her brother Tom to come up to London to set some of Dick's verses.

At nineteen Tom Linley was already considered to be one of the most eminent violinists and promising composers in the country. His anthem 'Let God Arise' was performed at the Worcester Music Festival[4] and he had completed and scored for orchestra twenty violin concertos 'many of which were performed at Drury Lane in the oratorio season, and were received with unbounded applause'. In contrast to his morose father, Tom's high spirits were infectious, and while he was staying at Orchard Street he kept Eliza delightfully entertained with his music and jokes. Day after day in the early summer months the music room at Orchard Street was bright and cheerful with Eliza, now clearly showing her condition, sitting between her young husband and even younger brother as they discussed *The Duenna*.

Their manner of composition was extempore. Dick would read out the words of his song, suggest a mood, and Tom would pick at his strings to find a note. Eliza would then hum his lead and establish a melodic line, Tom would go away and think about it, and perhaps after lunch come back with his first musical suggestions. Dick revised his words to fit in with the tune while Eliza repeatedly voiced the phrases. Sometimes Tom would be singing and strumming all day and even as she went to bed Eliza would be humming. By breakfast the next morning Tom would have the new song clear in his head for Eliza to copy out the score. As the summer days went on Dick was obliged to spend more and more time at the Garden. The brother and sister were left alone to their music, so that by the time a tired and cross Dick Sheridan arrived home they would greet him triumphantly with the present of another song, and he would have to approve the whole thing. Sometimes Eliza would try to teach him one of the new tunes but he was usually flat and quickly forgot it.

It was a happy time for Eliza. Once again her house was full of harmony. Both she and Dick were immensely grateful to Tom for filling his father's place. And because she was the first to sing the songs – even those for male performers – it was Eliza who advised Dick on the casting – though not without a pang of envy when she suggested names of other women to sing the songs she had come to regard as her own.

By late summer they were waiting for the arrival of Thomas Linley with an anxious impatience. Only Linley could hire the musicians, provide the scores, and rehearse the orchestra and soloists. Not even Eliza or Tom had the experience to do this. But their father did not come.

The trouble was that Linley had lost his nerve. Still in a panic that Garrick would cancel his Drury Lane booking, he went to ground in Bath in a paralysis of will. All he could do was occasionally set a song and send it to Dick by post. As the first night of the new opera approached, he decided to try to get Garrick's approval by explaining that it was his concern for his daughter which made him embark on such an enterprise. On 22 September he wrote to Garrick's friend Dr John Hoadley, knowing full well that the letter would be shown to Garrick himself.

> I have engaged to assist my son-in-law Sheridan in composing an opera, which he is to bring out at Covent Garden this winter . . . Sheridan thinks that he has been so honourably treated by Mr Harris, that he ought not to keep anything he has hitherto written from him. However, I hope Mr Garrick will not take anything amiss in my assisting him on this occasion; for it is a matter of absolute necessity that he should endeavour to get money by this means, as he will not be prevailed upon to let his wife sing.[5]

Linley told Hoadley that he relied upon Mr Garrick's 'enlarged sentiment' not to hold it against him for helping his son-in-law.

There was no reply, so Linley tried again, and on 28 September wrote to Garrick directly. As if to excuse his conduct he complained about Dick's manner of writing *The Duenna*:

> I have promised to assist Sheridan in compiling – I believe that is the properest term – an opera, which I understand from him, he has engaged to present at Covent Garden this winter. I have already set some airs which he has given me, and he intends writing new words to other tunes of mine. My son has likewise written some tunes for him, and I understand he is to have others from Mr Jackson of Exeter. This is the mode of proceeding in regard to his composition I by no means approve of. I think he ought first to have finished his opera with the songs he intends to introduce in it, and have got it entirely new set. No musician can set a song properly unless he understands the character, and knows the performer who is to exhibit it. For my part, I shall be very unwilling for either my name, or my son's, to appear in this business; and it is my present resolution to forbid it.

He assured Garrick that it was not disloyalty that had motivated his action but parental tenderness for his daughter, as she had married a man whose only income came from writing comedies.

> I would not have been concerned in this business at all, but that I know there is an absolute necessity for him to endeavour to get some money by this means, as he will not be prevailed upon to let his wife sing – and indeed at present she is incapable – and nature will not permit me to be indifferent to his success.[6]

Linley hung on in Bath waiting anxiously for a reply from Garrick but none arrived. Meanwhile matters were growing desperate, Covent Garden's Orchestra Leader, John Abraham Fisher, had walked out, presumably because he resented an absentee provincial being set over him. Tom Linley was too inexperienced to act as musical director while Dick certainly could not expect Eliza – who was eight months pregnant in October – even to listen in on the rehearsals. Without supervision, the musicians and singers each did what he thought best. Dick grew increasingly nervous at this musical anarchy and as the first night drew near, disaster threatened.

Linley still loitered down in the west country pleading prior commitments. So once again Dick wrote to his father-in-law, barely disguising his anxiety:

Dear Sir,

We received your songs today, with which we are exceedingly pleased . . . Betsey [Eliza] intended to have troubled you with some music for correction and with some stanzas, but an interview with Harris today has put me from the thoughts of it, and bent me upon a much more important petition. You may easily suppose it is nothing else than what I said I would not ask in my last. But, in short, unless you can give us three days in town, I fear our opera will stand a chance to be ruined. Harris is extravagantly sanguine of its success as to plot and dialogue, which is to be rehearsed next Wednesday at the theatre. They will exert themselves to the utmost in the scenery, etc., but I never saw any one so disconcerted as he was at the idea of there being no one to put them in the right way as to music. They have no one there whom he has any opinion of . . . He entreated me in the most pressing terms to write instantly to you, and wanted, if he thought it could be any weight, to write himself. Is it impossible to contrive this? Couldn't you leave Tom to superintend the concert for a few days? If you can manage it, you will really do me the greatest service in the world. As to the state of music, I want but three more airs, but there will be some glees and quintets in the last act, that will be inevitably ruined, if we have no one to set the performers at least in the right way. Harris has set his heart so much on my succeeding in this application, that he flatters himself we may have a rehearsal of the music in Orchard Street tomorrow se'n-night. Every hour's delay is a material injury both to the opera and the theatre, so that if you can come and relieve us from this perplexity, the return of the post must only forerun your arrival; or (what will make us much happier) might it not bring you? I shall say nothing at present about the lady 'with the soft look and manner' [Eliza], because I am full of more hopes of seeing you.[7]

Eliza added a postscript:

> Dearest father, I shall have no spirits or hopes of the opera unless we see you. Eliza Ann Sheridan.

Linley did not oblige. Writing to say that he could spare only a few days from his other concerts he suggested that in his absence a music master should be hired to put the performers in the right way of doing things. Although Dick told him that there was no such person it made no difference: he had to accept the fact that his father-in-law would not be appearing in London until late November just before the first night. Negotiations about the musical setting of the songs and choruses had to go on by post: thus Dick was obliged to describe situations, characters and singers by letter so that Linley could write the appropriate accompaniment. For example his instructions might read as follows 'The first [song] . . . a dialogue between Quick and Mrs Mattocks, I would wish to be a pert, sprightly air; for though some of the words mayn't seem suited to it, I should mention that they are neither of them in earnest in what they say'. and 'I like particularly the returning to 'O the days when I was young!' We have mislaid the notes, but Tom remembers it. If you don't like the words, will you give us one?'[8]

With such piecemeal communications it is hardly surprising that Thomas Linley was not the major contributor to the opera that Dick had intended. He supplied only some four or five of the thirty-three pieces in the final score[9] and was never available to discuss with his son-in-law the matching of melodies with words. Perhaps Linley had legitimate grounds for the excuse, because he was never told what the opera was about. Perhaps Dick was too embarrassed to tell Linley that the plot of his opera was based yet again on an elopement in which the girl's father was made to look ridiculous. On the other hand, Linley may have also kept Dick ill-informed because he had actually written less music than he wanted his son-in-law to realise.

Linley's failure was now apparent, and even more responsibility for the music inevitably fell on Eliza and Tom. She picked out suitable tunes from Italian opera and the work of contemporary composer, William Jackson, and Tom arranged five traditional Scottish and Irish melodies for the orchestra. About a third of the music was borrowed from previous material. As a composer, Tom rose to the challenge magnificently, writing the overture, the finale to Act 1, and most of the big set-piece songs – about half of the opera.[10]

On 2 November Dick wrote despairingly to Linley:

Our music is now all finished and rehearsing, but we are greatly impatient to see you. We hold your coming to be necessary beyond conception. You say you are at our service after Tuesday next; then 'I conjure you by that you do possess', in which I include all the powers that preside over harmony to come next Thursday night (this day se'n-night) and we will fix a rehearsal from Friday morning. From what I see of our rehearsing at present, I am become still more anxious to see you.[11]

Meanwhile with one father absent another made his reappearance. At fifty-six years old, Thomas Sheridan was enjoying something of a comeback. After the cast of *The Duenna* left Covent Garden theatre at the end of a long day of rehearsals, Thomas Sheridan would play to a packed house the lead role in a tragedy called *The Roman Father*. By now many people had written him off as the father of a famous dramatist, but here he was competing with his life-long rival Garrick as the centre of attention in the West End.

So pleased was he with his success that he may have actually nodded to his son as they bumped into each other one morning outside the theatre. Hopeful of an end to his father's silence, Dick confided to Linley: 'I think it will not be many days before we are reconciled.' But Eliza was painfully aware that even if the old man forgave Dick it did not follow that he would accept her.

At long last, in mid November, her own father turned up to take the baton at Covent Garden. Linley was a disciplinarian, and once he appeared he acted firmly and quickly. The Covent Garden band was taken in hand and the singers drilled with a rigour that soon brought them together.

Linley had probably planned his arrival to coincide with another family event. On 17 November, four days before the opening night of *The Duenna*, Eliza gave birth to a son. He was christened 'Tom' after both his grandfathers and his mother's favourite brother. It was a year to the day since Dick had written to his father-in-law to tell him that Eliza had had another 'disappointment'. But she was disappointed no longer. As for Dick, he rushed like a madman from her bedroom to the theatre in a frenzy of elation and anxiety. Naturally, Eliza could not be at the first night, but she knew the score so well that as she lay at home nursing her baby she could tell almost minute by minute what was going on in the theatre.

Dick had set *The Duenna* in Seville where two fathers oppose the hopes of two young lovers who come courting their daughters. The remedy is elopement. The trickster of the piece – Jack Absolute in *The Rivals* – is Isaac Mendoza the Jew, the suitor preferred by Don Jerome for his daughter Louisa. Isaac is simultaneously trying to cheat Jerome of the marriage settlement, but both men are tricked by the girl. She changes places with the ugly old Duenna to fly to her lover while Isaac woos *The Duenna* in error. So the trickster is tricked into marrying the penniless older woman, who soon makes it plain that she will be the master of the house. The dialogue is shot through with the amusing lines and good humour characteristic of Sheridan's work. Tom Linley's fandango provides the musical finale where Don Jerome announces: 'And I'faith we'll make a night on't, with wine and dance, and catches – then old and young shall join us'.[12] The whole thing was a charming confection ending on a note of irresistible cheerfulness.

The first night audience loved it. The next day the *Morning Post* announced that *The Duenna* had 'more merit, than any other comic opera we remember to have seen on the English stage'.[13] Soon the other papers took up the chorus and crowds packed into Covent Garden to see this new marvel. A set of verses appeared in the *Morning Chronicle* praising the play and signed 'T.S' which might have been Thomas Sheridan himself.[14] Eventually the opera proved to be 'one of the most successful theatrical entertainments of the century'. It ran for seventy-five nights, ten more than the *Beggars' Opera*. These were not continuous performances because the part of Carlos was sung by Signor Leoni, an orthodox Jew who might not appear on Fridays.[15] But it was such a triumph that in an unprecedented gesture, the King and Queen visited the opera twice within the first few days of performance. Queen Charlotte even ordered that a special copy of the music be made for her so that she might play it on the harpsichord.

Pirates very quickly got to work to steal the play, so that in March 1776 Dick and his music publisher were obliged to bring action against a man named Falkener at Peterborough who was selling eight songs from the show at a penny a page. The managers of

Covent Garden also brought a case against impresarios in Dublin named Ryder and Vandermere for putting on musicals named *The Governess* and *The Duenna* both from pirated versions. Another indicator of success was that only six days after the opening of Sheridan's opera the *Morning Chronicle*'s 'Adelphos' noted that:

> Among the various instances of national inconsistency that occur almost every hour in this strange metropolis, none has surprised me more than the sudden partiality of the Town to Covent-Garden Theatre, and their ungrateful desertion of Drury Lane; Mr Garrick, with a spirit undiminished by age, has beautified and adorned his playhouse, and made it the prettiest Assembly-room in the whole Town. He himself performs his best parts three or four times a week; and yet this new sing-song thing, the Duenna, brings crowded houses to Covent-Garden, and leaves Roscius almost in utter solitude.[16]

Garrick, however, was a supreme showman. Though exhausted by theatre management and his Shakespearean performances, he moved quickly to counter the Covent Garden success. In a brilliant exploitation of the name 'Sheridan' he revived *The Discovery* by Dick's mother. At the end of 1775, three Sheridans dominated the West End: Dick with his opera, Frances with her play, and Thomas as Cato in *The Roman Father*.

When *The Discovery* did not succeed Garrick tried reviving his most famous Shakespearian roles, but playgoers still preferred *The Duenna*. Adelphos concluded bitterly that 'it will be mentioned as among the many instances of our degeneracy, that we lose the favourable moment of beholding Garrick's Macbeth, Hamlet and Lear, to listen to a little Spanish Opera, and indulge in an unaccountable partiality for music'.[17] So Garrick began hatching a new scheme to save his beloved Drury Lane, one which would demand all his skills of acting and management. His plan permanently changed Eliza's life.

She had played no small part in the success of *The Duenna*: it was nearly as much her creation as her husband's. She was the first to think of it, she brought playwright and composer together, and she sung it, scored it, and cast it. Moreover her story was its inspiration, for though the opera was ostensibly a Spanish romance, it bore a remarkable similarity to some of her own recent adventures. For example, just as she had once planned to fly to a convent to take refuge from unwanted lovers, so does the heroine of *The Duenna*. Predictably though, Dick had turned the whole thing into a joke:

LOUISA: I protest Clara, I shall begin to think you are seriously resolved to enter on your probation.

CLARA: And, seriously, I very much doubt whether the character of a nun wou'd not become me best.

LOUISA: Why, to be sure, the character of a nun is a very becoming one – at a masquerade – but no pretty woman in her senses ever thought of taking the veil for above a night.[18]

At another point in the story Don Jerome reads out a letter, from his eloped daughter. It might very well have been written by Eliza to her father just three years before: 'My dearest father, how shall I entreat your pardon for the rash step I have taken, how confess the motive . . . If I have a spirit too resentful of ill usage, I have also a heart as easily affected by kindness'.[19] His courting of Eliza Linley still pervaded everything Sheridan wrote.

With *The Duenna* Eliza had attained all of her objectives. She had a new baby whom Dick adored; he enjoyed another theatrical success; they were making money again; she was reunited with her brother Tom; and once more the house was full of music. Her father had even talked of moving the Linleys to London. She saw it as the supreme expression of the combined Sheridan-Linley genius, a marriage of wit and lyric grace transformed into a family business.

Not everybody agreed. Even in the first reviews, the music by Tom and her father did not receive as enthusiastic a reception as her husband's libretto. *The London Packet* concluded its otherwise encouraging notice: 'Would we could add that the music deserved equal praise; but . . . instead of expressing the hilarity and merriment which should be heard at birth, it is for the most part as solemn and slow a dirge as a funeral.'[20] *The Morning Post* added to the criticism: 'As to the music, the compiled part (i.e. that taken from traditional airs) has the only claim to merit; – we know not the composer of the rest but we think he has not done justice to the words.'[21] The consensus of opinion was that the music was delicate, dull and too solemn for Sheridan's boisterous comic dialogue. The reviewers were probably right. This poor reception strengthened Linley's determination not to allow either his own name or that of Tom to be printed as the composer of the score and though the opera was subsequently revived many times in the years up to 1830, the Linley score was usually discarded in favour of settings by other composers. *The Duenna* served as a fitting emblem of the ill-matched sensibilities of Sheridan and his wife.

Nevertheless to Eliza *The Duenna* days were golden ones. Her carefully retrieved manuscript from the Garden served as a family memento, and one hundred and sixty years later her great-great-great-grandson, also named Richard Brinsley Sheridan set out from Algeria to England in his eighteen foot yacht, the *Clapotis*, with the manuscript on board. The money he hoped to raise by selling the opera and three Sheridan plays in England would save the Dorset family home Frampton Court, from demolition.[22] But off Tenes he met a cyclone, and although he was saved his boat was wrecked, and *The Duenna* went to the bottom of the sea. When he finally reached home he was greeted by the dismal sound of the crash of masonry and the felling of great trees in Frampton park. It was the wreck of his family hopes.

CHAPTER 20

Partners

In December 1773 Dick Sheridan was planning the most audacious project of his life. It all depended on Garrick. The fifty-eight year old actor-manager seemed dreadfully tired. Though they served rival theatres, Garrick was not too small-minded to chat, and in the course of conversations with Dick he let slip that he might soon retire from the stage. Suddenly a wonderful prospect opened up to Dick's imagination.

He guessed correctly that if Garrick retired from the stage, he would sell his share in the patent of Drury Lane. If so, Dick wanted to buy it. When at first he hinted his intentions to Eliza one morning in Orchard Street, she did not understand him. But once she realised that Dick was seriously proposing to borrow to make a bid for Drury Lane, she was appalled and apprehensive. In reply to her objections, he pointed out that the ownership of such a theatre would solve all their financial problems and might even make them rich in a few years. Eliza dreaded it might make them bankrupt in a few weeks.

For a young man with so few financial assets it was an incredible ambition. Perhaps the Sheridans had something left from Walter Long's gift to Eliza; perhaps Dick had realised the £600 from *The Rivals* that Harris had promised; perhaps Eliza's private concerts had brought in a few hundred pounds; and perhaps *The Duenna* had realised a few hundreds more. Set against this was their lavish lifestyle and over-generous hospitality at Orchard Street. Their total capital was therefore probably no more than about £200. By contrast Drury Lane had been recently valued at £70,000. Garrick had resolved he would take nothing less for his half-share in the patent than the full £35,000.

177

In astute hands the ownership of a patent was the key to a gold-mine. London's two 'patent' theatres, The Theatre Royal, Drury Lane and Covent Garden, had been granted an exclusive licence (or 'patent') from the King to present plays during the winter season which lasted from about September to May. None of the other theatres in the capital including Goodman's Fields, Sadler's Wells, the Pantheon and two houses in the Haymarket named the King's and the Little Theatre,[1] possessed such a winter-season patent. Covent Garden and Drury Lane were protected from all rivals save each other. In both cases the patents were vested in the buildings so that a half share in the patent meant a half share in the theatre.

Initially Eliza chose to regard Dick's interest in Drury Lane as a fantasy. He himself could hardly credit that the monarch of Drury Lane would throw away his kingdom. Nevertheless it soon became apparent to her that Dick really was trying to put together a financial package to make an offer to Garrick. Even more startling was the discovery that Dick was trying to recruit her own father as a partner. But though this news meant that her family would probably come up to live in London, at the same time she dreaded that Dick's failure would drag them down to destitution. She was already perfectly aware that Dick did not perceive that he could ever fail.

The days before Christmas were breathless with excitement and expectation. Dick wrote and sent secret emissaries to Garrick until on New Year's Eve he came home in a state of agitation to announce that because his agent Simon Ewart was ill, he had discussed the proposed purchase with Garrick in person. As a result he now believed that the great man was willing to sell. The only hitch was that Garrick had offered first refusal to his old friend George Colman, Harris's predecessor. Dick still had hopes that Colman would refuse. Garrick owned only half the theatre's patent; the other half was owned by a Willoughby Lacy, son of James Lacy, Garrick's business partner of twenty-eight years who had died two years previously. Coleman was reluctant to accept a partner as young, inexperienced, in debt and extravagant as Willoughby Lacy.[2] If he could not persuade Garrick to stay on as his business partner he wanted complete control. However, since Garrick was determined to go the question all revolved around whether or not Lacy would sell. Garrick had promised to discuss the issue with Colman and let Sheridan have the answer that evening.

As Dick excitedly described the situation all Eliza's caution melted away and she found herself buoyed up by his enthusiasm. He had that effect on people, even her own father. Nothing mattered more to her now than that Dick should achieve his ambition. That evening a letter was handed in from David Garrick. Dick scanned it quickly, groaned with frustration and handed it to her. It read:

> Mr Garrick presents his compliments to Mr Sheridan, and as he is obliged to go into the country for three days, he should be glad to see him upon his return to town, either on Wednesday about 6 or 7 o'clock, or whenever he pleases. The party has no objection to the whole, but chooses no partner but Mr G. — Not a word of this yet. Mr G sent a messenger on purpose. He would call upon Mr S. but is confined at home. Your name is upon our list.[3]

The note was ambiguous, though it certainly seemed as if Colman had turned down Garrick's offer. By 4 January however Dick felt sure enough of his success to inform his father-in-law in Bath that Colman had declined to have any partner but Garrick, and Lacy had refused to sell his share.

Dick Sheridan knew he was now in with a chance, provided that his financial consortium held steady. His chief doubt concerned his own fearful and hesitant father-in-law. Although Linley had long wanted to get a foothold in the lucrative London musical world, Dick had to work hard to offer him incentives. Not the least frightened by the figure of £70,000 – the now confirmed valuation of the property – Dick explained his simple financial philosophy. He pointed out to Linley that provided the proprietors could pay off the interest on Garrick's half share – only £1,750 per annum – they would be safe.[4] It was only five per cent of the mortgage. But he could see no reason why the box-office takings should not amount to at least ten per cent, therefore the purchase of Garrick's share would stand to make a handsome profit.

Sheridan's simplistic economics admitted no doubt. He was still only twenty-five, with little capital and no business experience. As he confused and enthused prospective business partners, they were swept away by his fervour. Dick dismissed their objections as trivialities which would take care of themselves, and simply held out golden opportunities. There could be no risk in purchasing Drury Lane, he told them, because the theatre building itself was their security and that could not disappear – unless it burned down. He wrote to advise his father-in-law that 'the surest way not to fail is to determine to succeed'.⁵

By late December he had trawled his acquaintances for backers for his enterprise. In addition to Linley, he had recruited his friend Simon Ewart (whose father John was a prosperous brandy merchant) and also theatre enthusiast and fashionable obstetrician Dr James Ford, also accoucheur to Her Majesty Queen Charlotte. His own lack of capital he regarded as a mere detail which he could sort out later. Negotiations went on during the early days of the New Year: Sheridan's lawyer Mr Philips examined the title deeds and the patent of Drury Lane; a firm of masons inspected the building; and Garrick himself collated the trading accounts of the theatre for the previous seven years. All this had to be done in some secrecy because, as Dick explained to Eliza, he still regarded Tom Harris at Covent Garden as his patron and he did not wish to act as if he was plotting against him. Ewart dropped out but Sheridan still regarded his own lack of capital as a mere detail he could sort out later. He coolly put pressure on Ford to provide more money. Of the £35,000 required, Linley and Sheridan would provide £10,000 each, while Ford was to put down £15,000.

As Eliza repeatedly and heatedly pointed out, Dick did not have £10,000. But his simple reply was another of his enigmatic smiles. Eliza never learned for certain of his final business arrangements but to raise his share he borrowed £7,700 from Ford and another £1,000 from Garrick's solicitor Albany Wallis.⁶ Of course he had to pay interest, probably of three per cent – but he was quite sure he would realise much more in profits. Although in the end he was obliged to find only £1,300 himself, it ran him so short that he did not pay his solicitor's bill until seventeen years later. On 17 January 1776, Sheridan at last made his offer, and on the same day he and his partners signed an agreement with Garrick to purchase his half share of the building and patent at Drury Lane for a sum of £35,000, to become effective the following June. Drury Lane was theirs.

Initially the whole business seemed miraculous to Eliza. Dick, practically penniless, was now the master of the finest theatre in the kingdom. On reflection, it seemed that the whole thing was perhaps not so much a miracle as the work of a guardian angel. It was Garrick who had selected Dick's note from among the 'numerous applications' to purchase his half share and Dr Ford was Garrick's close friend. Furthermore, Mr Albany Wallis, who had provided Dick with the last thousand he needed, was a partner in the legal firm of Garrick's solicitors. To Eliza as to many others it was obvious that to protect the interests of his beloved Drury Lane, Garrick had ensured all along that his successor should be the most popular and talented playwright of the day.

The public reacted sceptically to the news. Many people thought that young Sheridan was far too inexperienced to succeed. The retired actress Kitty Clive wrote to tell her old friend Garrick: 'what a strange jumble of people they have put in the papers as purchasers of the patent . . . I have some opinion of Mr Sheridan, as I hear every-body say he is very sensible; then he has a divine wife and I loved her mother dearly . . . I thought I should have died with laughing when I saw a man-midwife among them'. She added with a sly dig at Eliza: 'I suppose they have taken him in to prevent miscarriages.'[7] One playgoer remarked to Garrick: 'The Atlas that propped the stage has left his station,' but he replied: 'Has he? If that be the case, he has found another Hercules to support the office.'[8]

One afternoon in the late spring of 1776, Dick Sheridan went with his wife on his arm to inspect their new property. The season was over and the great theatre empty. It was larger than Eliza remembered, since Garrick's renovations prior to selling had taken in part of the old Rose Tavern. The frontage in Brick Street was now an imposing affair, with brick colonnades and a balcony over the entrance from which Eliza could imagine Dick accepting the plaudits of admiring theatre-goers. Above the balcony rose six Ionic columns with scrolled capitals and a pediment bearing the coat of arms. Across the apex of the roof a perky-looking lion and unicorn faced each other and above them was mounted 'a suit of ancient armour, resembling the trophies raised by a conqueror on slaying the leader of an army, such as were described by Virgil'. Eliza was not surprised to hear that a number of jokers had likened the suit to the management which Garrick had just hung up.[9]

When Dick led her out onto the empty stage she drew her breath in with delight. As a professional of long experience she realised that she was now standing in the best-equipped and most graceful of theatres in the world. Above her rose the proscenium arch, over which the Tragic and Comic muses supported a head of Shakespeare. An elegant ceiling copied from Garrick's town house at the Adelphi and new slender supports for the balconies – replacing the original heavy pillars – allowed a much better view for playgoers and gave the whole house a new delicacy and spaciousness. The boxes had been redesigned, the seats were re-upholstered with crimson plush and the walls lined with 'crimson spotted paper'. The new pillars were 'inlaid with plate glass on a crimson and green ground'.[10]

While Dick consulted with the scene-shifter, Eliza walked down to the front of the stage and gazed out onto the magnificent theatre. She imagined tier upon tier of fashionable playgoers, there once more to hear her sing. Perhaps she could not resist the temptation to release a quick trill from Handel and let it echo round the auditorium, almost catapulting a startled carpenter out of his seat in the gallery where he was taking his lunch-time nap. No doubt she would have quickly recollected herself and stepped back apologetically. She was no longer Eliza Linley the celebrated soprano but Mrs Richard Brinsley Sheridan, the wife of the proprietor of Drury Lane, and she wanted desperately to play her new part well. It was Dick's chosen task to make this great theatre successful again, and she was determined to prove his loyal help-mate and partner.

She was introduced to members of the company, chief among them the dignified Alsatian set designer, Philippe Jacques de Loutherbourg, who earned £500 a year for his amazingly inventive scenery and lighting effects. Of the rest, forty-eight of the company were male and thirty-seven female. First in dignity were the actors including such celebrities as Tom King, Mrs Abington, Mrs Yeates and Miss Youngue, all now at the top of their profession. Then there were eighteen adult and two juvenile dancers, thirty dressers, fourteen doorkeepers, four lobby-keepers and messengers, two numberers, a candle-woman, three box inspectors, seven office-keepers and two pensioners.[11]

Eliza was especially curious about the actresses whose well-publicised lives contrasted so vividly with her own. These women seemed so extraordinarily free: they controlled their own lives. Mrs Abington, for example, was said to have sold flowers once in St James Park where she was known as 'Nosegay Fan', and for many years she had paid her trumpeter husband thirty-six shillings a year to keep away from her.[12] Eliza would have liked to make friends among them, but she knew Dick would not have approved, and she had to respect his wishes; after all he was the manager. It was a sobering thought that her young husband, never before in his life manager of anything, was responsible now for all these people's livelihoods.

Dick Sheridan had taken on a task more formidable than he at first understood. As far as theatre business was concerned, Ford and Linley were only sleeping partners and Dick would not allow young Lacy to take a hand. Consequently he was personally responsible for every job at the Lane, from selecting the plays to running the box office. Even Garrick had had a business partner. Once he realised how much there was to do, Dick invited his own father to become artistic director, on the sole condition that he should never act himself. Initially Sheridan accepted, but this stipulation enraged him more and more every day. Soon he left in a huff.[13]

Eliza had been dying all along to help Dick in the business. Sheridan's departure gave her the opportunity to take on much of the secretarial work and the day-to-day administration. After leaving Tom in the care of his nursemaid, she began to make regular visits to the Lane, and quietly insinuated herself into its day-to-day running. She took charge of the finances which were in a terrible mess; she began to keep the books and theatre records in her own hand; and she helped Dick pick the singers for musical shows. But she was most useful to her husband when she took on the job of reading playscripts. Within weeks of arriving at the Lane, Sheridan's office tables and chairs were piled high with scripts he could not bring himself to read. Aspiring dramatists were at first disappointed and then furious that their manuscripts were neither acknowledged nor even returned and they began to hang menacingly around the stage door, looking out for the young theatre manager. Eliza came to the rescue. She would pick up a script, scan it briefly, and tell Dick what to say to the author. As a manager he was neither systematic nor businesslike. She was both.

Then just as she was beginning to feel useful, Eliza's little scheme fell to pieces. In August 1776, a few weeks before the opening of their first season, she became pregnant again. Predictably the Linleys anxiously urged Dick to take the greatest care of her. Consequently he became over-protective; she was not allowed to attend performances, and her daily visits backstage were discouraged. All he allowed her to do was to sit at home with her feet up reading interminably boring playscripts.

Unfortunately Dick was too excitable to stay at home with her. He always had to be doing something. Most nights he would go out drinking after the theatre closed, usually with his new friend Richard Tickell. Tickell was a would-be writer and hanger-on who imitated Dick in everything. Eliza took an instant dislike to him. Another crony was Willoughby Lacy, Dick's reckless partner in Drury Lane and one determined to drink away his fortune. Lacy had a town house and a mounting pile of debts. His recent marriage to a beautiful young woman had not sobered him: indeed Eliza thought that Lacy's only interest was to induct Dick into his riotous way of life. When they received an invitation to Lacy's birthday party, she wanted to turn it down, but at Dick's insistence they went. Down at Lacy's Thames-side mansion at Isleworth, the party was wildly cheerful rather than decadent, most of the guests getting very drunk. When it seemed that things might get out of hand Eliza simply went to bed. Henry Angelo later remembered;

> the high spirits of the guests at the supper-table; and Mr Colman in the fervent argument with Captain Thompson mounting the table, and declaiming with great energy. Our orgies lasted until day . . . when, about five o'clock, our party of *bon vivants* sallied forth to the garden, it being a bright summer morning. Sheridan and I had a fence match; and Jerry Orpin, brother of Mr Lacy, for a wager jumped from the lawn, his clothes on, into the stream and swam backwards and forwards across the Thames.[14]

They were just like schoolboys.

Eliza was much more comfortable with their friend Sir Joshua Reynolds, who frequently invited them to his house in Leicester Square. There she met Garrick again, the poet and critic Joseph Warton, the theatre manager George Colman and the historian Edward Gibbon. And of course, Johnson and Sheridan, two great celebrities of the day, were bound to meet. Dick was rather nervous about this, poised as he was to publish a sarcastic rejoinder to the old Tory's pamphlet on the American colonists entitled *Taxation No Tyranny*. The hostility between Johnson and Dick's father did not help. Even in Dick's company Johnson could not disguise his contempt for orthoepy and he made it known publicly to others, on one occasion telling Boswell, 'Sir, what influence can Mr Sheridan have upon the language of this great country, by his narrow exertions? Sir, it is burning a farthing candle at Dover, to show a light at Calais.'[15] Nor could he stop himself making disparaging remarks about Sheridan's character to Garrick: 'Sir, There is to be sure, in Sheridan, something to reprehend, and everything to laugh at; but, Sir, he is not a bad man.'[16]

Despite or perhaps because of his emnity with Sheridan, Johnson took a liking to Dick, and on 14 March 1777 proposed him as a member of his 'literary club', on the grounds that 'he who has written the two best comedies of the age [*The Rivals* and *The Duenna*] is surely a remarkable man'. So Dick acquired yet another set of jolly drinking companions and regularly dined at the Turk's Head in Soho.

The contrasting rhythms of their lives were now beginning to pull the Sheridans apart. In the mornings while Dick was still in bed recovering from the night before, Eliza would regularly slip out into the empty streets of Covent Garden to attend early morning service at St Clement Danes' or St Pauls'. However, sometimes – just to please her husband – she would put on her silks, take his arm and go out for the evening. As soon as she entered a fashionable drawing room, young men would sharply draw breath, startled by the vision of heart-piercing looks that had just come among them. There Eliza would sit patiently on her chair, trying hard not to hear the women gossiping about Dick and Mrs Crewe. But her preference now was for a quiet life and most nights she would sit up in bed, waiting for Dick to come home. In the early hours when the front door banged, her heart would turn over. Dick was always in good spirits as he bounded up the stairs. Sitting on the edge of the bed to pull off his boots, he would imitate the people he had met. His wicked impersonations could always make her laugh. Her Linley temperament was graver than his, but Dick had taught her gaiety; that was one of the reasons she loved him. In bed, they would giggle and talk baby-talk. He liked that.

But lying awake beside him in the dark hours she grieved for her dying marriage. Perhaps naïvely she had dreamed that they would always be together, work together, talk over everything, and know each other's thoughts. Yet that was not Dick's way. What he wanted of a wife was someone to bear his children, run his house, and act as a decorative companion. That was all that people expected of any society wife. They were never going to be partners.

CHAPTER 21

Scandal

It is rare that the climax of any human life may be assigned a precise date and time. It is even rarer when that moment determines not only the life of an individual, but also those of their families for generations to come. But such is true of Dick Sheridan and his descendants. At about nine o'clock on the evening of 8 May 1777 a friend of the old fencing master Domenick Angelo was passing through the passage of the Rose Tavern in front of Drury Lane when he was startled by an immense shout.[1] It was the roar of hundreds of people in the theatre, and was followed by a prolonged tumult of clapping and cheering. The fourth act of a new play by Richard Brinsley Sheridan had just finished, a screen fallen, and a door opened. On stage a young woman gazed aghast at an old man whose frail eyes blinked against the stage lights. The applause and laughter seemed to go on for ever. They continued staring at each other.

To understand how this came about we must return briefly to the autumn of 1776. Dick Sheridan's preparations for his first season as the manager of Drury Lane were at fever pitch. Dashing from Orchard Street to the theatre at all hours of the day to supervise business and rehearsals, he thrived under the fierce flow of adrenalin and creativity. To add to the tension, rumour had it that with Garrick gone, the new management would open the season playing to empty houses. But Dick was not afraid of such talk. Never before had he possessed such a toy to play with as this great theatre.

One might have thought that this work load would have constrained his amorous interests. But with Eliza's withdrawal from society, he was left at even greater liberty to enjoy the flattering attentions of Frances Crewe. No longer the innocent, devoted boy who had courted Eliza four years previously, he had now absorbed a quite different set of attitudes. Promiscuity was a way of life for his fashionable friends, and moreover celebrity had effected a change in him. He was more self-possessed, even arrogant, and persistent female admiration had sharpened the edge of his sensuality. In the autumn of 1776, though still technically faithful to his wife, he flirted with the delicious possibility of adultery, like a schoolboy who had broken into an orchard and was luxuriating in the choice of which apples to pick.

He opened the season with *The Rivals* which was still very popular, following it with a censored version of Congreve's *The Old Bachelor*. Then came Thomas Linley's opera *Selina & Azor* and later *The Tempest* for which he wrote new songs to be set by Linley. Star attraction for the festival season at the Lane was a revival of Garrick's *Christmas Tale* featuring de Loutherbourg's spectacular scene in which the fairy palace burns down. Later there was to be a new production of *Romeo and Juliet* with the female lead taken by a stunningly beautiful, but completely inexperienced *ingénue* named Mary Robinson. Even the ageing monogamous Garrick had been so smitten with this girl that he had insisted on coming down to the theatre for rehearsals.

Then came an event which threatened to upset all Dick Sheridan's plans and badly agitate Eliza. Desperate for money, Willoughby Lacy was clamouring to sell his half share in the Lane to his two friends, the auctioneer Robert Langford and the retired naval officer Captain Edward Thompson, and in return they promised to support his bid to become joint manager with Dick. Lacy was justified in arguing that Sheridan had no right to assume that he had inherited the artistic management with Garrick's half share. But he had no theatrical experience whatsoever and Dick was simply not prepared to put up with any artistic interference. To force Lacy's surrender, within three weeks of taking over the theatre Dick secretly fomented an actor's strike and the Lane closed down. The actors stopped turning up for rehearsals and most of them became 'ill'. They were taking a risk – the Lane was their livelihood – but they were not going to accept orders from an amateur. For a few days the outcome remained in doubt and Dick Sheridan refused to produce any plays. In the end Lacy could not even get a cast together and gave in. Amazingly, the actors recovered from their illnesses at once. Once Drury Lane reopened, Sheridan became its undisputed master.[2]

Meanwhile Eliza was discussing the theatre accounts with Dick.

She pointed out the scale of waste that she discovered, especially horrifying in view of the landlord's recent demand for £325 back-rent. But like her parsimonious mother Eliza could always see ways by which savings might be made and soon devised a programme of economies. They were to be strictly enforced.[3] The programme which her husband circulated to his fellow proprietors included a reduction in the numbers of actors, dressers and changing rooms; the ending of dressers' benefit money and their 'perk' of taking home candle ends; and a requirement for the actors to supply their own white silk stockings and gloves. The principal actors were also to have their annual salaries fixed at the start of the season, while those living at a distance from the theatre were responsible for providing their own porters to summon them to rehearsals. There was to be a property book to check 'straying' items and the plot of every play was to be transcribed into a record book kept by the proprietors, so that they might defend themselves against any charges from the censors. Had it not been precluded by her sex and social position, Eliza might well have become one of the most successful managers in theatrical history.

By the New Year, Drury Lane audiences were becoming restive. They wanted a new play from the manager. So on 24 February 1777 Dick presented his comedy, *A Trip to Scarborough*. However first-nighters were unamused to discover that it was not a new play at all, but a cleaned up version of Sir John Vanburgh's *The Relapse*. There was a lot of hissing from the audience and for a time things had looked dangerous. But it was the fine ladies who had rescued matters. Firstly, the splendid appearance of Frances Crewe and her elegant friends diverted hostility for a time, and then the Duchess of Devonshire herself saved the evening. Appearing in the Royal Box wearing an enormous crown of pink ostrich feathers, she provoked such prolonged applause that the house was good humoured for the rest of the evening. As one paper reported: 'her Grace's head-dress was the true bon-ton'.[4] It was as good as a show.

The display of female beauty on stage was equally distracting. There was Mrs Abington, forty years old but still the most joyous comedienne in London, and Miss Farren, sprightly and amusing. But neither of them could match the beauty of the young Mary Robinson, who in her memoirs claimed that it was her performance as the virtuous Amanda and not the Duchess's hat that saved the day. She wrote that the audience's hissing petrified her so much that she could only move when the 'late Duke of Cumberland, from the stage box, bade me take courage – "It is not you, but the play they hiss", said his Royal Highness.' She goes on: 'I curtsied; and that curtsy seemed to electrify the whole house; for a thundering peal of encouraging applause followed.'[5] Few could resist Mary Robinson's charms; even the painter James Northcote complained that Reynolds had failed to depict her adequately 'because her extreme beauty . . . was too much for him.' It seemed it was too much for Sheridan as well: Mary reported that in the first season he paid her 'flattering and zealous attentions . . . such as to fascinate and charm me'.[6] There is little doubt that they had an affair.

As the spring came on Eliza found herself even more isolated. As usual Dick had not allowed her to be at the first night of *A Trip to Scarborough*, and her visits to the theatre grew less and less frequent as her condition progressed. As a doting mother and a proud wife, she was content. Her one frequent guest was Mehetabel Canning, wife of the banker Stratford Canning, who sometimes invited her back to Putney Hill. Though a Quaker she was not solemn, and often wrote to Eliza addressing her jokingly as 'Sister Christian' and signing herself 'Patience Pure'. But Eliza longed for a visit from her brother or her sister Mary so that Orchard Street could be brought alive again with Linley music and humour.

In the New Year of 1777 the Sheridans moved to Great Queen Street to be nearer the theatre and because Dick thought that a grander house befitted their elevated status. Yet still the Linleys did not move. There was enough work for all the family at Drury Lane but Thomas Linley judged it more prudent to retain his music practice in Bath until he was quite sure that work in London would last. He became the theatre's musical director and that year he and Tom were both kept busy composing and performing for *Selina & Azor*, *The Beggar's Opera* and *The Tempest*.[7] Dick even suggested that Mary and fourteen-year-old Maria might like to sing at the theatre but their father soon put a stop to that. As for Mrs Linley, she was made responsible for the wardrobe and properties which gave her ample opportunity to exercise her flair for economy. As Drury Lane became a Linley family business, Eliza gradually saw more of them all and her contentment grew.

Meanwhile, since Eliza was still writing letters and reading scripts for her husband, Dick found the time to work on a new play entitled *The Slanderers*. For a while he had been experimenting with sketches about a married couple called the Teazles who some said were based on the Duke and Duchess of Devonshire. Characteristically, Dick Sheridan could not keep his working secrets to himself and in February the *Morning Chronicle* announced that two comedies were being prepared for representation at Drury Lane, both 'from the pen of the acting Manager'. Understandably there was scepticism about this from playgoers who had been misled into believing that *A Trip to Scarborough* was an original piece, but on 5 April the same paper hinted that having failed to secure the services of an Italian castrato, the manager was plugging the gap with his own 'last young colt, *School for Scandal*'. On 13 April the new play, though not finished, was in rehearsal.

Dick Sheridan's friends and critics were taken aback by his intention to introduce a comedy so late in the season. Drury Lane was a winter theatre; normally May was the month in which to ring down the curtain to let the cleaners go about their business, and for the actors to leave for provincial tours before the streets started to swelter and the Thames started to stink. Although he was taking a risk, Eliza and her family were sure he could pull it off. Betsy Sheridan remembered later that he had kept the characters of *The School for Scandal* in his head for years past, regularly claiming that the comedy was finished and that all he had to do was to write it. And Eliza had noticed that since Dick had gone into high society he had developed a fascination with scandal and gossip. It appealed to his secretive and manipulative nature; while pretending to despise it, he loved repeating snatches of conversation about assignations, affairs, elopements and intrigues that he had overheard in order to make his friends laugh.

That April he sat in the drawing-room at Great Queen Street surrounded by scraps of paper and his notes on *The Slanderers* and the Teazles, trying to fit both stories into one script. He did not dare use his elopement theme yet again and so at last was obliged to find a new story line. Then suddenly he recollected a scene at the opening of his mother's play *A Journey to Bath*:

STAPLETON: Oh I know you are wonderfully tender of reputations, you hate Scandal.

SURFACE: Ay, as I do poison. I do as I would be done by, Mr Stapleton.[8]

Surface and scandal: that was it. He told Eliza that the principal theme of his play was to be scandal-mongering. So he continued to work on his notes, re-naming characters and cutting whole scenes, but progress was slow.

Even if only partially aware of it, Dick Sheridan was now trying to find a pattern to his own emotional experience and to shape from it the elegant golden comedy that he wanted his own life-story to be. He distanced himself from the story of the central characters, the Teazles, by depicting the young wife, Lady Teaze-all – married to an old fool – as the one who appears to be contemplating adultery. Just as he felt his own motives for adultery innocent enough, so are hers. Taking the hint from his mother's play he devised the Surface brothers, each of whom is the reverse of what he seems. Joseph, the man of sentiment, is a scheming, canting hypocrite; Charles on the other hand, though apparently unprincipled and dissolute, is ultimately governed by a kind heart.

Old Sheridan later put his finger on it when he pointed out that Dick himself was both these characters. Dick saw himself as a well-meaning fellow, though indolent and too fond of women and wine. Nevertheless the insight he shows into Joseph Surface's scheming is itself a piece of self-revelation, for Dick too could act the innocent, feign surprise, play a part, lay a plot and utterly mislead creditors, playwrights, and partners. In fact he could even mislead his wife, and sometimes resented her for being too trusting, long-suffering and emotionally dependent on him. But he was still pained that his own father would not recognise her, and more than anything he wanted to bring them together.

Dick worked slowly through the April days until a perceptible sense of urgency hung over Great Queen Street like a cloud. Rehearsals had begun on 16 April but still the play was nowhere near finished. That day the *Morning Chronicle* reported optimistically that: 'Each actor in the Piece, it is said, is already in possession of a fourth part of his character, a second fourth it is imagined, will be delivered to the Company this week, and unless a fit of indolence seizes the Author, or a fit of Gout the Prompter, the remaining half will be ready before the end of the week.'[9] In fact it was a couple of weeks before Sheridan finished the play: meanwhile the frustrated actors worked on those scenes that had been completed, and there were frequent stoppages and rows while they waited for a few more pages to arrive. Fortunately some of the actors like Tom King and

Frances Abington were aware that what they were receiving, still wet with ink, was material which gave them the finest acting opportunities of their professional lives. Though to Dick's disappointment Mary Robinson was unable to take part because she was pregnant, Garrick himself was always on hand to encourage his old colleagues to be patient with the young dramatist.

Finally, one day late in April, with Hopkins the prompter standing over him in the office at Drury Lane, Dick scribbled the play's last words, to be spoken by Charles Surface:

You can indeed each Anxious Fear remove,
For even Scandal dies if you approve.

Below it he scrawled: 'Finished at last, Thank God!' With that he gave the manuscript to Hopkins, who was responsible for having it copied and distributed to the actors, and the prompter hurried downstairs with the manuscript, read it through and added a comment: 'Amen! W. Hopkins'.

Then came an emergency. The last job to be done was to get a performing licence, a mere formality. Dick wrote to the censor informing him that: 'if the following Comedy called *The School for Scandal* should meet his approbation, it would be performed at Drury Lane on the 8th of May'. Permission was refused. The censor thought that the play ridiculed the government candidate in a current by-election.[10] Round at the Lord Chamberlain's office the author explained to his friend Lord Hertford that he had no such intention. Hertford 'laughed at the affair and gave the licence' but the episode had put enormous strain on the Sheridan household.

On Tuesday 6 May Eliza went into labour. The following day a newspaper reported the single certainty that Mrs Sheridan was 'delivered of a son. The mother and child are likely to do well.' Even the sex of the child was a matter of dispute because some said it was a daughter. Eliza had picked her childbirth at precisely the moment when her husband was far too busy to give her attention, because his first night was only forty-eight hours away.

On the evening of 8 May, as Eliza lay critically ill in her bed in Great Queen Street, the Lane began to fill up with a fashionable audience: the Devonshires was there, as were the Lucans and many of Dick's other society friends. Of course, Garrick was there and almost certainly Samuel Johnson, come to witness the triumph of his protégé. Among the fashionable women present the radiant Amoret, Frances Crewe, sat smiling and chatting proprietorially among the audience as if she owned both the playwright and his work. Indeed, she and Sheridan were close enough for the author to present her later with a copy of the play with thirty lines of verse entitled 'A PORTRAIT, Addressed to a Lady with the Comedy of *The School for Scandal*, concluding with the apostrophe to 'Thee my Inspirer – and my Model – CREWE'.[11] There was also one other person present whose attendance would have meant a lot to Dick, had he known. It was his father, once again returned from his tour of Ireland.

In an upper bedroom in Great Queen Street that night lay a sleeping woman whose doctors were fast despairing of her. Had her bed been placed near the window to let in the fresh spring air, she too may have been dimly aware of sounds from the theatre just around the corner. At nine o'clock she would have heard the sudden roar and a cascade of applause, and though slumbering deep in laudanum dreams she might have known what it meant.

On stage the actors were just finishing the fourth act. The audience watched as Jack Palmer, all smooth suggestion and innuendo as the seducer Joseph Surface, had welcomed Mrs Abington (Lady Teazle) into his chamber. By calling on him alone Lady Teazle has compromised herself. Suddenly her husband Sir Peter Teazle is announced and in a panic she hides behind a screen. Sir Peter enters and confesses to Surface that though he and his wife do not get on together, he has decided to settle a sum of money on her before their separation. Sir Peter hears Charles Surface on the stairs and, believing him to be his wife's lover, insists on hiding so that he may overhear his conversation. For a brief moment he almost succeeds in getting behind the screen. But when he catches a glimpse of a petticoat in there, and Joseph Surface tells him it belongs to a little milliner, Sir Peter bundles into a closet instead. After Charles Surface arrives and has made plain his innocence with regard to Lady Teazle, he learns that Sir Peter is in the closet. He hauls him out and in Joseph's absence they decide to investigate the little 'French Milliner' whom he is keeping behind the screen. All in a moment Joseph returns, the screen falls and Lady Teazle is revealed.

In the theatre there was a great gasp and Drury Lane exploded with cheering and laughter. This commotion was the climactic moment in Dick's life, the commotion which Angelo's friend had heard in the Rose Tavern passageway and which carried through the bedroom window to the lady in Great Queen Street. Dick had always wanted to bring his father and wife together and now here they were, embodied as fictional characters on stage, confronting each other in astonished silence. Ironically both had been theatre stars before Dick Sheridan was even heard of, but he had triumphed beyond their fame. The old man and the young woman continued to gaze at each other, mute, while playgoers cheered and cheered.

After this scene, the audience were ecstatic in their reception of the rest of the play. Pouring into the lamp-lit Covent Garden piazza after the performance their talk was no longer of the reverses suffered by British troops in the American war but of the new glory Mr Sheridan had brought to the English stage. As for Dick, he knew very well that his comedy was fit to take its place beside the likes of *The Way of the World*. From now on as long as the English language survived he would be known as Richard Brinsley Sheridan, author of *The School for Scandal*. Sensing immortality, he was too excited to go home and strode from one roaring tavern to another to drown his joy in drink. Later, as he once told Lord Byron, 'he was knocked down and put in the watch-house for making a row in the streets, and for being found intoxicated by the watchman'.[12] But it was not so much wine that he had been gulping down, as glory.

The *London Evening Post* for 8 May reported:

On Tuesday last, Mrs Sheridan, wife of R.B. Sheridan, Esq., was delivered of a child still born. And,
On Thursday night, at her house in Drury Lane, Mr Sheridan's muse was delivered of a fine chopping female, likely to live for ever.[13]

So congratulations poured into Great Queen Street, while upstairs the sick woman slept deeply. In the next room the waxen form of a female infant was put into its coffin.

CHAPTER 22

Loss

It was June 1777. Among those who anxiously followed the bulletins about Eliza's health was an elderly couple living near Hampton Court. The soft-hearted Garricks had never met her, but they longed to offer comfort to this young lady with such a sad history. With no children of their own, they therefore sought objects on which to lavish their attention. So Garrick invited Dick to bring his wife and child down to their villa near the river for a summer holiday. Eliza certainly needed love and care. Her hosts were alarmed by her appearance when she first arrived because since the still-birth she was whiter and thinner than ever. And when after dinner of an evening she would sing to them some of Handel's poignant airs, they were deeply moved – like many before them – by the depth of feeling in her voice. Their parental instincts aroused, they wanted nothing more than to take care of this rare and delicate creature.

Although initially a little nervous, Eliza soon discovered that Mrs Garrick was a sympathetic and considerate hostess. The great actor Garrick was the sort of man who treated ladies with unfailing kindness. He had always admired beautiful women and had been especially fond of Dick's mother Frances in the days when he had put on her play at Drury Lane. As a young man he had many affairs, including one with the fiery actress Peg Woffington, but since he married the Austrian ballerina Violetta he had remained a faithful husband. As might have been expected, Eliza's ethereal beauty brought out all the old man's gallantry.

Though the Garricks often gave very grand receptions they also liked to welcome guests to more intimate house parties to spend lazy days by the river. Most mornings, Dick would ride off for London pleading important business at the theatre. His hosts did not mind a bit because it meant that with Eliza and little Tom to themselves, they might spoil them as much as they wished. While her husband was out Eliza would rest or go on a boat, or simply sit chatting all day on the terrace with her hosts, as she played with Tom and watched the barges glide lazily by.

The only other guest was the playwright Hannah More.[1] She had become a sort of adoptive daughter to the Garricks and had a suite of rooms in their house. Hannah was of a serious turn of mind, and disliked Eliza by reputation, assuming her to be a shallow, flirtatious, society woman. But she was pleasurably surprised, writing to her sister: 'We have been here a week, Mrs Sheridan is with us, and her husband comes down in the evenings. I find I have mistaken the lady; she is unaffected and sensible; converses and reads extremely well, and writes prettily.' She was less complimentary of the men: 'To be sure there may be wiser parties in the world than ours, but I question if there is one more cheerful. Ought one to own it, that the great English Roscius, and the best English dramatic poet . . . sit up till midnight, playing at cross-purposes, crooked answers, and what's my thought like? Yet it is true you never heard a set of half wits utter half so much nonsense!'[2]

One morning Garrick presented Eliza with some verses he had written. They were playful but clearly suggest the anxiety that her hosts felt about her state of health:

Verses of a Lady Singing

Whence are those sounds that raise the soul,
And tears of joy and grief draw forth;
A cherub sure has hither stole,
That we may taste of heaven and earth?

What! is it rosy, winged and sleek
The being that so sweetly sings?
Oh no! 'tis thin, and fair and meek
And with a covering hides its wings.

Tho' through the air the magic floats,
To fascinate our ears and sight,
Yet still we fear; for with such notes
She seems prepared to take her flight![3]

196

Yet Garrick had mistaken Eliza. She was no angel. Though weak and frail, she had far too much spirit in her to be thinking about taking her flight to heaven just yet, and she told him so:

Mrs Sheridan's Answer

What dost thou say, A cherub, Garrick? No,
Nor sounds divine, not wings concealed have I,
'Tis true I'm thin, and meek, for aught you know,
But though I still may sing, I cannot fly:

And though a shadowy form I may appear,
With your sweet wife much longer I should stay,
So kind is she, that had I wings, I fear
I soon should be too plump to fly away.

For the next year the Sheridan's lives were filled with the theatre. Dick would come home nightly buzzing with news of box-office takings, new productions and theatre politics. Then in the summer of 1778 he embarked upon a whole series of financial ventures. First of all he bought out Willoughby Lacy's share in Drury Lane for £45,000, £10,000 more than he had paid Garrick for his half. The shares in the patent were then re-divided between the three trustees so that Sheridan had a full half share, and Linley and Ford a quarter each.[4] Secondly, he joined forces with his old friend Tom Harris of Covent Garden to either lease or purchase the King's Theatre in the Haymarket as an opera house and possible third winter theatre, should the King be willing to grant a new patent.[5] Dick Sheridan still liked to keep his cards close to his chest and it is highly unlikely that he told Eliza about these deals. He knew that she would have been alarmed that he had just doubled his personal debt and had borrowed yet more money from her father. He knew that Eliza was always worrying about financial disasters at Drury Lane, whereas his plans were made on the assumption that things would always go right.

Dick Sheridan had other affairs which he kept secret from everyone. In the summer of 1778 the actress Mary Robinson gave birth to her second daughter, Sophia. The father was probably Mary's husband, the articled clerk Thomas Robinson, though he had tended to spend much of his time in the King's Bench Prison as a debtor who could not pay his gambling bills.[6] Sophia died when only six weeks old. Dick, now Mary's frequent visitor, called soon afterwards, and Mary recorded the visit: 'I had seen many proofs of his exquisite sensibility. I never had witnessed one which so strongly impressed my mind as his countenance on entering my apartments. I had not the power to speak. All he uttered was, "Beautiful little creature!" at the same time looking at my infant and sighing with a degree of sympathetic sorrow which penetrated my soul.'[7]

Meanwhile Dick's rising tide of confidence had buoyed Linley up with him, so that in the summer of 1778 the music master at last felt that he dare risk giving up his lease in Bath to settle in London. The Linleys chose a house in Norfolk Street, just off the Strand. It was not as commodious as the Royal Crescent but its fanlit front-door was fashionable enough, with sufficient room for all the 'nightingales' who would want to perch there. They brought only Tom, Mary and Maria with them; their younger children Ozias, William and Jane were left down in the west country and Samuel had gone to sea as a midshipman. They were close to Great Queen Street and every day Eliza was able to walk young Tom round to see his grandparents. As musical director at the Lane, Linley took his duties very seriously. With his long sought-after prestigious place in London artistic society and such a celebrated son-in-law, he felt confident about securing for himself yet more lucrative work as a society music tutor.

His son Tom's career as a composer and violinist also gave him cause for satisfaction. Tom was attracting wide attention in the musical world and few judges doubted that he had a brilliant future ahead. As if the gods had not rewarded the boy enough, he had also inherited the Linley good looks and charm. Moreover he was cheerful, generous and popular and Linley could hardly contain his pride in the boy. But then, out of the blue, disaster struck.

In August 1778 Tom and his sister Mary were invited to spend the summer as musical guest to the Duke and Duchess of Ancaster at Castle Grimthorpe. They accepted because their hosts made it clear that they were to be treated as house-guests who performed their music in the evening rather than a type of servant – which was usually the case in these situations. Tom was only twenty-two and Mary twenty, and as they rattled out on the dusty London streets the two young people relished the prospect of green fields, luxurious living and music-making among cultivated people. What happened there is best told in the words of the *Bath Chronicle* from 13 August:

> Mr Linley and Mr Olivarez, an Italian master, and another person agreed to go on the lake in a sailing boat, which Mr Linley said he could manage, but no sooner had they sailed into the middle of the lake, but a sudden squall of wind sprung up and overset the boat; however, they all hung by the masts and rigging for some time till Mr Linley said he found it was in vain to wait for assistance, and therefore, though he had had his boots and greatcoat on, he was determined to swim to shore, for which purpose he quitted his hold, but had not swam above 100 yards, before he sunk. Her Grace the Duchess of Ancaster saw the whole from her dressing-room window, and immediately despatched several servants off to take another boat to their assistance, but which unfortunately came only in time to take up Mr Olivarez and his companion, not being able to find the body of Mr Linley for more than 40 minutes.[8]

Mary Linley travelled back to London alone to break the news to her parents. She collapsed and was ill for several days afterwards. As Eliza and Dick were out of town, Thomas Linley had the melancholy duty of going up to Lincolnshire on 11 August to attend the funeral on his own.

Tom had been the pride of the Linleys and the hope of English music. As the news of his death spread among his colleagues there was universal recognition that a prodigious talent had perished. One prominent musician certainly thought so. Six years after Tom's death, Michael Kelly, the singer and friend of the Sheridans, met Wolfgang Amadeus Mozart in Vienna. When Kelly reminded Mozart of his schoolboy friend the composer replied: 'Linley was a true genius, and . . . had he lived, he would have been one of the greatest ornaments of the musical world.'[9]

But of course it was among Tom's family that the grief was most intense. Linley never really recovered from the loss. When some months afterwards he was sitting at the keyboard during a Drury Lane rehearsal, and someone tactlessly suggested that a young musician there was showing some promise, he did not argue. But the remembrance of his own brilliant son set the tears coursing down his cheeks. Eliza too felt the loss keenly for he was her favourite brother and the companion of her childhood. On seeing Tom's violin standing idle in the corner one day, she wrote some verses in which she imagined the instrument speaking for itself:

> *Those sounds melodious ne'er again shall please,*
> *No tuneful strains from me shall ever flow;*
> *Save o'er my trembling strings a sighing breeze*
> *To call one sad, soft note of tender woe.*
>
> *Else ah! forever mute let me remain,*
> *Unstrung, untuned, forgotten let me be:*
> *Guard me from curious eyes and touch profane,*
> *And let me rest in mournful sympathy!*
>
> *One fate with thee, dear Master, let me share,*
> *Like thee in silent darkness let me lie;*
> *My frame without thee is not worth my care!*
> *With thee alone it lived, with thee shall die!*[10]

To add to her misery, Dick began to come home with a nightly crop of worries from the theatre. Many concerned his father whom he had recently and unwisely brought in as artistic director. Sheridan's ill-tempered attempts to impose his will on the actors did not go down well and rehearsals at the Lane frequently deteriorated into shouting matches. With his antiquated notions of acting and production, a pompous manner and a short temper, he was supremely gifted at upsetting people. Garrick too was angry with him. Since his retirement Garrick had got into the habit of dropping into the theatre from time to time to offer Dick Sheridan his advice. His old rival Thomas Sheridan was now running the theatre, and believed that at last he had taken his rightful place as ruler of the Lane. He was not going to let Garrick interfere. Ungenerously taking advantage of his new position, he sent Garrick off with a flea in his ear each time he appeared. Yet Dick Sheridan let his father rule the roost for three more uneasy seasons before he let him go.

The actors at the Lane were realising that life with Dick Sheridan was going to be very different from their days under Garrick. Not only was his father's artistic direction rapidly sliding into disaster, but Dick failed to pay them regularly. It seemed as if the two Sheridans were conspiring to provoke dissatisfaction in the company. Furthermore despite Eliza and Mary's valiant play-reading efforts, the stage door was still haunted by disappointed authors aggressively demanding a word with the manager. Dick was equally unscrupulous in paying local tradesmen. But one of his creditors never complained. This was Mr Field, the chandler to whom Eliza and Dick had fled during their elopement.[11] He thought it an honour to supply candles to the theatre and never receive a penny. When Dick agreed to Eliza's economising by eking out the Drury candle-ends, he was forgetting that he had not paid Field for them in the first place.

Eliza's fears that Dick had taken on one more debt than he could manage were confirmed by another episode. Before he and his partners bought Lacy's portion, Dick was under obligation to pay Garrick a regular premium on the mortgage of his share. But he had recently spent so much on the theatre that he wrote to Garrick asking if he might defer payment for a set period. Garrick, whose comfort in his retirement depended on this regular payment, was furious. He replied to the triumvirate: 'Gentlemen, the rudeness of your letters, which is always a sign of a bad cause, I shall pass over with the greatest contempt. But as you have proposed to my friend, Mr Wallis, and my brother, an arbitration, I cannot, as an honest man, refuse to meet you on any ground.'[12] Garrick would have nothing to do with the partners except through his solicitor. Eliza was greatly saddened by this breach.

In contrast, she hated Tickell's growing influence over her husband. Whereas Dick saw him as his best friend, Eliza regarded him as his bad angel. Every night now they visited the clubs and taverns together and in Tickell's company Dick became a different man: loud, boisterous, hard-drinking and given to horse-play and practical jokes which Eliza despised.

She also disapproved of Tickell's morals. When she pointed out to Dick that Tickell had an illegitimate son and perhaps a daughter too, he dismissed them airily, arguing that at least Tickell was liberal enough to pay for the upkeep of his bastards. Even Mary was not sympathetic to Eliza on this matter: she seemed to find Tickell rather amusing.

In October 1788 Dick was planning a new 'Musical Entertainment' for the Lane to be called *The Camp*. Linley was still disconsolate over the death of his boy and could not work, so Dick recycled some of his tunes for the music. The Drury Lane publicity machine implied that Dick Sheridan had written the piece: in fact most of it was composed by Tickell. A simple tale of a Suffolk girl who dresses up as a boy and follows her soldier sweetheart to camp, the plot was poor, the characterisation thin, and the music second-hand. Dick was particularly worried that the scenery was not up to the usual Drury Lane standard and everything depended on the spectacle of the piece. Since de Loutherbourg was not available as a designer, he swallowed his pride, and asked Garrick to inspect it. Of course, with his customary kindness, Garrick forgot all about their dispute and came out in the chilly night air to the theatre. Looking at the flats, he pronounced they would do and hurried off, fearful of catching a cold.

If the production was moderately successful, it was probably because of the display of feminine charm on stage. In the *Morning Post* the comment was that 'Miss Farren, Miss Cuyler, and Mrs Robinson, appeared much to advantage in their Amazonian attire.'[13]

Throughout those autumn days, the Linleys sat at home nursing their grief, until in December they received yet more alarming news. *The Thunderer* had put into Portsmouth with cholera on board, and their eighteen-year-old son Sam was reported to be among the sick. Down in Portsmouth the distracted parents found him in a fever. They brought him home to Norfolk Street to be cared for by their thirteen-year-old maidservant Emma Hart, who became so attached to him in his sickness that she rarely left the room. But it did no good: in the same month Sam died. Eliza had lost a second brother.

Ironically, Sam's death brought about one of the most celebrated love affairs in English history. Emma Hart was so grief-stricken that she had to leave the Linley's service. The girl later became the kept woman of a young man of fashion who eventually handed her to his uncle, Sir William Hamilton. They married, and her new name made her, of course, Emma Hamilton, later lover of Horatio Nelson.

While Eliza was grieving, Dick also suffered a loss. On 3 December Mary Robinson appeared as Perdita 'the lost one' in a Command Performance of Garrick's *The Winter's Tale*. King George and Queen Charlotte were accompanied by their eldest son, the seventeen-year-old George, Prince of Wales. He was already engaged in an affair with a lady of the court, Mary Hamilton, but as soon as he saw Mary Robinson on stage as a 'poor lowly maid/ Most goddess like prank'd up' he became utterly infatuated with her and forgot his other love. At the curtain call he caught Mary Robinson's eye and with a look she said she would 'never forget' he 'gently inclined his head a second time. I felt the compliment and blushed my gratitude . . .'[14] The next day the Prince sent Mary Hamilton a farewell letter: 'Adieu, adieu, adieu, toujours chère. Oh! Mrs Robinson.' 'Perdita' now began to receive regular letters from the love-sick boy and eventually agreed to a tryst in Kew Gardens where he presented her with a miniature of himself. When he heard of it, Dick knew when he was beaten and gracefully withdrew. George had found a new mistress and young Sheridan had lost his leading lady. Due to the nature of his loss, Dick was forced to be discreet about his disappointment.

Meanwhile David Garrick had never quite recovered from the chill he had taken at Drury Lane when looking at the set for *The Camp*. This exacerbated his other medical problems. Although anxious, his wife Eva-Maria agreed that they should keep their promise of a New Year visit to their old friend Lord Spencer at Althorp in Northamptonshire. In some of the worst winter weather of the century they set out for home again on 14 January. Their coach-wheels churning in the thick snow, they began the worst journey of their lives, with Garrick taking laudanum all the way. When at last he reached his home in the Adelphi on Friday 15 January 1779 he was obliged to go straight to bed. Three days later Eliza and her husband were sitting in Great Queen Street when they received the grim news. Garrick was dead.[15]

Eliza did not attend the funeral but Dick was appointed chief mourner by Mrs Garrick.[16] Her choice was appropriate as there was now a general recognition that Dick Sheridan was Garrick's rightful successor as the leading figure of the English theatre. The funeral on Monday 1 February 1779 seemed like his greatest production. The cortège was to make its way from Garrick's home, at the Adelphi, down Whitehall to Westminster Abbey for the interment. From ten o'clock onwards the weather had turned mild, so onlookers lined every foot and housetop, while the bells of St Martin in the Fields and the Abbey kept up a continual tolling. A detachment of cavalry preceded the procession to clear the streets, but the huge crowds remained hushed and respectful to watch the great Garrick pass by. So many sightseers had come in their carriages that they blocked the road, and the fifty mourners' carriages took a full hour to reach the Abbey.

The church was so full that day that many people had to be turned away at the doors. As the carriages arrived, mourners were greeted by the Dean and Chapter and a Purcell anthem. The first six carriages carried Garrick's aristocratic friends, and the pallbearers included many notaries, such as the Duke of Devonshire, Earl Spencer, Viscount Palmerston, and Albany Wallis. Three of Garrick's nephews were there to represent the family.[17] Among other mourners were colleagues from Drury Lane – including the actors King, Smith, Palmer, Moody and Baddeley, and the treasurer, housekeeper, book-keeper and carpenter – and twelve actors from Covent Garden. Two of the patentees, Linley and Ford, were assigned the twenty-third coach. Of Garrick's old friends only Sheridan did not attend. From the Literary club came Burke and Samuel Johnson who was, according to Cumberland, bathed in tears.

As chief mourner, Dick Sheridan was able to arrange a fittingly dramatic entrance for himself. He arrived at the Abbey in the seventh coach, the first among commoners, dressed entirely in black. Onlookers saw an imperious young man step down to take his place at the head of the procession, then, head held high, he was followed into the Abbey by the two pages holding up his enormous train to the solemn strains of the funeral march.

The Bishop of Rochester read the service and at the interment at Poet's Corner Edmund Burke whispered to whoever could hear him that the statue of Shakespeare seemed to be pointing out the very place his great interpreter was to be buried. When the obsequies were over and the last farewells said, Dick returned to Great Queen Street to announce to Eliza that out of respect to Garrick's memory he would spend the rest of the day in silence. He sat at his desk thinking.

Dick was not mourning Garrick in his silence. In fact he was secretly elated by the scene at the Abbey. As he walked among England's greatest that morning, gravely bowing to the left and right, it occurred to him that if he were capable of orchestrating such a national drama, playing the lead role in what was almost a state funeral, there was nothing to which he could not aspire. Although there was enough of the actor in him to realise how much he enjoyed upstaging Garrick at his own funeral, he began to think of Drury Lane as a vulgar place compared with the Abbey and the life of a mere theatre manager a tawdry thing. For the first time he had glimpsed the higher stages of human endeavour that he might climb.

He went back to work but his heart was not in it. His monody *To the memory of Garrick*, delivered by Mrs Yates at the Lane on 3 March 1779, was a lifeless thing and received the tepid reception it deserved.[18] He was much more successful with his farce *The Critic or A Tragedy Rehearsed*, which was first performed on the 30 October that year to a delighted audience. But to concentrate on writing it was so difficult that Tom King had to lock him up in the office with a blazing fire, sandwiches and wine, and refuse to let him out until he had finished. The humour of *The Critic* derived from breaking every theatrical convention, especially those of heroic tragedy. His dramatic formula of a rehearsal observed allowed him to ridicule the theatre and all its arbitrary techniques on which illusion depends. For example, in the scene where three critics, Mr Puff, Mr Dangle and Mr Sneer, are on stage, their conversation consists chiefly of praising the actors, King, Palmer and Todd. Yet the actors who played the critics were actually those being praised. The situation was piquant and absurd and the audience loved it. The manager even included a reference to himself.[19] Sheridan was like a small boy cheerfully smashing china.

There were warning signs in all this. Eliza may have heard in *The Critic* echoes of that sniggering humour which Dick had recently picked up from Tickell. More seriously, in this farce he had begun to pull down that safety curtain of convention on which all theatre depends. It would clearly have been difficult for him to write another 'naturalistic' comedy afterwards: in fact, *The Critic* was Dick Sheridan's farewell to the comic stage. For many years afterwards he went about announcing that he would soon complete a new play called *The Foresters*, but he never did. On one occasion, his friend, the singer Michael Kelly, told him that he would never write a play again because he was afraid to do so. When Dick Sheridan asked him of whom he was afraid, Kelly replied: 'You are afraid of the author of *The School for Scandal*.'[20]

By the beginning of 1780 many of Dick's aristocratic Whig friends were urging him to join the political world. In January he agreed to chair a sub-committee to draw up proposals for parliamentary reform. In February these were put to a meeting of 3000 people at Westminster Hall presided over by Charles James Fox. The demand for universal suffrage was proposed by Alderman Sawbridge, seconded by John Wilkes, and passed by acclamation. Supporters included the Dukes of Richmond and Portland, and the Cavendish and Grenville families. It was a considerable boost for Dick Sheridan's political ambitions. Afterwards at home, he told Eliza that he wanted to enter parliament in the Whig interest.

Eliza was not surprised that her husband now tired of his expensive toy in Drury Lane. She knew that once he possessed something he ceased to value it. Besides, like his father, he had always affected to despise the theatre and even boasted that he never sat through a play. What it all meant for the future she could not guess. The Linleys were an artistic not a political family, and she did not understand how he could continue as manager of the theatre and as a member of parliament. Nobody had ever done such a thing before. Moreover, if he lost the Lane they would have no money.

But Eliza was still desperately in love with Dick Sheridan and determined not to lose him. She resolved to follow him anywhere. If it came to it, she would be a politician's wife.

PART THREE

One True Lover

CHAPTER 23

A Violent Politician

May 1784. For forty days and forty nights Covent Garden was consumed by the Westminster election campaign. Charles James Fox, the Whig champion, was fighting for his political life. Nightly the dark spaces of the great piazza were lit up by hundreds of torches flaring and sputtering in the fitful wind, and huge crowds jostled around the many booths and inns, flocking in for the excitement. The Tory rooms were at Wood's Hotel, while Fox kept his campaign headquarters at the Shakespeare Tavern. And there he was, Fox, 'the Jewish messiah' as they called him, short, obese, unshaven, ugly as sin and utterly charming, strolling with his bullies round the square and pulling in the votes. 'Fox and Liberty' he would shout, and then break off to fondle a servant girl or accept a swig of gin from a grinning admirer.

The theatres were almost deserted. Even though he was the manager of Drury Lane, Dick Sheridan seemed more interested in the hustings that in his own show, sometimes sauntering round the square with his friend Fox, sporting the campaign badge of a fox's brush and a sprig of laurel leaves, then disappearing for a few days to go and work on his campaign at Stafford. He was expecting a good result from his own seat since during the previous visits there he had bribed the grateful townsmen – using over £1,300 from the Drury Lane box office – with free dinners and ale.[1] It meant he could devote more of his time in Westminster helping Fox. Naturally Eliza, loyal wife as she was, also became involved.

The leader of the radical Whigs had a real fight on his hands. Westminster was the largest constituency in Britain, and its representation decided by popular vote. But it was the burgesses who were enfranchised and they were largely Pitt's men. In this election two seats were contested by three candidates: Fox, the naval hero Admiral Hood, and Pitt's man Sir Cecil Wray, or 'The Fox, the Lion and the Ass' as the crowds called them. From the beginning of the month's public voting Fox was behind. He could not hope to beat Hood of course but he stood a chance against Wray. Wray was unpopular, firstly because he wanted to demolish the Chelsea Hospital, and secondly because he had tried to impose a tax on hiring maidservants. But Chelsea pensioners and servant girls had no votes, whereas investors in the East India company generally had, and Fox had recently offended them by his abortive attempt to reform their government of India. So it very much looked as if Fox, who had served as His Majesty's Secretary of State for Foreign Affairs in the recent Whig administration, would soon be out of Parliament, unless he could find some way to turn the tide.

One way was to bring some of his famous friends down to Covent Garden to impress the voters. Foremost among these was the Prince of Wales. George was twenty-two and an enthusiastic boy about town. He visited Westminster more than once, and liked to preside over Fox's dinners at The Crown and Anchor where he would propose radical toasts such as 'Liberty of the Press'. Not surprisingly he got an ironic cheer when, with a fox's brush in his button-hole, he first stepped down from his carriage and strolled arm in arm with the candidate in the streets among labourers, shop-keepers, servant girls, pick-pockets, pimps and prostitutes. Though the crowds were good-humoured, he brought his bodyguard.[2] Whenever he appeared there was a great rush to see him, and a great deal of pushing and shoving round his carriage. Sometimes it got violent. One boy shouting 'Fox for ever' was knocked down by a constable, and another time an officer of the peace, Nicholas Casson, was trampled by Fox's supporters and died of his injuries. It was all a tremendous show and the crowd loved it, but still Fox was behind.

Then came an astonishing turn of events. It started slowly when plump Mrs Hobart was seen canvassing for Wray. As one of Fox's cast-off mistresses, everybody knew her motive was revenge, but any woman canvassing was a strange sight and Wray gained some very useful publicity. Fox knew he had to counter it. One morning as the piazza was coming to life, an open carriage drove round carrying the famous actress 'Perdita' Robinson, her superb figure outlined in silken blue and buff. Displaying a fox's brush on her breast, from time to time she would stand up to make a speech beseeching the electors to vote for Fox. And though she attracted a fair bit of sarcasm for her love-affairs, 'Perdita' certainly endowed Fox's campaign with more glamour than Mrs Hobart could command. A few days later she was joined in the campaign by Fox's current mistress, Mrs Armistead, driving a ducal carriage and solemnly bowing her thanks while the roughs shouted cheerful obscenities after her.

It was not entirely unknown at that time for a lady to take part in an election: Countess Spencer had recently supported her son in the family borough of Northampton.[3] But polite opinion still held that the hurly-burly of the hustings was no place for a respectable woman. Nobody considered Perdita Robinson or Mrs Armistead to be respectable, so their appearances in Covent Garden, though surprising were not shocking. But what happened next astounded the middle-classes, and provoked enormous gossip. For ladies, real society ladies, started walking round the square soliciting votes for Fox. One morning in a vision of finery the Countess of Carlisle, the Countess of Derby, the Viscountess Beauchamp and several others all appeared, arguing, wheedling and cajoling startled shopkeepers to go and support their hero. In so doing they were risking their reputations, especially since they were not related to Fox. What could be their motives? Could they all be his mistresses?

Of all these exotic creatures by far the most beautiful and fashionable were a trio of ladies who came almost every day; the Duchess of Devonshire, her sister Lady Harriet Duncannon, and Mrs Richard Brinsley Sheridan. Of these, the Duchess was the most outrageous. When confronted with such an astounding woman, only a brave tradesman would refuse to be led by the arm to the polling booth where he would tamely declare his vote for Fox. Georgiana canvassed everywhere. 'She was in the most blackguard houses in Long Acre by eight o'clock this morning' wrote one observer.[4] As news of their coming buzzed round the square each day, the Garden crowds turned out in force to see them. One commentator reported: 'the mob gaze and gaze and crowd until their senses are lost in admiration, and the pressure of those who push for the same pleasure drives them into areas, through windows, and rolls them along the kennel, bruised and be-muddled but not dissatisfied'.[5] As for Georgiana, one navvy exclaimed: 'Her eyes were so bright that I could light my pipe at them.' To what lengths these women would go was a matter of dispute. Whig accounts maintain that they confined themselves to talk, but hostile witnesses declared that they bought votes with kisses. The caricaturist Thomas Rowlandson published a cartoon of Georgiana and the Duchess of Portland embracing and kissing a couple of butchers to obtain their votes.[6] The Tories argued that if Fox was really a man of the people, it followed that Georgiana was a woman of the people and therefore by definition a prostitute.

But one of these women walked serenely among the worst vice in London and lost none of her reputation: Eliza. It was not that she was not politically active; she was everywhere in the fight and the acknowledged 'chairwoman of the petticoat committee' which supported Fox. Yet somehow she conducted herself with such an air of modesty and sincerity that even the most virulent of Tory pamphleteers dare not slander her. It was said that in canvassing throughout this roughest of campaigns, her 'sweetness' remained 'irresistible'.[7] And so at last the time came to see whether the chairwoman had influenced the result.

Four years previously Dick Sheridan had found it very difficult to get any nominations for a seat. Burke and Pitt were presented with their seats by rich patrons but no one had made a similar offer to him.[8] Nor did he have the money to buy himself a nice little pocket borough. Instead he was obliged to look for a 'free' constituency where he would need to canvass 'independent' voters. With a national reputation as a playwright and a free conscience, his assets were hardly calculated to impress local squires, and at first none of the Whig grandees who had encouraged him to go in for politics came forward to help. When an old friend of the Linleys, the artist Ozias Humphry, offered to sound out Dick's chances of partnering Sir George Yonge in Honiton on the Whig ticket, the local Whigs made it clear that they preferred another candidate.[9] For some months before the election of 1780 he continued without a nomination.

At last Georgiana stepped in suggesting that he might try his luck at Stafford where her own family the Spencers were influential. In August he arrived in the town with the overt support of the Duchess and a letter of introduction from Lady Spencer to her agent. Such backing guaranteed that he was chosen to run with a sitting member, Edward Monckton, as one of the Whig candidates for the two seats in the Borough. The small matter of actually getting enough votes remained. The electors of Stafford traditionally expected £5 apiece and a good dinner for each; fortunately, Dick Sheridan had already provided for this by drawing the requisite £1,000 from theatre profits. Eventually on 12 September Dick Sheridan and Monckton were duly returned as the members for Stafford. Dick told Eliza that it was the happiest day of his life.[10]

Eliza had not gone up to Stafford with him; there was no need for her to be there. Besides, somebody had to stay in London to look after five-year-old Tom and to keep an eye on the new season at Drury Lane. But when news came of Dick's election she was of course thrilled at his achievement. If she was still rather apprehensive about its implications, it was because membership of the House carried no salary and so he could not afford to give up the Lane. No manager of a major London theatre had ever been elected to the House of Commons, and she could not understand how Dick could do both jobs at once. She was right to be concerned. For the rest of their lives together Dick would lead a phrenetic existence, constantly rushing off to some business or other, and this was to have serious implications for their marriage.

But it was a proud day for them both when he first went off to take his seat that autumn, and on the nights that followed Eliza would listen eagerly to accounts of his adventures in the House. However, neither of them were prepared for the snobbery of the ranks of aristocratic Tory yobs who packed the opposite benches. They did not care twopence that he had written *The School for Scandal*. As far as they were concerned this young Sheridan was merely a presumptuous little scribbler, while his trade as a theatre manager should have ranked as a positive disqualification for membership of Parliament, the institution which they regarded as their club. So whenever he rose to speak they gave him a rough reception.

In his first speech Dick was obliged to defend his very presence in the House. The defeated member for Stafford, Benjamin Whitworth, presented a petition complaining that Sheridan's recent victory had been effected by bribery and corruption. This was true. But what Whitworth did not say was that Dick's conduct was in no way different from that of many other candidates. Even so, Dick had to get up and argue that Whitworth's petition was frivolous and malicious. There was some laughter and cat-calling but most members listened cautiously, since none of them wanted allegations of bribery pursued too closely. Besides, they were curious about this young man who was reputed to be a great wit.

The speaker ruled that there was no case to answer. But his opponents in the House never allowed Dick to forget his despised theatrical origins. One member named Rigby was always sneering about them, while a Mr Courtenay, having listened to Dick's over-earnest contribution to the debate on Burke's 'Bill for Regulating the Civil List Establishments' remarked that 'the Honourable Gentleman was an enemy to mirth and humour in any house but his own'. Relapsing into his familiar style Dick countered that 'the most serious part of [Courtenay's] argument appeared to [him] to be the most ludicrous'. He was beginning to understand that the only way for him to maintain his dignity in the House was to treat all this carping with wit and humour. It was just like Harrow.

Slowly he got the measure of the debates. His abilities did not go unnoticed, and as a reward he found himself ever more frequently invited to Devonshire House to confer with such rising Whig stars as Edmund Burke and Lord Holland's son, Charles James Fox. In 1780 Fox was thirty-one years old, full of rotund bonhomie, with a weak mouth, double chin, and thinning white hair. His gestures were limp and his hands womanly in their delicacy. But his looks betrayed him: Fox was a brilliant talker. A quick intuitive perception, a sharp wit and a liking for jokes made him the ugliest clever man alive, and even with Burke and Pitt as rivals, the most forceful politician of his age. Perhaps Fox's greatest gift was his charm, which impressed both men and women. He noticed Eliza at once.

In the years that followed, the Sheridans became part of the great Whig establishment. Not only did Georgiana introduce Eliza into the highest levels of aristocratic society, but she also encouraged Eliza's love of cards. On the many occasions Dick would be obliged to go back to London on business, his wife stayed on at some great country house, Croome or Crewe or Chatsworth. In the evening she would wander among the green baize tables until the others arrived and she could contrive to gamble her few pounds away. She wrote to Dick from Crewe:

> Oh, my own, 'ee can't think how they beat me every night. If it goes on, I shall soon be on the debtor's side of Mrs Crewe's book . . . It is the abominable whist they make me play – twenty-one guineas last night and fifteen before . . . I tell you this is what you may provide accordingly, for I very much fear you will find no little hoard here when you come. But, my soul,

when do you come? . . . Woodcocks are so plenty here that you may knock them down with your hat. Well, God thee bless, my soul. Me want to see 'ee eyes very bad. Your own.[11]

In 1780 Eliza was only twenty-three years old and still an unsophisticated girl from a provincial middle-class home. Despite the grand company she kept, she had not yet learned any other way of influencing her husband than by playing his impulsively affectionate child-wife. She obediently accepted the social role he had provided for her while keeping her reservations to herself.

She admired many of his friends, especially Georgiana, but these people often displayed attitudes which she found startling and which would have outraged her Bath relations. It was quite common among Dick's new friends for a man to proposition a married woman openly in a society drawing room, even with her husband standing near. Eliza herself had sometimes been approached in this overtly sexual way and she was embarrassed by it. At times she felt as if she was fighting off Captain Mathews again.

Aristocratic society was beginning to feel that it was beyond the moral restraints which necessarily bound inferior classes, especially in sexual matters. The Devonshires were a case in point: in the autumn of 1782 the Duke and Duchess returned from Bath with Lady Elizabeth Foster and set up a ménage-à-trois. She was introduced to Eliza as a friend of the Duchess but few efforts were made to disguise that she was in fact also the Duke's live-in mistress.[12]

In the early 80s Devonshire House was positively fizzing with sex and politics. Its society centred upon the Duke, his Duchess and mistress. Then there was Georgiana's passionate, intense sister Harriet, who had recently married Fred Ponsonby (Lord Duncannon), the son of Lord Bessborough. From the first it seemed to Eliza that Harriet was in some way dissatisfied with her new mate. Then there were the tensions between the rival politicians Fox and Burke, who watched each other suspiciously at the splendid receptions Georgiana gave for them. Fox and Burke were jealous of Dick Sheridan's easy success, and later Burke was touchy about Fox's greater preference for Dick to himself. In turn Dick was sexually jealous of Fox who had made a pass at Eliza. Fox was behaving entirely within the moral codes current in his circle: one of these was that only after a wife has borne her husband his first son was she fair game for anybody. But Eliza rejected him and despite the tension he and her husband remained friends.

Another frequent visitor to Devonshire House in the early 80s was the Prince of Wales. Lord North had turned his own Tory government into little more than the instrument of the King's will, and since the Prince was no favourite of his father, it was only natural that the Whigs should side with his cause. By 1781 he had already tired of the affections of the actress 'Perdita' Robinson. He had briefly set her up as his mistress in a small house in Cork Street. But now she was out of favour, every effort was being made to prise out of her not only the Prince's indiscreet letters, but also the bond for £20,000 which he had presented to her in the flush of youthful passion.

This ripely amorous young man had now begun to understand that he could have almost any woman he liked, provided that he acted with a certain respect for the proprieties. He was not yet the notorious rake of later years, when it was said that if a woman entertained him at home, she would end up in bed with him, and that it was considered grossly impolite for the woman or the husband to stand in the way of Royal inclination.[13] But even if he was still at the romantic stage, the Prince was constantly on the look-out for new conquests. Inevitably his gaze came to rest on Eliza. Though not yet to hand, she seemed within his reach. She was utterly ravishing and her husband so flatteringly obsequious when the Prince visited them. The fact that she was eight years older than he did not signify; George preferred older women. Then again, Mrs Sheridan was so angelic, so delicate and modest, that she seemed a shrine made to be violated.

To his amazement, when he signalled his intentions, she refused him absolutely. She seemed to have the odd notion that she should keep her favours for her husband. George was deeply affronted and embarrassed, cutting Eliza dead when next they met. When afterwards he reflected on his bad conduct, he was thoroughly ashamed of himself. The Prince was at bottom a person of generous impulses and disliked hurting peoples' feelings. He wrote to Eliza:

Windsor Castle, October 12th, 1781, Saturday evening 1/2 past five o'Clock,

Dear Madam,

If it is not inconvenient to you I should be excessively happy if you would allow me to call upon you early tomorrow morning, soon after 9 o'Clock, in order to explain to you my reasons for ye apparent indifference with which I behaved to you some little time back. Believe me nothing could be further from ye sentiments of my heart. I should be very unhappy could I suppose I meant to treat you ill, or indeed anybody in a manner unlike a gentleman.

I am dear Madam most affectionately yours, G.P[14]

He quickly consoled himself. While acting at Drury Lane 'Perdita' Robinson had a personal maid named Elizabeth Armistead, who after a brief sojourn in a 'notorious' and fashionable establishment had gone freelance. She was at that time the mistress of Charles James Fox, but it was not long before he discovered that he was sharing her favours with the Prince himself. It was a unifying element in what might prove to be a new Whig ascendancy.

Even if these men dismissed Eliza's fidelity to her husband as absurdly conventional, they would have been taken aback had they understood its true extent. Eliza persisted in remaining true to her husband, even though she was well aware that he was conducting an affair with Frances Crewe. She never condoned it and privately grieved at it; mostly she learned to accept it philosophically. Taking the attitude that even the best of men were spoilt children and could not be expected to feel that profoundly passionate fidelity of which some women were capable, she even tried to excuse Dick's unfaithfulness by arguing that, where a man was true to his wife, she usually had to pay for his self-denial. In a letter to her sister-in-law, Alicia Sheridan, she remarked: 'So Mrs — is not happy. Poor thing! I daresay if the truth were known he teases her to death. Your very good husbands generally contrive to make you sensible of their merits somehow or other.'

But even Eliza's patience was taxed by the repeated visits to Crewe Hall which Dick insisted they make. There she was obliged to accept protestations of undying friendship from a woman whom she knew to be her husband's mistress. At such times she could only rely on her sense of humour to see her through. On 23 November 1785 she wrote to her friend Mrs Canning: 'S [Sheridan] is in Town – and so is Mrs Crewe. I am in the Country and so is Mr Crewe – a very convenient Arrangement is it not? Oh the Tiddlings and Fiddlings that have been going on at C [Chatsworth] 'Twas quite a Comedy to see it.'[15]

Beneath her apparent serenity, however, Eliza was increasingly hurt and resentful about her husband's infidelities, and this led to blazing rows. The tension was exacerbated by pressures of political life, the late hours they kept, and constant worry about money, but it was Dick's deceitfulness and malicious hints about his affairs which at times provoked her to scream abuse at him, and when stung by her attack he would roar back. They were often past caring that there were other people present to witness these operatic displays. Once Mrs Mehetabel Canning saw Dick 'dashing his head frantically against the wall at one end of the room while Mrs Sheridan, as highly strung as her husband and much more sensitive, repeated the operation at the other'.[16]

Yet despite constant provocations to vengeance, she forgave him, preserving her romantic vision of the young hero who had once rescued her from misery. Her letters to friends reveal that for most of the time that she was still lost in a glow of admiration and affection for him, living her life through and for him. His success in the Commons especially delighted her and she would go to any lengths to help, whether by poring over the Drury Lane accounts, copying up notes for his speeches, or by secretarial duties. Notoriously unmethodical, Dick continued to lose playscripts and letters piled high on his desk without being opened. In 1781 Eliza wrote from Harrow to her sister Mary to complain that Dick allowed nobody to touch his correspondence, and did not even open letters from her when she was away from home. She added cheerfully that any papers in Dick's hands were 'irrecoverable'. But this verdict did not diminish her enormous faith in his abilities. For many years she clung to the belief that 'his power [was sufficient] to conquer all obstacles', and that there was 'nothing impossible for him'.[17]

This faith was vindicated in March 1782 when, after twelve years in office, North's Tory Government fell. Despite persistent pleas from King George that his minister should not desert him, the news of Cornwallis's surrender to the American colonists at Yorktown forced North to recognise that he could no longer command a majority for his policies in the House of Commons. He resigned. On 8 April a new parliament was summoned in which the Whigs under Rockingham were to form the administration. Dick Sheridan had always been a supporter of the American colonists, and welcomed a new government sympathetic to their rightful demands.

So far he had surprised both friends and opponents in the House by his assiduous attendance at debates and his sensible contributions to law-making. His passionate concern to defend the powers of Parliament and the magistracy against any further encroachment by the royal prerogative was apparent as soon as he entered the house. The Gordon Riots had taken place in the summer of 1780, just before he had become an MP, and the ensuing debate now provided him with a suitable occasion on which to make his point. In those riots the mob had rampaged through London and Westminster, yet the magistrates had held back because they were unsure of their powers and feared the law themselves. Control of the rampaging mob was left to army officers, servants of the King. Dick Sheridan argued that this situation was intolerable and that Parliament should clarify the role of magistrates. He asked: 'Why have the officers of the Crown, the Ministry of Parliament never been allowed to provide a remedy for the peculiar situation of the magistracy?'[18] Of course he knew very well why nothing had been done: North's government was packed with King's men who did not want to extend the magistrates' authority. With this speech he made his parliamentary reputation, and it brought him to the attention of Lord Rockingham. Rockingham appointed Charles James Fox as his Secretary of State for Foreign Affairs, and the post of Under-Secretary of State for the Northern Department was given to his friend. After just eighteen months in the House, Richard Brinsley Sheridan was in government. He became a true parliamentarian, laughing as loudly as other members did when William Pitt, son of the First Earl of Chatham, grandly announced that he would never accept a non-cabinet post in any administration.

The Sheridans were not enriched by Dick's promotion. As an under-secretary Dick would receive nothing like the £4,000 a year that Burke was rumoured to make as Paymaster-General to the Forces. Too proud and principled to line his pockets, he was always in debt; his income was furnished solely from the profits of the Drury Lane Theatre. Two years later Eliza wrote to her friend Mrs Canning: 'as you know, poor Dick and I have always been struggling against the stream and shall probably continue to do so to the end of our lives'.[19] As it happened, Dick's appointment did not last very long. Lord Rockingham, having planned to end the disastrous American war, died after only three months in government. His successor, Lord Shelburne, was by no means so committed to peace with the American colonists. Dick Sheridan resigned.

But while his own fortunes fell, another young politician was going up in the world rapidly. To Dick's amazement, William Pitt had been offered, and had accepted, the post of Chancellor of the Exchequer. Now he had the opportunity to study his performance from the back-benches, and though they were both nominally Whigs, a bitter rivalry soon grew up between them which other members were well aware of. Pitt began it. He could never resist making snide references to Dick's theatrical origins. Having listened to his rhetoric on the Articles of Peace with the Americans, Pitt acidly observed that 'no man admired more than he did the abilities of that Honourable gentleman, the elegant sallies of his thought, the gay effusions of his fancy, his dramatic turns, and his epigrammatic points; and that if they were reserved for the proper stage they would no doubt receive the plaudits of the audience'. The House laughed but Dick was ready. He rose smiling and replied that he declined to comment on the personal note introduced by the Right Honourable gentleman:

> the propriety, the taste, the gentlemanly point of it must have been obvious to the House. But let me assure the Rt. Hon. gentleman, that I do now, and will at any time when he chooses to repeat this sort of allusion meet it with the most sincere good humour. Nay, I will say more. Flattered and encouraged by the Rt. Hon. gentleman's panegyric on my talents, if I ever again engage in the compositions he alludes to, I may be tempted to an act of presumption, to attempt an improvement on one of Ben Jonson's best characters . . . [that] of the Angry Boy.[20]

The House chortled at this but Pitt was irate. As for Eliza, she had identified a villain in one who sneered at her beloved husband and from that time onwards she detested Pitt. This generous and entirely unmalicious woman had now found herself someone to hate.

Shelburne's government lasted barely a year. It was brought down in April 1783 by an unholy alliance of North's Tories and Foxite Whigs, united only by the desire to regain power. To general amazement, Fox and North then formed a coalition government, nominally headed by the Duke of Portland. Dick advised Fox against agreeing to such a pact because, like many others, he felt that no honourable coalition could be compounded between two parties of such opposing political interests. Eventually Fox persuaded Dick against his judgement to join the coalition as Secretary to the Treasury. This appointment provoked some hilarity among members because Dick's casual approach to Drury Lane's finances was now a matter of common knowledge. More that one wag demanded to know whether the inefficient paymaster of Drury Lane was an appropriate person to assist the Chancellor of the Exchequer. Nevertheless, having accepted the job, Dick soon proved himself rather good at it.

Meanwhile, Charles James Fox had once again become Foreign Secretary. His first project was to pilot a new India Bill through the House. This spelled trouble for Dick. For years the East India Company had been plundering the subcontinent, so Fox proposed that seven Parliamentary commissioners should be appointed for a four-year term to curb its worst excesses. In keeping with Whig doctrine Fox and Burke could claim that such a Bill would improve the lot of millions of exploited Indians. Naturally the Company opposed the Bill and lobbied hard to defeat it. King George also hated this proposal: it sought to replace his royal patronage on the vast subcontinent with a mere parliamentary committee. He decided to kill the Bill. First he got Pitt to agree to head a future administration of 'King's friends'. Next he took soundings in the country to learn that Fox's Bill was generally unpopular. Finally he let it be known among the Lords that anyone who supported the Bill would henceforward be regarded as his personal enemy. So even though it was passed in the Commons on 17 December 1783, it was defeated by 19 votes in the Lords. At once the King struck. In the early hours of the 18 December, he dismissed Portland and appointed a minority government headed by Pitt. The Fox/North coalition had endured barely nine months. Once again Sheridan found himself out of office.

He was not unduly perturbed. Pitt had only minority support in the House and it seemed only a matter of time before he would be thrown out and he himself would be back in office. But Pitt hung on for four months throughout the winter of 1783/4, wriggling to avoid defeat in the House. Circumventing votes of confidence, he worked hard to win over the Independent members who held the balance of power. Though he was very young, he was master of the house and a firm political leader. And when the election came at last in March, it was because he had chosen his moment.

Hanging on in Stafford, Dick knew that any hopes of office in the future depended on Fox's re-election. In the shires, Fox and North were deeply unpopular: 96 coalitionists were voted out, and Pitt returned triumphantly to Westminster. However the votes for Westminster had not yet been counted. On 14 May a huge crowd assembled in Covent Garden to hear the declaration of the poll. To an enormous roar of approval and hornpipe-dancing, it was announced that Admiral Hood had topped the poll with 6,694 votes. This was no surprise. But who had won the other seat? The answer came quickly: Charles James Fox 6,634, and Sir Cecil Wray 6,398. Fox was back.

Fox's supporters formed a great procession that wound all the way from Covent Garden to Piccadilly and past Devonshire House. Prominent in the cavalcade was a carriage bearing the arms of the Duchess of Devonshire with the inscription: 'Sacred to Female Patriotism'.[21] The carriage was empty but there was no doubt that it was the petticoat committee that had turned the election for him. One of his female admirers, Mrs Crewe, gave a great ball at her house in Lower Bond Street to celebrate the victory. The Prince of Wales attended in party colours to toast: 'True blue and Mrs Crewe', to which his hostess responded: 'True blue and all of you'.[22] The Sheridans attended the ball, Dick in a joyous mood. The recent political defeat of the Whigs seemed only a temporary set-back and he knew that he would be in government again very soon. Meanwhile, as he partnered his hostess all eyes were on them. Everybody in fashionable London knew he was her lover.

Eliza watched and smiled discreetly. She felt that she too had reason for self-congratulation. Had she not been the 'president' of the 'petticoat committee' and had she not stayed up half the night planning Fox's campaign? In fact her sister Mary had been very critical of her ill-disciplined life which sometimes involved 'going to bed at three, breakfasting at two and taking no regular exercise.' But Eliza ignored her advice. Partly out of necessity and partly out of loyalty to her husband she had now become an ardent radical, all for liberty and the citizen's rights. When Dick had first entered parliament she had written rather ironically to tell Alicia in Dublin: 'you don't know what a violent Politician I am perhaps'. But now she meant it. Her ultimate loyalty, however, was restricted to a rather small political party; its name was Richard Brinsley Sheridan.[23]

CHAPTER 24

Sisters

On the morning of Friday 4 June 1785 hundreds of Londoners might have been observed flocking across Westminster Bridge and from the direction of St James's and Whitehall towards the Abbey. Even before eight o'clock people had begun to take their places in the aisles. They had come to witness an event not usually staged at the Abbey, a concert to celebrate the life and work of a man who though not royal, nor military, nor even English had been interred among the most illustrious sons of the nation when he had died twenty-six years previously. This day marked the hundredth birth-day of George Frederick Handel, the favourite composer of the English people, and a splendid recital of his music was to be given to honour him.

Among those hurrying to the Abbey a little after nine o'clock was a Mr Luke Yarker, his sister and their guest, a little spinster named Miss Elizabeth 'Betsy' Sheridan. Twenty-seven years old, neither handsome nor fashionable, she had recently come over from Dublin and her sharp eyes surveyed everything with the ravenous gaze of a tourist. Though the party got to the Abbey soon after nine they only just managed to secure seats in the middle aisle from which they were able to see most of what was going on.

Having settled herself Betsy was able to take in the tremendous scene: some of the six hundred musicians and singers were clambering up to their places on the rows of wooden seats high above the congregation in the transept. Soon the bishops and senior clergy arrived to take their places in a huge box draped in purple cloth. Across the aisle an especially conspicuous enclosure had been made for society ladies, their outfits somewhat incomplete as there were to be no hats or feathers worn in the Abbey in order that people might see better. Provincial Betsy felt comfortably superior to the caps on display: 'A Mob of a most immense size, simply illustrated with blue or yellow ribbons – this over friz'd Heads and sallow complexions had a very bad effect – a few with fair skins and clear brown hair bore the disguise tolerably'.[1] By a quarter to twelve the Abbey echoed with the shuffling and coughing of about 3,000 people. The Linleys were there, and towards noon the Duchess of Devonshire swept in to her reserved place in the box with Eliza Sheridan. At the first notes of the national anthem all stood for the entry of the Royal family. Once they resumed their seats the Handel began with a 'Te Deum'. Four hours of music followed.

Betsy Sheridan was an emotional, impulsive woman and at times the music reduced her to tears. Later she wrote to tell Alicia back in Dublin that this music was 'the only homage worthy of the Devine [sic] being which I had ever heard offer'd up'. During the arias from *The Messiah* Betsy fancied – even at such a distance – that she discerned a wistful look on Eliza's face. The loyal Betsy understood at once: surely her famous sister-in-law should have been singing that day? Was she not the finest Handel soloist that people could remember? She felt quite jealous on Eliza's part and became more critical: 'the single songs appear'd to disadvantage I think after the glorious Band. Madame Mara[2] was the only real singer of merit – her voice is uncommonly fine perhaps beyond Mrs Sheridan's, but that something Angelic which was in the sound of hers is wanting as well as that beauty and expression which necessarily gave such additional charms to our sister's singing'.

The affection Betsy had always felt for Eliza had been renewed by the warm welcome her sister-in-law had recently given her. That was one of Eliza's most attractive qualities: even though she was accustomed to move in brilliant circles at Devonshire House, she never failed in her thoughtfulness and kindness to less fortunate women. Nor did her manners change to old friends; simplicity and sincerity remained natural to her. Furthermore, it might be assumed that possessed of such beauty, she would prefer the flattering company of male admirers, but it was not so. Perhaps because she had been so harassed in early life, her natural sympathies were chiefly for other women. In return they repaid her with fierce loyalty and affection. Her sisters and sisters-in-law received regular letters and invitations to her new home in Bruton Street.[3] She was closest of all to her sister Mary.

After her marriage to Tickell in 1780 Mary followed her husband to Wells in Somerset. Much to Eliza's pleasure she came back to London the following year because Dick had secured for his friend the sinecure of Commissioner of Stamps. At first the Tickells lived in a grace-and-favour apartment up a long flight of stairs at Hampton Court. In the mid-eighties, when they were more affluent, they rented a second home in Queen Anne Street, just a few blocks north of the Sheridans.

Tickell had long ceased to practise as a barrister and now spent much of his time involved in Dick Sheridan's business. Like Sheridan, on whom he modelled himself, he was amiable, unreliable and increasingly unprincipled. They egged each other on, especially when it came to drinking. Mary was a lesser Eliza, beautiful but not as much, a fine oratorio singer but not so consummate an artist. In one thing only was she Eliza's superior; she had a sprightlier sense of humour. Both Tickells seem to have been quite happy to live in the greater glow of the Sheridans. Mary was never jealous of her sister's status, just as Eliza never treated Mary with a hint of conde-scension. Their contrasting lifestyles amused them. When Eliza attended splendid banquets at Chatsworth, troops of footmen served her food on a silver platter; Mary stayed at home with a single maid to serve her beef off a tin plate. The sisters were exceptionally close; they remained each other's most intimate confidantes, writing almost daily when apart; they learned to tolerate their husbands together; and they shared family problems.

When Eliza was away in the country, Mary kept her informed about London life, painting humorous pictures of the domestic lives of the Linleys, Tickells and Sheridans.[4] Her surviving letters are chatty, funny and loving. She would enquire about Eliza's health and admonish her for late hours. One of their chief topics for amusement was their mother's proverbial meanness. In one letter Mary recounted how, in her role of wardrobe manager, Mrs Linley had greeted Tom King's suggestion that they should hire new extras for the latest Drury Lane production:

He [Tickell] found my Mother in the most violent agitation in the World. 'Oh! Tickell, I am fretted to death. Those Devils, but it is all Mr King's fault.' 'Why what's the matter Ma'am' 'Matter! Why, do you know they have hir'd a whole regiment of Guards almost for *Arthur* [an historical drama] and for what? as I said, for you know there's plenty of common men in our house' [the theatre] 'that always come on as Sailors and why should they not make as good soldiers.' 'What, because they can't march in Time, Ma'am', 'but my husband is such a fool'.[5]

Mary had three children: Elizabeth Ann Tickell was born in 1781, Richard Brinsley in 1782 and Samuel in 1785, when Eliza's own boy Tom was ten years old. From the first, the sisters took great interest in each other's children. Mary Tickell never made any secret of her hope that Tom Sheridan would marry her 'Betsy' in the course of time. Once at Eliza's request, Mary called with her sister Jane Nash Linley at Mrs March's School, a preparatory which Tom Sheridan attended, and where as so often happened she was mistaken for Eliza. Soon afterwards she wrote to the anxious mother a charming description of her reception:

I arrived at Mrs March's about four, and I walked directly up to the School – I was afraid at first the little Fry were all out as I walk'd quite thro' the House without seeing a single Boy – however, in the Garden there was such a Swarm and such a noise (as they were all at Play) that it was some time before I could make Enquiries for my worthy Nephew, but I believe I was taken for you, for in an instant all their little Voices set up at once a Hollow for 'Sheridan! Sheridan!' Tom was at the other end of the Garden but the Moment he heard himself call'd came running to me like a little Lapwing – the Picture of (I may say) beautiful Health –.[6]

In November 1785, Gainsborough made a permanent loan of his picture *The Linley Sisters* to Dick Sheridan, which was taken in by the Linleys while the Sheridans were away. Mary wrote to Eliza:

When I came home last night I found our picture come home from Gainsbro's very much improved and freshened up. My father and mother are quite in raptures with it; indeed, it is in my opinion, the best and handsomest of you that I have ever seen.[7]

During their protracted absences from London the Sheridans would lend their Drury Lane box to the Tickells. This way Mary could keep Eliza in touch with the news of the theatre. In the early eighties the fortunes of the Lane had declined to such an extent that Thomas Linley, now the manager, often dreaded to go through the accounts, and was driven to near despair when the King visited the rival Covent Garden two nights running. But on 10 October 1782, everything changed when a relatively unknown actress appeared at the Lane to play Isabella in the tragedy *The Fatal Marriage*. It was Sarah Siddons. She had failed at the Lane before and both Tom King and Garrick had turned her down, but Thomas Sheridan had seen her act in Bath and recommended that she be given another chance. Her performance was a triumph. The audience was 'nearly drowned with tears' and her infant son was so deceived by the death scene that he could not be restrained from prolonged howling.'[8] And just as Mrs Siddons reigned supreme in tragedy at the Lane, so Mrs Jordan's splendid legs (especially popular in male hose) became the new sensation in comedy.

The careers of these two actresses were now of enormous importance to the Sheridans because they depended upon their success for their own income. In writing theatre news to her sister, Mary was therefore providing her not just with entertaining gossip but also vital information about the family business. She nearly always tried to present her news optimistically in order to calm Eliza's ever-present anxiety about money. On January 1784 Mary saw Mrs Siddons as Lady Ranulph in *Douglas*, and confided to Eliza: 'Mrs Siddons is as much the rage as when she first appeared – this illness has given an amazing fillip to people's curiosity to see her – and I think she played better than ever she did.' Later in the year, Mrs Siddons' performance as Margaret of Anjou in *The Earl of Warwick* brought out all Mary's gifts as a theatre and social critic:

> I may tell you Mrs Siddons was charming and very different from what we had ever seen of her. If you remember the part, there is not only a great deal of ranting, that is in the style of Sara, but also a sort of irony and level speaking, or rather familiar conversation that placed her quite in a new light. I thought her very great indeed . . . She had amazing applause, yet it was rather the fashion I found, after the play, to speak rather slightingly of her, for Mr Fitzpatrick came into the box and gave his fiat against her.

As for Mrs Jordan, Mary went to see her on her opening night on 18 October 1785 and declared: 'I went last night to see our new Country Girl, and I can assure you, if you have any reliance on my judgement, she has more genius in her little finger than Miss Bruton in her whole body.'[9]

Mary was a great admirer of Dick Sheridan and would have forgiven him anything except an injury to her sister. Perhaps to spare both Eliza and herself from a true acknowledgement of their husbands' behaviour it was she who contrived the fiction that both Sheridan and Tickell were thoughtless, unreliable but essentially well-meaning boys. With this maxim to guide her, she was able to forgive their undisciplined lives and their jolly parties in her own dining room. Peopled by such cronies as Richardson and Reid, they kept Mary awake by 'every cruel Pop of that odious five shilling claret from downstairs. Even when pregnant she forgave Tickell flirting with other women. She told Eliza:

> As for T – , he danced the whole night – the redoubtable Mrs Arabin was as handsome as ever yet I did not feel at all uneasy about her tho' like a good wife I staid most of the evening in the other rooms . . . but then I knew I had a precious little spy in Jane and that I should have a particular account of all their flirtations.[10]

So when Eliza was absent from London, Mary also kept a wary eye on her brother-in-law. Sometimes, rather clumsily, she tried to keep him away from other women by getting him to sleep at her house. On one such occasion in 1784, with Eliza at Chatsworth, Dick declined her offer of a bed. She was taken aback but in her customary letter to Eliza she sought to pass the whole thing off by making her sister smile; they were not spies, she seemed to be saying, but adults tolerating the foolish antics of children:

> I was afraid we should have incommoded S[heridan], who I took it for granted slept here, but I find my Gentleman prefers a bed at the Hummums [an hotel in Covent Garden],[11] I take it for granted I am making no mischief in mentioning this; as you know he always tells me everything himself . . . I suppose we shall see little of him. Charlotte and Amoret, Amoret and Charlotte, hey?[12]

'Amoret' of course was Mrs Crewe; 'Charlotte' probably Mrs Love.

> Monday Morning. Well, Ma'am I've seen the Man of Men. He
> is just gone and left me a Trump. He promises to see me every
> day and to give a good account of himself for I told him I
> should report him to you accordingly. I laughed at him a good
> deal about his Hummums – indeed, we had a few jokes .. but
> I must tell you what I believe his Chief Business here was –
> truly, to get my Mother's box for Mrs Crewe . . . so I suppose
> they will be very snug . . . don't know whether I shan't peep
> upon them about the third Act.[13]

Perhaps because they did not trust their mother's perception and
good sense at all, both Eliza and her sister kept a parental eye on the
younger women of the Linley family. In 1784 Maria was twenty-one,
some nine years Eliza's junior, and Jane Nash was sixteen. Maria was
a talented singer, though becoming difficult for her parents to handle.
Jane Nash, (whose twin sister Charlotte had died in infancy) had
been brought up in Wells, and first came to London when her
parents moved into Norfolk Street. Neither a singer, nor particularly
talented at anything, in fact she was an ordinary girl, so overawed
in the presence of her gifted elder sisters, that she admitted that she
'felt so sensibly their superiority that [she] scarce ever spoke'. She had
to live at home, dressing herself from her father's very small
allowance, subject to the continual complaints from her mother
because she did not help keep herself.

Both Eliza and Mary contrived to call upon their parents in
Norfolk Street every day. Mary was deputed to 'take on' Maria but
she was rejected. As a child Maria had seemed to be a true Linley,
yet another of the beautiful angelic nightingales who had so amazed
Dr Burney. Later she too was trained by her father and sang in the
Drury Lane oratorios. David Garrick had even tried to book her for
the opera and had been refused. But as she approached womanhood
Maria became a difficult, very 'un-Linley-ish' sort of person,
described by her older sisters as 'eccentric'. To get away from home
she consented to Mary's offer of a bed at her house but she was not
a bit grateful: in fact when she arrived and discovered that she had
been allotted an upper bedroom, she stormed out with the words,
'I don't chuse to sleep in the Garret Mrs Tickell.' It is possible that
she was struggling with lesbian impulses that she barely under-

stood. She marched off to live with a friend, a Mrs Troward, with whom she shared a bed, and from then on was sometimes seen going about in a man's overcoat. In 1784, when only twenty-one, she went to stay with her grandparents in Bath and became suddenly ill. Yet again Thomas Linley was to need comfort for the dramatic death of one of his children. One day in her sickbed, Maria 'raised herself up, and with unexpected and momentary action, sung a part in the anthem "I Know that my Redeemer Liveth"' before being 'carried away by brain fever'.[14] Once more Eliza wrote verses for an epitaph. A pupil of Thomas Linley at this time, the singer Mrs Crouch, reported that whenever she attempted to sing a song which Maria used to sing, '[Linley's] tears continually fell on the keys as he accompanied her'. Maria was the last of his children to sing professionally.

Eliza's two sisters-in-law were both living in Dublin at this time. Her old friend and contemporary Alicia had married Joseph LeFanu in 1781. He was the son of Thomas Sheridan's trustee and banker in that city and in 1874 they had their first child Tom. However, 'Betsy' – as the family called her – had no settled home. For three years following her sister's marriage she had moved from Alicia's to the house of her brother Charles.

There she was treated little better than a servant. In her letters to Alicia she made scarce secret of her detestation and contempt for Charles, whom she referred to as 'Joseph' – Joseph Surface, the hypocritical villain of *The School for Scandal*. In contrast, she and Alicia were tremendously proud of her brother Dick. But relations between the two branches of the family were difficult: Thomas Sheridan had still not forgiven his son for sacking him as manager at Drury Lane, and treating him (as he maintained) with contempt. From time to time both Betsy and Eliza had tried unsuccessfully to repair the rift which Thomas Sheridan's residence in Ireland aggravated. Now, in 1784 their chance came, for Sheridan senior decided to return to England, bringing Betsy with him.

Betsy Sheridan was not talented, nor specially handsome: Eliza later wrote that she was a 'very sensible and amiable woman – but Misfortunes and ill Health [had] thrown a gloom & reserve over her w[hic]h does not prejudice Strangers in her favour'.[15] Of course this is only a partial view for Betsy also possessed the Sheridan sense of humour and a very sharp critical eye, qualities much in evidence in the letters she wrote to Alicia.

Old Sheridan made it clear to her that he would never consent to meeting Dick and his wife though he had no objection to her doing so. Accordingly, once settled in London on 30 September – having first called on the Angelos, and visited the Pantheon to see the balloonist Lunardi and his cat and dog which had ascended with him into the London sky – she summoned up the courage to call on the Linleys. She knew she would find Dick and Eliza there but because of her father's hostility to Dick and old Linley she was apprehensive of their reception. She need not have feared. The warmth of the greetings she received from both the Sheridans surprised and touched her and she found the Linleys equally kind. The evening must have recalled for many of them that first meeting of the Sheridan and Linley families at the Royal Crescent in Bath all those years before.

Betsy wrote to Alicia:

Dick received me more affectionately than I expected, he ask'd a thousand questions about you and then immediately turned the conversation on my Father. He said he hoped now I was come that all would be made up as there was nothing he wished so much as to be on terms. If he is in earnest and I think he is I am pretty sure all will end well. We sat some time together and when summon'd to Dinner I was introduced to the Linleys. I am very angry with the Old Man [Thomas Linley] but as his Guest was obliged to be civil to him. Mrs Linley is grown older than any one I have ever met. She had lost all her teeth and looks a complete Witch but in manner she remains the same. She gave us a bad dinner not to make a stranger of me and hoped I would often come and play Pool. Jenny is with them and is grown up what she promised. Poor Maria did not seem to be remember'd among them. Dick sat by me and ask'd me a thousand questions about Ireland that made me smile as one would have supposed I had come from the farthest part of America. When dinner was over Mrs Sheridan [Eliza] and I went to Drury Lane. We found Mrs Tickell seated in the Box. She came up to me with the warmth of an Old Friend and I was really happy to see her. She is grown a compleat little Matron. She looks I think much older than Mrs S. and has more compleatly lost her beauty than I thought possible for so young a woman.[16]

Throughout the performance Dick sat behind Betsy's seat. He had put on weight since she last saw him and she noticed 'a good deal of scurvy in his face'. But her chief impression of Eliza was one of kindness. Eliza understood very well the unenviable situation of this penniless spinster tied to a grouchy old father, and both women agreed their tactics for trying to bring the Sheridan father and son together again. A few days later Eliza and Mary called upon the Sheridans in their lodgings, apparently unexpectedly. Betsy recalled:

> At half past three enter Mrs Sheridan and Mrs Tickell. After some time they ask'd for my Father. I went down to prepare him for the Visit but he positively refused to hear of it – I used every possible argument but at last he left the Room and said he would leave the House if I persisted in urging him to what was so very disagreeable to him. I return'd a good deal vex'd to Mrs S. – and tho' I soften'd the refusal as much as possible yet I could see she was greatly hurt. I think she should not have left off seeing my Father and bringing her son as she certainly did so for a length of time after the disagreement between him and Dick. This circumstance is a very great Bar in my way. She enter'd on the subject with great warmth and from her representation you would have thought my father a most unreasonable Man who had persecuted and distrest a most affectionate and generous son. Mrs Tickell told her with her usual honesty that of course she thought her Husband right but that all retrospect had better be laid aside . . .[17]

Despite these tensions, Betsy was grateful for the continued interest Eliza showed in her during her two years in England. The gesture was by no means negligible considering the social gap between them, yet Eliza made a point of sending notes to enquire after Betsy's health, of including her in the Sheridan party wherever possible, and of making available for her a place in their box at Drury Lane. In return, Betsy became more and more fond of her sister-in-law and concerned about her. On 1 June 1785 Eliza looked in on her for a few minutes just before dinner to say 'How do you do?' The time was awkward but by now Betsy had given orders that Mrs Sheridan should never be refused entrance. Not for the first time Betsy was struck by the fact that her sister-in-law looked very pale, and as soon as Eliza rushed off to yet another engagement, Betsy scribbled a note to Alicia: 'She enquired kindly for you but did not seem so well, she complained much of her head but indeed the life she leads would kill a horse, but she says one must do as people do.'[18]

Betsy's letters to Alicia continued to provide glimpses of Eliza's day-to-day life: sitting chatting in her parlour for two hours and planning with her sister-in-law how to bring the two Sheridans together; scribbling a note to Betsy to enquire after her health; at the Handel anniversary concert with the Duchess of Devonshire; in her box at the Lane; crying at the breakfast table after parting with Tom whom they had sent away to Dr Parr's school. But these sketches are often coloured by Betsy's obvious disapproval of Eliza's hectic way of life and concern for her health. Nevertheless her opinion had little effect. By October 1786 Dick had still done nothing to put his father in the way of theatre work and Thomas Sheridan left for Dublin again, taking his daughter with him.

Betsy's worries about Eliza were justified: her sister-in-law was overworking herself to promote Dick's interests. This still involved keeping the Drury Lane accounts, reading plays, copying out Dick's speeches for the House, entertaining his friends, and playing her part in the Whig social world. She had no more children but suffered a number of miscarriages. She became instead a second mother to Mary's children, especially the oldest who was named Elizabeth after her. Despite Betsy's imaginings at the Handel concert, Eliza no longer dreamed of the theatrical career she might have had, even after hearing Nancy Storace talk about her triumphant operatic career in Milan and Vienna.[19] Music had somehow departed from Eliza's life. She rarely performed now, even at private gatherings. She once tried another form of artistic expression, an opera entitled *The Haunted Village*, but foolishly handed her manuscript to her husband to look at. He lost it – or claimed to have lost it. On reflection, she realised that he would never have tolerated another Sheridan as successful playwright. Frustrated, she set her heart on a retired life in the country, so that Dick might appease their financial worries by disposing of his Drury Lane interests and buying an annuity with the proceeds. But though he was always hard pressed by his three roles of theatre manager, politician and socialite he never seriously contemplated such a course. Rush, bustle, excitement and intrigue were meat and drink to Sheridan.

With tears Eliza packed off Tom to go to school at Dr Parr's early in 1786, but as the summer came on, the parliamentary term ended and the theatres closed, she, Mary and their husbands were free to take a jaunt into Dorset. Her spirits lifted and there followed the most care-free time of her life in the company of the two people she loved best. For Mary's sake she was prepared even to tolerate Tickell. They had all been invited to stay at Lord Palmerston's house at Broadlands in Hampshire, and it was from there on 14 August that she reported to Mehetabel Canning:

> here we are . . . at Broadlands, where we arriv'd to dinner . . . There you would have seen a very beautiful Place, a comfortable House, a good-nature'd, Poetical, Stuttering Viscount, and a pleasing, unaffected Woman, who tho' She did squeeze thru' the City Gates into a Viscountess, bears her bustling Honours without shaking them at you every Moment. There you w[oul]d have seen Water Works by Day, and Fire-works by Night. The first perform'd by your dearly beloved Brother in the Faith, [an ironic reference to the pagan Sheridan] and his Dear Brother-in-law . . . by going every Morning in different Boats, on the River wh[ic]h runs thro' Lord P's Grounds, and splashing one another till one confesses himself conquer'd by running away, after w[hic]h they us'd to come puffing to us like two Tritons in a Sea piece . . . dripping from all parts . . .[20]

The breezy tone is maintained to describe a clergyman's wife, a Mrs Parton, whom Eliza had known many years before at Bath and who was now oddly 'more blooming, more youthful, more everything of that kind than ever I remember her'. Her friend Miss Harvey was just as 'smartly ugly' as when she used to traipse on the Parade there.

After Broadlands, they went two miles out of their way to call on 'poor Mrs F.', and then proceeded to Christchurch:

> where our gentlemen promis'd to meet us at dinner – but having seen all the Curiosities of the Place . . . clamber'd up to the top of the Tower at the risque of our Necks . . . and admir'd a fine Head of Beautiful Brown Hair w[hic]h had been taken up on the Skull of a woman that had been buried 300 Years, ornamented with Ribbon in the fashion of those Days, we return'd to our Inn, eat our boil'd Chicken, and having some reason to suppose our Gentlemen were gone on some frolick, and had left us to our own discretions, we thought

proper to proceed on our Journey without them, and having left them a Letter of Instruction, drove to Wimborn, where we always Intended to sleep – we waited with great patience till Eleven o'Clock, and then I confess my Courage began to fail me, for having discovered by this time that they were gone over from Lymington to the Isle of Wight, and that from thence they meant to coast it to Christchurch my Horror of the Water acted so powerfully on my busy Mind, that I was completely wretched . . . at one o'clock I sent off an Express to Christchurch to gain some tidings of them, thank God my fears were soon remov'd, as the man return'd in a Quarter of an Hour, having met a Servant coming to order Supper for them at that Hour – as my fears subsided my Anger rose, and . . . I went to Bed and left them to eat their Supper by day light . . .[21]

The only way to cope with such callous and inconsiderate behaviour was to tolerate it, but it was some hours before the 'naughty boys' were forgiven. Then the party drove on to Weymouth, where the sisters took a warm bath as preparation for a sea bathe the following morning. But Mary did not swim: she was not feeling well. The painful stitch in her side lasted for three or four days.

She never really got better, coughing her way through the following winter and spring, and by May 1787 it was clear to Tickell and to Eliza that she was suffering from consumption. The disease played its usual tricks: there were times of lassitude, sweats and coughing, and others of boisterous energy and buoyant, flushed high spirits. As the days passed Mary became thinner and weaker. Her pessimistic doctor thought her only hope was to get to some spa for fresh air, good food, and healing waters. They chose the Hotwells at Clifton, Bristol.

On 15 June 1787 Eliza accompanied her sister from Queen Anne Street to Hampton Court and four days later Mary, Elizabeth and Tickell left for the Hotwells. Their journey was to take them via Salt Hill, Reading, Speen Hill and Cirencester. From each inn or room at which they stopped for one or two nights to allow Mary to recover her strength, Eliza wrote an account of their journey to Mehetabel Canning. She was just as close a friend to Mary as she was to Eliza and although Mrs Canning's husband 'Stratty'[22] had just died, knowledge of this was kept from Mary for fear of its effect upon her. At times it seemed that she was well aware of her likely end but in periods of apparent remission she talked cheerfully about plans for the future.

On Mary's last night in London Eliza wrote to Mehetabel Canning that she was already 'inclin'd to despair about her'. At Reading she wrote again of her miserable forebodings, apologising that she did so to one already 'tutor'd in affliction'. Mary was beginning to spit blood and her condition, Eliza said, had 'struck a damp in my Heart'. Though she had laughed, she said, 'in our giddy Hours . . . nobody has more true Religion at heart than I have, tho' I profess to think less seriously of forms and Ceremonies than some do'.[23] At Chippenham Mary was so ill that the travellers stayed all night. Tickell had to get his wife a room in a private house because 'the inn (was) a sad dirty Place, where nobody thinks of sleeping'.

This long pilgrimage to the Hotwells was one of the defining experiences of Eliza's life. Until then she behaved as if human existence were one of Dick's comedies, all exuberance, style and wit, just like the thrilling adventure she had started on when she and Dick first ran away. The vexations of theatre business, reverses in politics, lack of money, and her husband's infidelities had not really disturbed her equanimity. But now with the threat to Mary's life, perhaps for the first time she seemed to sense the doom hanging over her family. Since the earliest nightingales, Tom, Sam and Maria departed, the nest had grown strangely empty of the young geniuses with whom she had grown up in Bath.

They arrived in Bristol on 25 June and Eliza wrote from Clifton to say that Mary was a little better. She hoped against all evidence that the magic of the sulphurated waters had begun to work: 'She woke this Morning very much refresh'd and in great Spirits, we took her down to the Wells, and She walk'd with the assistance of T[ickell] and me, across the Pump Room, to the Pump, with more strength than She has done [for] a long time – at her return, She eat her breakfast with relish, and afterwards slept'. Later, however, Mary became unwell again and had to go to bed with a sleeping draught. Eliza confessed:

the Dear Creature does not seem apprehensive herself of her Danger, and at times talks chearfully [sic], and lays Schemes for the future, that rend my Heart when I listen and look at her – we have got a very good Airy House on the Hill but the Weather is very unfavourable. It has rain'd constantly, and we were not able to get to the Wells the second time today for the Damp, w[hic]h likewise prevents her from receiving the Benefit of the Air, but I hope to God it will clear up tomorrow – for we want every Advantage and assistance Nature can give.[24]

Mary lingered on another month and by 22 July Eliza wrote that in the previous week they had been daily expecting 'the fatal event to relieve her from the most dreadful sufferings'. And then this sophisticated woman, imbued with the deistic views of her class, almost imploringly attempted to argue out the ethics of death and judgement in these letters to her pious friend Metahabel:

you perhaps would have thought it right to undeceive her – but I trust it is better not. She has no need of preparation – her life has been as actively Virtuous, and as free from Sin as Human frailty will allow. I do not think the Supreme Being whatever is its Nature can be influenc'd by our vain supplications to reward or punish. The first & greatest of his Attributes is Mercy – and I can never bring my Heart to believe, that fore-knowing he c[oul]d create us poor Wretches to Doom us to everlasting Punishment in another World. I am convinced my Mary will be happy eternally I have Confidence and faith in the goodness and justice of God . . .[25]

In late July, Thomas Linley, his wife, and Ozias arrived at the Wells to take a last farewell of Mary and on 27 July she died.

No blow afflicted Eliza as greviously as this loss of the enchanting youthful companion who stood by her side for Gainsborough's portrait. She had lost the dearest friend of her life, the woman she referred to as 'my more than sister'. Her immediate impulse, once the burial at Wells Cathedral was over, was to quit the 'House of Mourning' and to take charge of Mary's three children, Elizabeth, Richard and Samuel, which Tickell had agreed.

Mary's death taught Eliza Sheridan two things. The first was medical. She now understood very well that at any time she too might contract the same disease as her sister: if she saw it she would know it and would not, she told Mehetabel, 'mistake any alarming symptom'. Secondly, though she had continued to play her part in the hedonistic society her husband loved, she had little enjoyment in it. Mary's death had made her a graver, more thoughtful woman. But it was partly also due to Mehetabel Canning's influence that she became a moral being. Nevertheless her later course was perhaps not quite one that the Quaker lady would have wished for her.

CHAPTER 25

Indian Summer

While Eliza was busy nursing her sister, Dick Sheridan was engaged in an enterprise which was to make him at least for a short time a chief player in the national political drama and the star of two great parliamentary occasions. These events seemed to promise him promotion to the highest level of government.

The first of these was the question of India. It was India that had brought the Whigs down. The reception given in 1783 to Fox's India Bill – when jealous of its privileges, the East India Company had conspired with the King and Pitt to overthrow the Whig government – proved that corruption and money-grubbing could outdo the country's democracy. Four years later the Whigs were still burning with indignation. However, their chance to punish the East India shareholders came in 1785 with the return from the subcontinent of a rather undistinguished-looking, fifty-two year old man. He was the chief servant of the Company and also Governor General of India. His name was Warren Hastings.

For years past stories had reached England of the plundering and corruption practised by East India officials, of the numerous 'nabobs' returning home from India enriched by extortion and loaded with ill-gotten wealth which they converted to untaxable diamonds. For this reason successive governments under Lords North and Rockingham attempted to curb such activities and bring company officials under parliamentary control. They had been largely unsuccessful.

Then in 1785 Edmund Burke discovered someone whom he felt might provide the Whigs with their just revenge. Philip Francis had been a member of the council appointed in the early eighties which went to India to root out corruption in public life. He knew little of the country. By contrast the Governor General of India, Hastings, had lived most of his life there. He understood the culture, spoke native languages and respected local traditions. His rule was pragmatic: that is to say he sternly repressed large scale corruption by senior officials but tolerated the vast apparatus of small bribes which by custom oiled the workings of the country's finances. A struggle ensued between them but eventually Francis was defeated and left for home; Hastings meanwhile went from success to success. Before he came back to England he had enlarged British India, fought off French influences in the subcontinent, and substantially increased his company's profits.

But Frances could not forgive Hastings his success. He landed in England before his rival and soon began to fill the ear of Edmund Burke with tales of the wickedness of the Company's rule. By his account, the Governor General was the source of all corruption in India. When Hastings at last arrived home, intending to enjoy his fortune of £100,000 and fully expecting to receive a peerage, he found instead that he was widely regarded as a criminal. Soon he was arraigned for impeachment before the House of Commons. Burke was so anxious to involve Dick Sheridan in the proceedings as a prosecutor that he wrote to Eliza beforehand:

> I am sure you will have the goodness to excuse the liberty I take with you, when you consider the interest which I have and which the public have . . . in the use of Mr Sheridan's abilities. I know that his mind is seldom unemployed; but then, like all such great and vigorous minds, it takes an eagle flight by itself, and we can hardly bring it to rustle along the ground with us birds of mean wing, in coveys. I only beg, that you will prevail on Mr Sheridan to be with us this day, at half past three, in the Committee. Mr Wombell, the Paymaster of Oude, is to be examined there today. Oude is Mr Sheridan's particular province . . .[1]

Oudh (or 'Oude' as Burke preferred) certainly was.

Hastings attended the opening and Sheridan – who had agreed to act as one of the prosecutors – must have marvelled with many others that this pale little man, dressed in a red suit and only five foot six inches high, should have once ruled a subcontinent.[2] The first charge against him concerning his conduct in the war against the

Rohilla tribesmen was presented by Burke and strongly supported by Fox. Since Pitt had decided against the charge and his Tory majority naturally followed his lead, the motion to impeach was defeated by 119 votes to 67. Following on from this it was generally assumed that Pitt was Hastings' ally and that therefore the Governor General's reputation was in no danger. Pitt however wanted both to control the company in India and to emphasise his independent stance. When the second charge was presented on 13 June 1786 concerning the collector of Benares, Chait Singh, Pitt voted once more against Hastings. This time the move to impeach was carried by 119 votes to 79. Everything now depended upon the next charge: it alleged that Hastings had conspired with Asaf-ud-daula, the Nawab of Oudh, to extort the private fortunes of the Begums, his own mother and grandmother. This charge was to be presented by Dick Sheridan.

The progress of the impeachment proceedings was excessively slow and it was not until 7 February 1787 that he first rose to address members. His speech of that day came to be regarded as one of the greatest pieces of parliamentary oratory of the century. Once and for all it was demonstrated to the House that though it numbered among its members such fine orators as Fox, Burke and Pitt, it was Dick Sheridan who excelled and set the impeachment proceedings alight. True, Burke had got the business under way by accepting the doubtful evidence of Francis, and it was Burke who had needled Dick into supporting him. But it was Dick who endowed the hearings with a solemn grandeur elevating them to the status of a crusade against the brutality visited upon millions of subjects of the British monarch throughout the vast subcontinent.

His theme was humanity and he decorated it magnificently. For five-and-a-half hours members listened with rapt attention while he painted scenes of a sunburnt land, of helpless dark-eyed women, of treacherous plots, of avarice, cunning, brutality and rape. The story they heard was immensely detailed. Dick and Eliza had assembled a huge dossier of evidence from statements, letters and official reports, and these he twisted into a skein of narrative which was by turns pathetic, mysterious, dramatic and splendid. He spoke rapidly and fluently, his voice rising and falling in tones of mystery, horror, outrage and pity. His language was gorgeously caparisoned, like some great rajah's favourite she-elephant. With noble and impassioned sentiments, Dick told the House how he saw the Begums as representative of countless numbers of oppressed Indians. The justice these women cried out for was universal in its implications. Even though after Hasting's machinations the Begums remained highly-privileged and very wealthy aristocratic women, Dick Sheridan persisted in regarding them as ladies in distress. He could never tolerate any form of cruelty, especially to women, and he could not bear to see them suffer. Thus in attacking Hastings, he was displaying his own gallantry. This knight errant spoke on right through the day, and as wisps of evening fog began to creep through the House and the candles were placed before the Speaker's chair, he came to his conclusion. Dick knew very well how to work up an audience and the language of his final flourish was both idealistic and sexually climactic. *The London Chronicle* reported the end of Dick's speech, noting that there were many factions and parties in the House, and that:

> There was scarcely a subject on which they were not broken and divided into sects . . . But when inhumanity presented itself, it found no division among them. They set upon it as their common enemy, as if the character of the land were involved; in their zeal for its ruin they left it not till it was completely overthrown. It was not given to the House, as it was to the officers (to behold) the objects of their compassion (and their) ecstatic emotions of gratitude in the instant of deliverance. They could not behold the workings of the hearts, the quivering lips, the trickling tears, the loud and yet tremulous (?) joys of millions whom their vote of this night would snatch or save from the tyranny of corrupt favour.[3]

It is difficult for us to credit the emotionalism which greeted this oratory. Members cheered, clapped, embraced one another and burst into tears. Burke pronounced the speech to be unequalled in record or tradition: Pitt – not one given to hyperbole – declared that 'an abler speech had, perhaps, never been delivered' and another political opponent, Sir Gilbert Elliot, wrote that:

> This last night, though the House was up soon after one, and I was in bed before two, I have not slept one wink. Nothing whatever was the matter with me, except the impression of what had been passing still vibrating in my brain . . . You may

241

imagine the quantity of matter [the speech] contained. It was by many degrees the most excellent and astonishing performance I ever heard, and surpasses all I had ever imagined possible in eloquence and ability . . . It is impossible to describe the feelings he excited. The bone rose in my throat . . .[4]

This speech had the same effect on other members. His motion on the Begums of Oudh was passed by 175 votes to 68, and the decision to impeach Hastings became inevitable.

The proceedings became the most popular show in town, and Dick Sheridan the man of the hour. His oratory drew larger crowds than even *The School for Scandal*. Amongst the general adulation, relatives felt it a privilege to be connected with him. His toadying brother Charles wrote from Dublin to congratulate him on the high credit he had done to his country (ie Ireland), while Alicia's letter to Eliza declared: 'I wish you joy – I am sure you feel it: "O moments worth all ages past, and all that are to come". You may laugh at my enthusiasm if you please – I glory in it'.[5] The proceedings were almost too much for Eliza. She sat with Mrs Siddons while Burke formally introduced the motion to impeach Hastings and at the climax of his speech the great actress dissolved into tears, while she herself fainted away. When Dick's turn came she was pale as death and almost incapable from agitation. Years of her own life were invested in this moment, for she had often toiled at Bruton Street from breakfast to the early hours searching through documents, transcribing letters and organising her husband's notes. At last she realised the enormity of his success, and she was flushed with ecstasy. She even dared to think that she too might claim a little of the credit; on reflection, however, she acknowledged to herself that this triumph belonged entirely to Dick, her man of men, the prodigy she had married.

Unfortunately Dick had to go through the whole business again. It was the Commons who decided that Hastings was to be impeached but it was the Lords, who constituted the high court of Parliament, that had to try him. Proceedings began in Westminster Hall in the summer of '88, with 186 peers present. It was an absolute sell-out. Ticket touts demanded and got £50 for standing room to hear Dick Sheridan speak. As might have been expected, he was selected to prosecute the charge concerning the Begums of Oudh, and booked to speak on 3 June. So once again Eliza and he sat up all of the previous night going through the evidence.

From six a.m. that morning the approaches to Westminster Hall were crowded with people trying to get in, and by ten o'clock the hall was packed with hundreds of spectators, many in full morning dress. They included the Prince of Wales, and the Duke of Orleans; in fact almost every important figure in London society. Both Dick and Eliza understood full well the danger he ran on this occasion: It could be an anti-climax. Dick had had to decide whether he should simply repeat his previous speech, which might bore his audience, or deliver an entirely new address, which might disappoint them. He chose novelty. His three-day speech was another tremendous rhetorical display, stuffed with argument, exhortation, and morality, garnished with a language rich in metaphor and conceit, and delivered with a solemn grandeur of tone. But most telling was its simple conclusion, when, breathing heavily and apparently close to collapse, Dick finished with the words: 'My Lords, I have done', and sank into Burke's arms.

Sir Gilbert Elliot made a note of the last day: 'He was finer yesterday than ever. I believe there were few dry eyes in the assembly; and as for myself, I never remember to have cried so heartily and so copiously on any public occasion'.[6] The historian Edward Gibbon had been present throughout the speech, and was especially flattered by Sheridan's reference to his 'luminous' (or was voluminous?) page. Gibbon, like many observers, had been concerned by signs of Dick's increasing weakness and illness throughout the speech, but calling on him the day afterwards, was amazed to find the great orator not only gleeful, but fit and well. The whole scenario of illness and exhaustion, and the collapse into Burke's arms, had been contrived effects. He was, noted Gibbon dryly, 'a good actor'.

Eliza, however, was truly exhausted. She had done nothing else for weeks but prepare for these proceedings, supplying the detail to her husband's argument which, to judicious listeners at least, was perhaps more persuasive than all his rhetoric. The resulting tension and excitement had taken a considerable toll of her health. It was four whole days before she was recovered sufficiently to write to Alicia LeFanu:

I have delayed writing till I could gratify myself and you by sending you the news of our dear Dick's triumph! – of our triumph, I may call it; for, surely, no one in the slightest degree connected with him, but must feel proud and happy. It is impossible, my dear woman, to convey to you the delight, the astonishment, the adoration he has excited in the breasts of every class of people! Even party prejudice has been overcome by a display of genius, eloquence and goodness which no one with anything like a heart about them, could have listened to without being the wiser and the better for the rest of their lives. What must my feelings be! – you can only imagine. To tell you the truth it is with some difficulty that I can 'let down my mind', as Mr Burke said afterwards, to talk or think on any other subject. But pleasure, too exquisite becomes pain, and I am at this moment suffering for the delightful anxieties of last week . . . I hope by next week we shall be quietly settled in the country, and suffered to repose, in every sense of the word; for indeed we have both of us been in a state of constant agitation, of one kind or another, for some time back.[7]

When Dick Sheridan first delivered his Commons speeches for the Hastings impeachment, it seemed they would be the making of him. At a time when his friends were out of office, conversely the Hastings case brought him employment, an aim in life, and enormous fame. Yet as the years dragged on, and Pitt's hold on power became ever more secure, the achievement was gradually revealed for what it was – mere rhetoric. After Hastings was finally acquitted in 1795, by chance he and Dick Sheridan bumped into each other at Brighton, and were introduced by the Price of Wales. Dick immediately began to excuse his previous antipathy to Hastings by claiming that it was political, not personal, and that no one had more respect for Hastings than he. 'Old Hastings said with great gravity that "it would be a great consolation to him in his declining days if Mr Sheridan would make that sentence more public"; but Sheridan was obliged to mutter and get out of such an engagement as best he could.'[8] By that time, Dick understood very well that the Hastings business had simply been a dazzling chimera. He had wasted his talent and worn out his wife's health in a cause which counted for absolutely nothing.

CHAPTER 26

Last Stages

About seven weeks after Dick Sheridan had made his Westminster Hall speech an unusual couple picked their way down the gangway from the Irish packet at Liverpool. The coughing man was sixty-nine years old, heavily built and with an extraordinarily mannered way of talking; the companion whom he so abruptly ordered about his daughter. She was thirty, rather plain, and evidently did not resent his sharp temper because she answered him mildly and took great care for his comfort. Once off the boat they enquired about the first coach for Chester, announcing their destination as Crewe Hall. After a two-year absence Thomas and Betsy Sheridan had returned to England.

The old actor did not intend to stay long. Despite the fact that he had a son, grandson and daughter-in-law in England he still argued that he had no family left there. Besides, he was not well; he was unable to digest most foods and he suffered terribly from cold even in the hottest summer. His immediate remedies were enormous roasting fires and, now his daughter had persuaded him to give up spirits, as much Madeira wine as he could afford. Yet he knew full well that these things could only briefly restore his comfort; what he really wanted was to progress to London by easy stages and then set off from some south coast port for Lisbon, where he intended to retire cheaply, just as Henry Fielding had done thirty-four years before him.[1] He dreamed of warming himself into life again like some ancient lizard come out into a southern sun. But though he talked loudly about his plan his daughter said nothing.

Staying briefly with Mrs Crewe at the Hall they then took the coach as far as Stone in Staffordshire. There an odd thing happened at the inn. Each dish of their dinner was brought in by a new set of waiters, and on each occasion there seemed to be far too many of them for such a humble place. Not till the next morning did Betsy discover the reason for this prolific attendance: somehow the innkeeper had discovered the identity of their elderly guest, and every single one of his numerous family had begged to take in the dishes so that they might catch a glimpse of 'Mr Sheridan's father'.[2] Betsy dared not tell him for he would have been furious to have been regarded as merely an appendage of the famous son with whom, after all, he was still not reconciled.

Things were no different when they got to London, where they were welcomed by their old friends Mrs Kitty Angelo and Doctor Morris. At dinner the serving man, Thompson, would not stop talking about the famous speech that young Mr Sheridan had recently made. Even old Sheridan's most fearsome scowls could not shut him up. Thompson was loyal but not very bright and understood only that 'dear Master Richard' was now 'the first Man in England', which he repeatedly reminded old Sheridan. What gave Thompson most pleasure was to repeat over and over the last words of Dick Sheridan's recent speech in Westminster Hall – he did not understand the rest but loved the simple drama of the moment – My Lords I have done', he would say and then he would bow solemnly and burst into laughter.[3]

On 24 July, the day after she arrived in London, Betsy went round to Bruton Street to see her brother and his wife. When Dick first caught sight of her his eyes filled with tears; he took both her hands for some time just looking at her and then sighed and asked in a kindly way after their father. He took her into the sitting room to meet Eliza. As befitting a great political lady she was found sitting on a sofa amid a heap of gorgeous yellow and blue election ribbons, favours for Lord John Townshend's current campaign. She was just as affectionate as ever but excused herself because she said she had promised to go out canvassing and must leave almost immediately. She invited her sister-in-law to accompany her but when Betsy hurriedly explained that she had to get back to her father, Eliza contented herself by pinning one of Townshend's ribbons to her handkerchief.

Betsy had not seen Eliza since Mary's death and she noticed the great changes that event had wrought in her. Despite her current flurry of political energy, Eliza had never fully recovered her spirits since her loss. Besides that she was overworked. With Tickell's agreement she was bringing up her sister's three little children as her own, and they now treated her as their mother. Responsibility for them had become her *raison d'etre* and chief motivation for struggling against the ill health which dogged her days. The previous August she had visited Crewe Hall for the first time since Mary's death. Entering a house in which she had spent many hours writing to her sister gave her 'Heart a wring' and particularly upset her delicate constitution. As a result she developed a nervous cough and pains in the 'Hand, Breast & Bowells'. Not a woman given to hypochondria – indeed she was normally an animated person more interested in the welfare of others than her own health – so often now she found herself in a state of physical wretchedness brought on by a host of ailments. She wrote from Crewe Hall to describe her medical regimen to Mehetabel Canning:

> I know you are half angry at my writing so much without mentioning my Health, but to say the truth I am so weary & sick of advice, medicine and all the Paraphernalia of Physic, that I detest the thought of even mentioning the Subject – but for your Satisfaction I must tell you that since my last I have been at Chester to consult a very famous Physician there, under whose direction I at present am. I have been Emetic'd & dos'd the other way. I have had five horrible Leeches fasten'd to my poor Breast w[hic]h continued bleeding from eleven in the Morning till twelve at Night. I take Pills for I cannot swallow their abominable Draughts three times a day, and drink a large Cup of Hore Hound Tea after each Dose – w[hic]h is in itself as dreadful a Mass as ever came out of an Apothecary's Shop – last night, my poor Breast not quite heal'd from the Leeches, I had a Blister clapt on to amuse me –[4]

Nor had her husband been quite the support to her that she would have wished. Nowadays Dick was constantly worried about money and often left her stranded and embarrassed either at the house of friends or even in completely strange surroundings on the pretext of attending to business or simply acquiring some cash. That September he had taken her to Tunbridge Wells for a brief holiday but after a day or two with her, promptly went off to London on the plea that he must raise some money to pay their expenses and would return the following day. Though she waited 'with fidgety impatience' from breakfast to supper time he did not come.

Despairingly she went to bed, and was woken at four o'clock in the morning, when he got back. Even though such neglect was upsetting, it still hardly impinged upon the deep grief for Mary which continued to occupy her 'whole Heart & Mind'.

In October she was little better, still bitten by leeches and wrapped in warm poultices, but more able now to sympathise with others. Her heart went out especially to her father who grieved as deeply as she did. He was, she told Mehetabel, 'the shyest of creatures' and she understood very well that his timidity and depression were becoming pathological. To cheer him up she was constantly devising little schemes such as the time she sent him to ramble round Normandy with a friend. When he came to stay with her she was always trying to divert him with a 'Game of Whist or a Story Book or something of that sort'. She longed for rural peace and quiet, and dreamed of a small house in Wales where, except in the theatre season, she and Dick might be quiet and cheerful together and live quietly within their means. Of course her plans were only day-dreams. At the moment Dick could not think of giving up political life, especially now that he had become so important to the Prince of Wales. She did not press the issue. Though her spirits were still only partially recovered by the summer of 1788 when Betsy came to England, she had already resumed her old loyalties, determined once more to promote Dick's career with all the energy she could muster. To do so she planned to re-enter the fashionable world.

This was the woman Betsy Sheridan encountered swathed in Townshend's ribbons. Their first meeting was short, but three days later, Betsy's heart was gladdened when after being 'dragg'd' out by a well-meaning Kitty Angelo, she came home to find her sister-in-law sitting in the parlour with her father. Old Sheridan had little strength now to keep up past hatreds and at last Eliza's persistence had won him over. She could not have been more considerate. She apologised for the fact that both she and Dick were heavily involved in Townshend's election at that time but insisted that once it was over, her father-in-law and Betsy should come to stay with them at Deepdene, set in the peaceful Surrey countryside. She explained that Dick had recently been offered the use of this home by his friend the Duke of Norfolk, and she painted the old man a wonderful picture of the place, an ideal retreat in which he might recover his health. When Sheridan protested that they would have no room for him she made him laugh despite himself by claiming that 'Dibden' (as she called it) was 'large enough to accommodate Soloman and all his wives'. It was not beautiful, she said, but the air there was sweet and healthy. She was determined to help him get better. At Deepdene she would nurse him, amuse him, play cards with him and provide him with every comfort. Even cantankerous old Sheridan could not help but be touched by such kindness, and cautiously promised to consider going to Deepdene – provided that he had not already sailed for Lisbon. Privately Eliza was moved to pity by his stubborn independence of mind, since both she and Betsy knew that Thomas Sheridan was far too ill to undertake such a sea journey. Yet she said nothing to him, other than to suggest he go to Margate for the intervening month, where he would start to regain his strength. He agreed.

On 5 August Dick and Eliza went down to the resort where they found Betsy and her father grilling themselves in front of an enormous fire in a small house in 'the Highest part of the town'. Their lodgings comprised of a parlour, a kitchen, two good bedrooms, two garrets, with china, glass and linen provided, all for two guineas a week.[5] For the whole day Dick, Eliza and Betsy conspired to amuse the old man. Betsy told them brightly that her father loved the fresh country air of Margate and their view of the channel with its many sailing boats plying to and fro. She hoped to bathe, she said, and her father intended to try the warm sea bath the following day. Dick and Eliza told stories of London political life and Dick made them all laugh by recounting how in Bow Street, during Townshend's recent election campaign, when he heard that the justice Sir Sampson Wright had called out troops to control excitable Whig supporters, he had seized the gentleman and shaken him until his ribs rattled. Eliza told Betsy confidentially that she had made a collection to present a purse of ten guineas to a poor black man who had risked his life in protecting Charles James Fox and had got a sabre slash across the skull as a reward. Eventually the Brinsley Sheridans were obliged to say their 'goodbyes' and go back to London and their politics.

So Betsy returned to a life of daily country drives with her father, alternating at night with fires big 'enough to kill [them]' in the parlour. This process, which she referred to as 'airing and roasting' only delayed Sheridan's demise. Soon he began to complain of pains in his stomach and as a result he could hardly eat a thing. On 11 August Dick and Eliza hurried down to Margate again, only to hear Thomas Sheridan declaring that he hoped to embark for Lisbon very soon. Eliza wrote to Mehetabel:

249

S[heridan] intends to go to Margate for a short time, to see his Father who, with Miss Sheridan [Betsy] is come to England, on a hopeless Errand I think, for at his time of Life, It seems an almost impossible thing to recover a broken Constitution . . . I was really astonish'd to hear him! for I have no notion that a Sensible Man can so Deceive [*sic*] himself with a Love of Life as to be insensible to his Situation, or even hear with patience (much less propose himself) a long Voyage at 70 year[s] old, when he can scarce [*sic*] walk across the Room for feebleness & Diseise! [*sic*].[6]

Thomas Sheridan retained just enough strength to be obstinate. A local doctor, Mr Jarvis, advised him that it would not be wise to take the hot salt-water bath, so of course contrarily he did. Soon afterwards he developed a violent fever. His symptoms were sufficiently alarming for Betsy to send for Dick who came at once. Thomas Sheridan's friend, Dr Morris, who arrived at about the same time witnessed a scene of reconciliation between father and son. The old man suddenly bursting out with 'Oh! Dick, I give you a great deal of trouble'. Afterwards, Eliza wrote to tell Alicia in Dublin that: 'My Dick had the delight of seeing his poor father sensible of and grateful for the dutiful attention and affectionate tenderness shown to him, and though he acknowledged the worth of such a son too late, I thank God he did at last look on him with tenderness, and appeared touched with the anxiety he expressed about him'.[7]

Old Sheridan's final agony began. Eliza was not present but on hearing the details from Dick she later told Mehetabel Canning that 'his Death was dreadfully painful, & the Scene more shocking than you can imagine'. Betsy could not bear to describe their father's death to Alicia, save to say that Dick had seen his father 'and never quitted him till the awful moment was past – I will not dwell on the particulars'.

Thomas Sheridan died at Margate in the afternoon of 14 August. His friend and physician Dr Morris, and his younger son were with him. Immediately afterwards Dick left town with his sister Betsy, intending to return next day to supervise the interment. Thomas Sheridan's will, completed at Richmond in Yorkshire in 1774, requested that his dust should rest in the parish next to the one in which he died, so Dick made arrangements for this to be done. His father had not much to leave but he had made some small provision for both his daughters, Alicia and Betsy, and also for his elder son, Charles, even though he had recently come to dislike him. There was no mention of his younger son. In his grief Dick barely noticed: he never wanted anything more from his father than his love and approval. For some time after his father's death, he was inconsolable. Yet despite the gravity of the occasion, he promised more than he performed. He left Margate with heartfelt assurances to the vicar that he would send money to have a memorial erected over his father's grave. But the money did not materialise, and so the memorial was never built.

CHAPTER 27

Secret Service

After the death of Thomas Sheridan, Eliza took Betsy to live with her. This was no mean feat because Betsy did not easily fit into the Sheridan's social world. But Eliza insisted that Miss Sheridan should go everywhere with her, introducing the poor, dowdy young woman to her aristocratic friends at some of the grandest social occasions in London. Eliza saw Betsy as a gentlewoman, a member of the family, and a sister in distress. That status and her recent bereavement entitled her to nothing but sympathy and consideration from her relatives. Eliza wrote about her to Mehetabel Canning:

> poor thing, her Life has been a Miserable one, and She seems surpriz'd at every little attention, or at least the appearance of kindness from me. She will most probably remain with me some time – what her future Plans are I don't know. I have assured S[heridan] of my readiness to contribute to her future Comfort, & happiness, if he wished her always to remain under his Protection – and however unpleasant such an Arrangement would be to me, I sh[oul]d certainly reconcile myself to it very chearfully, if I thought it would give him any Pleasure, for I am sure his kindness to all my Family deserves any sacrifice from me, but I rather think he w[oul]d not like this scheme himself, & that some other more eligible will be thought of by and by.[1]

Not surprisingly, Betsy's devotion to her sister-in-law now became total. At Deepdene where Dick Sheridan would sometimes leave his wife for long periods Eliza had only Betsy and the Tickell children for company. Betsy wrote to tell Alicia all about it, at first naïvely

252

informing her that all was well: Mrs Sheridan seems now quite reconciled to these little absences, which she knows are unavoidable.'[2] She reported that Eliza spent much of her day at Deepdene teaching her niece Elizabeth Tickell, and with her music, books and household duties. Often before dinner the two Tickell boys, aged five and three, would be allowed to come in and say goodnight to their 'Mamma-Aunt' (as they called Eliza) and she would take all the children into the music room and play and sing to them until their bed time. They were her most loving audience.

But as time went on Betsy began to pick up on the tensions between the Sheridans, and was increasingly critical of her brother's neglect and thoughtlessness towards his wife. On one occasion at the end of September he had promised to return from London bringing fish and game with him for the four o'clock dinner. He did not turn up. Eliza was not particularly worried by such broken promises: they were routine. Left by herself she would happily have sat down to a plate of bread and cheese. But to her consternation their landlord, the 'good honest Gentleman Farmer' the Duke of Norfolk suddenly descended on them for dinner. Eliza could only order up the vegetables and such scraps of joint as were left in the house. Despite the genial Duke's amusement, Eliza was hugely embarrassed, and after dinner tried to pass matters off by taking him into the music room and singing duets with her sister Jane, until Dick bounced in, brimming over with excuses and anecdotes. Betsy watched and judged. And in her admiration for Eliza's singing, she wrote to assure Alicia that their sister-in-law still possessed: 'that same peculiar tone that I believe is hardly to be equalled in the world'.[3]

Late hours did not suit Eliza. While the Duke stayed with them she would sit up past midnight playing cribbage but Betsy noticed that she looked dreadfully tired afterwards. Things were no better when she filled in for her father at Drury Lane. Linley was still nominally responsible for providing the music there but seemed progressively confused, exhausted and incapable of the work. Fearing that he had suffered a mild paralytic attack Eliza helped him by spending hours scoring new music for the theatre. Betsy thought she was driving herself too hard and 'exhausting her spirits'.

But when she was unwell, even the company of her family became a wearing trial for Eliza. Her father was constantly depressed, complaining of pains in his head, while Mrs Linley insisted on all her guests in Norfolk Street, including Eliza, sitting up night after night for whist. Betsy hated cards and was quite sorry for Thomas Linley who was obliged both to play and to listen to his wife's 'incessant prate'. She wrote in her journals 'If the poor Man had no other cause of illness, such constant teasing would be sufficient to account for his headaches'. Mrs Linley, she concluded, was 'incurably vulgar' yet she had some redeeming qualities. She was 'really affectionate and fond of her family' where 'their health or comfort was concern'd'.[4] Her thoughtfulness, however, did not extend to her daughter. But Eliza bore all these impositions of domestic life without complaining, even though they undermined her health – resigning herself to the idea that from that time onwards she was destined to a life of growing obscurity and service to others. After all it was what she often said she longed for.

It was not to be so: she had caught the disease of restlessness from her husband. When they returned to London in the autumn of 1788 she was soon willingly caught up with him in a great political adventure which offered them both the chance of a glittering future. The King was ill. Stories of the monarch's eccentric behaviour had been circulating since July, when one morning in the early hours he had insisted on dragging the startled Dean of Worcester out of his bed, declaring excitedly to the old gentleman that together they must watch the dawn rise in his cathedral. By late November, the King's mind was deeply confused, and he was swept by irrational passions that had to be restrained. During a twelve-week period, he was raving so much that he was expected to die at almost any minute. It seemed quite certain that the Prince of Wales would soon become King, or if his father continued alive, Regent. It was a great opportunity for all the Whigs, especially Dick Sheridan.

George III had appointed Pitt as Tory Prime Minister in a House of Commons with a Whig majority. Now the Whigs hoped that his son would replace him with Fox in a Tory House and that they would come in with the succession, just as Pitt had ruled as a friend of the King. During parliamentary terms the foremost Whig statesmen of the 1780s, Fox and Burke, met the Prince almost daily either at Devonshire House or at Carlton House, his personal residence.[5] Dick Sheridan, however, was even closer to the Prince, and had become his chief confidant and drinking companion. Under the Prince's influence, Sheridan became used to consuming two or three bottles a day, and as a result by his late thirties his figure became heavy and his features red.

He was also agreeable to doing the Prince's dirty work for him, even at the cost of his own reputation. After word had gone round in 1785 that the prince had secretly and illegally married a Catholic lady, Maria Ann Fitzherbert, Fox defended the Prince's reputation and denied the rumour to the House, only to discover later that it was true. Understandably he was furious with the Prince and would not speak to him for days afterwards, refusing to represent him in the House any further. So the Prince chose Sheridan to answer on his behalf, and when a member demanded to know about the Prince of Wales's domestic arrangements, Dick got up and gave an answer so equivocal that it earned him the contempt of the House.

This close friendship with the Prince now came to dominate the Sheridans' lives and induced Dick to a lifestyle far beyond anything the Drury Lane box office could finance. The Prince was often present at supper parties in Bruton Street where Sheridan offered him lavish hospitality. Inevitably he over-reached himself, and ran up huge bills for goods and services with the tradesmen and servants of Mayfair. Most people would have been arrested for it and imprisoned with other debtors in the Marshalsea, or at least shut up in a 'sponging house'.[6] But because of his position as a Member of Parliament, Sheridan was protected from arrest. Nevertheless, creditors had the right to seize his goods and the house in Bruton Street was frequently under threat from the bailiffs, sometimes with bizarre consequences. On one cold night, when the Prince of Wales was at dinner with the Sheridans, the bailiffs stood outside stamping their feet, waiting for their chance to serve him with a writ for the distraint of goods. The story goes that Sheridan took pity on them, invited them in, and let them keep warm by waiting on the table till his guest left. Such was the influence of the Prince on Sheridan, and it was ruining him.

But in December 1788, it looked as if he would get his reward. If his friend became King, then the least he might expect was to be promoted to Chancellor of the Exchequer, and his personal financial difficulties would be over. All that was required was for George III to die.

The King refused to do so. Raving he may have been, but he was physically strong. So throughout that time which came to be known as the 'Regency Crisis', the Prince of Wales and his brother and ally, the Duke of York, waited and watched and took advice and conspired about what they should do. The question was, should the Prince press to be made Regent at once, or wait to see whether the King was likely to recover his senses? The Prince had two enemies:

Queen Charlotte, who had never favoured her son, and William Pitt, who knew very well that if the Prince became Regent he himself was unlikely to remain Prime Minister very long. But his allies were the Whigs. Unfortunately Charles James Fox was in Bologna at the start of the crisis. Though he was sent for immediately and travelled home faster than was good for his health, he did not arrive in London until 24 November. In the meantime Dick Sheridan who some called the Prince of Wales' Prime Minister was his chief adviser, and so, during this frantic struggle for power, Bruton Street became the headquarters of the Prince's party. Eliza, as the mistress of Bruton Street, played a central role in the making of history.

Events at the house were recorded by Eliza and Betsy. On 11 November Eliza wrote: 'the times are Eventful and Interesting the K'[ing]s situation is desperate – his death is not Immediately apprehended tho' his life cannot be long – his Senses are irrecoverably gone – a Regency will be formed – the Prince is warmly attach'd to S – whatever Change takes place (and change of some sort is inevitable)'. A few days later she wrote that the King's madness was more and more confirmed every day and that in the House Pitt would move a fortnight's adjournment of any decision on the regency question. She believed he would get his way but also that in the end 'all wise People [would agree] that there must be a Regency, in which the Prince would be 'absolutely invested' with 'royal Powers'. Dick, she said, was 'harrass'd to death'.[7]

Meanwhile, as Eliza watched events, Betsy watched her. Though she was never impressed by the 'grand people' in the Sheridan's social life, Betsy was very concerned about the possible effects of these intense days upon her sister-in-law's health. On 16 November she reported: 'I am here in the midst of news and politics. Ever since breakfast Mrs S – has had a constant Levée and the present situation of the king of course the only topic of conversation.' On 21 November she reported that they had dined home alone with 'Tickell and Richardson as usual' but that Dick was so engaged in thought he hardly seemed to see or hear them. 'Chère Frère' she told Alicia, was the head of all their consultations, and if things 'turn out as we have reason to expect [he will be] just what he chuzes'. After the dinner party everyone except Dick went to the theatre to see Mrs Jordan, and then 'the usual intimates . . . came home to eat oysters. I now have got the method of going to bed as I could not hold out a month of Mrs Sheridan's town life.'[8]

Eliza's work was not restricted to Crisis management. She still had

Mary's children to look after, and she was still quietly helping her father by taking on as much as she could of his duties as musical director of Drury Lane. In January, writing late without candles in 'utter darkness', she reported that though she had been very ill, she was just finishing a musical chore for her 'poor Father', who had been too unwell to attend to it. This was probably the orchestration of a song in Stephen Storace's comic opera *The Haunted Tower*.[9]

She was also engaged in copying more important documents. On his return to England, Fox had made a disastrous error. Announcing to the House of Commons that any Prince of Wales had a right to the Regency without the consent of Parliament he opened himself up to immense criticism. Pitt had no difficulty in beating off this proposal and inaugurating a deliberately prevaricating debate on the nature of the Regent's powers. However, even he could not put the matter off indefinitely, and in reluctantly preparing a Regency Bill he sent off what Betsy Sheridan called: 'impertinent restrictions to the Prince and in an impertinent manner by a common Livery Servant'. The Prince now had to consider his response carefully. He deputed Loughborough, Burke, Fox and Elliot to draw up appropriate replies for him, and gave all their best versions to Sheridan, so that he might distil them into one lucid, diplomatically couched letter. Dick of course turned to Eliza for help. He made a précis of the various suggested drafts, she amended his version, made further suggestions, and copied out the resulting letter. It was some thirteen hundred words long, and as might be expected, each clause was couched in language both stiff and cautious:

> The Prince has only to add that if Security for his Majesty's repossessing his rightful Government, whenever it shall please Providence in Bounty to this Country to remove the Calamity with which he is afflicted, be any part of the Object of this Plan, the Prince has only to be convinced, that any Measure is necessary, or even conducive to that End, to be the first to urge it as the preliminary and permanent Consideration of any Settlement in which he could consent to share.[10]

Eliza later explained to Mehetabel the role she had played:

> The P[rince of Wales] has consented to take the Regency even tho' all Mr Pitt's Restrictions should be carried, and he has

257

written an Answer to the Ministers explaining his Reasons for so doing. I s[houl]d think the Answer will appear soon in the Papers – It is vastly well done, and I am sure must all unprejudiced Persons love the P & hate Pitt; I have had a great hand in it, for I copied it twice, and the Copy actually sent to the Cabinet was written by Me and signed by the Prince. I intend when he is Regent to claim something good for myself for Secret Service.[11]

It is doubtful whether any other common-born English woman in the entire eighteenth century ever played a closer part in the struggle for supreme political power.

Now all eyes were on the Regency Bill in the Commons which Pitt had so successfully delayed. The atmosphere was tense at Bruton Street that January. Eliza would sometimes sit up without a fire till six in the morning to hear the result of the previous night's debate. Betsy presents a vivid picture to Alicia of the Sheridan sitting room in the evenings, with Richardson gossiping, Tickell fidgeting and sentimentalising over the dead Mary, and Eliza herself, white with fatigue and worry. 'They are all' said Betsy, 'here upon the look out'.[12] So they were. They knew that their fortunes would be made the moment that Sheridan burst through the door to announce that George III was dead.

But by the next month, though Sheridan was 'quite worn out with fagging' in the Prince's cause – so much so that even when he tried to take a day off he was dragged from home by the Duke of York and the Prince himself – all this effort seemed to be getting no-where. New rumours were circulating. On 13 February Eliza broke the astonishing news to Mehetabel: 'I verily believe this tormenting K[ing] is going to recover in earnest', she wrote. The rumours were right. Two weeks later it was clear the King had regained his sanity, and the Regency Bill was dropped. In April Sheridan, with his customary cheerfulness, attended the great service of thanksgiving for the King in St Paul's Cathedral. Nevertheless the appalling implications of the King's recovery for the Sheridans' personal fortunes were quite apparent. Pitt was once again pre-eminent and there was now no hope that the Whigs might return to power in the foreseeable future. It was even less likely that Sheridan himself would ever regain office. Now his political career was in ruins, they were to be denied the financial security which Eliza craved. With little to look forward to but a life plagued by creditors and bailiffs, she dreaded her future.

CHAPTER 28

Baby Talk

The Duke of Devonshire was 'Canis'. That is what they called him, 'Canis', the dog. His mistress, Lady Elizabeth Foster, was 'Racoon' because she had a pointed face. His wife, and Racoon's intimate friend, The Duchess, was 'Rat' and her lover, Crawford 'Fish'. Another of the Duchess's close friends, possibly Charles Grey, was referred to as 'Tamphosbine'. The ladies of Devonshire House liked nicknames and baby talk.[1]

Eliza walked warily among these aristocratic beasts. They were friends but she kept them at arm's length. Their language was not hers. Of course the Linley brothers and sisters had also used their own private 'little language' but this had been affectionate and humorous rather than suggestive. She too had made up nicknames for people. She had privately referred to her father-in-law as 'old surly boots' an expression which she defended because it had done him no harm. Anyway he *had been* surly. And sometimes when she and Dick were parted, she would write him letters in her little girl's language. She knew he liked that:

> I did not mean to lecture 'ee my soul, in my first letter; me only vex that you should ever fret yourself or be unhappy without the shadow of a cause . . .

or:

> Nothing to say but I love 'ee dearer than life and miss 'ee ever so bad.[2]

and after having read out part of Dick's letter to the Crewes:

259

And how I was envied by them . . . for having such a kind good natur'd attentive little Body of a Husband, but I told 'em 'ee didn't love me a bit better than I deserv'd, for that I cared for nothing in the world but 'ee.[3]

But as Eliza grew older she tired of this sort of talk and began to write to Dick simply and without any pretences, just to tell him how she missed him and wanted him to come back to her: 'my dearest love . . . I know you will like to have a line from me every day and I am willing to set you a good example, but I have nothing to say but that I love you dearer than my life and miss you ever so bad.' This is how she wanted to be with him, direct and sincere, for her sensibility was maturing and she was no longer content with the role of a decorative doll wife. Yet somehow Sheridan could not respond to such conversation. He understood wit and speech-making, flirting and flattering, but quiet, sober, loving talk was beyond him. He simply could not take anything seriously. Emotionally he was still a little boy.

By the spring of 1788 the Sheridans were apparently once again the devoted couple that Fanny Burney had described nine years earlier: 'they are extremely happy in each other. He evidently adores her, and she as evidently idolises him.'[4] His long liaison with 'Amoret' (Frances Crewe) was evidently over and Eliza had forgiven him. He had always regarded these affairs as a species of amusement. Eventually Mrs Crewe's self-pitying, depressive nature got him down. She as also indiscreet which exasperated him immensely. Even after he had broken the affair off, she still tried to extend and prolong it. She gave it retrospective importance by discussing it with their mutual friends. Gossip was meat and drink to her. From Crewe, Sheridan wrote to the Duchess of Devonshire:

[Mrs Crewe] has asked me a thousand questions [about the Duchess's latest affair] to all of which I have answered as I would to the town Cryer if I was questioned by him. I believe that she feels that my heart is shut against her, and behaves accordingly . . . she is of an unhappy disposition, and there are moments when, in spite of her behaviour, I feel inclined to pity her.[5]

What made the situation worse for Frances Crewe was that

another of the great Whig hostesses, the charming Mrs Bouverie, now began to pursue Sheridan. Eliza had to put up with it. Furthermore she was obliged to endure these women when they welcomed her to their homes and called her their 'dearest friend', for Dick still insisted that they pay their annual visits to Chatsworth, Wynnstay, Delapré Abbey and Crewe Hall. In their splendid salons she would sit nightly at the card tables glancing up from time to time towards the great mirrors to catch glimpses of the small but intense dramas of jealousy played out behind her back. Betsy Sheridan, in a letter from Deepdene on 27 November 1788 left an account of the backbiting and bitchery between Frances Crewe and Mrs Bouverie. They were fighting over Sheridan:

> As to your questions concerning Mrs Crewe and Mrs Bouverie I can not entirely satisfy you as you do not know the cause of their difference. That Mrs Crewe hates Mrs B– is certain – and to such a degree as to be distress'd if they accidentally meet. Mrs B– neither seeks nor avoids her and by what had drop'd from Mrs Sheridan I fancy She is the injured person of the two. Some love affair I believe to be the origin of the quarrel. As to Mrs Crewe's coldness with regard to Mrs S– it is partly jealousy of Mrs B– to whom Mrs S– certainly gives the preference. You know also that Mrs Crewe among other Lovers (favor'd ones I mean) Has had our brother in her train. As his fame and consequence in life have increased, her charms have diminished, and passion no longer the tie between them, his affection, esteem and attentions return'd to their proper channel. And he never has seem'd or I believe never was in truth so much attach'd to his wife as of late, and this her dear friend cannot bear. And Mrs S– tells me that while they were at Crewe Hall, she took little pains to conceal her jealousy. A strange system you will say altogether and for such people to associate and disgrace the name of friendship is truly disgusting. Yet such I am told is the universal practice of the great world . . .[6]

The affair with Mrs Crewe had undermined the relationship between the Sheridans for many years and now that it was over both of them felt a strong sense of relief. Eliza did not mind Mrs Bouverie, whom she recognised as no more than a passing distraction for

Dick. She accepted that if one's husband were to figure prominently in the Devonshire House clique, one could hardly expect him to regard sexual fidelity as a cardinal virtue. She was content that he was consistently kind, both to herself and her family.

He possessed many other qualities: he was well-meaning, affectionate, cheerful and generous. And he was still the brilliant wit and talker she had married. Eliza had to weigh against these things the fact that he rarely kept his promises, that he was not always truthful, and that his vanity was at the mercy of any pretty woman who flattered him. But she forgave him his little erotic escapades. One such occasion in January when she was absent at Crewe Hall was a ball he attended for 'women of no character'.

Eliza's chief worry in 1788 was not to do with her husband's fidelity, but their profligate way of life which, she kept telling herself, could not go on. Their expenditure was vastly beyond their income. But Dick would never listen to suggestions that they should cut back, and when his drinking cronies from the Prince's clique spent their money freely, Sheridan felt that he must at least pay his share. So he entertained his friends lavishly at Bruton Street, and presented them with box seats for performances at Drury Lane, even though he was undercutting his own income.

The Lane was now a cause for concern to them both. Without telling Eliza where he got the money from, in 1788 Sheridan bought out Ford's share, and as a result faced the prospect of even higher interest repayments. Then he found out that the building itself was not safe. In June 1789 the King's Theatre in the Haymarket burnt down and a year later the Pantheon went the same way. The builders warned Dick that the structure of Drury Lane was unsafe, as it had been built one hundred and seventeen years ago with very inflammable timbers. He knew that something would have to be done.

To add to all these troubles, when he paid his daily visits to the theatre, Sheridan now found himself pursued by creditors demanding their premiums. He could not pay them but would often buy them off with free boxes at the next performance. Once again he was mortgaging part of his income. Nor could he easily dodge the impoverished actors, whom, by a curious oversight, he had neglected to pay, or the small tradesmen who clustered round the stage door hoping to get their bills attended to. Dick Sheridan had become a master of tricks of evasion. For example, he would go into the box office early, so that unnoticed he might quickly raid the till for his daily drinking money. Sometimes, however, he would duck out onto Covent Garden only to find himself confronted by a desperate comedian or a shopkeeper waving his bill. At times like these he had to bluff them. He would make promises to them, and make them laugh with tall tales and jokes. More often than not he would get away with it.

After the Regency crisis Eliza realised that Sheridan had no future in politics and wanted him to concentrate his energy on his theatre. She told him so in a note written in 1790 when he was recontesting his Stafford seat:

> I am more than ever convinced we must look to other resources for wealth and independence, and consider politics merely as an amusement – and in that light 'tis best to be in Opposition, which I am afraid we are likely to be for some years again.[7]

Dick could never see it like that. He was still a political animal; he loved intrigue, policy, the clash of parties, speech-making, the hustings, and the House. He would never give it up.

Then once again he began to neglect Eliza. At first the reason was not obvious. He would explain that business in the House or the theatre compelled him to go back to London for a few days, and promptly leave her stranded at some large country house. She did not argue: she had become used to it. Once in the late 1780s he left her for a whole summer at Delapré, and she reverted to using her baby talk to bring him back, promising to 'kiss 'ee up ever so'.[8] But these days it was no good: he was no longer susceptible. Betsy Sheridan confirmed this growing neglect. She told Alicia in April 1789 that: 'Mrs Sheridan is going to the country next week. Her sister [Jane] has gone to Norwiche [sic] and I could not decently leave her to go alone, for alone She would be, as Dick never stays two days at a time with her.'[9] From Richmond in August, Eliza wrote to tell a friend: 'I have been leading a solitary Life here till a few days ago when Mrs B[ouverie] came to settle. As for S– I really do not see him four and twenty Hours in the whole week – he has lately been most vexatiously harrass'd by Money Matters.'

At this time Eliza was still devoted to her husband's welfare. Although she appreciated the pressures he was under from his theatrical and political responsibilities, and from the demands of his 'evil genius' the Prince, nevertheless she was increasingly concerned about his drinking and tried to get him to cut down:

> When you tell me how vexed and grieved you was at not being able to speak that Monday, on account of your making yourself so ill on Sunday, would you have me say, drinking to that excess is not an abominable habit . . . ?[10]

She also warned him against a number of people he counted among his friends. One of these was his old business partner, Thomas Harris, manager of Covent Garden:

> I can't make out what business you are settling with Harris . . . I have no opinion of Mr H. nor ever had. He is selfish, that is, quite a man of the world, of course you are no match for him; but I trust you do not deceive me when you say you shall settle things well, though (as the poor sailor said) I'll be hanged if I see how, for you seem all poor and pennyless, I think, not able to play whist when the fine ladies wanted you, nor nothing.

When it came to it, in the middle of another theatrical deal he and Harris had planned, Harris went off to Boulogne leaving Dick Sheridan to pay the creditors. Once again, the bailiffs began to sniff round Bruton Street.

Despite all these worries, Eliza could still console herself with the idea that she and Dick had a marriage that had worked. He had been faithful in his fashion, unlike his romantic friend Tickell. For him, she had the most profound contempt. When Mary had died in 1787, Tickell had gone wild with grief; in fact Sheridan had to prevent him from inscribing Mary's headstone with a declaration that he, her husband, was inconsolable and would never marry again. Tickell had then spent a year 'sentimentalising' as Betsy put it, over Mary. But by July 1789 Eliza had proof that he was involved in an affair with a young woman. She told Mehetabel that when Tickell had driven her back from her stay in Richmond, he:

> kept me in the Phaeton all the way to Town during w[hich] time he never ceas'd making the most violent protestations, against any Idea of [re]Marrying – and assur'd me . . . by the Faith & Honor of a Gentleman that so far from having any

serious thoughts of Miss Q he was very unhappy at the scrape he had got into with Miss Q . . . and . . . at the very time he was uttering these Falsehoods to me he was absolutely engag'd to go with her in the very Phaeton I was in w[hic]h he had hir'd for the purpose of driving her to Eastbourne where her Brother has a House & where Mr T has a House next door.[11]

To Eliza's grim satisfaction, her original opinion of Tickell was soon confirmed. In October 1789, against the orders of her father, Richard Tickell married not Miss Q but a Miss Lee, the pretty, eighteen-year-old daughter of a sea-captain. Nevertheless he agreed that Eliza might go on bringing up her sister's three children.

This was a considerable consolation to her, especially because in the September of that year she had suffered the last of a long series of miscarriages. The Tickell business depressed her. It was, she told Mehetabel Canning, 'a hard thing after living in habits of Friendship & Confidence with a Person for such a number of Years to be oblig'd to consider them as worthless & unworthy . . .'[12] She was now able to discover the real truth of this sentiment.

The discovery came with a great change in the Sheridans' relationship. While Eliza had been absorbed in family matters, her husband had fallen desperately in love with a younger woman. It happened during the Regency crisis when Sheridan went almost every day to Devonshire House to consult his Whig colleagues. In those great apartments he often found himself in the company of Georgiana's sister, Henrietta (Harriet) Spencer, who had been, since 1780, the wife of Frederick Ponsonby, Viscount Duncannon. Harriet was twenty-seven years old (ten years younger than Sheridan). Unlike Georgiana, she had children – a son and a daughter – and therefore she had done her duty to her husband by providing him with an heir. Now she might consider herself free for any emotional adventure that appealed to her. Harriet was more intelligent than her famous sister but just as animated and passionate: her behaviour was impulsive, sometimes almost disturbed. She loved gambling, dancing and talking, and she was a fervent Whig. Sheridan was mad about her.

Domestic relationships at Devonshire House in the 1780s were more than usually complicated. The Duke still kept his two women, Georgiana, and Lady Elizabeth (Bess) Foster who had left her husband and two children to live with the Devonshires. Both of the

Devonshires were said to be fond of her. The Duchess and Bess then became pregnant simultaneously, though for appearance's sake Bess was sent abroad to have her baby, taking with her an illegitimate child of the Duke by yet another woman. When Bess returned, both she and Georgiana became pregnant again, as did Georgiana's sister Harriet Duncannon, despite the fact that she was virtually separated from her husband and lived mostly with her sister at Devonshire House. So Bohemian was the life of this family that even their friends were perplexed about the relationships between them. But it was the Spencer girls, Georgiana and Harriet, who had the worst reputations of all, with their lovers, their gambling, and their disgraceful behaviour in the recent Westminster election.[13]

What particularly upset their mother, Lady Spencer, was not that her daughters' behaviour was immoral, but that they seemed deliberately to flout convention. Though she privately accepted the doctrine that people of their own class were above the dictates of ordinary morality, she believed that to advertise this was to undermine society itself. Dick Sheridan meanwhile increasingly took his lead from these people. He admired their charm, their taste, and the dramatic significance they gave to their smallest whims. He was more and more attracted by their languorous, almost offhand attitude towards sexual morality and intrigued by their urbane contempt for conventions. Under their influence, his once delicate sensibility coarsened.

He had known Harriet Duncannon since about 1780 and when in the heady amorality of Devonshire House, they were thrown into each other's company, their affair blossomed swiftly. Harriet had a choice of admirers, including Lord John Townshend, Colonel Fitzpatrick and Charles Wyndham. But when he wanted to make himself charming, there was no man to compare with Sheridan. In the winter of 1788-9 he wrote flattering letters to her, couched in the authentic Devonshire House 'baby language'. At first he presented himself as her moral guardian, the only one who was really concerned for her welfare. He also pretended to reprimand her lax, uncaring husband for allowing Harriet to visit her sister's unconventional house every day, where she would be surrounded by potential lovers:

> I must bid oo good Night for by the Light passing to and fro near your room I hope you are going to bed, and to sleep happily, with a hundred little cherubs fanning their white

wings over you in approbation of your goodness. Yours is the sweet untroubled sleep of purity.

Grace shines around you with serenest beams and whispering Angels prompt your golden dreams and yet and yet – Beware!! Milton will tell you that even in Paradise Serpents found their way to the ear of slumbering innocence.—

Then to be sure poor Eve had no watchful guardian to pace up and down beneath her windows or clear sighted friend to warn her of the sly approaches of T's and F's and W's and a long list of wicked letters. And Adam I suppose was – at Brookes's – 'fye Mr S' – I answer 'fye fye Lord D'. Tell him either to come with you or forbid your coming to a House so inhabited. Now dont look grave. Remember it is my office to speak the truth. –

I shall be gone before your Hazel eyes are open tomorrow, but for the sake of the Lord D. that you will not suffer me to blame – do not listen to Jack's [Townshend's] Elegies or smile at F's [Fitzgerald's] epigrams, or tremble at C.W.'s [Wyndham's] frowns but put on that look of gentle firmness, and pass on in Maiden Meditation fancy free – now draw the Curtain Sally.[14]

The following March and April they were often in each other's company, and by the summer they were lovers. In June it was reported by one of the gossiping 'Ladies of Llangollen' that 'S. had been caught with Lady Duncannon and that her husband had begun divorce proceedings'.

Quite how Eliza was affected by all this is a matter for speculation but there is no doubt that Dick was now obsessed with Harriet Duncannon and could not have kept it a secret from his wife. So Eliza underwent the torment of meeting her on public occasions, for they continued to move in the same social set. One such event was a Masquerade held at Hammersmith by a Mrs Sturt, on Saturday 13 June 1789. Betsy Sheridan went with Mrs Bouverie and Eliza, all three dressed as gypsies. There was a fine marble pillared gallery, in which the Duke of York's Band was playing, and the ante-rooms were filled with flowers and decorated with coloured lamps. Guests of honour were the Prince of Wales and the Duke of York, and they arrived together at about one o'clock in the morning dressed as highland chiefs.

Dick Sheridan by now had interests other than his wife and soon became detached from her party. The Prince came straight over to Eliza to enquire where Sheridan was and to discover the identity of Betsy, who was promptly presented to him. He then invited Eliza into his own private supper room, but she insisted on Betsy coming with her, and kept a tight hold of her hand as they went in. Perhaps she thought they would be a protection for each other. Once inside, they sat at table with the Prince, the Duke of Clarence, and Dick who had reappeared with a partner. Betsy wrote to tell Alicia about it: 'Opposite to us Lady Duncannon as a Soeur Grise, casting many tender looks across the table which to my great joy did not seem much attended to.'[15] She was wrong. The affair was becoming yet more intense.

Then came a charming and unexpected event. When supper was over the company was entertained by catch singing from members of the 'Je ne sais quoi' Club. As they finished, the Prince, splendid in his kilt, walked over and requested Eliza join him in a song, though (as Betsy said) 'she has not practised anything of the kind for many months.' Indeed she had not sung in public for years, but after her splendid voice finished resonating round the room, this new audience, startled by its depth and feeling, began to applaud wildly. Then the Prince humbly approached. He was about to beg her for another song, when he caught a glimpse of the exhaustion in her face and desisted.[16] Soon afterwards Dick Sheridan entered in a black 'domino' (or loose cloak with a half mask) and went from table to table, fooling about and getting the young women to guess his name. He still had to be the centre of attention.

Relations between the Sheridans grew worse. For Dick was never at home any more but always at Devonshire House in pursuit of Harriet. Things finally came to a head during the Christmas holiday at Crewe Hall. Letters from Eliza to Mehetabel Canning tell the story. On 10 January 1790 she apologised for not having written recently but explained that she had wanted to delay the bad news because she knew it would give her friend pain:

It is impossible in a Letter to detail the thousand Causes I have for Vexation – but dont let it make you too unhappy if you hear that S and I shall next probably come to an amiable Separation when I return to Town – we have some time been separated in fact as Man and Wife – the World my Dear Hitty is a bad one – and We are both the Victims of its Seduction – S has involved himself by his Gallantries and cannot retreat – the duplicity of his Conduct to me, has hurt me more than anything else and I confess to you that my Heart is entirely Alienated from him – and I see no prospect of Happiness for either of us, but in the Proposal I have made him of parting . . . you may rely on the propriety of my Conduct in regard to him for many sakes – but I will in future live by myself, and to my own Tastes – and not suffer what I have done for so many Years – in sacrificing everything I really like, to the Caprice, and conveniences of others . . .[17]

When she wrote again on the 27th of the month, things seemed a little better:

it will give you Pleasure to hear that, Matters are in some degree made up between S & Me – I wrote under the influence of violent irritations, and at the time was perfectly determin'd to part from him entirely – but time, and Reflection, has brought other objects to my View and taught me to think I have no right to sacrifice the Happiness and Interests of many that are so very Dear to me, to my selfish feelings of Resentment – and S's sorrow too, for having made me so very unhappy, and for having expos'd Me so often to Temptations and Dangers (w[hic]h God knows I have hitherto escaped) has made some impression on my Heart, and in short, I have been soften'd into forgiveness . . . We are both now descending the Hill pretty fast, and though we take Different Paths, perhaps We shall meet at the Bottom at last, and then our Wanderings and Deviations may serve for Moralizing in our Chimney Corner some twenty years hence.[18]

Only in early February when she was safely back in her home in Bruton Street was Eliza able to gather her emotions sufficiently to write to tell her friend the end of the story. But even as she sat quietly in her own room, the business of scratching these black lines of ignominy across her white note paper was a dreadfully upsetting task for her. For she had to describe how in those final appalling hours at the Hall, in front of her husband's ex-mistress and the whole goggling 'Crewe', she had been humiliated more savagely than at any time in her life:

> you will not be sorry to hear that I have at last consented to pass an Act of Oblivion over all S's vagaries, and that we are at present on very comfortable terms – I don't know in my life that I ever pass'd so many Miserable Hours as I did for the last Weeks [when] I was at Crewe [Hall] – S had so completely involv'd himself with Lady D[uncannon] that a suit was actually commenced against them in Drs Commons – and if the Duke of D[evonshire] had not come over to England, and exerted his influence with L[ord] D[uncannon] by this time S w[oul]d have been an Object of Ridicule and abuse to all the world – however, thank God! the Business is hush'd up – I believe principally on old Ld Bessborough's [Harriet's father-in-law] account – and She is going abroad very soon I believe to her Sister; you will imagine this affair gave me no little uneasiness, but can you believe it possible, that at the very time when S was pleading [for] forgiveness to me, on this Account, before it was certain that it w[oul]d be hush'd up, at the Moment almost in w[hic]h he was swearing and imprecating all sorts of Curses on himself, on Me & his Child Tom, if ever he was led away by any Motive to be false to me again – he threw the whole family at Crewe into Confusion, and Distress, by playing the fool with Miss Jd [little Emma Crewe's governess] and contriving so awkwardly too, as to be discover'd by the whole House lock'd up with her in a Bed-Chamber in an unfrequented part of the House.[19]

It was the end for Eliza. No longer could she perceive her husband as the romantic hero of their youth, the gentle young man who had eloped and fought two desperate duels for love of her. All she saw, when he emerged shamefaced from a bedroom with his young governess in tow, was what he had now become – a boozy, blowsy, con-man, still brilliant but utterly unprincipled. In a moment she changed. What she saw destroyed all the innocent adoration she had felt for him over many years, and a firm resolve began to grow in her. She was sick of his infantile infidelities. He would baby-talk her no more.

CHAPTER 29

A Little Affection

Even before her humiliation at Crewe, Eliza had been living apart from her husband for several months. Their separation was not formalised but they had contrived as far as possible not to occupy the same house at the same time. Though he could not really afford it, Sheridan was in the habit of acquiring leases on various properties that took his fancy. These included Deepdene, for which the Duke of Norfolk probably charged some rent, Willoughby Lacy's villa at Isleworth near Richmond, a house at Brompton, and the one in Bruton Street. Eliza generally preferred to stay out of town, leaving Sheridan in London so that he might see Harriet Duncannon more often. As a result she was not merely neglected but also as she would say 'unprotected', and because her recent poor health had rendered her complexion even more exquisite, any number of men were only too willing to console her for her husband's indifference.

She remained more or less faithful to Sheridan throughout their marriage, though a phrase in a letter she wrote to Mehetabel Canning as far back as August 1785 suggests that she may have had a brief affair at that time: 'We visited our old House at East Burnham the other Day – and I wish'd for you to keep me Countenance, I piped [i.e. wept] so pittifully at the Sight of all my old Haunts, in the days of Happiness, and innocence and Eighteen – but . . . *I have tasted the forbidden fruit since that time, I have gained the knowledge of good and evil*'. [Author's Italics][1] But it seems more likely that she was unswervingly faithful. In May 1788, a year after Fox had first propositioned her, he did so again. No doubt Eliza's fragile beauty made a refreshing contrast to Mrs Armistead's more generous charms which Fox shared with the Prince of Wales and several other members of the House of Lords.[2] But once again Eliza rejected

271

him. It was not Fox's attentions which depressed her but Sheridan's neglect, for he was now so besotted with Harriet that he seemed to have lost all concern for his wife's reputation or even her welfare.

Eliza's health deteriorated and her mood became fitful. She wanted more than anything to retire to the country where she might avoid Sheridan's whole pack of friends. At other times she would pursue a 'racketting' social life, indifferent to her doctor who had advised a strict regime of 'blistering . . . and . . . bleeding'. In April 1789, she insisted on attending a ball at Brook's Club because she had spent money on a pretty dress and did not want to waste it. So she summoned Dr Turton and her hairdresser to her toilette on the morning of the ball and together they prepared her for the event. While the coiffeur festooned her head with curling papers and whispered the very latest gossip, the doctor patched her up, mixed her medicines, and cautioned her for that evening not to dance. She did not dance – or not very much. Most of the time she sat in a box watching the 'magnificent' spectacle below, taking care of course that she was seen to advantage.[3]

Of those who watched her admiringly was a man eleven years her junior, short, with straight fair hair, a long head, and the rolling walk of a sailor. He was a naval officer just back from the West Indies station. With a confident, downright way of speaking and a bold convivial laugh, he also happened to be the third son of King George III. He had just been created Earl of Munster and the Duke of Clarence and St Andrews. Though unimaginable at the time, forty years later he became King William IV. Once introduced to him, Eliza was not at all surprised when she and Sheridan were invited to Clarence's ball on 2 June. She had sensed immediately that the young Duke was of a romantic disposition and keenly interested in her.

Soon Clarence began to pursue her. It was he who had prompted the Prince of Wales to invite Eliza and Betsy into his private room on the night of the Hammersmith masquerade, and it was he who had persuaded his brother not to insist that she sing a second time because she looked unwell. He was so considerate, but he was also very pressing, and it was this aspect of his behaviour which alarmed her. In her time she had been ogled by the King, and propositioned by the Prince of Wales; now she was being harassed by the Duke of Clarence. Really, she felt at times that she could have dispensed with the whole royal family.

Her miraculous pregnancy in the summer of 1789 after one of Dick's rare visits home concluded in her final miscarriage that September. It came as something of a relief. Afterwards, exhausted and depressed, she decided to go down to the Thames-side villa at Richmond where she and Dick had long ago attended the party given by Willoughby Lacy. There she planned to rest and practise living on her own. But she was given little chance of isolation, and was disappointed when her admirers followed her. She told Mehetabel:

I have been living an idle kind of Life here lately Ma'am . . . Mr Fitzpatrick & L[or]d John Townshend (who . . . live in this Neighbourhood) seldom miss calling in of a Morning . . . Mr Hoare has been here once or twice lately – in short Ma'am as Sheridan says, all the gentlemen are obliging indeed – Ch[arles James Fox] is at present on a visit to Mrs B[ouverie]. Mr B[ouverie] is gone into Suffolk to shoot, so L[or]d Robert & Ch[arles James Fox] thinking no doubt that they should have as good Sport here are supplying his place – they all meet here every Evening . . .

She had one other regular visitor: 'People have taken to drop in as they say, of a Morning and interrupt me in my occupation of School Mistress – the D[uke] of Cla[rence] lives within a hundred yards of me, and he generally pays me a Visit most Mornings'. Aiming to please, the impetuous Duke insisted on presenting a set of drums each to little Richard and Samuel Tickell, so that even after he had gone it was difficult for Eliza to forget him.

At Christmas she paid the dreadful visit to Crewe Hall when she was obliged to endure humiliating scenes of Sheridan begging forgiveness, both for his affair with Lady Duncannon and for swearing fidelity to her for ever then contriving to get locked in a bedroom with the governess. But even while she suffered all this, Eliza was deeply troubled by quite another fear. For though her first reaction to Sheridan's behaviour was to pack her bags and go home to London alone, she realised that Clarence would be there waiting for her.

Before she left for Crewe he had become quite hysterical when telling her how much he loved her. Prince William (as he was known then) was no innocent; he had had his love affairs, had frequented the brothels of Hanover and Westminster, and was even at that time keeping the *demi–mondaine* Polly Finch. However he had become sick of his previously dissolute life and now he wanted love. Moreover he had developed a genuinely romantic passion for Eliza. She was briefly tempted, but in the end wrote to tell Mehetabel:

> – I do not suppose that I will do anything that is likely to disgrace myself or my family – the D[uke] of Clarence (tho' I own to you I am not indifferent to his devoted Attachment for Me, and have thought more favourably of him still, since I have had reason to make Comparisons between his Conduct and S[heridan]'s) has nothing to do with this determination, nor does he even guess my intentions – you may rely on the propriety of my Conduct in regard to him for many sakes . . .[4]

She had finally realised that love with a man who was third in line to the throne was likely to prove unrewarding. Besides, it was not passion she wanted, and so she resolved not to be forced into a foolish affair merely out of disgust at her husband's conduct.

But shaking Clarence off was not easy. While still at Crewe, Eliza had begun to receive passionate, imploring letters from him. So she decided to stay on at Crewe for a few weeks after Christmas to enjoy a little uninterrupted repose. She told Mehetabel that if the Duke:

> persist[ed] in his Passion – and writes Me letters here enough to melt a Heart of Stone – I have been endeavouring (lately especially) to put an entire end to this Business, and have been reasoning and preaching as well as you c[oul]d do – but all to no purpose – he insists on living with Me as a Friend as Usual – but as I know that can only make him more unhappy, and will probably create a great deal of Vexation to me, I still hope to carry my point before I see him in Town – he is very ill poor Man, and confin'd to his Bed – and a Person in his Confidence wrote Me Word yesterday that his illness was entirely occasion'd by my refusal to answer his Letters, and entreated Me so earnestly, and frightened Me so much, by his Account of him, that I have written to him again – God knows how it will end – but I confess I am very wretched about it – for tho' I most earnestly wish to get rid of the thing – I cannot find it in my Heart to be harsh and brutal to him . . .[5]

Eliza was now genuinely alarmed by the business with Clarence.

He was obsessed with her and she felt out of her depth. If she refused to live with him he might kill himself or fade away in melancholy and she would be responsible for the death of a royal Duke. If she accepted him she would destroy what was left of her marriage and get herself into a royal entanglement – it would surely be the end of her. She was eleven years older than Clarence and understood that his elevated social status was an insuperable barrier between them. What was more, she did not love him, so in the end her common sense and notions of propriety overcame her depression and indifference. She wrote and turned him down.

Still he would not accept her decision. So when she finally returned to London in February, exhausted with the ordeal of Dick's affairs and the endless marital arguments at Crewe, she was confronted as she had dreaded by a Royal Duke close to breakdown. Again, she wrote to Mehetabel:

> you know I left Town persecuted, and at last quite oppress'd by the Violence and Passion of the D.C. [Duke of Clarence] – the Sentiment of Compassion and Gratitude, I don't know well what to call it, but most certainly it was not Love, I felt for him, was not decreas'd by comparing his persevering Attachment to S[heridan]'s fickleness & indifference – but when I came to reflect the Circumstance of my being 160 miles off was probably the only thing which prevented Me from bringing eternal Disgrace and Misery upon myself & all that I lov'd, I began to be seriously alarm'd, and to reproach myself, for having so long, from any Motive amus'd myself by dancing on the brink of a Precipice; and then I determin'd to put an entire end to all Correspondence and particular Acquaintance with the D of C. I therefore began to remonstrate with him on the folly & impropriety of his pursuit w[hic]h he knew himself to be [in] vain, but I find more difficulty in laying the Spirit than [in] raising it – in short when I came to Town, I found him like one out of Bedlam, and so completely did he frighten me by his Violence & Passion that I really was made very ill for some days, but at last with the assistance of my friends, Mrs B[ouverie] & C[harles] Fox back'd by the P[rince] of W[ales], who began to be very seriously alarm'd at it, I am now freed from this Entanglement – till he was brought to promise that he w[ould] only speak to

me as a friend, I did not dare to stir out – I have now met him twice and except [for] the first time he has behav'd very well – his Health is still very bad – and he went Yesterday into the Country for a fortnight – his house at Rich[mond] is burnt down, as I suppose you have heard – so he has taken the House we liv'd in [at Richmond] – the P[rince] of W[ales] is moving Heaven and Earth to bring him to himself, but hitherto all in vain- he will not speak to S[heridan] for he thinks the alteration in my Behaviour is on his Account – the P[rince] is vex'd at his Obstinacy, but a little time, and a new Mistress will do more for him than all the preaching in the World – for my own part I feel very happy at having got out of this Scrape so well . . .'[6]

In this Eliza's opinion was sound, and royal William finally looked elsewhere. He had not far to look. In 1790 all London was captivated by the tomboy actress Dora Jordan, whom Sheridan had hired at Drury Lane to display her splendid legs to universal acclaim. As William watched her, within a few minutes he discovered a new admiration rising within him. In just a few months' time he made her his mistress. A year later he wrote to his brother: 'Mrs Jordan, through a course of eleven months' endless difficulty, has behaved like an angel'.[7] He had forgotten Eliza already.

Meanwhile Harriet Duncannon had left the country. Betsy wrote to tell her sister: 'Lady Duncannon is thank God, gone to Bruxelles. I should not be sorry to hear that she was drown'd on her way thither.' She added: 'I see by the 'Herald' that Mrs S. is giving great parties and making up for last year's moderation. I am sorry to see the Pharaoh table always makes a part of the entertainment, as I know her passion for it and the result of ill luck must be dreadful.'[8]

In 1780, the election year, Sheridan was obliged once more to go up to Stafford to defend his seat. But though Sheridan was again successful, throughout the country the Whigs lost ground, and he soon found himself sitting on the impotent benches of opposition. Still politically loyal to her husband and the Whig cause, this result depressed Eliza further.

'Black Dog' was now her familiar. Wherever she looked she saw few reasons for optimism. The long Tory hegemony gave Dick little chance of office which meant that the Sheridan finances were unlikely to improve. What made things worse was that the Drury

Lane theatre, chief source of their income, was said to be falling down. Closer to Eliza's heart, however, was the real fear that Tickell would come to reclaim his children as soon as they were old enough for him to bring up. Her own son Tom was a comfort, but although he had inherited her looks and his father's charm, he was a wild boy and, Dr Parr reported, too impatient to study. Sometimes she glimpsed in his face that fragile look of Mary's and would worry about his health. Normally Eliza was a cheerful person and would have bravely confronted all these troubles, if only she did not have to contend with almost constant sickness and her husband's complete lack of attention.

Nevertheless she had received one piece of news recently which gave her great pride and contentment. Betsy Sheridan, who had lived with Eliza since her father's death, had come through many troubles and was now to be married. Her husband-to-be was Henry (or 'Harry') LeFanu, the brother of Joseph LeFanu who had married Alicia in 1781.[9] Betsy was of course deeply grateful to Dick, who had taken her into his home, introduced her into high society, and even secured for the young couple that same apartment in Hampton Court which the Tickells had occupied years before. But above all others it was to Eliza that Betsy was grateful for her continued affection and kindness.

There was a touching moment when Eliza visited Betsy at Hampton Court a few days after her marriage. Betsy told Alicia:

in the Eveng Mrs Sheridan sung to us at my request as the best celebration of the day I consider'd as happy. The moment of parting from her was another trial and my shedding tears in abundance could hardly be considered as in any way derogatory to my affection to Harry. She had received me with the affection of a Sister at the most melancholy period of my Life, and during the Eleven months I had been with her I could only look back to constant kind and friendly treatment – And that when my situation was most dependent. She was affected too, tho' She reiterated her request that we would consider her House as our home when ever we should chose to be from Hampton. I dried up my tears as soon as I could and the rest of the Eveng was cheerful.[10]

After Lady Duncannon's departure for the continent Dick

Sheridan quickly found a new romantic interest. He was attracted to young girls. This one was sixteen and her name was Pamela. She had lived for most of her life in France and with her friend, the daughter of Philippe Égalité (the one-time Duke of Orleans) and her guardian Mme de Genlis, she was now on a visit to England. Though some said that the aristocratic trio were simply sitting out revolutionary excesses in their own country until they might return home safely, their expressed intention was to meet English society. It was whispered that Pamela 'Seymour' was actually the natural daughter of the Duke of Orleans and Mme de Genlis herself. Sheridan did not care much. He intended to have the girl, despite the fact that Mme was hunting for an English husband for her and already had her sights set on the young Viscount Castlereagh. Sheridan was twenty-four years older than Pamela and no longer good looking, and though he was aware sometimes that his breath and clothes stank of gin, Sheridan remained confident that his old charm could win her over. Promising Mme that he would introduce Pamela into the best English society, he started with his wife. Eliza was indifferent. She did not care now that Sheridan was embarked on yet another liaison. But when she first met Pamela she was impressed, and when others saw the two women together they often remarked on the extraordinary likeness between them.

Then against her every intention Eliza fell in love again. She had thought she had done with that sort of thing. In 1790 she was thirty-six, ill, and tired of life. All she wanted now was retirement in some country cottage where she could escape from the hot-house of London society with its endless, wearisome amours. But appearances had to be kept up, and she was still required to pay her visits, even to houses she had come to detest. Consequently one day at Devonshire House she fell into conversation with an interesting young man. She had first glimpsed him standing at a great window and staring moodily over the vistas of Green Park. He aroused her curiosity. Not conventionally handsome, he was too short and his head was too big. Yet he had a way of lowering his long dark eyelashes which was very pleasing, and soon Eliza found herself warming to his unusually frank, straightforward manner. By Devonshire House standards he was a bit naïve but his sincerity was refreshing. It was clear that he was no intellectual, though he obviously meditated on things and felt about them deeply. He was contemptuous of the sexual goings-on in the house, because, he said, he did not regard love as some species of entertainment. But what most intrigued Eliza about him was that like her, he was so very unhappy. Something had happened to make him bitter.

His name was Lord Edward Fitzgerald. He was Irish and in that year, at twenty-seven, was nine years younger than Eliza. His dead father had been the first Duke of Leinster and an uncle was the Duke of Richmond. Of course he was a Whig and some said he was extremely radical with startling views about Irish independence. On arriving in London he had soon become a friend of Fox and also of Eliza's husband. Fitzgerald's personal history was extraordinary: one of seventeen children, he was only ten when his father the Duke had died. His mother had then married her steward William Ogilvie, who later educated young Edward. He revered his stepfather, but adored his mother, and was very close to her. He confided that he had come to London to be with her as she was staying at her house in Harley Street.[11]

By profession Fitzgerald was a soldier. He had served in the Americas, in 1788 moving cross-country from Halifax in Newfoundland to join his regiment at St John in New Brunswick. Eliza noticed that he became especially animated when talking about the simple farmers of Nova Scotia. When she ventured the idea that such people must be very uncouth, he sharply corrected her. He said that one could not help admiring 'The equality of . . . their manner of life . . . There are no gentlemen, everybody is on a footing provided he works, and wants nothing, every man is exactly what he can make of himself'.[12] He told her about an old couple he had met who had lived for over thirty years right out in the woods by the banks of a great river with no other human company for sixty miles. It was, he said, just like the noble, natural life in *Emile*. Had she read Rousseau?

As he spoke he surveyed the splendid moulding of the Devonshire House ceiling with some distaste. Eliza did not know whether to be amused or moved. Such talk of human equality and a simple natural life was incongruent with the opulence, decorum and calculated licence of the society in which they were both moving. Yet somehow the pictures he had conjured up attracted her and she wanted to know more of his story. He said that two years before he had gone with a companion on a trip from Frederickton, New Brunswick, to Quebec, and thence southwards by way of Niagara down the Mississippi to Louisiana. He told her of huge torrents of water, of immense silent forests and of the great river flowing serenely through the pine woods. He told her of the Indian tribes he had met and how at a settlement called Detroit he had been to admitted as a chief of the Bear people. Later, sitting alone in Bruton Street, she became lost in thought, following him in her mind's eye as he drove his canoe down the rapids or trekked across the wilderness until he suddenly came in sight of his destination – New Orleans.

It was not until he told her of his arrival in that splendid city that Eliza understood the cause of his moroseness. He confessed that throughout his long journey he had been encouraged by visions of his cousin, Georgiana Lennox. In his mind he had heard her voice coming from the grey woods at morning and seen her face flickering in the camp fire at night. It was because of Georgiana that he had accepted his commission in the first place, believing that he might make his name and his fortune as a soldier and so go home and marry her. But when he emerged from the woods that day and marched into New Orleans he had found a letter which had lain waiting for him for months. It was from England. When he opened it he learned that Georgiana had married Lord Bathhurst.

His story brought out all Eliza's maternal feelings. In return Fitzgerald began to treat her with a compassion and sympathy she had not experienced for years. They had both been cruelly hurt by life but both were revived by their mutual tenderness. Their intimacy grew so rapidly that Eliza quickly realised things between them could not go on as they were for much longer. Fitzgerald was obviously no womaniser but sooner or later he would want them to become lovers. She had to decide now whether or not to encourage him further. That she was contemplating an affair with this young man she knew would shock her friend Mehetabel, but the thought of Sheridan's unfeeling treatment was almost driving her into his arms. He had no time for her, and she was sick of his incessant infidelities, and his complete failure to treat her as a valued companion. Edward was different. He appreciated her and was completely devoted. He brought calm into her life and something else she had craved for years – a little quiet affection.

When it came to morality Eliza was to some extent a free-thinker. She had picked up that attitude from the society in which she had moved for most of her life. Provincial Betsy Sheridan was quite shocked by her views:

Mrs S– always amiable and obliging has adopted ideas on

many subjects so different from what mine must be that we can never converse with that freedom that minds in some sort of the same kind indulge in. She told me last night she . . . was not without hopes of bringing me over to her way of thinking. I assured her . . . that my opinions on some points were as fix'd . . . and that I was now too old to change either – That I allow'd others to indulge their own ways of thinking and should no more quarrel with a woman for thinking differently in a point of morals than I should on religious matters if She had happen'd to be brought up a Mahometan. In this manner I always treat the subject and we end in good humour.[13]

But Sheridan's affair with Lady Duncannon had finally destroyed Eliza's love for him, and with neither morality nor sentiment to stop her she was now seriously considering an affair. She had nothing to lose and might even gain a little solace from it. What harm would it do to anyone if she became Fitzgerald's mistress?

There was a sense of things drawing to an end in the summer of 1791. Sheridan had at last seen sense and ordered that the rickety old Drury Lane theatre should be demolished and a new one built on the site. On 4 June he and Eliza had gone together to the last night of old Drury and from the director's box watched performances of *The Country Girl*, and a farce *No Song, No Supper*. These titles reminded Eliza of those days when, aged only seventeen, she had come up from Bath to sing from this same stage Handel's triumphant music.[14] The following day the workmen arrived to smash up the Drury Lane of Nell Gwynne, John Dryden and David Garrick. In the next few weeks Eliza regularly walked over there to see the building come down. Sheridan did not feel the pathos of it. He cheerfully told her that he had removed his company to a temporary home in the Haymarket but was taking with him a plank from the Lane to be built into the stage of his new theatre. To Eliza, however, the gloomy rubble-strewn site seemed like a symbol of her failed marriage.

Soon afterwards she became Fitzgerald's lover, and did so without regrets. It was an uncomplicated and quiet relationship and if at times her conscience was uneasy it was not because of Sheridan but because she felt she was too old for Edward. Eliza was not a selfish or jealous mistress. She was more like a mother to him. She even advised him to leave her and take up with a younger woman, like

Pamela, for example. Eliza knew that Pamela was looking for a husband and suggested to Fitzgerald that he should propose to her. He laughed and would not even meet the girl. He was interested only in Eliza.

What worried her more than anything was how she should break the truth to Mehetabel Canning. She did not want to lose her best friend for she needed every scrap of kindness she could get and she dreaded risking Mehetabel's good opinion. So when she wrote to beg her 'Sister Christian' to come and stay she only hinted at her relationship with Fitzgerald:

> you will drive the Black Dog away and admit me once more as your Dear Betsey [Eliza was sometimes known by this name] – I have been leading a strange rakish Life lately – but my Sins of all kinds are too numerous to be detailed on paper. I shall reserve them till we meet, and then as Usual I will come to a true Confession and submit to any Penance that you think proper – if it is not severer tho' than the one you threaten Me with, I feel I shall be tempted to sin again.[15]

The wording suggests that she wanted to confess her affair to Mehetabel and then draw upon her friend's strength so that she might give up Fitzgerald. She did not do so. Eight months later she was still 'sinning' and still evading 'Sister Christian's' questions. She also contrived not to tell Sheridan directly about Fitzgerald. Of course Sheridan suspected the affair – he even received a poison-pen letter about it – but they never at this stage acknowledged it. Eliza treated both her husband and best friend on a need-to-know basis, so that neither might be compromised. On 1 April 1791 she told Mehetabel:

> do you know I was very near coming to spend a Week with you some little time ago, if I had not been afraid of my D[ea]r sister Christian's purity, bringing my peccadillos into a Scrape that I know she w[oul]d have been sorry for – seriously I was coming – but I thought if I did – that S[heridan] w[oul]d most probably pay me a Visit & then if he s[houl]d have asked a Question about the Anonymous Letter, I felt sure that your face at least w[oul]d betray Me, w[hic]h now that everything is blown over, w[oul]d have been attended with disagreeable Consequences . . .[16]

Yet her 'peccadillo' with Fitzgerald had not blown over, and in July or August 1791 she became pregnant.

Eliza was alarmed, not because of the effect on her reputation, but because of her age and poor health. Another miscarriage was more than likely, but if her child were born it would have no legal father. This worried her dreadfully. What was she to do? She was sure of Edward's continuing affection but not of his family's. So to understand the Leinsters better she agreed to a visit from Edward's mother. Fortunately Sheridan was rarely at home and the lady might call without his knowledge. One day in late August Eliza welcomed the Duchess to Bruton Street. Fortunately she turned out to be an extremely sympathetic woman, very inclined to like anyone who loved her son. Nevertheless despite her obvious admiration for Eliza, the Duchess was conventional and a stickler for propriety. She was obviously uneasy about her son and the illegitimacy of her future grandchild.

The next day Sheridan came home looking dreadfully ill and went straight to bed. At once Eliza became immersed in the task of nursing him and was soon unwell herself. She told Mehetabel that she was as 'Yellow as a Golden Cup – a composition of Bile and Nerves . . . dying of a sick headache'. She took to her bed for several weeks and lay there worrying about the future. As the months went on and Eliza began to show, certain decisions had to made. Sheridan must be told.

His response surprised her. He did not blame her, but himself. He seemed to understand that it was his neglect which had caused this situation and he was ashamed of himself. For the first time in years he began to show her some tenderness and he expressed great concern for her state of health and her predicament. He even suggested that if she wished, he would stand as father to the child and acknowledge it as his own. He was at his most magnanimous. Eliza was touched.

As her confinement approached she longed for anonymity and peace to deal with her situation. In January 1792 she left for Southampton to get away from society. Sheridan went down later to check that she was comfortably settled in her little house and meanwhile Eliza assured Mehetabel she was not consumptive: 'I trust the Air & regularity of my Life will remove my remaining Complaints & that I shall return in a Month or two quite stout.'[17] She refused to make any new acquaintances and declined cards from the neigh-bours. All she wanted were letters from her friend. She did not get any. Mehetabel had decided to have nothing more to do with her.

In offering to stand as father to the child, Sheridan had presented Eliza with a way out of her trouble. She understood very well that she could not rear a child in respectable society and go on with her love affair: she was not the Duchess of Devonshire. So she summoned Fitzgerald to Southampton to talk things over and he arrived full of endearments. When she told him what she was going to do he was taken aback. She said that their baby must take priority, and it was best that it should be brought up as a Sheridan. She said that for the sake of the child, she had to accept her husband's generous offer. But they had to break off their affair and Fitzgerald must promise never by word or deed to seek to intervene in the child's upbringing. After a great deal of desperate pleading he agreed. Within a month he had sailed for France.

At the end of February 1792, Eliza left Southampton and went to Brompton where Sheridan had taken Cromwell House. Her baby was born there in March or April, and was christened Mary Sheridan. She was, said her mother, a 'little badge of affection'. In May Eliza received a letter from the Duchess of Leinster, the baby's grandmother, congratulating her on having returned to the path of 'peace and Comfort in this World'. The Duchess particularly remarked on the 'generosity and noble proceding . . . of Mr R.B. Sheridan'. The letter promised continuing friendship and expressed delight that 'little Mary' would be brought up with the principles of Religion which afforded Eliza herself so much comfort, and begged that Eliza would 'Kiss [the baby] from me, with all my heart'.[18] The note was well meaning but too late. For by May 1792 it was beyond anyone's power to help Eliza at all.

CHAPTER 30

Poor E

On the evening of 7 May 1792 a man got out of a chaise on King's Down near Bristol and climbed alone to the top of King's Down Hill. Stopping at the top to get his breath, from there he watched the vehicle continue slowly down the road until it drew to a halt at the bottom to wait for him. On impulse he had come up here to spend a few minutes on a sentimental journey. The climber was Richard Brinsley Sheridan, now stout, florid and forty. In the carriage below sat his thirty-seven year old wife Eliza, frail and pale and desperately trying not to cough.

Twenty years before, Sheridan had fought his second duel against Captain Mathews here and had nearly died from loss of blood. Now curiosity had brought him back: he wanted to see if he still recognised the place. To his surprise he found a great stone set up to mark the very spot where he had fallen. Not far from that was the same hovel into which he had been carried. When he knocked on the door an old man answered, the very person who had taken him in as he lay bleeding. A few minutes conversation was enough for Sheridan to discover that this man had since made a small income by telling curious sightseers about the day the famous Mr Sheridan had fought a duel here and how he had saved the great man's life by giving him a drink of water. The cottager proudly displayed a few pathetic relics for Sheridan: there were some bits of broken sword blade, a sleeve button from his coat and the smashed frame of a miniature. Sheridan remembered well how the picture frame from Eliza's portrait had once hung over his heart and so saved his life from the desperate sword-jabbings of the enraged Mathews.[1]

He was overcome with remorse. The following evening he wrote to his mistress Lady Harriet Duncannon, now in France: 'What an interval has passed since, and scarce one promise that I made to my own soul have I attempted to fulfil. I looked at the carriage that bore her down the same road, and it wrung my heart to think of the interval and the present and too probable conclusion.'[2]

He had not been really apprehensive about his wife's health until early March during his second visit to Southampton. He went down from London late at night with a friend, Dr Moseley, and since there had been no sense of urgency about their journey, they had stopped at Bagshot for a jolly dinner with Richard Tickell and his new wife. Early next morning the pair arrived in Southampton where Moseley examined Eliza and announced that he thought her very well. Sheridan was reassured.[3] However the next day she became very ill and started spitting blood. At midnight Sheridan walked gloomily by the sea and afterwards in a letter to Harriet, told her:

> I wrote to you in rather good spirits yesterday . . . for I like the Quiet of this spot and E. seemed much better and I wrote in the morning when the gloom upon everybody's mind is lighter. But now I am just returned from a long solitary walk on the beach. Night Silence Solitude and the Sea combine to unhinge the cheerfulness of anyone . . . reflecting on many past scenes, and to offer slender hope in anticipating the future . . .

He remembered the time when he had eloped to France with Eliza and thought that the boat was sinking:

> How many years have pass'd since on these unceasing restless waters which this Night I have been gazing at and listening to, I bore poor E. who is now so near me fading in sickness from all her natural attachments and affections, and then loved her so that had she died as I once thought she would in the Passage, I should assuredly have plunged with her body to the Grave . . .[4]

What shocked Sheridan especially was that Eliza appeared to be utterly friendless in Southampton. When he enquired about Mrs Canning, Eliza was forced to admit that she had not received a letter from Putney for weeks past. She suspected that Mehetabel wanted nothing more to do with her as she considered her life to be immoral. On hearing this Sheridan privately wrote to Mrs Canning, telling her about Eliza's condition and begging her to forgive her friend:

> I am confident you do not know what her situation is, or what effect may arise, and has indeed taken place in her mind, from the impression . . . that the Friend she loved best in the world appears, without explanation even, to be cooled and changed towards her . . .
>
> My Dear Mrs C. you do not know the state she has been in, and how perilous and critical her situation is, or indeed you would upbraid yourself for harbouring one alter'd thought or even abating in the least degree of warmest Zeal of friendship . . . Pray forgive my writing to you thus, but convinced as I am that there is no chance of saving her life, but by tranquillizing her mind, and knowing as I do and as I did hope you knew that God never form'd a better heart, and that she has no errors but what are the Faults of those whose conduct has created them in her against her nature, I feel it impossible for me not to own that the idea of unkindness or coldness towards her from you smote me most sensibly, as I see it does her soul. . .[5]

The letter was successful and Mehetabel wrote to Eliza again. And despite having a young family of her own, from this time onwards she spent as much time as she could with her sick friend.

Sheridan then persuaded his wife to come back to London so that she could be near Mehetabel. He took a house near the Cannings in Brompton and it was there that the baby was born. Everybody hoped that the event would signal Eliza's return to health and for a time it seemed to do so. But then came more alarms. For a time she would cough and sweat and then just as abruptly recover her vitality and spirits. Dr Moseley was not deceived, however, and advised a change of scene, recommending the fresh air and healing waters of a spa. It was decided that Eliza should go to Bristol where she could visit the Hotwells and be near her old home in Bath.

The journey was dreadful. They started on Thursday 3 May, Eliza travelling in a closed chaise attended by her maid Faddy and Mrs Canning. Sheridan had originally intended to accompany Eliza only as far as Maidenhead Bridge and then to return to London for a week before going down to Bristol, but on the day of the journey she was so ill that she begged him not to leave her. It worried him so much that as soon as he had seen her off he hurriedly tidied up his affairs at the theatre, and started after her on horseback. He caught up the carriage at Speen Hill near Newbury on the Great West Road where they stopped at an inn. After Eliza had been put to bed he sat up with a bottle of wine and wrote to Harriet:

> E is in bed very very ill – eager to get there, and sanguine of the Event. But many gloomy omens have told me our Hopes will be disappointed. I have been in long and great anxiety about her – flying from my Fears and yet hoping, one event safely over [he means the birth] that all would be well. But this day se'enight every favourable appearance exceeded our most sanguine hopes, since Friday when the infant was christen'd and she has been steadily falling back . . .'[6]

It was not until the Sunday evening that Sheridan paused to look out from King's Down over Bristol. The city was now in shadow against the declining sun, a sight which held many poignant recollections for him. The small dark shape of Eliza's carriage was almost swallowed up by the gloom below. With a sigh he shook his head and set off downhill hoping that they might reach the Hotwells before nightfall.

Bristol Hotwells was a major centre of the Georgian 'death industry'. Its prosperity depended on the milky-white water that gushed out of St Vincent's Rock at Clifton and discharged itself into the River Avon at the rate of sixty gallons a minute. Long famed for its miraculous curing properties, once its commercial potential was noticed by a number of sharp-witted Bristonians, a considerable industry of bottling the water had sprung up around the Wells. It was sold around the country and exported as far as the West Indies. Only once was this industry threatened. On 1 November 1755 the spring-water foaming out of the rocky throat of St Vincent was as red as blood and quite undrinkable. Later on, however, people learned that on that very day there had been a great earthquake at Lisbon.

As a summer health resort, the Hotwells attracted a wide range of visitors, and began to host public breakfasts, dances, card-playing and gossip. But when at the end of the century, the bottled water prices rocketed, fewer visitors came, and the Hotwells were left chiefly to the pale people, desperate consumptives investing their last hope of a cure in the effervescent waters.

Eliza endured her journey to Bath with courage. She had come to meet her one true lover, he who admired the pale faces, delicate physiques and dreamy eyes of all the Linleys. Dr Moseley had recognised him instantly. Although he realised that she was dying of tuberculosis, he did not say so directly but resigned to give her up to his embrace. He was consigning her to the Hotwells as a last hope. As Eliza arrived with her husband, her friend, her maid and Sheridan's long-serving butler George Edwards, her entire faith also lay in this water. It seemed to be all that stood between her and extinction.

As soon as she got there she was put to bed and seen by Dr Bain, a kindly, cheerful young Scot. He had once practised in Bath. His opinion carried added weight because he had been cured of consumption by Hotwells water. Leaving Eliza's bedroom that first night his manner was so grave that Sheridan feared the worst. But with caution Bain said that though Mrs Sheridan's lungs were undoubtedly ulcerated she might yet improve from drinking the water.

Following a good night's rest Eliza felt refreshed and stronger and the doctor was more optimistic. The exact whereabouts of her lodging-house is not known though it was probably just above the colonnade. Eliza soon discovered other streets built for polite visitors to the Wells; there was Dowry Square and Dowry Parade and most recently, Albermarle Row. It is unlikely that Eliza was told about the terrace nicknamed 'Death Row' or about the 'Strangers Burial Ground' situated discreetly up the hill. However she may have noticed that the staircase in her lodging was rather shabby and needed repainting. When asked about this by a visitor one of the landladies admitted that the paintwork was knocked so often by the coffins going downstairs that repainting was a waste of money. It was a matter of sensible economics in the death industry.

So Eliza began to lead her new life. Each morning she was driven down to the Pump Room where she would drink one or two glasses of water, while trying at low tide to ignore the stink coming up from the mudflats below the room. She was never well enough to take a hand at cards, but sometimes she would enjoy sitting there listening to the small orchestra or chatting to other visitors. She already knew a number of them including Lady Sarah Napier, Edward Fitzgerald's aunt, who was there with her debilitated husband. Dr Bain had prescribed moderate exercise for her so that when she was feeling robust enough, Dick or Mehetabel would accompany her in the carriage for a ride up the Down. Sometimes instead she chose to walk along the tree-lined promenade, or, if it were raining, within the thoughtfully erected colonnade for visitors by the side of the Pump House. There she could peer out onto the grey tree-covered slopes across the misty river, or watch the cargo boats mysteriously gliding past. Then after a light lunch she would rest for a while on her bed and after that would be driven out again onto the Down. After dinner she would visit the Pump Room once more to drink her two or three glasses of water before she went to bed at eight or nine o'clock.

Inevitably she became involved with the gossip of the place. The talk was all about the rise in prices and the consequent decline of the Hotwells. In previous years it had cost only ten shillings per annum for a whole family to drink the waters at the Pump Room, whereas now the new landlord Samuel Powell charged twenty-six shillings for a single person. Carriage prices on the Down had rocketed too. The assembled consumptives were indignant. Was it any wonder they asked that there were far fewer people at the Wells this season, and that hardly anyone came for the social life? The terraced lodgings were already noticeably emptier than in the previous year and the atmosphere of the whole place was gloomier. However, few of the complainants dared to draw the obvious conclusion from this. For if the Hotwells was no longer a pleasure resort but only a haven for last-hopers, then they had unwittingly consigned themselves to that number.

During her first few days at the Wells, Eliza's condition improved to such an extent that Sheridan thought he might leave her for a night to take a short business trip to London. Eliza urged him to go because she worried that he was neglecting important parliamentary and theatre matters for her sake. She said that she would be quite alright without him: she had Mehetabel and also Mrs Leigh, the wife of a local clergyman, to sit with her. Besides, there was a general optimism about Eliza's progress from the small party. Mehetabel Canning wrote to tell her daughter that her friend was on the road to recovery, and Mrs Leigh announced that she thought Mrs Sheridan was 'by no means desperately ill'.

Both women were wrong. A week after she arrived, Eliza's condition suddenly worsened, with renewed bouts of weakness, sweating, and spitting blood, so that her husband despaired and called a clergyman to administer the sacrament. From then on she was restricted to her bed for most of the time. Eliza knew now how close she was to death.

In Sheridan's words 'she [could] not be deceived about the Danger of her situation'. Long months of nursing her sister Mary five years before had familiarised her with the guileful nature of the disease, how it often fooled a patient with abrupt remissions, and then just as suddenly came on again with renewed bouts of coughing. So she prepared herself for death. She exchanged her lending-library novels for books on religious subjects and sometimes lay in bed crooning to herself snatches of arias she had performed in years gone by. In those days she had been too preoccupied with the triumph of the occasion to pay much attention to the words. Now, however it was the awful truths they embodied that occupied her thoughts and dreams.

Her friends noted the change. Eliza had always been regarded among her acquaintances as almost saintly but this disease now gave her an ethereal radiance. Dick told Mehetabel that if she could recover 'there never was on earth anything more perfect than she will be'. A determination to lead a better life made her eager to go on living. Her manner to her friends became even more patient and affectionate and Sheridan was often moved to tears by her consideration for his distress. He was now obsessed with the idea that if he had remained faithful to her she would never have become ill. Devoting all of his time to her, he was trying desperately to make amends. So each evening, in a Bristol lodging house, the author of *The School for Scandal* sat by a consumptive's bedside, a Quakeress on one side and a clergyman on the other, reading aloud improving sermons. He would spend hours with Eliza in their little parlour holding her hand, soothing and comforting her, and trying to keep her spirits up. But sometimes they both found it difficult, especially when it grew dark outside, the candles were lit and she had to climb wearily upstairs to face yet another night of bad dreams and sweats.

It was time for her last concert. She had spent hours in bed thinking about her childhood in Bath and the nest of nightingales in which she had grown up. In her mind's ear she could still faintly hear their music as she saw the Linley children playing together in Orchard Street. She could picture the faces of her brothers and sisters: Tom laughing triumphantly as he lowered the violin from his chin; Sam at his oboe and Mary, arm outstretched, trilling an aria.

Now she, the last of the nightingales, was dying and she had to perform once more. Although her breathing was almost too weak to sing she hoped she could still play a few notes. Once she came downstairs, others helped her to the piano. Sheridan wrote:

> Last Night she desired to be placed at the Piano-Forte. – Looking like a Shadow of her own Picture she played some Notes with the tears dropping down her thin arms. Her mind is become heavenly, but her mortal Form is fading from my sight – and I look in vain into my own mind for assent to her apparent conviction that all will not perish.[7]

Her friends were moved to tears by the sight. Her husband was struck by how closely the scene resembled Reynold's famous portrait of Eliza as St Cecilia.

Sheridan's only relief during this time was to scribble a daily journal to Harriet Duncannon. On 16 May he reported that Eliza was very poorly, had been bled that day, and was put to bed with a 'Blister'. While she had slept that evening he had ridden out

> to a Place where I remember she made me drive her when poor Mrs Tickell was dying here – it is a spot on the side of Brandon Hill where she and her sister used to play when they were at boarding-school close by. And I remember how bitterly she cried here and lamented her sister's approaching Fate – O . . . I cannot describe to you how sunk I am and how horrid the solitude of the Night is to me. I now watch half the Night in the expectation of being called for some new alarm.[8]

At four o'clock in the morning of 20 May, he was summoned to Eliza's bed to be told that she had suffered a violent pain in her side for three hours. He went at once to Bain who prescribed the application of leeches. These creatures seemed to give her some relief. Next day she was more cheerful but contrary to Bains's instructions she insisted on eating a piece of chicken. Digesting this quickened her pulse-rate. Later that week she seemed a little better and once again urged Dick to go up to London to see to his business. On 21 May she received the sacrament and spent most of the day writing a long paper which she handed to Mehetabel to be given to Dick should she not recover.

Mrs Canning, Mrs Leigh, and the maid Faddy took turns to watch at her bedside with Sheridan so that occasionally he might leave Eliza to snatch some sleep or write a few letters.[9] But he could barely keep his mind on business: his thoughts were always upstairs in the sick-room. His devotion to his ill wife was according to Dr Bain 'that of a lover'. Then once again at the end of the month she rallied and he was able to go to town for a day to talk to Albany Wallis, Henry Holland and the Duke of Bedford's agent about the work on Drury Lane. As yet not a brick had been laid. At times it must have seemed to him that his whole life was in ruins.

Meanwhile Eliza was making her will. To Eliza Canning her goddaughter she left her watch, chain and some jewels, and to her sister Jane, her pearls. She instructed that the 'fine linen' of all kinds she had lately made up was so far as suitable to be reserved for her 'dear little infant' Mary. Her wardrobe was to go to a servant: she particularly instructed that her mother must not interfere in this. The Leighs and the LeFanus were to get £50 in mourning rings while the 'fausse montre, containing my dear husband's picture' she left to her 'dear and beloved friend' Mrs Canning. Mehetabel was also to have a portrait of Eliza painted by anyone 'but Cosway', as well as rings for herself and her daughter. Little Betsy Tickell was to receive a locket 'of my dear Mary', to which Eliza's own picture was to be added and the hair intertwined. Eliza dared to hope that the second Mrs Tickell would allow the little girl to wear this memorial of 'her two poor Mothers'. To her own mother Eliza left 'a new black cloak which will be comfortable for her in winter'. George Edwards the Sheridan's butler and Faddy her maid were to get £25 each.

While Dick was away in London Eliza suddenly became worse again. Though she was quickly put to bed she would not rest until Mehetabel had brought her pen and paper to write a codicil to her will, but after a few minutes of sitting up, desperately gasping for breath, she could not finish it. She handed the paper to Mehetabel for safe-keeping. The fragmentary instructions consisted of two sentences. The first was addressed to Mehetabel and referred to the infant child Mary:

I have – do most solemnly promise My Dear Friend Mrs S, to protect & guard her poor Child thr[ough] Life, & to do my utmost to breed her up like my own – that is saying enough –[10]

In the second she tried to bind Fitzgerald not to interfere in the upbringing of their child:

> I here solemnly promise my Dear Betsey never to interfere on any account with Mrs C[anning] in the Education or in any other way of my poor Child – I cannot write all I wish but he knows my heart – swear or I shall not die in peace – [11]

That was all she could manage. She sank back exhausted.

When Dick Sheridan arrived back at Hotwells, tired and famished, he discovered that Eliza's condition had worsened with the weather. He prayed fervently for a hot spell. The *Wolverhampton Chronicle* reported that Mrs Sheridan was 'in a dreadful way. When the fickleness of our climate chears her with a sky unclouded, her mind as well as her frame revive, and she converses with spirit that gives her friends the liveliest hopes; but with the changing elements, she becomes languid and silent, an affecting spectacle of beauty and accomplishments sinking to the grave.'

Dick had already sent for Tom who came in the middle of June. Towards the end of the month Mr and Mrs Linley arrived with Ozias. They were staying in Bath and so could come over daily. When together the family kept up the fiction that Eliza was recovering and they chattered cheerfully and even hopefully. At first Eliza was clearly buoyed up by their visits. But then on 27 June there came a rapid deterioration in her condition and it became plain to everyone that she was dying. The Linleys were sent for immediately, this time to take their farewells. Mehetabel Canning described the scene to Betsy Sheridan:

> They were introduced to her one at a time at her bedside and were prepared as much as possible for this sad scene. The women bore it very well, but all our feelings were awakened for her poor father. The interview between him and the dear angel was afflicting and heart-breaking to the greatest degree imaginable. I was afraid she would have sunk under the cruel agitation – she said it was indeed too much for her. She gave some kind injunction to each of them, and said everything she could to comfort them under this severe trial. They then parted in the hope of seeing her again in the evening, but they saw her never more. Mr Sheridan and I sat up all that night with her,

– indeed he had done so for several nights before, and never left her one moment that could be avoided. About four o'clock in the morning we perceived an alarming change, and sent for her physician. She said to him 'If you can relieve me, do it quickly; if not, do not let me struggle but give me some laudanum,' His answer was, 'Then I will give you some laudanum.' Before she took it, she desired to see Tom and Betty Tickell, of whom she took a most affecting leave. Your brother behaved most wonderfully, though his heart was breaking; and at times his feelings were so violent, that I feared he would have been quite ungovernable at the last. Yet he summoned up courage to kneel at the bedside, till he felt the last pulse of expiring excellence and then withdrew. She died at five o'clock in the morning . . . For my part I never beheld such a scene – never suffered such a conflict – much as I have suffered on my own account. While I live, the remembrance of it and the dear lost object can never be effaced from my mind.[12]

Dick Sheridan was in torment. He could not bear the thought now that he must be part from Eliza for ever. At last when he went to his room and sat down on the bed, he could only scribble distractedly on a scrap of paper. 'The loss of breath from a beloved object, long suffering in pain . . . is not so great a privation as the loss of her beautiful remains . . . The victory of the Grave is sharper than the sting of Death.' A misty dawn broke over the Avon and in the lodging-house bedroom a cold grey light began to caress the still-handsome features of the woman on the bed. Below her, water from St Vincent's Well pumped unceasingly into the dirty river.

Afterword

Dick Sheridan hated the funeral. It took place at Wells Cathedral on the evening of 7 July 1792. The cortège started at half-past seven in the morning from the Hotwells, but during the twenty-mile journey stopped for five hours, outside what Mehetabel described as a very uncomfortable inn. There Sheridan got his first inkling of what they were in for when a whispering, gaping irreverent crowd gathered outside to inspect the bier. To them the name 'Sheridan' meant a show. After the unaccountably long wait the procession started off again through midsummer Somerset. All along the way the country people gathered on village greens and haymakers working in the fields looked up to see Mrs Sheridan pass.

At about seven o'clock that evening the coffin arrived at the cathedral where it was met by the choir. Sheridan led the mourners, including his son Tom, old Thomas Linley, Ozias and Jane Nash Linley, Joseph Richardson, Mehetabel Canning, little Betty Tickell, and the servants 'Faddy' and George Edwards. The cathedral was packed. The Reverend Leigh read the psalms and lessons but although he almost shouted, Mehetabel could hardly hear him, and there was such a pushing and jostling that she thought she was going to faint. The coffin then was let down into the vaults already containing the remains of Mary Tickell. The crowd pressed in so hard for a better view that the Reverend Leigh feared that he was going to be thrown into the grave.

During the service Mehetabel managed to get a glimpse of Dick Sheridan's face. She saw 'a wildness in his look' which terrified her. Later he spoke with hatred of the 'gaudy parade and show, where all the mob, high and low' had turned his wife's funeral into a farce. That night he crept back into the church and knelt over Eliza's

296

coffin in silent prayer, remaining there until the mechanical figures on the great medieval clock came out to strike midnight.

In the course of time Eliza Sheridan became something of a cult figure. Stories about her circulated widely, emphasising her ravishing looks, her innocence, and the profound spirituality of her singing voice. Portraits by Gainsborough bore witness to her great beauty and that by Reynolds permanently coupled her name with St Cecilia, so that by the end of the century she was regarded as something of a protestant saint. In 1793 a publication appeared in Bath entitled *The Female Mentor* which demanded of its readers 'Who that ever heard the late Mrs Sheridan sing . . . "Brighter scenes I seek above/ In the realms of peace and love" . . . did not feel a rapture blended with devotion, which is more than mortal?' Not averse to having it both ways, the same book told the story of Clara [Eliza] a girl of 'amiable disposition' and 'great genius' in music, who married young and wasted her life 'in fashionable amusements' so that when she died of consumption in Bath aged thirty-seven she was both terrified and friendless. The fact that Eliza Sheridan was neither of these things when she died did not seem to matter. Her story was useful to evangelical Christians as both inspiration and an awful warning to young girls.

The cult of Eliza Sheridan continued to flourish into the next century. On 8 May 1813 her portrait was prominently displayed at the British Institution before the curious inspection of the Prince of Wales. William Wilberforce, who was standing behind the Prince, recounted that on spying the picture, his friend Sheridan took him by the arm and led him up to it. There, the Prince stood stock still for some minutes, simply gazing at Eliza's portrait. Twelve years later in October 1825 the editors of the *Gentlemen's Magazine* thought there was still enough interest in the Linley legend to publish an 'original letter', apparently written by Eliza in 1772 and telling the story of her elopement with Sheridan. It was a fake but served to promote the story once more. During the Victorian period there were frequent revivals of interest in Eliza's story, prompted either by yet another biography of Sheridan or else the exhibition of 'Sheridan' paintings by Jerry Barrett, where scenes such as *The Elopement* or *Miss Linley at Home* could be admired.

True to his promise Sheridan took Mary (Fitzgerald) Sheridan into his care and hired a nurse at an 'extraordinary salary' to look after the child at his house at Wanstead. It did no good. On the night of a party in October 1793 Mehetabel Canning rushed out of the nursery shouting 'the child is dying'. Mary was having fits. By the time the doctor arrived it was too late. Aged only eighteen months, Mary was buried with her mother in Wells Cathedral. Two years later, in November 1795, Thomas Linley died. He too was buried at Wells in the same grave as his two daughters and grand-daughter. There is a memorial to them all on the east wall of the cloister.

Sheridan's grief did not last long. He was a man of quick but not profound feelings and very soon found solace in a couple of bottles of wine a day. Surprisingly his friend Richard Tickell proved to have greater depths of feeling. Though he had married quickly after Mary's death he seems never to have got over it. Long afterwards he was still in the habit of visiting their old apartments in Hampton Court, the very ones that Betsy Sheridan and her husband had occupied afterwards. On 4 November 1793 Tickell committed suicide by throwing himself from the parapet there. Sheridan hushed everything up.

Only a few months after Eliza's death Sheridan held a grand fête for six hundred people at Isleworth and invited Madame de Genlis and her two wards to be his guests. He also invited Lord Edward Fitzgerald who excused himself on the grounds that he wished to avoid Madame de Genlis because he had a 'terror of learned ladies'. Since the Duke of Orleans had recently cut off her allowance, Madame was only too pleased to accept Sheridan's hospitality and she arrived in the most gracious of moods. She even allowed Pamela to hand out the ices. Soon Sheridan and Madame had a tacit agreement that he would become Pamela's husband, on one condition: that Madame should first go back to France to obtain the consent of Pamela's friends – by which she meant the Duke. Reluctantly Sheridan agreed. It was not easy in those revolutionary times for anyone to get a permit to cross the Channel and it took the combined efforts of Sheridan and Fox to get one for them. Sheridan accompanied them to Dover and for years afterwards Madame recollected how this middle-aged lover had kept them amused by playing practical jokes all the way down the Dover road.

A few weeks later in November 1792, Fitzgerald also crossed the Channel to France. He was trying desperately to forget Eliza. It was then in Paris he first caught sight of Eliza's double, Pamela, in the Théâtre Feydeau. But though he was appalled to learn from Madame that the girl was engaged to Sheridan, he did not allow that to deter him. He proposed to Pamela and she returned his love. For a few days more, however, Madame insisted on carrying out the Duke's instructions and pressed on for Belgium, so Fitzgerald accompanied the little party to Rancy. In December in Tournai he reached his goal and married Pamela. Sheridan's wife's lover had become the husband of his fiancée. Their marriage was a happy one, lasting for six years until Fitzgerald died in Newgate Gaol on 4 June 1798. While resisting arrest for his part in a United Irishmen conspiracy, he had been wounded in the shoulder by a pistol bullet. The wound proved fatal.

Sheridan was not deeply upset by Pamela's defection. In 1795 he married Hester Ogle, daughter of the Dean of Winchester. At twenty-two, she was just a year older than his son.

Eliza's only surviving child, Tom Sheridan, eloped with Caroline Callender of Craigforth after a brief and unsuccessful army career. He decided to go into politics. At first two constituencies turned him down flat and when he finally gained the Whig nomination for his father's old seat at Stafford, he was defeated. So he turned his attentions to the financial management of Drury Lane. To everybody's surprise he was rather good at it. Chiefly owing to him, the theatre's finances were kept afloat for many years to come. In the meantime, Caroline had presented him with six children. But their father had begun to show tubercular symptoms. In 1813 Dick Sheridan pulled some strings and secured Tom an appointment as Treasurer to the Colonial Governor of the Cape of Good Hope. Leaving five of the children behind, he, Caroline and their eldest daughter left for the Cape in search of good health. It was hopeless. There, in September 1818, he died, just two months after the death of his father in England.

Tom had received the Linley inheritance. Within four generations the tubercular bacillus had destroyed many Linleys: apart from Eliza, her sister Mary and possibly Maria, it took Eliza's only son Tom; two of his sons, Frank and Charles; and two of Eliza's grandsons, Fletcher and Brinsley Norton.

Drury Lane was eventually rebuilt and on 21 April 1794 the first night audience packed in to watch Mrs Siddons play Lady Macbeth. This huge theatre held 1,828 people, and the management was especially proud of the new fire-curtains. In her opening address the actress Mrs Farren declaimed: 'The very ravages of fire we scout/For we have wherewithal to put it out/In ample reservoirs of firm reliance/When streams set conflagration at defiance.' But all these devices eventually proved of little use. Fifteen years later, on the night of 24 February 1809, Sheridan was speaking in the House of Commons when he noticed that its windows had turned dark red. Fire had broken out at Drury Lane. The Speaker courteously offered to adjourn the sitting but Sheridan gratefully declined. Accompanied by the Duke of York he hurried down to the theatre. The Lane was an inferno, and he could see at a glance that it would be largely destroyed.

Sheridan never failed in a dramatic gesture. He retired to the Piazza Coffee House in Covent Garden, took a seat at a table and ordered a bottle of wine. When, as he had anticipated, his friends remarked on his calmness he had his one-liner ready: 'May not a man be allowed to drink a glass of wine at his own fireside?'

Privately, however, he saw his own ruin in the flames. He still owed huge sums of money on the Lane and now he had no way of paying them off. With the destruction of his theatre he had lost his sole source of income. It meant that he would be unable to bribe the electors of Stafford at the next election, he would lose his seat in Parliament, and would no longer be free from arrest for debt. In the flames that crackled and roared before him he glimpsed an ignominious future of ducking and dodging creditors while he drew ever closer to destitution. And that was exactly what happened.

For some hours longer he sat in Covent Garden watching the spectacle. Theatrical history was going up in smoke. That last plank from Nell Gwynne's theatre was now blazing away, along with the famous screen which had fallen to reveal everything in *The School for Scandal*. There were many such treasures stored beneath the great theatre, among them the scores of Thomas Linley's operas and nineteen of Tom Linley's violin concertos, some the only copies. Towards dawn the fire sank down. Above the glowing mass there was now a huge pall of smoke carrying innumerable shreds of charred manuscript paper into the sky. And as Sheridan turned to go, perhaps for a brief moment a woman's voice sounded in his ears, before the Linley music finally faded away.

Notes

PART ONE
The Beauty of Bath

CHAPTER 1
Incident at the Théâtre Feydeau

1. Moore, Thomas, *The Life and Death of Lord Edward Fitzgerald* (2 vols, London, 1832), vol. 1
2. Dictionary of National Biography
3. For supporting the seditious toast to abolish 'all hereditary titles and feudal distinctions' Fitzgerald was subsequently dismissed from the army.
4. The incident at the Théâtre Feydeau is recounted also by Patrick Byrne in *Lord Edward Fitzgerald* (London, 1955), pp.115-17

CHAPTER 2
All Geniuses

1. Black, *The Linleys of Bath* (London, 1911), p.20
2. The Portico leading to Orchard Street is still to be found off Pierrepont Street. The Linley House just beyond it served at the time of writing as the publicity office for the Bath International Festival of the Arts.
3. Black, *The Linleys of Bath*, pp.10-11
4. Ozias Humphry's sketch owned by the Victoria Art Gallery in Bath. Reproduced in Waterfield et al, *A Nest of Nightingales* (London, Dulwich Picture Gallery, 1988), p.55
5. Black, *The Linleys of Bath*, p.20
6. Fraser Rae, W., *Sheridan* (2 vols, London, Richard Bentley & Son, 1896), vol. 1, p.91
7. Fiske, Roger, *English Theatre Music in the Eighteenth Century* (Oxford University Press, 1986), p.268
8. LeFanu, William (ed.) *Betsy Sheridan's Journal* (London, 1960), pp.50-1
9. Waterfield, Giles et al, *A Nest of Nightingales*, p.10
10. Ibid., p. 10
11. Fiske, *English Theatre Music in the Eighteenth Century*, p.413
12. Ibid., pp.10-12
13. Ibid., p.62
14. Ibid., p.12
15. Black, *The Linleys of Bath*, p.23
16. Waterfield, Giles et al, *A Nest of Nightingales*, p.31

301

CHAPTER 3
Entertaining Strangers

1. We can assume that the Linleys had already moved to the Royal Crescent by October 1770 although Black, *The Linleys of Bath*, p.20, argues that they were still at Orchard Street. We are informed that the Orchard Street house had been 'void for half a year since Midsummer 1771' and since the traditional quarter day for settling rents and tenancies was 29 September that is likely to be the date the Linleys vacated it.
2. The Sheridans lodged when in Bath at Kingsmead Street, presently close to 9, New King Street, where a plaque reads;
    'Near this site between 1770-1772 lived Thomas Sheridan, actor and orthoepist, Richard Brinsley Sheridan, dramatist, 1751-1816'
3. Price, Cecil, *The Letters of Richard Brinsley Sheridan* (3 vols, Oxford University Press, 1966), vol. 1, p.20

CHAPTER 4
An Enemy

1. The history of the earlier Sheridans is told in Fitzgerald, P., *Lives of The Sheridans* (2 vols., London 1888), vol. 1
2. Watkins, John, *Memoirs of the Public & Private Life of the Right Honourable R.B. Sheridan with a Particular Account of his Family and Connnexions* (2 vols., Henry Colburn Public Library, London, 1817), vol. 1, p.45
3. Ibid., p.48
4. LeFanu, William (ed.) *Betsy Sheridan's Journal* (London, 1960), pp. 55-6
5. Watkins, John, *Memoirs of the Public & Private Life of the Right Honourable R.B. Sheridan*, vol. 1, pp. 57-64 gives a comprehensive account of the Kelly riots
6. Sheridan's publications on rhetoric include
    i. *British Education* (1765) in which he purported to show how 'immorality, ignorance and False taste' might be cured by a 'Revival of the Art of Speaking, and the Study of our own Language'.
    ii. *A Discourse delivered in the Theatre at Oxford, in the Senate House* (1759), for which he was awarded an MA.
    iii. *A Course of Lectures in Elocution* (1762)
    iv *A Dissertation on the Causes of the Difficulties which occur, in learning the English Tongue With a scheme for publishing an English Grammar and Dictionary* (1762) and addressed to 'a certain Noble Lord'.
7. Boswell, David, *Life of Dr Samuel Johnson* (London, 1791, reprinted Dent, London, 1962), vol. 1, p.239
8 LeFanu, William (ed.) *Betsy Sheridan's Journal*, p.260-5. Alicia LeFanu (nee Sheridan) recollected the years in France in her biography of her mother.

CHAPTER 5
Lovers

1. Watkins, John, *Memoirs of the Public & Private Life of the Right Honourable R.B. Sheridan with a Particular Account of his Family and Connnexions* (2 vols., Henry Colburn Public Library, London, 1817), vol.1, p.178
2. Sichel, Walter, *Sheridan* (2 vols., Constable, London, 1909), vol. 1, p.334
3. Dick Sheridan's literary partnership with Nat Halhed consisted chiefly of translating and updating obscure classical texts. Among these were a burletta *Ixion*

which Dick retitled *Jupiter* and the translations of a Greek poet named Aristenaetus. The only item of their joint labours ever to be published was the Aristenaetus which came out in August 1771. It sank with little trace.

4. Fraser Rae, W., *Sheridan*, (2 vols., London, Richard Bentley & Sons, 1896), vol. 1, pp. 149-50
5. Ibid.
6. Moore, Thomas, *Memoirs of the Life of the Right Honourable Richard Brinsley Sheridan*, 3rd edition (2 vols., Longman, Hurst, Green, et al, London, 1825), vol. 1, pp.418 ff
7. Ibid.
8. Fraser Rae, W., *Sheridan*, vol. 1, pp.151-55

CHAPTER 6
Farce

1. Watkins, John, *Memoirs of the Public and Private Life of Richard Brinsley Sheridan with a Particular Account of his Family and Connnexions* (2 vols., Henry Colburn Public Library, London, 1817), vol. 1, p.175
2. Ibid.
3. Moore, Thomas, *Memoirs of the Life of the Right Honourable Richard Brinsley Sheridan*, 3rd edition (2 vols., Longman, Hurst, Green, et al, London, 1825), vol. 1, p.43
4. Black, *The Linleys of Bath* (London, 1911), p.34
5. Belden, Mary Megie, *The Dramatic Works of Samuel Foote* (New Haven, Yale University Press, 1929), Caps. 1 and 2
6. Foote, Samuel, *The Works of Samuel Foote* (2 vols., Glasgow, John Murdoch, and London, Robinson & Verbnor & Hood, 1799), vol. 1
7. Black, *The Linleys of Bath*, pp.41-2
8. Ibid., p.42
9. Sir William Herschel (1738-1822) discovered Urarus in 1781 and later several of its satellites. He became Astronomer Royal to George III. He also discovered the motion of the double-stars and his son Sir John Herschel became an eminent astronomer.

CHAPTER 7
Local Hero

1. Moore, Thomas, *Memoirs of the Life of the Right Honourable Richard Brinsley Sheridan*, 3rd edition (2 vols., Longman, Hurst, Green, et al, London, 1825), vol.1, p.4
2. Watkins, John, *Memoirs of the Public and Private Life of Richard Brinsley Sheridan with a Particular Account of his Family and Connnexions* (2 vols., Henry Colburn Public Library, London, 1817), vol. 1, p.163
3. Ibid., vol. 1, pp.164-5
4. Moore, Thomas, *Memoirs of the Life of the Right Honourable Richard Brinsley Sheridan*, vol.1, pp.14-16
5. Angelo, Henry, *The Reminiscences of Henry Angelo* (2 vols., reprinted Benjamin Blom, New York/London, 1831), vol. 1, pp.230-31
6. Reproduced in Fraser Rae, W., *Sheridan* (2 vols., London, Richard Bentley & Sons, 1896), vol. 1, pp.144-45
7. Ibid., vol. 1, p.139
8. Ibid., vol. 1, p.140
9. Ibid., vol. 1, p.142

10. Moore, Thomas, *Memoirs of the Life of the Right Honourable Richard Brinsley Sheridan*, vol. 1, p.45

CHAPTER 8
Gone!

1. Thomas Gainsborough (1727-88) lived and worked in Bath from 1759 to 1774. According to the Dulwich Picture Gallery catalogue, the 'beggar' portrait of Eliza and Tom was painted probably in 1768. It is now in the Sterling and Francis Clark Institute, Williamstown, Mass., USA
2. Black, *The Linleys of Bath* (London, 1911), p.24
3. Thicknesse is reported in the Dulwich papers
4. Gainsborough to Lord Mulgrave, 31 March 1772, Dulwich papers
5. Brereton's letter reproduced in Fraser Rae, W., *Sheridan* (2 vols., London, Richard Bentley & Sons, 1896), vol. 1, p.172
6. Mathews' advertisement reprinted by Moore, Thomas, *Memoirs of the Life of the Right Honourable Richard Brinsley Sheridan*, 3rd edition (2 vols., Longman, Hurst, Green, et al, London, 1825), vol. 1, p.71

CHAPTER 9
Mrs Harley's Adventure

1. Fraser Rae, W., *Sheridan* (2 vols., London, Richard Bentley & Sons, 1896), vol. 1, pp.144-45, p. 166
2. Lamb, Charles, ed., 'My First Play' in *Essays of Eliza* (London, Dent, Dutton, 1911), p.114
3. Reproduced in Sichel, Walter, *Sheridan* (2 vols., London, Constable, 1909), vol. 1, p.344
4. Fraser Rae, W., *Sheridan*, vol. 1, pp.167-8
5. Ibid.
6. Price, Cecil, *Letters of Richard Brinsley Sheridan* (3 vols., Oxford University Press, 1966), vol. 1, p.125
7. Ibid.

CHAPTER 10
Hysterics

1. Sichel, Walter, *Sheridan* (2 vols., London, Constable 1909), vol. 1, p.358
2. Price, *The Letters of Richard Brinsley Sheridan* (3 vols., Oxford University Press, 1966), vol. 1, p.28
3. Ibid., vol. 1, p.27. Price notes that this letter to the printer may not have actually been sent.
4. Angelo, Henry, *The Reminiscences of Henry Angelo* (2 vols., reprinted Benjamin Blom, New York/London, 1831), vol. 2, p.314
5. Price, *The Letters of Richard Brinsley Sheridan,* vol. 1, p.31
6. Sichel, *Sheridan*, vol. 1, p.369
7. Fraser Rae, *Sheridan* (2 vols., London, Richard Bentley & Sons, 1896), vol. 1, pp.182- 6

CHAPTER 11
Love Letters

1. Sichel, Walter, *Sheridan* (2 vols., London, Constable, 1909), vol. 1, p.358

2. Black, *The Linleys of Bath* (London, 1911), pp.75-6
3. Fraser Rae, *Sheridan* (2 vols., London, Richard Bentley & Sons, 1896), vol. 1, pp.190-191
4. Black, *The Linleys of Bath*, pp.76-77
5. Ibid., p.77
6. Fraser Rae, *Sheridan*, vol. 1, pp.192-3
7. Ibid., vol. 1, pp.193-4
8. Black, *The Linleys of Bath*, p.80
9. Sichel, *Sheridan*, vol. 1, p.381
10. Ibid., vol. 1, p.358
11. Price, *The Letters of Richard Brinsley Sheridan* (3 vols., Oxford University Press, 1966), vol. 1, p.244

CHAPTER 12
Doubts and Suspicions

1. Fraser Rae, *Sheridan* (2 vols., London, Richard Bentley & Sons, 1896), vol. 1, pp.200-201
2. Moore, *Memoirs of the Life of the Right Honourable Richard Brinsley Sheridan*, 3rd edition (2 vols., Longman, Hurst, Green, et al, London, 1825), vol. 1, p.99
3. Ibid., vol. 1, p.92n.
4. Fraser Rae, *Sheridan*, vol.1, p.199
5. Moore, *Memoirs of the Life of the Right Honourable Richard Brinsley Sheridan*, 3rd edition, vol. 1, p.102n
6. Black, *The Linleys of Bath* (London, 1909), p.90. The wording of this and some of the letters following are damaged by their seals, hence the blanks in parentheses.
7. Fraser Rae, *Sheridan*, vol.1, p.207
8. Moore, *Memoirs of the Life of the Right Honourable Richard Brinsley Sheridan*, 3rd edition, vol. 1, p.106
9. Black, *The Linleys of Bath*, p.93
10. Sichel, *Sheridan* (2 vols., London, Constable 1909), p.273
11. Ibid., vol.1, p.275
12. Ibid., vol. 1, p.94

CHAPTER 13
At Waltham Abbey

1. Price, *The Letters of Richard Brinsley Sheridan* (3 vols., Oxford University Press, 1966), vol. 1, p.38
2. Ibid., vol. 1, p.35
3. Ibid., vol. 1, p.41
4. Fraser Rae, *Sheridan* (2 vols., London, Richard Bentley & Sons, 1896), vol. 1, p.223
5. Price, *The Letters of Richard Brinsley Sheridan*, vol. 1, pp.45-46
6. Fraser Rae, *Sheridan*, vol. 1, pp.230-31
7. Price, *The Letters of Richard Brinsley Sheridan*, vol. 1, p.60
8. Ibid., vol. 1, p.62
9. Ibid., vol. 1, p.66
10. Ibid., vol. 1, pp.68-9
11. Ibid.
12. Ibid., vol. 1, p.77

CHAPTER 14
Lady in Distress

1. Fraser Rae, *Sheridan* (2 vols., London, Richard Bentley & Sons, 1896), vol.1, p.243
2. From *The Bath Chronicle* of 15 April 1773, reproduced in Sichel, *Sheridan* (2 vols., London, Constable 1909), vol.1, p.423
3. Concert bill for the Drury Lane Oratorio, 26 February 1773, reproduced in Waterfield et al, *A Nest of Nightingales*, (London, Dulwich Picture Gallery, 1988), p.11. A later bill of 3 March is reproduced in Sichel, *Sheridan*, vol. 1, p.418
4. From *The Bath Chronicle*, 1 April, reproduced in Black, *The Linleys of Bath* (London, 1911), p.115
5. From Fanny Burney's *Early Diaries*, reproduced in Black, *The Linleys of Bath*, p.112
6. Ibid., p.113
7. Ibid., p.114
8. The following appears in a supplement to *The Bath Chronicle*, 15 April 1773, addressed to Miss Linley from Lord M:

> *Yes, my fair, to thee belong,*
> *All the noblest power of song.*
> *Trust me, for I scorn deceit,*
> *Nought on earth is half so sweet*
> *As the melting, dying note,*
> *Warbling through thy liquid throat;*
> *Save the breath in which it flows,*
> *Save the lips on which it grows.*

Reproduced in Fraser Rae, *Sheridan*, vol. 1, p.262

9. Ibid., p.262
10. Letter from Horace Walpole to Lady Ossory, dated 16 March 1773, reproduced in Black, *The Linleys of Bath*, p.116
11. Fraser Rae, *Sheridan*, vol. 1, p.253
12. Black, *The Linleys of Bath*, p.109
13. Price, *The Letters of Richard Brinsley Sheridan* (3 vols., Oxford University Press, 1966), vol.1, p.77
14. Ibid.
15. Fraser Rae, *Sheridan*, vol.1, p.255
16. Ibid., p.256
17. Ibid., pp.256-7
18. The crucial account of exactly how Linley was persuaded to allow Eliza to marry Dick Sheridan are missing from Alicia (LeFanu) Sheridan's account of their courting. The pages were lent to Thomas Moore for material for his biography (see bibliography) and were never returned. Moore's own account is sketchy.

PART TWO
A Theatrical Marriage

CHAPTER 15
Bliss and After

1. From *The Morning Chronicle*, 16 April 1773, reproduced in Price, *Letters of Richard Brinsley Sheridan*, vol. 1, p.79

2. Price, *The Letters of Richard Brinsley Sheridan* (3 vols., Oxford University Press, 1966), vol. 1, p.83
3. Ibid.
4. Moore, *Memoirs of the Life of The Right Honourable Richard Brinsley Sheridan*, 3rd edition (2 vols., Longman, Hurst, Green, et al, London, 1825), vol. 1, pp.119-121
5. Price, *The Letters of Richard Brinsley Sheridan*, vol.1, p.83, n.1
6. Ibid., p.83
7. Watkins, *Memoirs of the Public and Private Life of the Right Honourable Richard Brinsley Sheridan, with a Particular Account of his Family and Connexions*, (2 vols., Henry Colburn Public Library, London, 1817), vol.1, p.193
8. Ibid., p.195
9. Price, *The Letters of Richard Brinsley Sheridan*, vol. 1, pp.79-80
10. Ibid., p.80
11. Ibid., pp.80-81
12. Fraser Rae, *Sheridan* (2 vols., London, Richard Bentley & Sons, 1896), vol. 1, p.278
13. James Beattie's London Diary quoted by Bor, Margot and Clelland, Lamond in *Still the Lark* (London, 1962), p.73
14. *Gloucester Journal* quoted in Bor and Clelland, *Still the Lark*, p.73

CHAPTER 16

Miscarriages

1. Price, *The Lettters of Richard Brinsley Sheridan* (3 vols., Oxford University Press, 1966), vol. 1, p.81 n.2
2. Ibid., p.81 n3
3. Fiske, *English Theatre Music in the Eighteenth Century* (Oxford University Press, 1968), p.384
4. Ibid.
5. Ibid., pp.492-499 for details of the careers of Stephen and Nancy Horace
6. Price, *The Letters of Richard Brinsley Sheridan*, vol. 1, p.84 n.2
7. Ibid.
8. Sichel, *Sheridan* (2 vols., London, Constable 1909), vol. 1, pp.629-30. Sheridan's poem 'On His Wife Ceasing to Sing' runs to thirty-six lines and rambles enough to be considered incoherent. After suggesting that Eliza is actually a better writer than singer it tells us that she was 'no mortal Maid' but Euterpe the maid of Harmony, whom the god Phoebus fell in love with. The only lines pertinent to the title are 'So well her mind and voice agree/That every thought is melody.'
9. Ibid.
10. Boswell, *Life of Dr Samuel Johnson* (London, 1791, reprinted London, Dent, 1962), vol. 1, pp.560-561
11. Price, *The Letters of Richard Brinsley Sheridan*, vol.1, p.85
12. Ibid., p.85
13. Ibid., p.84
14. Ibid., p.84 n3
15. Ibid., p.84 n2
16. See Fanny Burney's *Early Diaries*, quoted in Bor and Clelland, *Still the Lark*, (London, 1962), p.74
17. Ibid., p.74
18. Fraser Rae, *Sheridan* (2 vols., London, Richard Bentley & Sons, 1896), vol.1, p.280

19. Price, *The Letters of Richard Brinsley Sheridan*, vol. 1, p.84
20. Ibid.

CHAPTER 17
Rivalry

1. It is possible that Sheridan was optimistic about making his fortune with *The Rivals* as far back as May 1773 when he wrote from his honeymoon cottage about his 'slight gale or two of Fortune' (see note 9, Chapter 14).
2. Price, *The Dramatic Works of Richard Brinsley Sheridan* (2 vols., Oxford University Press, 1973), vol. 1, p.37. Price adds that the resemblance between *The Rivals* and *A Journey to Bath* shows that Sheridan had read his mother's play 'with care'.
3. *A Journey to Bath* from The British Library, MS Add 25975, dated (wrongly) 1749. Percy Fitzgerald and others sometimes referred to this play as *A Trip to Bath*, see Fraser Rae, *Sheridan* (2 vols., London, Richard Bentley & Sons, 1896), vol.1, p.52
4. Frances Sheridan's career as a dramatist is summarised in Fraser Rae, *Sheridan*, vol. 1, p.51-54
5. Ibid., vol. 1, p.52
6. *A Journey to Bath* quoted, ibid., vol.1, p.53
7. Price, *The Letters of Richard Brinsley Sheridan* (3 vols., Oxford University Press, 1966) vol. 1, p.88, RBS to T Linley, 17/11/74
8. The Bath plays connected with the Sheridans make a remarkable dramatic sequence but as far as I know have never been published together. They are: *The Journey to Bath* by Frances Sheridan (1764); *The Maid of Bath* by Samuel Foote (1771); *The Rivals* by Richard Sheridan (1775)
9. Price, *The Dramatic Works of Richard Brinsley Sheridan*, vol. 1, p.39 n3
10. Ibid.
11. Moore, *Memoirs of the Life of The Right Honourable Richard Brinsley Sheridan*, 3rd edition (2 vols., Longman, Hurst, Green, et al, London, 1825), vol. 1, p.137
12. Price, *The Dramatic Works of Richard Brinsley Sheridan*, vol. 1, p.40
13. Ibid.
14. Watkins, *Memoirs of the Public and Private Life of Richard Brinsley Sheridan, with a Particular Account of his Family and Connexions* (2 vols., Henry Colburn Public Library, London, 1817), vol. 1, p.198, agrees that the outlines of *The Rivals* 'will be found to correspond with the history of Mr Sheridan's marriage' and that the characters had before been dramatised in a 'ludicrous manner' by Foote.
15. The literary ancestresses of Mrs Malaprop's linguistic solecism are Mrs Slipslop in Fielding's *Joseph Andrews* (1742) and Mrs Winifred Jenkins in Smollett's *Humphrey Clinker* (1771). Sheridan would have known both novels well.
16. *The London Chronicle*, 21-24 January 1775, reproduced in Sichel, *Sheridan* (2 vols., London, Constable 1909), vol. 1, p.499 n.1
17. From the *Morning Post* 31/1/1775, quoted in Price, *The Dramatic Works of Richard Brinsley Sheridan*, vol.1, p.51
18. Ibid., p.41
19. Ibid., p.42
20. Ibid., p.44
21. Note from Eliza to RBS, Sichel, *Sheridan*, vol.1, pp.500-1
22. Ibid., p.501
23. Price, *The Dramatic Works of Richard Brinsley Sheridan*, vol. 1, p.45, from the

Morning Post, 1/1/1775
24. *The Rivals*, Act II, sc. 1, from Price, *The Dramatic Works of Richard Brinsley Sheridan*, vol.1, p.105
25. Ibid, Act 1, sc. 1, p.93. In this scene, Sheridan is making jokes about Eliza's singing. The song 'My Heart's Own Will is Free' is a jumbled version of one from *Love in a Village* which had been a favourite of Eliza's since as a little girl she had sung it to the lodger, Ozias Humphry.
26. Price, *The Dramatic Works of Richard Brinsley Sheridan*, vol.1, p.50
27. Ibid., p.51, quoted from the *London Evening Post*
28. Ibid., p.50
29. Moore, *Memoirs of the Life of The Right Honourable Richard Brinsley Sheridan*, 3rd edition, vol. 1, pp.137-8
30. Fraser Rae, *Sheridan* (2 vols., London, Richard Bentley & Sons, 1896), vol. 1, p.291

CHAPTER 18
At Play

1. Angelo, *Reminiscences of Henry Angelo*, quoted in Bor and Clelland, *Still the Lark* (London, 1962), p.74
2. Sir Joshua Reynolds' *Mrs Sheridan as St Cecilia* is reproduced in Waterfield, Giles et al, *A Nest of Nightingales* (London, Dulwich Picture Gallery, 1988), p.68
3. The provenance of Reynolds' picture is ibid., pp.67-69
4. Ibid., p.68
5. Fanny Burney quoted in Bor and Clelland, *Still the Lark*, p.91
6. Ibid.
7. Dictionary of National Biography
8. Battiscombe, Georgina, *The Spencers of Althorp* (London, 1984), pp.84-7. The Duke of Devonshire was a member of the inarticulate and cold Cavendish family. On one occasion the Duke and his brother were given a three-bedded room at an inn. The third bed, curtained off, contained a corpse. Neither of the brothers mentioned it to the other until morning.
9. Dictionary of National Biography
10. Most of the Silvio/Laura sequence is reproduced in Moore, *Memoirs of the Life of The Right Honourable Richard Brinsley Sheridan*, 3rd edition (2 vols., Longman, Hurst, Green, et al, London, 1825), vol. 1, pp.201-7

CHAPTER 19
Family Matters

1. Fraser Rae, *Sheridan* (2 vols., London, Richard Bentley & Sons, 1896), vol.1, p.299
2. *St Patrick's Day*, Act 1, sc.1, from Price, *The Dramatic Works of Richard Brinsley Sheridan* (2 vols., Oxford University Press, 1973), vol.1, p.166
3. Reviews of *St Patrick's Day* are taken from Price, *The Dramatic Works of Richard Brinsley Sheridan*, vol.1, pp.151-2
4. Tom Linley's career is summarised by Fiske, Roger, *English Theatre Music in the Eighteenth Century* (Oxford, 1986), p.414
5. From Garrick's correspondence, quoted in Price, *Dramatic Works of Richard Brinsley Sheridan*, vol. 1, p.199
6. Ibid., p.200
7. Price, *Letters of Richard Brinsley Sheridan* (3 vols., Oxford University Press,

1966), vol. 1, pp.86-87, RBS to Linley, October 1775.

8. Ibid., pp.88-89, RBS to Linley, October 1775.

9. Fiske, *English Theatre Music in the Eighteenth Century*, p.416

10. Ibid.

11. Price, *Letters of Richard Brinsley Sheridan*, vol.1, p.92, RBS to Linley, 2 November 1775

12. *The Duenna*, III, viii, in Price, *The Dramatic Works of Richard Brinsley Sheridan*, p.283

13. *Morning Post* of 22/11/1775, quoted in Price, *The Dramatic Works of Richard Brinsley Sheridan*, vol. 1, p.208

14. These complimentary verses to Sheridan for his *Duenna* appeared in the *Morning Chronicle* for 30 November 1775. The twelve lines began:

> Hail to the bard who writes with grace and ease,
> And plainly, by the plainest rules, can please.
>
> No musty plot throughout thy piece prevails,
> Stale, aukward, and uncouth, from twice-told tales,
> But witty, lively, interesting, new,
> Such thy Duenna Sheridan we view.

If the signatory 'T.S.' really was Sheridan senior than he must have decided to 'puff' the play as a peace offering to his son.

15. An account of the critical reception of the opera is provided in Price, *Dramatic Works of Richard Brinsley Sheridan*, vol. 1, pp. 206-214

16. Ibid., p.209

17. Ibid.

18. *The Duenna*, III, iii, Price, *Dramatic Works of Richard Brinsley Sheridan*, vol. 1, p.270

19. Ibid., III, i, p.263

20. Ibid., p.207

21. Ibid., p.208

22. Ibid., p.23 and Sheridan, Clare, *To the Four Winds* (London, 1957). Clare Sheridan was the wife of Richard Brinsley Sherdian's great-great grandson, Wilfred, and a cousin of Winston Churchill. Her son, RBS IV, set out on his disastrous voyage in the spring of 1935, carrying manuscript copies of *St Patrick's Day*, *The Critic*, and *The Duenna*. That year Frampton Court was almost completely demolished. He died within a year.

CHAPTER 20
Partners

1. Fiske, Roger, *English Theatre Music in the Eighteenth Century* (Oxford, 1986), pp.252-4

2. Price, *Letters of Richard Brinsley Sheridan* (3 vols., Oxford University Press, 1966), vol. 1, p.96 n.1

3. Ibid., p.94, Garrick to RBS, 31/12/1775

4. Ibid., pp.94-95

5. Ibid., p.102, RBS to Linley, 1776

6. Ibid., p.100, n.3

7. Fraser Rae, *Sheridan* (2 vols., London, Richard Bentley & Son, 1896), vol.1, p.314 and Bor and Clelland, *Still the Lark* (London, 1962), p.82

8. Watkins, *Memoirs of the Public and Private Life of Richard Brinsley Sheridan*,

with a Particular Account of his Family and Connexions (2 vols., Henry Colburn Public Library, London, 1817), vol. 1, p.214

9. Oman, Carola, *David Garrick* (London, 1958), p.336
10. Kendall, Alan, *David Garrick: A Biography* (London, 1985), pp.169-70
11. Information on the company at Drury Lane in the late eighteenth century is collated from Price, *Letters of Richard Brinsley Sheridan* (3 vols., Oxford University Press, 1966), vol. 1, p.111f. and Macqueen, Pope, *Theatre Royal, Drury Lane* (London, 1945), pp.180-83
12. Macqueen, Pope, *Theatre Royal, Drury Lane*, p.178
13. Henry Angelo reported in Fitzgerald, P., *Lives of the Sheridans* (London, 1888), vol.1, p. 188-89
14. Price, *Letters of Richard Brinsley Sheridan*, vol.1, p.101, n.1
15. Boswell, David, *Life of Dr Samuel Johnson* (London, 1791, reprinted Dent, London, 1962), vol.1, p.280
16. Ibid., vol. 1, p.366

CHAPTER 21
Scandal

1. Fitzgerald, P., *Lives of the Sheridans*, (London, 1888) vol.1, p.161
2. Moore, *Memoirs of the Life of The Right Honourable Richard Brinsley Sheridan*, 3rd edition (2 vols., Longman, Hurst, Green, et al, London, 1825), vol. 1, pp.193-4 and Price, *Letters of Richard Brinsley Sheridan* (3 vols., Oxford University Press, 1966), vol. 1, pp.105-7
3. Price, ibid., vol.1, pp.111-16, RBS to the proprietors of Drury Lane, September 1777
4. Sichel, *Sheridan* (2 vols. Constable, London, 1909) vol.1, p.534
5. *Memoirs of the late Mrs Robinson Written by Herself* (1801), in Price, *Dramatic Works of Richard Brinsley Sheridan* (2 vols, Oxford University Press, 1973), vol.2, pp.560-61
6. Quoted in Ingamells, John, *Mrs Robinson and her Portraits* (London, Wallace Collection Monographs, 1978), p.9
7. The list of musical items provided by Thomas Linley and his son Tom from Fiske, *English Theatre Music in the Eighteenth Century* (Oxford University Press, 1986), pp. 413f.
8. British Library Manuscript collection, Add MSS 25975
9. Price, *The Dramatic Works of Richard Brinsley Sheridan* (2 vols., Oxford University Press, 1973), vol.1, p.297
10. The difficulties came about because through the character of Moses, the money-lending Jew, Sheridan was having a dig at Hopkins, the government-sponsored candiadate in the City of London by-election who had recently been accused of money-lending to those who were below the legal age to act as debtors. The fact that Sheridan quickly won round Lord Hertford was evidence that his assiduous cultivation of the nobility was proving its value.
11. Price, *The Dramatic Works of Richard Brinsley Sheridan*, vol.1, p.354
12. Fitzgerald, P., *Lives of the Sheridans* (London, 1888), vol.1, p.161
13. Quoted in Price, *The Dramatic Works of Richard Brinsley Sheridan*, vol.1, pp.315-6

CHAPTER 22
Loss

1. Hannah More (1745-1833) bluestocking, dramatist and moralist. Garrick

produced her tragedy *Percy* in 1777, the year of the Sheridans' visit.

2. From *The Letters of Hannah More*, ed. William Roberts (London, 1834), quoted in Bor and Clelland, *Still the Lark* (London, 1962), p.92

3. Ibid.

4. Sichel, *Sheridan* (2 vols., Constable, London, 1909), vol.1, pp.527-8

5. Price, *Letters of Richard Brinsley Sheridan* (3 vols., Oxford University Press, 1966), vol.1, p.123 n.4

6. Ingamells, *Mrs Robinson and Her Portraits* (London, 1978), p.8

7. Fitzgerald, *Lives of the Sheridans* (London, 1888), vol.1, p.148

8. From *Bath Chronicle*, 13/8/1778 in Waterfield et al, *A Nest of Nightingales* (London, Dulwich Picture Gallery, 1988), p.83-4

9. Ibid., p.13

10. Annual Register quoted in Black, *The Linleys of Bath* (London, 1911), pp.145-6

11. See Lamb, Charles, 'My First Play' in *Essays of Eliza* (London, Dent, Dutton, 1911), p.114

12. Oman, Carola, *David Garrick* (London, 1958), pp.361-2

13. Price, *Dramatic Works of Richard Brinsley Sheridan* (2 vols., Oxford University Press, 1973), vol. 2, p.714

14. Ingamells, John, *Mrs Robinson and her Portraits* (London, Wallace Collection Monographs, 1978), p.11

15. Oman, *David Garrick*, p.372

16. Kendall, Alan, *David Garrick: A Biography* (London, 1985), p.158

17. Oman, *David Garrick*, pp.374-5

18. Moore, Thomas, *Memoirs of the Life of the Right Honourable Richard Brinsley Sheridan*, 3rd edition (2 vols., London, Longman, Hurst, Rees, et al, 1825), vol.1, p.265

19. *The Critic* in Price, *Dramatic Works of Richard Brinsley Sheridan*, vol.2, p.503

20. Kelly, Michael, *Life of Henry Kelly* (2 vols., London, 1826), vol.2, pp.308-9

PART 3

One True Lover

CHAPTER 23
A Violent Politician

1. Fraser Rae, W., publishes facsimiles of two of Sheridan bribe tickets in *Sheridan* (2 vols., Richard Bentley and Son, 1896), vol.1, p.355

2. Sichel, Walter, *Sheridan* (2 vols., London, Constable, 1909), vol.2, pp.61-4

3. Colley, Linda, in *Britons: Forging the Nation 1707-1837* (London, 1992), pp.242-8, for an estimate of women's contribution to Fox's Westminster Election Campaign of 1784

4. Battiscombe, Georgina, *The Spencers of Althorp* (London, 1984), p.93

5. Ibid., p.94

6. Ibid., p.95

7. Sichel, *Sheridan*, vol.1, p. 61-5, for an account of the Westminster election

8. Charles James Fox entered Parliament through his father's (Lord Holland's) control of Midhurst; Edmund Burke was presented with the Wendover seat by Lord Burney; William Pitt, having been defeated in the contest for the Cambridge University seat, was brought into the house as a member for Appleby by Sir James Lowther.

9. Price, Cecil, *Letters of Richard Brinsley Sheridan* (3 vols., Oxford University Press, 1966), vol.1, pp.132-3 for letters from RBS to Ozias Humphry dated

August 1780, 18 August 1780 and July-September 1780.

10. Ibid., pp.135-6, for letter from RBS to Duchess of Devonshire
11. Sichel, *Sheridan*, vol.2, p.97
12. For an account of the Devonshire's love-life see Battiscombe, *The Spencers of Althorp*, pp.84-104
13. A measure of the Prince of Wales' amorous propensities in later life can be found in a letter from Lord Nelson then on active service, to Lady Hamilton after she had written to tell him that she had received a visit from the Prince: 'Did you sit alone with the villain for a moment? No, I will not believe it. Oh God! oh God! keep my senses. Do not let the rascal in. Tell the Duke you will never go to his house.' See Simpson, Colin, *Emma: The Life of Lady Hamilton* (London, 1983), pp.169-70
14. Fraser Rae, *Sheridan*, vol.2, p.80 for the letter from the Prince to Eliza, 12 October 1781
15. Sichel, *Sheridan*, vol.2, p.64, reprinted from the Bath Manuscript
16. Sichel, *Sheridan*, vol.1, pp.73-4
17. Ibid., p.24
18. Fraser Rae, *Sheridan*, vol.1, 371-8 provides an account of Sheridan's early parliamentary performances
19. Sichel, *Sheridan*, vol.1, p.74
20. Fraser Rae, *Sheridan*, vol. 1, p.399. Kastrill, the angry boy, is a character from Ben Jonson's *The Alchemist*, 1610
21. Colley, *Britons: Forging the Nation*, p.248
22. Sichel, *Sheridan*, vol.2, p.64
23. Ibid., p.391, for extract from letter from Eliza to Alicia LeFanu, 20/12/1781

CHAPTER 24
Sisters

1. For an account of the Handel anniversary concert see LeFanu, William, (ed.), *Betsy Sheridan's Journal: 1784-86 & 1788-90* (London, 1960), pp.50-1
2. Mme Gertrud Mara (1749-1843) was the leading German singer of the period
3. The Sheridans moved to Bruton Street early 1784. RBS wrote to a Joseph Cradock from the new address on 23 March. See Price, *Letters of Richard Brinsley Sheridan* (3 vols, Oxford University Press, 1966), vol.1, p.160
4. Of the letters between Eliza and Mary only the latter's survive. Clementina Black reprints them in *The Linleys of Bath* (London, 1911), pp.157-174
5. Ibid., p.169
6. Ibid., p.171
7. Fraser Rae, W., *Sheridan* (2 vols., London, Richard Bentley & Son, 1896), vol.2, p.15
8. Details of Mrs Siddon's Drury Lane career are supplied by W. Macqueen Pope, *Theatre Royal, Drury Lane* (London, 1945), pp.202-3
9. Fraser Rae, *Sheridan*, vol.2, pp.11-12
10. Black, *The Linleys of Bath*, p.162
11. The Hummums was an old coffee house and hotel on the south-west corner of Russell Street, Covent Garden, founded about 1631, demolished 1865
12. Black, *The Linleys of Bath*, p.168
13. Ibid.
14. Alicia LeFanu, *Memoirs of The Life and Writings of Mrs Frances Sheridan* (London, G&B Whittaker, 1824), p.417
15. Gillaspie, John A., *The Catalogue of Music in the Bath Reference Library I*, MSS, Letters, Indexes (London, Munich, New York, Paris, GK Saur, 1986), ES

to MC, 10/10/1778, Alb.1560

16. William LeFanu, ed., *Betsy Sheridan's Journal*, pp.24-5
17. Ibid., pp.26-7
18. Ibid., p.49
19. Nancy Storace returned to England in February 1787 with the tenor Michael Kelly. She had sung at La Scala at the age of fifteen and triumphed in Vienna in *Le Nozze di Figaro*. Married to the musician John Abraham Fisher, she afterwards became the mistress of the Emperor Joseph II. The lover of Wolfgang Amadeus Mozart, she was hoping to hear news that he had followed her to England on the night she called in on the Linleys
20. Gillaspie, *The Catalogue of Music in the Bath Reference Library I*, ES to MC, 1?/8/1786, Alb.1540
21. Ibid.
22. Stratford 'Stratty' Canning was a Quaker banker who was partner in the banking firm of French, Borroughess & Co which failed in 1787. He died that year. Uncle of George Canning (1770-1827) who served as Prime Minister in 1827
23. Gillaspie, *The Catalogue of Music in the Bath Reference Library I*, ES to MC, 21/6/1787, Alb.1544
24. Gillaspie, *The Catalogue of Music in the Bath Reference Library I*, ES to MC, 26/6/1787, Alb. 1545
25. Gillaspie, *The Catalogue of Music in the Bath Reference Library I*, ES to MC, 27/7/1787, Alb.1546

CHAPTER 25
Indian Summer

1. Watson, J. Steven, *The Reign of George III* (Oxford University Press, 1985), p.332. Hasting's career is summarised in pp.306-322
2. Fraser Rae, W., *Sheridan* (2 vols., London, Richard Bentley & Son, 1896), vol.2, pp.55-6
3. Ibid., pp.63-4
4. Ibid., pp.59-60
5. Ibid., p.67
6. Ibid., p.71
7. Ibid., p.74
8. Bor, Margot & Clelland, Lamond, *Still the Lark* (London, 1962), p.128 quoting Thomas Creevey who was present at the meeting between RBS, the Prince and Hastings. See the *Creevey Papers*, ed. Sir Herbert Maxwell (London, 1903)

CHAPTER 26
Last Stages

1. Henry Fielding sailed for Portugal in 1754 in the hopes of improving his health. On the journey he wrote *A Journal of a Voyage to Lisbon*. He died two months after his arrival
2. See LeFanu, William, (ed.), *Betsy Sheridan's Journal: 1784-86 & 1788-90* (London, 1960), pp.102-3
3. Ibid., p.105
4. Gillaspie, John A., *The Catalogue of Music in the Bath Reference Library I*, MSS, Letters, Indexes (London, Munich, New York, Paris, GK Saur, 1986), ES to MC, 17/8/1787 Alb. 1555
5. LeFanu, William, (ed.), *Betsy Sheridan's Journal*, p.110
6. Gillaspie, *The Catalogue of Music in the Bath Reference Library I*, ES to MC,

11/8/1788, Alb.1555

7. Fraser Rae, W., *Sheridan* (2 vols., London, Richard Bentley & Son, 1896), vol.2, pp.29-32

CHAPTER 27
Secret Services

1. Gillaspie, John A., *The Catalogue of Music in the Bath Reference Library I*, MSS, Letters, Indexes (London, Munich, New York, Paris, GK Saur, 1986),, ES to MC, 17/8/1788, Alb. 1555
2. LeFanu, William, (ed.), *Betsy Sheridan's Journal: 1784-86 & 1788-90* (London, 1960), p.118
3. Ibid., p.119
4. Ibid., p.122
5. The Prince of Wales residence, Carlton House, was designed by Henry Holland and opened with a grand fête on 19 May 1784. The house was demolished in 1826 but the Ionic columns that once rose above Pall Mall now stand at the entrance to the National Gallery on Trafalgar Square
6. The Marshalsea Prison in Southwark from the 1430s onwards accepted mainly admiralty prisoners and debtors. Charles Dickens' father was incarcerated there. It was closed in 1842. A 'sponging house' was where debtors were kept for twenty-four hours during which time a bailiff would try to 'sponge' the prisoner of all his money. If he could not, the debtor would go to prison.
7. Gillaspie, *The Catalogue of Music in the Bath Reference Library I*, Es to MC, after 11/11/1788 (?), Alb. 1559
8. LeFanu, William, (ed.), *Betsy Sheridan's Journal*, pp.130-1
9. Gillaspie, *The Catalogue of Music in the Bath Reference Library I*, ES to MC, 9/1/1789, Alb.1562
10. The Prince Of Wales' letter to Pitt (written by the Sheridans) is reproduced in Sichel, Walter, *Sheridan* (2 vols., London, Constable, 1909), vol.2, pp.393-6
11. Gillaspie, *The Catalogue of Music in the Bath Reference Library I*, ES to MC, 9/1/1789
12. LeFanu, William, (ed.), *Betsy Sheridan's Journal*, pp.136-7

CHAPTER 28
Baby Talk

1. Battiscombe, Georgina, *The Spencers of Althorp* (London, 1984), pp.92-3
2. Sichel, Walter, *Sheridan* (2 vols., London, Constable, 1909), vol.2, p.74,n.1
3. Ibid., p.100
4. Ibid., p.74
5. Ibid., p.102
6. LeFanu, William, (ed.), *Betsy Sheridan's Journal: 1784-86 & 1788-90* (London, 1960), pp.132-3
7. Bor, Margot & Clelland, Lamond, *Still the Lark* (London, 1962), p.147
8. Sichel, Walter, *Sheridan*, vol.1, p.458
9. LeFanu, William, (ed.), *Betsy Sheridan's Journal*, p.156
10. Bor and Clelland, *Still the Lark*, p.147
11. Gillaspie, John A., *The Catalogue of Music in the Bath Reference Library I*, MSS, Letters, Indexes (London, Munich, New York, Paris, GK Saur, 1986), ES to MC, July 1789, Alb.1564
12. Ibid.
13. For a summary of the Devonshire's domestic lives, see Battiscombe, *The Spencers*

of Althorp, pp.87-112. Harriet (or 'Harriot') Ducannon's third child by her husband Frederick Ponsonby (afterwards Lord Beesborough) was named Caroline (1785-1828). She married William Lamb (later Lord Melbourne) and later became the Caroline Lamb who infatuated Byron. Lord Melbourne subsequently enjoyed an intimate friendship with Caroline Norton, Eliza's granddaughter. See *A Scandalous Woman* by the present author.

14. Price, *Letters of Richard Brinsley Sheridan* (3 vols., Oxford University Press, 1966), vol.1, pp.207-8
15. LeFanu, William, (ed.), *Betsy Sheridan's Journal*, pp.67-9
16. Ibid., pp.168-9
17. Gillaspie, *The Catalogue of Music in the Bath Reference Library I*, ES to MC, 10/1/1790, Alb. 2303
18. Gillaspie, *The Catalogue of Music in the Bath Reference Library I*, ES to MC, 27/1/1790, Alb. 2305
19 Gillaspie, *The Catalogue of Music in the Bath Reference Library I*, ES to MC, 5/2/1790, Alb. 2304

CHAPTER 29
A Little Affection

1. Gillaspie, John A., *The Catalogue of Music in the Bath Reference Library I*, MSS, Letters, Indexes (London, Munich, New York, Paris, GK Saur, 1986), ES to MC, 6/8/1785, Alb. 1535
2. Mrs Armistead was an actress and a demi-mondaine. Her lovers included Fox, the Prince of Wales, the Duke of Dorset, Lord Derby and Lord Cholmondely. For twelve years (1783-95) she was the more or less exclusive mistress of Fox whom she married in 1785
3. Gillaspie, *The Catalogue of Music in the Bath Reference Library I*, ES to MC, April 1789, Alb. 2209
4. Ibid., 10/1/1790, Alb. 2303
5. Ibid.
6. Ibid., 5/2/1790, Alb.2304
7. Tomalin, Claire, *Mrs Jordan's Profession* (London, 1994), p.113
8. LeFanu, William, (ed.), *Betsy Sheridan's Journal: 1784-86 & 1788-90* (London, 1960), p.195
9. The fact that the two Sheridan girls Alicia and Betsy both married LeFanu brothers, Joseph and Henry respectively, has caused innumerable confusions and errors in Sheridan biographies.
10. LeFanu, William, (ed.), *Betsy Sheridan's Journal*, p.195
11. Material on the life of Edward Fitzgerald has been taken from
    (a) Moore, Thomas, *The Life and Death of Lord Edward Fitzgerald* (2 vols, London, 1832), and
    (b) Byrne, Patrick, *Lord Edward Fitzgerald* (London, 1955)
12. Byrne, Patrick, *Lord Edward Fitzgerald*, p.53
13. LeFanu, William, (ed.), *Betsy Sheridan's Journal*, p.140
14. W. Macqueen Pope, *Theatre Royal, Drury Lane* (London, 1945), p.214
15. Gillaspie, *The Catalogue of Music in the Bath Reference Library I*, ES to MC, 19/8/1790, Alb. 1568
16. Ibid., 1/4/1791, Alb. 1565
17. Ibid., 17/1/1792, Alb. 1570
18. Ibid., 23/5/1792, Alb. 2113

CHAPTER 30
Poor E.

1. Price, *Letters of Richard Brinsley Sheridan* (3 vols., Oxford University Press, 1966), vol.1, pp.244-5
2. Ibid.
3. Ibid., pp.238-9
4. Ibid., pp.239-40
5. Ibid., pp.236-7
6. Ibid., pp.241-3
7. Price, *Letters of Richard Brinsley Sheridan*, vol.1, pp.246-7
8. Ibid., pp.248-9
9. While at the Hotwells Sheridan passed his time usefully . He wrote letters to get Ozias Linley a church living and a girl named Mary Haydock pardoned for horse-stealing. Ozias eventually got his living but Mary was transported
10. Gillaspie, John A., *The Catalogue of Music in the Bath Reference Library I*, MSS, Letters, Indexes (London, Munich, New York, Paris, GK Saur, 1986), June 1792, MSb 2308
11. Ibid.
12. Sichel, Walter, *Sheridan* (2 vols., London, Constable, 1909), vol.2, 223-4

Select Bibliography

On the Linleys

Black, Clementina, *The Linleys of Bath* (London, 1911)

Bor, Margot and Clelland, Lamond, *Still the Lark* (London, 1962)

Gillaspie, John A., *The Catalogue of Music in the Bath Reference Library I*, MSS, Letters, Indexes (London, Munich, New York, Paris, GK Saur, 1986)

Waterfield, Giles et al, *A Nest of Nightingales* (London, Dulwich Picture Gallery, 1988)

On the Sheridans

British Library Department of Manuscripts (London, British Library Manuscripts)

Watkins, John, *Memoirs of the Public and Private life of the Right Honourable R.B. Sheridan with a particular Account of His Family and Connexions* (2 vols., London, Henry Colburn Public Library, 1817)

Moore, Thomas, *Memoirs of the Life of the Right Honourable Richard Brinsley Sheridan*, 3rd edition (2 vols., London, Longman, Hurst, Rees, Orme, Brown and Green, 1825)

Fitzgerald, P., *Lives of the Sheridans* (2 vols., London, 1888)

Fraser Rae, W., *Sheridan* (2 vols., London, Richard Bentley and Son, 1896)

Sichel, Walter, *Sheridan* (London, Constable, 1909)

LeFanu, Alicia, *Memoirs of the Life and Writings of Mrs Frances Sheridan, By her Grand-daughter* (London, G & B Whittaker, 1824)

LeFanu, William, (ed.) *Betsy Sheridan's Journal 1784-86 & 1788-90* (London, 1960)

Price, Cecil, *The Letters of Richard Brinsley Sheridan* (3 vols., Oxford University Press, 1966)

Price, Cecil, *The Dramatic Works of Richard Brinsley Sheridan* (2 vols., Oxford University Press, 1973)

Sheridan, Clare, *To the Four Winds* (London, 1957)

Contemporaries

Angelo, Henry, *The Reminiscences of Henry Angelo* (2 vols., New York, London, 1831)

Battiscombe, Georgina, *The Spencers of Althorp* (London, 1984)

Belden, Mary Megie, *The Dramatic Works of Samuuel Foote* (New Haven, Yale University Press, 1929)

Boswell, David, *Life of Dr Samuel Johnson* (London, 1791, reprinted London, Dent, 1962)

Byrne, Patrick, *Lord Edward Fitzgerald* (London, 1955)

Cecil, David, *A Portrait of Charles Lamb* (London, 1983)

Derry, John W., *Politics in the Age of Fox, Pitt, and Liverpool* (London, 1990)

Fiske, Roger, *English Theatre Music in the Eighteenth Century* (Oxford University Press)

Foote, Samuel, *The Works of Samuel Foote* (2 vols., Glasgow, John Murdoch and London, Geo. Robinson and Verbnor & Hood, 1799)

Fraser, Flora, *Beloved Emma: The Life of Lady Hamilton* (London, 1986)

Ingamells, John, *Mrs Robinson and her Portraits* (London, 1978)

Jarrett, Derek, *Pitt the Younger* (London, 1974)

Kelly, Michael, *The Life of Henry Kelly* (2 vols., London, 1826)

Kendall, Alan, *David Garrick: A Biography* (London, 1985)

Moore, Thomas, *The Life and Death of Lord Edward Fitzgerald*, 3rd edition (2 vols., Longman, Rees, Orme, Brown, Green & Longman, 1832)

Oman, Carola, *David Garrick* (London, 1958)

Reilly, Robin, *Pitt the Younger* (London, 1978)

Simpson, Colin, *Emma: The Life of Lady Hamilton* (London, 1983)

Tomalin, Claire, *Mrs Jordan's Profession* (London, 1994)

Periods and Places

Colley, Linda, *Britons: Forging the Nation 1707-1837* (London, 1992)

Craig, Maurice, *Dublin 1660-1860* (London, 1992)

Macqueen Pope, W., *Theatre Royal, Drury Lane* (London, 1945)

Summerson, John, *Georgian London* (London, 1962)

Waite, Vincent, 'The Bristol Hotwell' in *Bristol in the Eighteenth Century* (Newton Abbott,1972)

Watson, J. Steven, *The Reign of George III* (Oxford University Press, 1985)

Index